United States Constitutional Law

An Introduction

PAUL RODGERS

McFarland & Company, Inc., Publishers

Jefferson, North Carolina, and London

LIBRARY OF CONGRESS CATALOGUING-IN-PUBLICATION DATA

Rodgers, Paul, 1933–
    United States constitutional law : an introduction / Paul Rodgers.
        p.   cm.
    Includes bibliographical references and index.

    ISBN 978-0-7864-5940-7
    softcover : 50# alkaline paper ∞

    1. Constitutional law—United States.   2. Constitutional
law—United States—Cases.   I. Title.
    KF4550.R579   2011
    342.73—dc22   2010049322

BRITISH LIBRARY CATALOGUING DATA ARE AVAILABLE

Cover image: Howard Chandler Christy, *Scene at the Signing of the
Constitution of the United States,* oil, 240" × 360", 1940; (background)
first page of the Constitution of the United States, 1787 (National
Archives and Records Administration)

Manufactured in the United States of America

*McFarland & Company, Inc., Publishers
    Box 611, Jefferson, North Carolina 28640
    www.mcfarlandpub.com*

This book is dedicated to those 22 lawyers of the 39 delegates who signed the Constitution of the United States in Philadelphia, Pennsylvania, on that Monday afternoon, September 17, 1787, and to their successors whose advocacy of constitutional principles have raised the rights and dignity of Americans to the highest level in the history of humankind.

Acknowledgments

Great appreciation is expressed to the George Mason University Law School for the use of its excellent Library at 3301 North Fairfax Drive, Arlington, Virginia 22201.

Great appreciation is also expressed to my daughter, Marsha King, for her computer skills in assisting with the preparation of this book, and also to my wife, Barbara, for her steadfast encouragement for all the work required to write this book.

United States Constitutional Law

Table of Contents

Preface

The purpose of this book is to provide a basic understanding of the United States Constitution, and to explain the awesome power of the Supreme Court whereby a bare majority of five justices, with lifetime tenure, can overrule the President, the Congress, state and local governments, and declare the rights and obligations of persons and organizations across the land. Five justices can instantaneously change the meaning of a constitutional provision, whereas the Congress and the states are required to pursue a long and laborious process to amend the Constitution.

The United States Constitution is one of the great political documents of all time. Crafted by able men in secret session in the hot Philadelphia summer of 1787, it split the power of kings into three parts: legislative, executive and judicial, with intertwined checks and balances. This was followed in 1791 by the adoption of the ten amendments of the Bill of Rights to protect persons against the tyranny of government. Over the years additional amendments were adopted, most notably the Fourteenth Amendment in 1868 which imposed on the states the obligation to afford persons under their jurisdiction with the due process of law and the equal protection of the laws.

The original Constitution is divided into seven articles and further into numbered sections and unnumbered paragraphs. Most of the 27 amendments are also divided into numbered and unnumbered paragraphs. For ease of reference, these paragraphs are often referred to as clauses, such as the "Commerce Clause," the "Necessary and Proper Clause," the "Advise and Consent Clause," the "Faithful Execution Clause," and the "Supremacy Clause." Within the main text, the meaning of each constitutional clause is explained, and key Supreme Court decisions that have interpreted the clause are reviewed. The decision is briefly described and the vote, such as 5–4, is usually reported so that the reader may assess the potential for modification or reversal later on.

The present work references over 950 Supreme Court decisions, which are reported without opinionated commentary. Unlike so many other books on the subject, there is no attempt to offer praise or criticism about various decisions, and it is left to the reader to formulate his or her own view. No one agrees with all the decisions—especially the Supreme Court justices, as shown by their many dissents.

The titles of the clauses in the text and in the Constitution (presented without commentary in Appendix B) are not stated in the original Constitution and its amendments, but are added here for ease of reference. Most other books do not add the titles to constitutional text, thereby making it more difficult to find sought-after provisions. In the topical index, page references are given to a clause both as it is addressed in the text and as it appears in the Constitution. Most works about the Constitution do not tie the two together.

Article II, Section 1, concerning the electoral college and presidential succession, has been amended by the 12th, 20th and 25th Amendments, making it difficult to reconcile all of them to determine the present meaning. Accordingly, this provision is here presented in its current amended form so that the reader is spared having to piece together the changes so as to divine the present status of the law, as would be required in many other books.

The great liberties and guarantees of the Constitution are stated as general principles so that they may be perpetuated and reapplied to meet the needs of a changing America. Traditionally, the Supreme Court abides by the doctrine of stare decisis under which it adheres to precedent on questions of law in order to promote consistency in the administration of justice. However, when convinced of former error, the Court has never felt constrained to follow precedent, and has freely exercised its power to reexamine the basis of constitutional decisions (e.g. *Smith v. Allwright*, 321 U.S. 649, 665 [1944]).

In essence, the power of the Supreme Court rests on its moral authority, on the respect accorded to it by the other branches of government and by the general public. The Court does not have the ability to finance itself or to enforce its decisions. It must rely on the Congress for annual appropriations and legislation to support the Court's decisions, such as the civil and voting rights acts of the 1960s. Also, the Court must rely on the President to use his military authority to implement the decisions when necessary, such as in the enforcement of racial desegregation following *Brown v. Board of Education of Topeka*, 347 U.S. 483 (1954). Justice Felix Frankfurter said it well in his dissent in *Baker v. Carr*, 369 U.S. 267 (1962): "The Court's authority—possessed of neither the purse or the sword—ultimately rests on sustained public confidence in its moral sanction."

The judicial power has not always been respected, as shown by the conduct of two of our most prominent presidents. In *Worcester v. Georgia*, 31 U.S. 515 (1832), the Supreme Court, in an opinion by Chief Justice John Marshall, confirmed the supremacy of federal authority over the states by holding that the Cherokee Nation was entitled to federal protection from the actions of Georgia which would infringe on tribal sovereignty. President Andrew Jackson refused to enforce the decision, supposedly saying: "John Marshall has made his decision, now let him enforce it!" Next, President Abraham Lincoln, after the outbreak of the Civil War, suspended the writ of habeas corpus and authorized the military to arrest and indefinitely detain anyone suspected of aiding the rebels. Chief Justice Roger Taney, sitting as a circuit judge, ruled in *Ex parte Merryman*, 17 F Cases 144 (CC MD 1861), that the writ can only be suspended by the Congress, not by the President. Lincoln ignored the ruling. Congress formally suspended the writ in 1863.

So here we will review the high drama of constitutional conflicts that have challenged the Supreme Court since its inception, as we travel the clauses of the Constitution and see the handiwork of the framers, the advocacy of the litigants, and the decisions of the justices.

Prologue

Events Leading to the Ratification of the Constitution

Origins

We begin with the Magna Carta (Great Charter) that the barons compelled from King John of England (1166–1216) on June 15, 1215, at Runnymede on the River Thames near Windsor Castle. It expressed the principle that no man is above the law, and it required the king to renounce certain rights, respect legal procedures, and accept that his will would be bound by law. The Magna Carta grew in importance over the years as succeeding generations interpreted its chief principle to guarantee the fundamental rights and liberties of all citizens. According to popular legend, Robin Hood opposed the tyranny of John, both as Prince and during his reign as King (1199–1216).

English common law evolved from the Magna Carta as reflected in the *Commentaries on the Laws of England* produced by the English jurist and professor Sir William Blackstone (1723–1780). The *Commentaries* are an historical and analytic treatise on the common law that were first published in four volumes over the period 1765–1769. They remain an important source on classical views of the common law and its principles.

Englishmen brought with them to the New World colonial charters guaranteeing that they and their heirs would have "all the rights and immunities of free and natural subjects." When American colonists rebelled against the British government, they fought to preserve liberties that dated to the Magna Carta. Accordingly, the delegates drafting the state and federal constitutions relied heavily on the English common law.

Two political theorists had great influence on the creation of the Constitution. One was the English philosopher John Locke (1632–1704), who in his *Second Treatise of Government* (1690) argued that the ultimate sovereignty resides in the people, not rulers; that restraints are necessary to prevent the exercise of arbitrary power by the executive or the legislature; and that the social compact may be revoked by the people when power has been arbitrarily used against them. The political state emerges from a social compact among the people, who consent to government in order to preserve their lives, liberties and property. In the words of the Declaration of Independence, which drew heavily on Locke, governments derive "their just powers from the consent of the governed." Locke also pioneered the idea of the separation of powers.

The French philosopher and jurist Charles-Louis de Secondat, Baron de Montesquieu (1689–1755), was the second major intellectual influence on the Constitution. He further developed the concept of a separation of powers in his treatise *The Spirit of the Laws* (1748) by arguing that despotism could best be prevented when different bodies exercised legislative, executive and judicial power, in which all were bound by the rule of law.

Accordingly, the founders of the United States government were given a blueprint for a new kind of political architecture that did not need to be discovered or invented, only applied. They did not meet to reform society, but to create a government for society as it existed.

The Continental Congress

The First Continental Congress was the first *de facto* national government of the 13 original American colonies: Connecticut, Delaware, Georgia, Massachusetts, New Hampshire, Maryland, New Jersey, New York, North Carolina, Pennsylvania, Rhode Island, South Carolina, and Virginia. It had no legal basis and was dependent on the colonies for political direction and support. The First Congress met in Philadelphia, Pennsylvania, September 5–October 26, 1774, to petition the British government for the redress of grievances.

The Second Continental Congress met from May 10, 1775, to the ratification of the Articles of Confederation by all 13 states on March 1, 1781. The Second Congress adopted measures of resistance against the British government, and became the responsible political agency for carrying on the Revolution against the British.

The Declaration of Independence

The Declaration of Independence, drafted principally by Thomas Jefferson of Virginia, was issued by the Second Continental Congress on Thursday, July 4, 1776, to list the colonies' grievances against King George III and thereby to justify independence. The delegates had spent over two days making editorial changes to the draft of the Declaration that addressed the grievances. However, the beginning of the second paragraph of the Declaration received little comment: "We hold these truths to be self-evident, that all men are created equal, that they are endowed by their Creator with certain unalienable rights, that among these are Life, Liberty, and the pursuit of Happiness. That to secure these rights, Governments are instituted among Men, deriving their just powers from the consent of the governed." These 55 words defined the ideals of the new nation, the essence of the American creed. While these sentiments are not part of the law of the land, they continue to exert a profound influence on American political thinking. (The phrasing of this part of the Declaration was influenced by paragraph 1 of the Virginia Declaration of Rights drafted by George Mason and adopted by the Virginia Convention on June 12, 1776.) With the issuance of the Declaration of Independence the English colonies declared themselves independent states.

Fifty-six men from all 13 states signed the Declaration of Independence. The average age of the signers was 45. The youngest signer was Thomas Lynch, Jr. (age 26), South Carolina; Benjamin Franklin (age 70), Pennsylvania, was the oldest. Two future presidents signed: John Adams, Massachusetts, the second president, and Thomas Jefferson, Virginia, the third president. Adams, Jefferson and Charles Carroll, Maryland, were the longest surviving signers. Adams and Jefferson both died on July 4, 1826, the 50th anniversary of the Declaration of Independence. Carroll died in 1832 at age 95.

President Abraham Lincoln, in his Gettysburg Address on November 19, 1863, directly referenced the Declaration of Independence, invoking its principle of equality, and stating that the Civil War was fought not only to preserve the Union, but also for "a new birth of freedom" that would bring true equality to all Americans.

The Confederation Congress

On November 15, 1777, the Second Continental Congress adopted the Articles of Confederation, which served as the *de facto* system of government used by Congress until the Articles became *de jure* by ratification of all 13 states on March 1, 1781. The ratification of the Articles legally united the states by compact into the "United States of America." Ratification also transformed the Second Continental Congress into the Congress of the Confederation, which governed from March 1, 1781, to March 4, 1789, when it was succeeded by the United States Congress.

The Constitutional Convention

The Confederation Congress, sitting in New York City on February 21, 1787, called a convention in Philadelphia for the purpose of revising the

Articles of Confederation. The Articles had proved inadequate for effective governance because: (1) Congress was a unicameral body in which each state, irrespective of population, had one vote; (2) Congress was not empowered to levy and collect taxes, and had no means to compel the sovereign states to pay the amounts apportioned among them for the support of the Confederation; (3) Congress could not regulate foreign and interstate commerce; (4) Congress had a ceremonial presiding officer, but there was no executive to enforce congressional acts; (5) there was no federal judiciary; (6) the enactment of legislation required a two-thirds majority vote; and (7) the amendment of the Articles required unanimous consent. It had become obvious that the Articles were insufficient to support a national government strong enough to unify the states and protect the country against foreign aggressors.

There were advantages to having a special convention to address the revision of the Articles of Confederation, rather than having Congress attempt the revisions. One advantage was that convention delegates would not be distracted by the usual legislative business of the Congress. Another was that the convention permitted the contributions of eminent individuals who were not members of Congress.

The Constitutional Convention assembled with a quorum of delegates from seven states in the East Room of the State House (Independence Hall) in Philadelphia on Friday, May 25, 1787, and continued its deliberations in secret during the long, hot summer until Saturday, September 15. The East Room was the site of past sessions of the Continental Congress and was also where the Declaration of Independence had been signed. The Convention delegates—usually no more than 30 at a time, due to their comings and goings—sat at tables of three or four delegates each. The presiding officer occupied a desk on a dais facing the other delegates. George Washington of Virginia was unanimously elected as the president of the Convention. James Madison of Virginia took meticulous notes on the proceedings. Thomas Jefferson, away in Paris as minister to France (1785–1789), called the delegates "an assembly of demigods." John Adams was also absent as minister to Great Britain (1785–1788) in London. Rhode Island, fearful that a strong national government would injure its lucrative trade, opposed revising the Articles of Confederation and sent no delegates.

Of the original 55 delegates, 35 were lawyers. The average age of the delegates was 42, ranging in age from the 26-year-old Jonathan Dayton (10/16/1760) of New Jersey to the 81-year-old Benjamin Franklin (1/17/1706) of Pennsylvania. Eight delegates had signed the Declaration of Independence: Roger Sherman of Connecticut; George Read of Delaware; Elbridge Gerry of Massachusetts; George Clymer, Benjamin Franklin, Robert Morris, and James Wilson of Pennsylvania; and George Wythe of Virginia.

Fourteen of the 55 delegates had returned home over the summer and were not present at the conclusion of the Convention. They were, from Connecticut, Oliver Ellsworth (later served as U.S. Supreme Court justice, 1796–1800); from Delaware, John Dickinson (signed Constitution by proxy); from Georgia, William Houstoun and William Pierce; from Maryland, Luther Martin and John Francis Mercer; from Massachusetts, Caleb Strong; from New Jersey, William Churchill Houston; from New York, John Lansing, Jr. and Robert Yates; from North Carolina, William Richardson Davie and Alexander Martin; and from Virginia: James McClurg and George Wythe.

On September 8, the Committee on Style and Arrangement, composed of Alexander Hamilton of New York, William Samuel Johnson of Connecticut, Rufus King of Massachusetts, James Madison of Virginia, and Gouverneur Morris of Pennsylvania, was appointed to draft the final version of the Constitution to reflect the agreements that had been reached by the delegates. The Committee condensed the agreements into seven articles, written in plain, brief language with occasional vagueness to accommodate future developments. The Committee's submission, with few changes, became the Constitution that was adopted by the delegates and ratified by the states.

Three delegates, Elbridge Gerry (1744–1814) of Massachusetts and George Mason (1725–1792) and Edmund Randolph (1753–1813) of Virginia, opposed the Constitution and refused to sign because they were fearful of an all-powerful government and wanted a bill of rights to protect the rights of the people. Randolph also argued that the Constitution should not be submitted for ratification without affording the states an opportunity to amend it.

The Constitution was signed on Monday afternoon, September 17, 1787, and submitted to the states for ratification. The members aligned themselves geographically for the order of signing, beginning with New Hampshire and followed by Massachusetts, Connecticut, New York, New Jersey, Pennsylvania, Delaware, Maryland, Virginia, North Carolina, South Carolina and Georgia. The delegate signatories were the following 39 men from twelve states: *Connecticut*: William Samuel Johnson* (1727–1819), Roger Sherman* (1721–1793); *Delaware*: Richard Bassett* (1745–1815), Gunning Bedford, Jr.* (1747–1812), Jacob Broom (1752–1810), John Dickinson* (1732–1808) (Dickinson was absent, but had authorized George Read to sign for him), George Read* (1733–1798); *Georgia*: Abraham Baldwin* (1754–1807), William Few* (1748–1828); *Maryland*: Daniel Carroll (1730–1796), Daniel of St. Thomas Jenifer* (1723–1790), James McHenry (1753–1816); *Massachusetts*: Nathaniel Gorham (1738–1796); Rufus King* (1755–1827); *New Hampshire*: Nicholas Gilman (1762–1814), John Langdon (1739–1819); *New Jersey*: David Brearley* (1745–1790), Jonathan Dayton* (1760–1824), William Livingston* (1723–1790), William Paterson* (1744–1806);

New York: Alexander Hamilton* (1757–1804); *North Carolina*: William Blount (1744–1800), Richard Dobbs Spaight (1758–1802); Hugh Williamson (1735–1819); *Pennsylvania*: George Clymer (1739–1813), Thomas Fitzsimons (1741–1811), Benjamin Franklin (1706–1790), Jared Ingersoll* (1749–1822), Thomas Mifflin (1744–1800), Gouverneur Morris* (1752–1816); Robert Morris (1734–1806); James Wilson* (1742–1798); *South Carolina*: Pierce Butler (1744–1822); Charles Cotesworth Pinckney* (1746–1825); Charles Pinckney* (1758–1824); John Rutledge* (1739–1800); *Virginia*: John Blair* (1732–1800); James Madison, Jr. (1751–1836), George Washington (1732–1799). William Jackson, South Carolina, attested the signatures as the secretary. The following four signers of the Constitution later served as U.S. Supreme Court justices: John Blair, Virginia, 1790–1795; William Paterson, New Jersey, 1793–1806; John Rutledge, South Carolina, 1790–1791, 1795; and James Wilson, Pennsylvania, 1789–1798.

William Jackson, convention secretary, carried the Constitution to the Congress in New York City. The Congress on September 28, 1787, transmitted the Constitution to the state legislatures with the recommendation that the issue of ratification be considered by special state conventions, instead of state legislatures, in order to demonstrate that the action thereon was the will of the people rather than a compact among the states.

The Federalist Papers

To promote the ratification of the Constitution, Alexander Hamilton, James Madison and John Jay wrote the 85 essays comprising *The Federalist Papers* that were printed anonymously in New York City newspapers between November 1787 and March 1788, and were widely reprinted elsewhere. They appeared under the pseudonym "Publius," in honor of the Roman consul Publius Valerius Publicola (died 503 BC) for his role in establishing the Roman Republic. Hamilton wrote about two-thirds of the essays.

The Federalist Papers are a primary source for interpretation of the Constitution, as they outline the philosophy and motivation of the proposed system of government. The authors wanted to both influence the vote in favor of ratification and shape future interpretations of the Constitution.

Madison is generally credited as the "Father of the Constitution" and became the fourth President of the United States. He died in 1836 as "The Last of the Founders."

Hamilton became the first Secretary of the Treasury. Jay became the first Chief Justice of the Supreme Court.

---

*One of the 22 lawyers who signed the Constitution.

Ratification of the Constitution

Delaware was the first state to ratify the Constitution (Friday, December 7, 1787), and the last to ratify was Rhode Island (Saturday, May 29, 1790). With the ratification of the ninth state, New Hampshire, on Saturday, June 21, 1788, Congress passed a resolution to make the Constitution operative as provided in Article VII, and set dates for choosing presidential electors and the opening session of the new Congress.

The Constitution provides for a representative government based on the principle of popular sovereignty. Articles I, II and III of the Constitution allocate the lawmaking, law-enforcing and law-interpreting functions to coequal branches of government, thereby creating checks and balances in order to preserve liberty from the tyranny of combining these powers in the same entity. The Constitution promotes an entrepreneurial market-driven economy fueled by the energies of unfettered citizens, provides for a secular state unaffiliated with any official religion, and mandates the rule of law that presumes the equality of all citizens. The so-called Great Compromise made representation proportional to population in the House of Representatives, and equal for all states in the senate.

The Constitution vested the federal government with only those enumerated sovereign powers essential for preservation of the union. All residual sovereign powers remained with the states. However, beginning with Supreme Court interpretations under Chief Justice John Marshall (1801–1835) the power of the federal government has grown at the expense of state sovereignty. On the state side, some have likened it to playing against a team that supplies the umpires.

Associate Justice Joseph Story, in delivering the opinion of the Court in *Martin v. Hunter's Lessee*, 14 U.S. 304, 326 (1816), described the capacity of the Constitution to address changing circumstances: "The Constitution unavoidably deals in general language. It did not suit the purposes of the people, in framing this great charter of our liberties, to provide for minute specifications of its powers, or to declare the means by which those powers should be carried into execution. It was foreseen that this would be a perilous and difficult, if not an impracticable, task. The instrument was not intended to provide merely for the exigencies of a few years, but was to endure through a long lapse of ages, the events of which were locked up in the inscrutable purposes of Providence. It could not be foreseen what new changes and modifications of power might be indispensable to effectuate the general objects of the charter, and restrictions and specifications which at the present might seem salutary might in the end prove the overthrow of the system itself. Hence its powers are expressed in general terms, leaving to the legislature from time to time to adopt its own means to effectuate legitimate objects and to mould and model the exercise of its powers as its own wisdom, and the public interests, should require."

Chief Justice John Marshall observed in *Cohens v. Virginia*, 19 U.S. 264, 387 (1821), that a "constitution is framed for ages to come, and is designed to approach Immortality as nearly as human institutions can approach it."

The Constitution of the United States

Ratified June 21, 1788

The Constitution is composed of the preamble, seven articles and 27 amendments, the first ten of which are the Bill of Rights. The complete text of the Constitution is printed again, without commentary, in Appendix B. Joseph Story (1779–1845), an Associate Justice of the Supreme Court (1812–1845) and a close colleague of Chief Justice John Marshall (1801–1835), authored the *Commentaries on the Constitution of the United States* (3 volumes, 1833), an authoritative treatise on the development of the Constitution.

Preamble

We the People of the United States, in Order to form a more perfect Union, establish Justice, insure domestic Tranquility, provide for the common defense, promote the general Welfare, and secure the Blessings of Liberty to ourselves and our Posterity, do ordain and establish this Constitution for the United States of America.

The declaration that the "People" established the Constitution clarifies that the federal power was given directly by the people and not the states. *Martin v. Hunter's Lessee*, 14 U.S. 304, 324 (1816), 6–0 vote. Thus a fundamental feature of the Constitution is that sovereignty reposes in the people who created it. However, the Preamble is merely declaratory and does not grant or limit power. *Jacobson v. Massachusetts*, 197 U.S. 11, 22 (1905).

Article I
The Legislative Branch

Article I, Section 1. Legislative Vesting. All legislative Powers herein granted shall be vested in a Congress of the United States, which shall consist of a Senate and House of Representatives.

Although the Constitution separates legislative, executive and judicial powers, the separation is not precise, for each of the three branches does exercise powers logically belonging to the other two as a means of more effectively handling its role. A prime example is the establishment of numerous independent administrative agencies to carry out important government services with each exercising combined legislative, executive and judicial powers.

The legislative branch cannot impair the exclusive authority of another branch. In *United States v. Klein*, 80 U.S. 128 (1871), Congress enacted legislation providing that persons whose property was seized during the Civil War could recover it, or be compensated for it, upon proof that they had not aided the rebels, but prohibited presidential pardons being used as an element of proof. The Supreme Court held 7–2 that Congress had exceeded its authority by invading the province of the judicial branch by restricting the use of proof in judicial proceedings. "It is the intention of the Constitution that each of the great coordinate departments of the government— the Legislative, the Executive, and the Judicial—shall be, in its sphere, independent of the others." 80 U.S. 147.

The Supreme Court, recognizing the difficulty of drawing a precise line of separation, held that a conditional exercise of legislative power, by enactment of a statute with a provision that takes effect upon the presidential

16

making of a certain factual finding, is not an unlawful delegation of legislative power. *Cargo of the Brig Aurora v. United States*, 11 U.S. 382 (1813), 6–0 vote. The Supreme Court in *St. Louis, Iron Mountain and Southern Railway Co. v. Taylor*, 210 U.S. 281 (1908), upheld 9–0 an authorization under the Safety Appliance Act of 1893 for the uniform height of drawbars on interstate rail freight cars to be determined by a private railway association and declared by the Interstate Commerce Commission.

In *United States v. Grimaud*, 220 U.S. 506 (1911), the Supreme Court upheld 9–0 a statute authorizing the Secretary of Agriculture to make regulations governing the use of public lands, where varying local conditions made precise congressional legislation impracticable, and imposed criminal penalties for the violation of the regulations. The Court observed: "The legislature cannot delegate its power to make a law, but it can make a law to delegate a power to determine some fact or state of things upon which the law makes or intends to make its own action depend. To deny this would be to stop the wheels of government. There are many things upon which wise and useful legislation must depend which cannot be known to the lawmaking power, and must therefore be a subject of inquiry and determination outside of the halls of legislation." 220 U.S. 520.

In *J. W. Hampton, Jr. & Co. v. United States*, 276 U.S. 394 (1928), the Supreme Court upheld 9–0 a statute delegating to the President the power to adjust tariffs to any rate, within a wide range, he found necessary to equalize the cost differences in the United States and the competing country. The Court set out the governing standard by holding that a legislative action is not a forbidden delegation of legislative power if the Congress lays down by legislative act an intelligible principle to which the person or body to whom the power is delegated is directed to conform.

In *Schechter Poultry Corp. v. United States*, 295 U.S. 495 (1935), the National Industrial Recovery Act (NIRA) authorized business groups to establish fair codes of competition in various industries and to set wages and work hours with the approval of the President. Schechter violated the poultry trade code by paying low wages and selling sick chickens at reduced prices. The Supreme Court declared 9–0 that the NIRA was an unconstitutional delegation of legislative powers to the President. The case became known as "The Sick Chicken Case." Similarly, in *Panama Refining Co. v. Ryan*, 293 U.S. 388 (1935), the Court invalidated 8–1 an NIRA ill-defined authorization for the President to stabilize oil prices by prohibiting the interstate shipment of oil produced in excess of state quotas. However, since *Schechter* and *Panama*, the Court has generally permitted the Congress to delegate difficult and divisive legislative issues to agencies in the executive and judicial branches, apparently recognizing the practical need for the delivery of government services that continue to increase in volume and complexity.

In *National Broadcasting Co. v. United States*, 319 U.S. 190 (1943), involving regulations issued by the Federal Communications Commission pertaining to associations between broadcasting networks and their affiliated stations, the Supreme Court held 7–2 that the standard of "public interest" governing the exercise of the powers delegated to the FCC by the Communications Act is not so vague and indefinite as to create an unconstitutional delegation of legislative authority. The Court in *Lichter v. United States*, 334 U.S. 742 (1948), upheld 7–2 executive authority under the Renegotiation Act to recover "excessive profits" from private contractors for war goods in time of war. "It is not necessary that Congress supply administrative officials with a specific formula for their guidance in a field where flexibility and the adaptation of the congressional policy to infinitely variable conditions constitute the essence of the program." 334 U.S. 785. The Court in *Arizona v. California*, 373 U.S. 546, 594 (1963), upheld 6–3 a law giving the Secretary of the Interior broad discretion in allocating water among southwestern states during shortages.

Chevron USA, Inc. v. Natural Resources Defense Council, Inc., 467 U.S. 837 (1984), concerned a congressional amendment to the Clean Air Act in 1977, requiring those states that had not attained national air quality standards prescribed by the Environmental Protection Agency (EPA) to establish a permit program regulating new or modified stationary sources of air pollution. Under the EPA implementing regulation, a state could allow a plant that contained several pollution-emitting devices to install or modify one piece of equipment without meeting the permit conditions if the alteration would not increase the total emissions from the plant. On appeal, the question was whether the EPA's decision to allow states to treat multiple pollution-emitting devices as though they were encased within a single "bubble" was based on a reasonable interpretation of the statutory term "stationary source." The Supreme Court upheld the EPA 6–0, ruling that courts must defer to an administrative agency's interpretation of its statutory authority, unless the interpretation conflicts with an unambiguous statute, or the interpretation is unreasonable.

In *Whitman v. American Trucking Associations, Inc.*, 531 U.S. 457 (2001), the Supreme Court held 9–0 that Congress constitutionally delegated legislative power under the Clean Air Act to the EPA administrator by authorizing the promulgation of national ambient air quality standards that "are requisite to protect the public health" with "an adequate margin of safety."

Independent administrative agencies are established by Congress to carry out government programs and are usually lodged in the executive branch. They typically exercise in their assigned spheres of jurisdiction the powers of the three branches of government by making rules (a legislative function), administering and enforcing the rules (an executive function), and interpreting the rules and imposing sanctions for their violation (a judicial function.) These agencies, often called the "fourth branch" of government, have multiplied in modern times to respond to a growing public demand for services and to deal with the increasing complexities of government programs.

The combination of investigative and adjudicative functions does not, in itself, constitute a due process violation as creating an unconstitutional risk of bias. *Withrow v. Larkin*, 421 U.S. 35 (1975), 9–0 vote. The value of evidence in administrative proceedings varies, and the weight to be given to it is peculiarly in the body experienced in regard to the intricacies of the subject matter. *Interstate Commerce Commission v. Louisville & Nashville Railroad Co.*, 227 U.S. 88 (1913), 9–0 vote. Agencies, within the limits of the law and of fair and prudent administration, may adapt their rules and practices to meet the needs of a volatile, changing economy. *American Trucking Associations, Inc. v. Atchison, Topeka & Santa Fe Railway Co.*, 387 U.S. 397, 416 (1967), 6–3 vote. Agencies may adjudicate private rights provided they use court-like procedures and their decisions are subject to review by Article III courts. *Crowell v. Benson*, 285 U.S. 22 (1932), 6–3 vote.

The United States *Statutes at Large* is the official record of the laws passed by Congress at each session, with laws arranged in the chronological order of passage. The *Statutes* is not a convenient research tool because the laws addressing the same or related topics may be scattered across many volumes. This problem is solved by the publication of the *United States Code* (USC), which compiles and codifies the general laws into 50 titles (Title 1, General Provisions, to Title 50, War and National Defense). The *Code* is continually updated to eliminate repealed or expired provisions, and to reflect additions and amendments. The *Code of Federal Regulations* (CFR) compiles and codifies into 50 titles (Title 1, General Provisions, to Title 50, Wildlife and Fisheries) the general and permanent rules and regulations published in the *Federal Register* by the executive branch agencies. The CFR is also continually updated to keep it current. The agencies promulgate their rules and regulations under the Administrative Procedure Act whereby the public is permitted to comment and to seek judicial review of decisions for alleged legal wrongs.

Article I, Section 2, Clause 1. House of Representatives. The House of Representatives shall be composed of Members chosen every second Year by the People of the several States, and the Electors in each State shall have the Qualifications requisite for Electors of the most numerous Branch of the State Legislature.

The elector equality defined by "one person, one vote" was not contemplated by the framers. However, the malapportionment of population among districts grew excessive as state legislators in many cases failed to redistrict in order to avoid transferring political power to the rapidly growing urban areas. In 1964, the Supreme Court in *Wesberry v. Sanders*, 376 U.S. 1, held 6–3 that Article I, Section 2, of the Constitution mandated that congressional districts be equal in population "as nearly as practicable." This decision was spawned by *Baker v. Carr*, 369 U.S. 186 (1962), holding 6–2 that federal courts must consider on the merits suits challenging the apportionment of state legislatures as allegedly violating the Equal Protection Clause of the Fourteenth Amendment. In *Reynolds v. Sims*, 377 U.S. 533 (1964), the Court 8–1 extended the "one person, one vote" requirement to both houses of state legislatures under the Equal Protection Clause.

In *Kirkpatrick v. Preisler*, 394 U.S. 526 (1969), the Missouri congressional redistricting law created districts with population variances ranging from 12,260 (2.84 percent) below to 13,542 (3.13 percent) above the statewide average. The Supreme Court invalidated 6–3 the law because of these population variances and the failure of the state to explain why they were unavoidable and justifiable. In *Karcher v. Daggett*, 462 U.S. 725 (1983), the New Jersey congressional redistricting law created 14 districts with an average population per district of 526, 059, each district, on the average, differing from the "ideal" size by 0.1384 percent. The Supreme Court invalidated 5–4 the law because the population variances among districts, although small, were not the result of a good faith effort to achieve population equality.

Although the Court has taken a strict view on population equality among districts, it has avoided addressing the gerrymandering of districts for partisan political advantage, except in cases of racially motivated districting found in violation of the Equal Protection Clause of the Fourteenth Amendment. In *Vieth v. Jubelirer*, 541 U.S. 267 (2004), the Supreme Court in a 5–4 opinion recognized the difficulty of developing a standard for assessing political gerrymandering claims.

The term "gerrymander" was derived from a sprawling, salamander-shaped legislative district that was created in Massachusetts in 1812 and signed into law by Governor Elbridge Gerry. He had also signed the Declaration of Independence and the Articles of Confederation, but had refused to sign the Constitution because it did not include a bill of rights.

While Article I, Section 2, gives authority for determining elector qualifications to the states, this authority is superseded by other provisions of the Constitution that forbid the exclusion of voters on grounds such as race (Fifteenth Amendment), sex (Nineteenth Amendment), failure to pay poll tax (Twenty-fourth Amendment), and age of 18 years or above (Twenty-sixth Amendment).

Representatives are not assigned seating in the House Chamber, and may sit where they choose. Traditionally, Democrats occupy the east side of the Chamber, on the Speaker's right, and Republicans occupy the west side on the Speaker's left.

Article I, Section 2, Clause 2. Qualifications for Representatives. No Person shall be a Representative who shall not have attained to the Age of twenty five Years, and been seven Years a Citizen of the United States, and who shall not, when elected, be an Inhabitant of that State in which he shall be chosen.

This Clause, and Section 3, Clause 3, prescribe that the qualification of a Representative and a Senator shall include being a "Citizen of the United States" for prescribed times and an "Inhabitant" of the state from which chosen, with no prescribed residency. Accordingly, such a U.S. citizen may satisfy the habitation qualification by merely being a resident of the state without any minimum period of residence.

The Supreme Court in *Powell v. McCormack*, 395 U.S. 486 (1969), held 7–1 that Congress had no authority to exclude Representative Adam Clayton Powell, Jr., from Congress when he had been elected by his constituents and met the qualifications prescribed by Clause 2. The Supreme Court in *United States Term Limits v. Thornton*, 514 U.S. 779 (1995), held 5–4 that the qualifications in Clause 2 were exclusive and could not be altered, meaning in this case that states cannot apply term limits to members of Congress.

Article I, Section 2, Clause 3.1. Apportionment. Representatives and direct Taxes shall be apportioned among the several States which may be included within this Union, according to their respective Numbers, which shall be determined by adding to the whole Number of free Persons, including those bound to Service for a Term of Years, and excluding Indians not taxed, three fifths of all other Persons.

"Direct taxes," also referred to in Section 9, Clause 4, are those imposed directly upon property or upon the person (capitation), as distinguished from taxes based on privilege or use. Under apportionment, if a state had 10 percent of the population, then the people of that state would be required to pay no more than 10 percent of the direct taxes levied by Congress. The Sixteenth Amendment (1913) permits Congress to levy taxes upon income from whatever source derived without apportionment among the states.

The "Three-fifths Clause" referred to slaves and was a compromise between the North and the slaveholding South. The latter urged that slaves should be counted fully, whereas the North objected that such a count would increase the political power of the South beyond what its free population would warrant. The "three-fifths" count was nullified by the adoption of the

Fourteenth Amendment (1868) with the result, ironically, that Southern representation was increased in the House.

Article I, Section 2, Clause 3.2. Enumeration. The actual Enumeration shall be made within three Years after the first Meeting of the Congress of the United States, and within every subsequent Term of ten Years, in such Manner as they shall by Law direct.

The entire population of the country must be counted every ten years for the purpose of allocating the House of Representatives among the states. The basic question here is whether the Constitution requires that this census consist only of the actual counting of individuals or whether estimates may be relied on. In *Department of Commerce v. United States House of Representatives*, 525 U.S. 316 (1999), the Supreme Court invalidated 5–4, as unduly broad, a statistical sampling method that uses information on a portion of the population to infer that it accurately reflects the population as whole. However, in *Utah v. Evans*, 536 U.S. 452 (2002), the Supreme Court upheld 5–4 the use of the more accurate census method called "hot-deck imputation" in which information derived from a current census is used to infer that an address about which there is uncertainty (such as failure to return a mailed census form) has the same population characteristics as those of its geographically closest neighbor of the same type. Imputation fills in missing data as part of an effort to count individuals one-by-one, whereas sampling seeks to extrapolate features of a large population from a small one.

Article I, Section 2, Clause 3.3. Allocation of Representatives. The Number of Representatives shall not exceed one for every thirty Thousand, but each State shall have at Least one Representative; and until such enumeration shall be made, the State of New Hampshire shall be entitled to chuse three, Massachusetts eight, Rhode-Island and Providence Plantations one, Connecticut five, New-York six, New Jersey four, Pennsylvania eight, Delaware one, Maryland six, Virginia ten, North Carolina five, South Carolina five, and Georgia three.

Accordingly, the House began with an allocation of 65 Representatives. Since each state must have at least one Representative, the population of single-state congressional districts varies widely across the nation. The phrase that: "The Number of Representatives shall not exceed one for every thirty Thousand" is interpreted to mean that that there shall be at least thirty thousand persons for each Representative.

To keep the House membership from becoming unwieldy, the Congress passed a law in 1911 that fixed the size of the House at 433 members, with provision for adding one member each for Arizona and New Mexico when they became states. The House size has remained at 435 since then, except for a temporary increase to 437 at the time Alaska and Hawaii became states in 1960. The existing apportionment for the other 48 states did not change at that time, but the House size returned to 435 after the reapportionment based on the 1960 census. According to the 2000 census, the population ratio per representative is about 1 for every 646,000 citizens.

The Supreme Court in *Franklin v. Massachusetts*, 505 U.S. 788 (1992), upheld 9–0 the inclusion of federal military and civil personnel and their independents in the apportioned populations.

Article I, Section 2, Clause 4. Vacancies. When vacancies happen in the Representation from any State, the Executive Authority thereof shall issue Writs of Election to fill such Vacancies.

In *Jackson v. Ogilvie*, 426 F2d 1333 (7th Cir 1970), the court of appeals ruled that the Clause imposes a mandatory duty on governors to issue writs of election to fill vacancies in the House of Representatives. However, the district court in *American Civil Liberties Union v. Taft*, 217 F Supp 2d 842, 850 (SD Ohio 2002), held that the governor possessed substantial discretion in the timing of a special election to fill a vacancy, and that, if the unexpired term was short, he could forego calling the election so that the vacancy could be filled in the upcoming general election.

Article I, Section 2, Clause 5. Speaker of the House; Impeachment. The House of Representatives shall chuse their Speaker and other Officers; and shall have the sole Power of Impeachment.

SPEAKER OF THE HOUSE

The Speaker of the House is the highest officer in the legislative branch, and is chosen by the majority party. Under the Presidential Succession Act of 1947, the Speaker is in line after the Vice President to become President.

IMPEACHMENT

Impeachment is the process by which a civil officer in the executive or judicial branch of the United States is charged with wrongdoing. Article II, Section 4, provides that "[t]he President, Vice President, and all other civil officers of the United States, shall be removed from office on impeachment for, and conviction of, treason, bribery, or other high crimes and misdemeanors." Article I, Section 3, Clause 6, provides that, "[t]he Senate shall have the sole power to try all impeachments."

In an impeachment proceeding, the House, acting similar to a grand jury, brings charges against an executive or judicial official, and presents evidence of guilt to the Senate for its determination.

The House has only twice impeached a President: Andrew Johnson in 1868 after his attempted dismissal of Secretary of War Edwin M. Stanton; and William Clinton in 1998 on charges of perjury and obstruction of justice arising from a scandal involving a sexual relationship with White House intern Monica Lewinsky and a sexual harassment suit filed by Arkansas state employee Paula Jones. Both Jackson and Clinton were acquitted by the Senate. The House Judiciary Committee voted to impeach President Richard Nixon in July 30, 1974, but he resigned ten days later on August 9 before the full House voted on the charges. The Supreme Court has ruled that the Senate's sole power to try impeachments is not subject to judicial review. *Nixon v. United States*, 506 U.S. 224 (1993), 9–0 vote.

Article I, Section 3, Clause 1. Senate. The Senate of the United States shall be composed of two Senators from each State, chosen by the Legislature thereof for six Years; and each Senator shall have one Vote.

The formulation of the Senate was the result of the Great Compromise that provided for proportional representation of the states in the House and equal representation in the Senate. The Seventeenth Amendment (1913) amended Clause 1 to provide for direct election of Senators by the people of each state.

In the Senate Chamber, Senators are assigned specific desks and locations. When facing the presiding officer, Democrats sit on the left side of the main aisle, Republicans on the right. Desks are shifted back and forth across the aisle to allow the Senators of the same party to sit together. Senators, in order of seniority, choose their desk location at the start of each new session. Some desks of historical significance are reserved for certain Senators, such as Daniel Webster's desk being assigned to the senior Senator from New Hampshire.

Article I, Section 3, Clause 2. Senatorial Classes and Vacancies. Immediately after they shall be assembled in Consequence of the first Election, they shall be divided as equally as may be into three Classes. The Seats of the Senators of the first Class shall be vacated at the Expiration of the second Year, of the second Class at the Expiration of the fourth Year, and of the third Class at the Expiration of the sixth Year, so that one third may be chosen every second Year; and if Vacancies happen by Resignation, or otherwise, during the Recess of the Legislature of any State, the Executive thereof may make temporary Appointments until the next Meeting of the Legislature, which shall then fill such Vacancies.

Accordingly, one-third of the Senate is elected every two years, whereas the House of Representatives is elected in its entirety every two years.

Under the Seventeenth Amendment, vacancies are filled by elections of the people, although state legislatures may empower governors to make temporary appointments until an election can be held.

Article I, Section 3, Clause 3. Qualifications for Senators. No Person shall be a Senator who shall not have attained to the Age of thirty Years, and been nine Years a Citizen of the United States, and who shall not, when elected, be an Inhabitant of that State for which he shall be chosen.

The Senate has interpreted the age and citizenship requirements to apply at the time of assuming office, but not at the time of election. The Supreme Court has held that the specified qualifications are exclusive and that the states have no authority to alter qualifications. *United States Term Limits v. Thornton*, 514 U.S. 779 (1995), 5–4 vote.

Article I, Section 3, Clause 4. Vice President as Presiding Officer. The Vice President of the United States shall be President of the Senate, but shall have no Vote, unless they be equally divided.

The Vice President is the only U.S. official who is a member of two branches of government, the executive and the legislative. Authorizing the Vice President to cast a tiebreaking vote permits the Senate to come to a definitive resolution.

Article I, Section 3, Clause 5. President Pro Tempore. The Senate shall chuse their other Officers, and also a President pro tempore, in the Absence of the Vice President, or when he shall exercise the Office of President of the United States.

The President Pro Tempore is typically the longest serving Senator of the political party with the majority of Senate seats. He presides in the absence of the Vice President, and is the third in line of succession to the presidency after the Vice President and the Speaker of the House. The political head of the Senate is the Majority Leader who is elected by the majority party.

"Other Officers" of the Senate include the Majority and Minority Leaders, the Sergeant at Arms and Doorkeeper, the Chaplain, the Secretary of the Senate, the Chief Clerk, the Executive Clerk and others.

Article I, Section 3, Clause 6. Trial of Impeachment. The Senate shall have the sole Power to try all Impeachments. When sitting for that Purpose, they shall be on Oath or Affirmation. When the President of the United States is tried, the Chief Justice shall preside: And no Person shall be convicted without the Concurrence of two thirds of the Members present.

The requirement for the Chief Justice to preside over a presidential impeachment trial avoids the possible conflict of interest of a Vice President presiding over a trial in which conviction of the President would result in the Vice President's assuming the office.

The proceeding is not a criminal trial, so different rules apply as established by the Senate. The House appoints "managers" who act as prosecutors, and the accused may be represented by counsel. The Senators, once the evidence has been presented, deliberate in closed session and then vote in open session. In *Nixon v. United States*, 506 U.S. 224 (1993), the Supreme Court upheld 9–0 the appointment of a small number of Senators to operate as a trial committee to gather evidence and take testimony, instead of requiring the entire Senate to conduct a full trial. The Court accepted the Senate's argument that it had complete authority over how to fashion its proceedings, and that Senators' political accountability was the only check on this authority.

Article I, Section 3, Clause 7. Punishment for Impeachment. Judgment in Cases of Impeachment shall not extend further than to removal from Office, and disqualification to hold and enjoy any Office of honor, Trust or Profit under the United States: but the Party convicted shall nevertheless be liable and subject to Indictment, Trial, Judgment and Punishment, according to Law.

Whether the Senate convicts or acquits, an impeached official can still be prosecuted under any criminal law that applies. Such prosecution does not violate the Fifth Amendment's prohibition of double jeopardy because impeachment is not a criminal proceeding. Clearly, officials other than the President may be convicted and imprisoned before impeachment. Since the executive branch is headed by a single official, the imprisonment of the President, prior to conviction on impeachment, would disrupt the executive branch.

Article I, Section 4, Clause 1. Election Regulations. The Times, Places and Manner of holding Elections for Senators and Representatives, shall be prescribed in each State by the Legislature thereof; but the Congress may at any time by Law make or alter such Regulations, except as to the Places of chusing Senators.

In *Ex parte Siebold*, 100 U.S. 371 (1880), the Supreme Court upheld 7–2 the right of Congress to enact legislation making state officials liable for prosecution if they committed fraud (ballot-box stuffing) in congressional elections. In *United States v. Classic*, 313 U.S. 299 (1941), the Supreme Court upheld 5–3 congressional authority under this clause to redress corruption and discrimination in primary elections and political party nomination procedures where state law made them an integral part of the process for choosing candidates for federal office.

The "Manner of holding Elections" has been curtailed by: the Fifteenth Amendment (1870) prohibiting voter discrimination on the basis of race; the Nineteenth Amendment (1920) prohibiting voter discrimination on the basis of sex; the Twenty-fourth Amendment (1964) prohibiting the poll tax in federal elections; and the Twenty-sixth Amendment (1971) fixing voting age at 18 or older. The Voting Rights Act of 1965 imposed stringent prohibitions on racial discrimination in voting, such as requiring certain Southern states to obtain federal pre-clearance for new voting practices. The Supreme Court in *South Carolina v. Katzenbach*, 383 U.S. 301 (1966), upheld 8–1 the constitutionality of the pre-clearance requirement.

The "Places of chusing Senators" applied to the selection of Senators by the state legislatures, which was changed by the Seventeenth Amendment (1913) providing for the election of Senators by the people.

In 1842, Congress required the election of Representatives by single-member districts. This requirement was repealed in 1929, but the single-member district was restored by Congress in 1967. Also, from 1842 until 1929, Congress required that each district's territory be compact and contiguous with substantially the same number of inhabitants. *Wood v. Broom*, 287 U.S. 1, 6 (1932). In 1964, the Supreme Court in *Wesberry v. Sanders*, 376 U.S. 1, held 6–3 that Article I, Section 2, Clause 1, mandated that the "one person, one vote" formula be applied to each congressional district.

In *Shaw v. Reno*, 509 U.S. 630 (1993), the Court ruled 5–4 that, under the Fourteenth Amendment's Equal Protection Clause, congressional redistricting based on race must be held to a standard of strict scrutiny. Gerrymandered districts can be an indication of an unconstitutional, racially motivated redistricting plan. The case was remanded to the district court to determine whether or not some compelling government interest justified the North Carolina plan for a district that was 160 miles long to connect areas having large black populations.

Article I, Section 4, Clause 2. Meetings of Congress. The Congress shall assemble at least once in every Year, and such Meeting shall be on the first Monday in December, unless they shall by Law appoint a different Day.

This clause was changed by Section 2 of the Twentieth Amendment (1933), which provides: "The Congress shall assemble at least once in every year, and such meeting shall begin at noon on the 3d day of January, unless they shall by law appoint a different day." Section 1 of the Amendment provides that the terms of Senators and Representatives shall end "at noon on the 3d day of January, of the years in which such terms would have ended if this article had not been ratified; and the terms of their successors shall then begin."

Article I, Section 5, Clause 1. Qualifications and Quorum. Each House shall be the Judge of the Elections, Returns and Qualifications of its own Members, and a Majority of each shall constitute a Quorum to do Business; but a smaller Number may adjourn from day to day, and may be authorized to compel the Attendance of absent Members, in such Manner, and under such Penalties as each House may provide.

The Supreme Court in *Powell v. McCormack*, 395 U.S. 486 (1969), ruled 7–1 that the House of Representatives could not refuse membership to a candidate who met the qualifications stated in Article I, Section 2, Clause 2. The case involved Representative Adam Clayton Powell, Jr., of New York, who had been found by congressional investigators to have misused federal funds. The Court held that the proper remedy was expulsion under Article I, Section 5, Clause 2, instead of an attempt to enlarge the constitutional qualifications.

In *Roudebush v. Hartke*, 405 U.S. 15 (1972), Hartke was certified by the state as the winner of a close senatorial election. Roudebush filed a timely recount petition in state court. Hartke opposed the recount, claiming that the Senate under this clause was the judge of the elections, returns and qualifications of its members. The Supreme Court held 5–2 that the clause does not prohibit a state recount of the ballots, and that the recount would not prevent an independent Senate evaluation of the election any more than the original count did.

In *United States v. Ballin*, 144 U.S. 1 (1892), the Court upheld 9–0 the House of Representatives' rule that a quorum is satisfied if a majority of members are present, even if they withhold their votes. The authority to compel the attendance of absent members is a safeguard against a minority's preventing the formation of a quorum for the transaction of business. Parliamentarians define the quorum as a majority of those elected, sworn in, and living.

Article I, Section 5, Clause 2. Rules and Expulsion. Each House may determine the Rules of its Proceedings, punish its Members for disorderly Behaviour, and, with the Concurrence of two thirds, expel a Member.

The Supreme Court has held that there are no judicially enforceable constitutional standards limiting the use of the expulsion power other than the supermajority requirement. *In re Chapman*, 166 U.S. 661 (1897), 9–0 vote. On occasion each House has punished its respective members by censure, reprimand, loss of seniority, removal of chairmanship, and fine.

Article I, Section 5, Clause 3. House Journal. Each House shall keep a Journal of its Proceedings, and from time to time publish the same, excepting such Parts as may in their Judgment require Secrecy; and the Yeas and Nays of the Members of either House on any question shall, at the Desire of one fifth of those Present, be entered on the Journal.

Each House possesses complete discretion over what proceedings shall be secret. *Field v. Clark*, 143 U.S. 649 (1892). The journal is not the same as the *Congressional Record* which Congress started in 1873. The *Record* is neither the official or actual record of congressional proceedings. It includes legislative texts, floor speeches (whether delivered or not), revisions of remarks, and correspondence from constituents. The court in *Gregg v. Barrett*, 248 U.S. App DC 347, 354 (1985), held that the rules allowing a member of Congress to edit his remarks before publication in the *Congressional Record* are not subject to judicial review.

Article I, Section 5, Clause 4. Adjournment. Neither House, during the Session of Congress, shall, without the Consent of the other, adjourn for more than three days, nor to any other Place than that in which the two Houses shall be sitting.

If the two Houses cannot agree upon a time of adjournment, the President, pursuant to Article II, Section 3, Clause 1, "may adjourn them to such Time as he shall think proper." While the two Houses are required to meet together, they are not required to meet in the Capitol, which was especially important during the War of 1812 when the British burned Washington.

Article I, Section 6, Clause 1. Compensation; Privilege from Arrest; Speech and Debate. The Senators and Representatives shall receive a Compensation for their Services, to be ascertained by Law, and paid out of the Treasury of the United States. They shall in all Cases, except Treason, Felony and Breach of the Peace, be privileged from Arrest during their Attendance at the Session of their respective Houses, and in going to and returning from the same; and for any Speech or Debate in either House, they shall not be questioned in any other Place.

COMPENSATION

As to the question of who should be able to change the level of legislative compensation, the court in *Humphrey v. Baker*, 848 F2d 211 (DC Cir 1900), upheld the constitutionality of a statute under which a commission made recommendations for salary increases to the President, who in turn had statutory authority to recommend increases to the Congress. The presidential recommendations would become effective as law unless Congress enacted a joint resolution of disapproval within 30 days. The court reasoned that the pay increase procedure (delegation to the President and disapproval option) was itself "ascertained by Law."

The Twenty-seventh Amendment (1992) provides that no change in compensation for Senators and Representatives shall take effect "until an election of representatives shall have intervened." Oddly, this Amendment was proposed in 1789 as part of the original Bill of Rights and took over 200 years to be ratified.

PRIVILEGE FROM ARREST

The Supreme Court in *Williamson v. United States*, 207 U.S. 425 (1908), 9–0 interpreted "in all Cases, except Treason, Felony and Breach of the Peace" to encompass all crimes and held that this clause does not provide Congress with any immunity from criminal prosecution. In *Long v. Ansell*, 293 U.S. 76 (1934), the Court held 9–0 that the clause does not provide any privilege from civil process and that civil litigants can compel members of Congress to appear in court to defend against civil actions.

SPEECH AND DEBATE

The Supreme Court has applied the immunity of this clause to protect the independence of Congress when exercising the legislative responsibilities assigned to it by the Constitution. *Eastland v. United States Servicemen's Fund*, 421 U.S. 491 (1975), 8–1 vote. Such protected activities must be clearly part of the legislative process. *United States v. Brewster*, 408 U.S. 501 (1972), 6–3 vote. An activity is deemed to be within the legislative process if it is "an integral part of the deliberative and communicative processes by which Members participate in committee and House proceedings with respect to the consideration and passage or rejection of proposed legislation or with respect to other matters which the Constitution places within the jurisdiction of either House." *Gravel v. United States*, 408 U.S. 606, 625 (1972). The clause protects such acts as voting, conduct of committee hearings, issuance and distribution of committee reports, and the subpoenaing of information required in the course of congressional investigations. *Doe v. McMillan*, 412 U.S. 306 (1973). A congressman may not be held accountable for a speech made on the floor of the House allegedly in pursuance of a criminal conspiracy and in return for compensation. The clause forecloses inquiry not only into the content of a speech, but also the motives for making it. *United States v. Johnson*, 383 U.S. 169 (1966), 7–0 vote. In *Gravel*, the Court declared that the clause applies "not only to a Member but also to his aides insofar as the conduct of the latter would be a protected legislative act if performed by the Member himself." 408 U.S. 618.

However, the Supreme Court in *Hutchinson v. Proxmire*, 443 U.S. 111 (1979), held 8–1 that a "Golden Fleece Award" given by Senator William Proxmire (D-WI) to recipients of alleged government waste was not protected by the clause because it was disseminated in news releases and constituent newsletters which are not essential to Senate deliberations.

Article I, Section 6, Clause 2. Sinecure; Incompatibility. No Senator or Representative shall, during the Time for which he was elected, be appointed to any civil Office under the Authority of the United States, which shall have been created, or the Emoluments whereof shall have been encreased during such time; and no Person holding any Office under the United States, shall be a Member of either House during his Continuance in Office.

SINECURE

This clause applies to those members who have taken their seats, not to those who are elected but not yet sworn in. "Appointed" means at the moment of nomination for civil office, not at the time of approval. The prohibition cannot be avoided by resignation from Congress because the clause applies for the term "for which he was elected," not to the time during which the member actually holds office. "Civil office" refers to an office in which the appointee exercises an authoritative role, and not to temporary, honorific, advisory or occasional postings. *United States v. Hartwell*, 73 U.S. 385 (1867).

"Emoluments" include more than salary. *McLean v. United States*, 226 U.S. 374 (1912). Congress has occasionally avoided the "emoluments" increase prohibition by temporarily reducing the salaries of certain offices so that members who had voted for increases could be appointed.

INCOMPATIBILITY

This clause reinforces the separation of powers by prohibiting a member of Congress from simultaneously holding an office in the executive or judicial branch.

Article I, Section 7, Clause 1. Origination. All Bills for raising Revenue shall originate in the House of Representatives; but the Senate may propose or concur with Amendments as on other Bills.

The purpose of the Origination Clause is to require revenue bills to originate in the House of Representatives which is deemed closer to the people than the Senate. However, as a practicable matter, the clause is largely ineffective since the Senate may amend the bills. Also, the clause does not apply to bills that impose user fees. *United States v. Munoz-Flores*, 495 U.S. 385 (1990), 9–0 vote.

Article I, Section 7, Clause 2. Presentment of Bills; Pocket Veto. Every Bill which shall have passed the House of Representatives and the Senate, shall, before it become a Law, be presented to the President of the United States; If he approve he shall sign it, but if not he shall return it, with his Objections to that House in which it shall have originated, who shall enter the Objections at large on their Journal, and proceed to reconsider it. If after such Reconsideration two thirds of that House shall agree to pass the Bill, it shall be sent, together with the Objections, to the other House, by which it shall likewise be reconsidered, and if approved by two thirds of that House, it shall become a Law. But in all such Cases the Votes of both Houses shall be determined by Yeas and Nays, and the Names of the Persons voting for and against the Bill shall be entered on the Journal of each House respectively. If any Bill shall not be returned by the President within ten Days (Sundays excepted) after it shall have been presented to him, the Same shall be a Law, in like Manner as if he had signed it, unless the Congress by their Adjournment prevent its Return, in which Case it shall not be a Law.

PRESENTMENT OF BILLS

The Presentment Clause defines the law-making process involving bicameralism and presentment to the President. When there is any difference in the bills passed by the two Houses, the bills are referred to a conference committee, composed of members of both Houses, to resolve the difference. Afterwards, the legislation must be passed in identical form by both Houses before being presented to the President. Upon presentment, the President has several options. First, he may sign the bill into law. Second, he may veto the bill and return it to Congress with his objections. If the bill is re-passed by each House with a two-thirds majority vote, the bill becomes law without the President's signature. Third, the President may do nothing, and the bill will become law within ten days if Congress is still in session. However, if Congress is in adjournment at the end of the ten days, the unsigned bill does not become law. This de facto veto is called a pocket veto.

In *Clinton v. City of New York*, 524 U.S. 417 (1998), the Supreme Court struck down 6–3, as a violation of the Presentment Clause, the Line Item

Veto Act of 1996 that authorized the President to cancel specific items in tax and spending measures. The Court held that the line item veto allows a partial veto which conflicts with the clause. Accordingly, the use of line item veto would require a constitutional amendment.

POCKET VETO

If the President refuses to approve or return a bill within the allotted time, the bill automatically becomes law. However, if the Congress is in adjournment at the end of the allotted time, the bill dies if the President has not signed it. In *The Pocket Veto Case*, 279 U.S. 655 (1929), the Supreme Court held 9–0 that "adjournment" applied to *sine die*, inter-session and intra-session adjournments of both Houses. In *Wright v. United States*, 302 U.S. 583 (1938), the Court held that a three-day recess by a single House did not meet the clause's definition of adjournment. Since some federal courts have subsequently raised the issue that a pocket veto applies only to *sine die* adjournments, the Presidents now often exercise the pocket veto with a "protective return" declaring their objections to the bill so that if a pocket veto is found invalid, the bill will be treated as vetoed in the regular manner, rather than becoming law by default.

LEGISLATIVE VETO

In *Immigration and Naturalization Service v Chadha*, 462 U.S. 919 (1983), the Supreme Court considered the constitutionality of the legislative veto, a commonly-used practice authorized in 196 different statutes at the time. Under this practice, Congress reserved the right to disapprove executive branch regulations without formally passing a law subject to the President's veto. The Court held 7–2 that the legislative veto violated the Presentment Clause. Once the Congress delegates authority to an executive branch agency, it cannot overturn that agency's regulations without passing another law for presentation to the President.

SEPARATION OF POWERS

In *Bowsher v. Synar*, 478 U.S. 714 (1986), the Supreme Court addressed a key provision of the Balanced Budget and Emergency Deficit Control Act of 1985. This Act provided for annual cuts in the federal budget deficit and stipulated that if the Congress could not agree on the cuts, they would be specified by the Comptroller General, a legislative branch officer. The Court invalidated the provision, holding 7–2 that the specification of budget cuts was an execution of laws, and that the attempted vesting of this executive function in a legislative branch official violated the principle of separation of powers.

Article I, Section 7, Clause 3. Presentment of Resolutions. Every Order, Resolution, or Vote to which the Concurrence of the Senate and House of Representatives may be necessary (except on a question of Adjournment) shall be presented to the President of the United States; and before the Same shall take Effect, shall be approved by him, or being disapproved by him, shall be repassed by two thirds of the Senate and House of Representatives, according to the Rules and Limitations prescribed in the Case of a Bill.

This clause ensures that the President participates in the legislative process, whether the law in question is labeled a bill or a resolution. However, the President is not presented with resolutions that are not laws, such as simple resolutions that apply only to the operations of one House, or concurrent resolutions passed by both Houses that prescribe procedures, express public policy or set revenue or spending goals.

Also, pursuant to Article V, proposed constitutional amendments are not presented to the President before they are sent by the Congress to the states for ratification.

Article I, Section 8, Clause 1. Taxes; Spending. The Congress shall have Power To lay and collect Taxes, Duties, Imposts and Excises, to pay the Debts and provide for the common Defence and general Welfare of the United States; but all Duties, Imposts and Excises shall be uniform throughout the United States [...].

Section 8 defines the enumerated powers of Congress which have been broadly interpreted by the Supreme Court. The purpose of this clause, known as the "General Welfare or Uniformity Clause," is to prevent geographic discrimination that would give one state or region a competitive advantage or disadvantage in its commercial relations with the others. In *United States v. Ptasynski*, 462 U.S. 74 (1983), the Supreme Court held 9–0 that any tax in which the subject is defined in nongeographic terms satisfies the Uniformity Clause, and that where the subject is defined in geographic terms, the tax will be scrutinized for actual geographic discrimination.

TAXES

"Duties" are indirect taxes on imported goods. "Imposts" are indirect taxes imposed on imports and exports. "Excises" are indirect taxes levied on goods produced, manufactured, sold, used or transported within the country, or upon various privileges. The power to tax under this clause did not include the income tax, which was authorized by the Sixteenth Amendment (1913).

The Supreme Court in *McCray v. United States*, 195 U.S. 27 (1904), upheld 6–3 a federal tax on the production of oleomargarine which had been advocated by the dairy industry to reduce competition. McCray contended that the tax was a misuse of the taxing power because it was used for regulation and not for revenue. The Court reasoned that the judiciary is without authority to void a congressional act lawfully exerting the taxing power even where it appeared that the tax was unwise or oppressive; nor can the judiciary inquire into the motive of Congress in levying a tax within its constitutional power.

In *New York v. United States*, 326 U.S. 572 (1946), the Supreme Court held 6–2 that the state, in the sale of mineral waters taken from state owned property, is engaged in a nongovernmental function and, hence, is not immune from the federal tax imposed on mineral waters. This decision followed *Ohio v. Helvering*, 292 U.S. 360 (1934), holding that, while state governmental instrumentalities and operations are exempt from federal taxation, state engagement in a business of a private nature is not immune from the federal taxing power.

SPENDING

The authority for the Congress to tax and spend to pay debts and provide for the common defense and general welfare was strictly construed for much of U.S. history. However, in *United States v. Butler*, 297 U.S. 1, (1936), the Supreme Court broadly interpreted congressional authority to tax and spend for the general welfare, and held that it was not limited to authorizations contained elsewhere in the Constitution. Nevertheless, the court ruled 6–3 in this case that the particular tax and regulatory program to increase farm income by reducing crop acreage, at issue under the Agricultural Adjustment Act of 1933, was unconstitutional because it sought to regulate and control agricultural production that violated the reserved powers of the states under the Tenth Amendment (1791). As stated in *Fullilove v. Klutznick*, 448 U.S. 448, 474 (1980), the power to provide for the general welfare "is an independent grant of legislative authority, distinct from other broad congressional powers."

In the *Social Security Cases* (*Steward Machine Co. v. Davis*, 301 U.S. 548 [1937], 5–4 vote, and *Helvering v. Davis*, 301 U.S. 619 [1937], 7–2 vote), the Supreme Court upheld the constitutionality of provisions of the Social Security Act of 1935 to tax employers to finance unemployment compensation insurance, and to tax employers and employees to finance old-age benefits. The Court ruled that Congress may spend money in aid of the general welfare, that the congressional determination of general welfare must be respected by the courts unless it is plainly arbitrary, and that the concept of the general welfare is not static, but adapts itself to the crises and necessities of the times. The rationale of the *Social Security Cases* reflected a reversal of that used to invalidate Agricultural Adjustment Act in the *Butler* case.

In *South Dakota v. Dole*, 483 U.S. 203 (1987), the Supreme Court indicated that whatever limitation the spending clause might impose is essentially a nonjusticiable political question. In *Dole*, the Court held 7–2 that Congress could use its spending power to encourage certain activities by the states, as a condition of receiving federal funds, such as in this case of withholding highway funding from states that did not raise the minimum drinking age to 21. Earlier, in *Massachusetts v. Mellon*, 262 U.S. 447 (1923), the Congress had enacted legislation to provide grants to states that agreed to establish programs to protect the health and welfare of infants and mothers. The validity of the legislation was attacked as coercion upon the states by the federal government that resulted in taxation for illegal purposes. The Supreme Court ruled 9–0 that the issue was nonjusticiable, but observed that the legislation did not force the states to do anything or to yield any rights, except if they voluntarily chose to participate in the program.

Article I, Section 8, Clause 2. Borrowing. [The Congress shall have Power] To borrow Money on the credit of the United States [...].

The clause does not limit the amount of debt that the United States may incur.

In *Knox v. Lee* and *Parker v. Davis (Legal Tender Cases)*, 79 U.S. 457 (1871), the Supreme Court relied in part on the borrowing clause in holding 5–4 that Congress had authority under the Legal Tender Act of 1862 to issue treasury notes and to make them legal tender in satisfaction of antecedent debts. The Act enabled government to force creditors to accept paper money instead of gold coins for debt. In *Perry v. United States*, 294 U.S. 330, 351 (1935), the Court held that when the Congress borrows money "on the credit of the United States," it creates a binding obligation to pay the debt as stipulated and cannot thereafter vary the terms of its agreement. A law purporting to abrogate a provision in government bonds calling for payment in gold coin was held to contravene this clause, although the creditor was denied a remedy in the absence of a showing of actual damage.

Article I, Section 8, Clause 3. Commerce. [The Congress shall have Power] To regulate Commerce with foreign Nations, and among the several States, and with the Indian Tribes [...].

The Commerce Clause is one of the great sources of congressional power, and its interpretation has generated extensive litigation. It is also referred to as Dormant Commerce, Indian Commerce, Interstate Commerce, or Negative Commerce Clause.

FOREIGN NATIONS

Congressional power over foreign commerce is qualitatively greater than its power to regulate commerce among the states because it is part of the federal government's complete sovereign power over foreign relations, in which the states have no standing. *Brolan v. United States*, 236 U.S. 216 (1915).

INTERSTATE COMMERCE

Gibbons v. Ogden, 22 U.S. 1 (1824), involved the power of states to grant monopolies over steamboat navigation in their waterways. In striking down New York's steamboat monopoly, the Supreme Court declared 7–0 that congressional power to regulate foreign and interstate commerce embraced every species of commercial intercourse between the United States and foreign nations and every commercial transaction that was not wholly carried on within the boundaries of a single state; that in the case of interstate commerce, its power did not stop at the boundary line of any state but was applicable within the interior of a state; and that the term "commerce" included navigation.

The following are later key cases in which the Supreme Court has interpreted the scope of the Commerce Clause.

1. *Wilson v. Black Bird Creek Marsh Co.*, 27 U.S. 245 (1829), upheld 6–0 a state law permitting a company to erect a dam across a minor navigable stream to drain a swamp, in the absence of conflicting congressional legislation. Hence, when Congress chose to allow its commerce power to lie dormant, states could exercise concurrent power to regulate interstate commerce. This case is the origin of the "dormant" or "negative" commerce clause doctrine holding that if Congress has not enacted laws regarding the subject, a state may regulate local aspects of interstate commerce if it does not discriminate against or unduly burden interstate commerce. Otherwise, the state law would be invalidated by the doctrine. *American Trucking Associations, Inc. v. Michigan Public Service Commission*, 545 U.S. 429 (2005), 9–0 vote.

2. *United States v. Coombs*, 37 U.S. 72 (1838), upheld 9–0 a federal law punishing the theft of shipwrecked goods above the high water mark on the coast of New York State. "Any offense which thus interferes with, obstructs, or prevents such commerce and navigation, though done on land, may be punished by congress, under its general authority to make all laws necessary and proper to execute their delegated constitutional powers." 37 U.S. 78.

3. *Cooley v. Board of Wardens*, 53 U.S. 299 (1851), involving local pilotage regulations, held 6–2 that the commerce power of Congress is not exclusive but that, on the contrary, where a uniform national rule is not required, the states may apply their own regulations to foreign and interstate commerce until such time as Congress may decide to supersede them.

4. *Crandall v. Nevada*, 73 U.S. 35 (1867), involving a state tax of $1 for every person leaving the state by stage coach or railroad, invalidated 6–2 the tax, holding that a state cannot inhibit persons from leaving the state by taxing them. "We are all citizens of the United States, and as members of the same community must have the right to pass and repass through every part of it without interruption, as freely as in our own States." 73 U.S. 49.

5. *Welton v. Missouri*, 91 U.S. 275 (1876), invalidated 9–0 a state tax on peddlers selling out-of-state goods, but not on peddlers selling goods produced in-state, as discrimination against interstate commerce in favor of local interests.

6. *Wabash, St. Louis & Pacific Railroad Company v. Illinois*, 118 U.S. 557 (1886), invalidated 6–3 a state law seeking to regulate interstate railroad rates as a direct burden on interstate commerce, even in the absence of federal legislation on the subject. The *Wabash* case led to the establishment of the Interstate Commerce Commission in 1887 to regulate interstate railroad rates.

7. *In re Debs*, 158 U.S. 564 (1895), upheld 9–0 federal injunctive relief to end the violent strike by a labor union against the Pullman Company in 1894 under the authority of the Commerce and Post Office clauses in order to facilitate railroad ability to carry on commerce and the mail for the general welfare.

8. *Addyston Pipe & Steel Co. v United States*, 175 U.S. 211 (1899), held 9–0 that companies engaged in price-fixing and marketing schemes were engaged in interstate commerce and subject to congressional regulatory power.

9. *Champion v. Ames*, 188 U.S. 321 (1903), declared 5–4 that congressional power to regulate interstate commerce includes the authority to prohibit interstate traffic in lottery tickets.

10. *Northern Securities Co. v. United States*, 193 U.S. 197 (1904), upheld 5–4 the application of the Sherman Antitrust Act of 1890 to break up the holding company Northern Securities Company as an unreasonable restraint on interstate and international commerce. The holding company was established by financiers J. Pierpont Morgan and James J. Hill for the control of two competing railroads, the Northern Pacific and Great Northern, which operated across the northern United States between the Great Lakes and Puget Sound.

11. *Swift & Co. v. United States*, 196 U.S. 375 (1905), held 9–0 that

goods in the "stream of interstate commerce," such as cattle at the Chicago stockyards and slaughterhouses on the way from farm to nationwide distribution, were under congressional regulatory power.

12. *Standard Oil Company of New Jersey v. United States*, 221 U.S. 1 (1911), held 8–1 that the Standard Oil Company, owned by John D. Rockefeller, was guilty of monopolizing the petroleum industry by "unreasonable" contracts and combinations in restraint of trade in violation of the Sherman Antitrust Act, and upheld the dissolution of the company into several competing firms. On the same rationale, the Supreme Court in *United States v. American Tobacco Company*, 221 U.S. 106 (1911), ordered 8–1 the reorganization of the tobacco trust on the basis of the "rule of reason." In *United States v. Trenton Potteries Co.*, 273 U.S. 392 (1927), the Supreme Court held 5–3 that an agreement, among those controlling the manufacture and distribution of sanitary pottery, to fix and maintain uniform prices violated the Sherman Act whether the prices in themselves were reasonable or not.

13. *Southern Railway Company v. United States*, 222 U.S. 20 (1911), upheld 9–0 the application of the Safety Appliance Act of 1893 to intrastate trains because intrastate rail traffic has a substantial connection to interstate traffic.

14. *Minnesota Rate Cases*, 230 U.S. 352 (1913), upheld 9–0 state authority to regulate intrastate rates of interstate railroads, but suggested that where intrastate and interstate commerce were so intermingled as to render separation impracticable, Congress might regulate both under the Commerce Clause.

15. *Houston E. & W. Texas Ry. Co. v. United States (Shreveport Rate Case)*, 234 U.S. 342 (1914), held 7–2 that Texas had fixed unreasonably low rates between Texas points near state borders to the disadvantage of shippers in other states, and ordered Texas to raise its rates to conform with those fixed by the Interstate Commerce Commission for interstate shipments to avoid unjust discrimination.

16. *Buck v. Kuykendall*, 267 U.S. 307 (1925), invalidated 8–1 a requirement that interstate common carriers using the highways obtain a state license declaring the public need for their services. The Court found that the licensing was primarily to restrain competition, and not for highway safety or conservation. However, the Supreme Court in *Bradley v. Public Utilities Commission of Ohio*, 289 U.S. 92 (1933), upheld 9–0 a state denial of licensing for an interstate common carrier to operate over a particular highway as justified by the promotion of public safety in order to reduce highway congestion. The effect on interstate commerce was found to be incidental. The same result was reached in *South Carolina State Highway Department v. Barnwell Brothers, Inc.*, 303 U.S. 177 (1938), where the Court upheld 7–0 state limitations on the weight and width of interstate vehicles in order to conserve the highways and promote public safety.

17. *Ashwander v. Tennessee Valley Authority*, 297 U.S. 288 (1936), upheld 8–1 the construction of hydroelectric installations in the Tennessee Valley, and the acquisition by the Tennessee Valley Authority of transmission lines for the distribution and sale of its electric power, as a means to improve river navigation pursuant to congressional commerce powers, and to assure abundant electric energy for the manufacture of munitions in the event of war pursuant to congressional war powers (Article I, Section 8, Clause 11).

18. *National Labor Relations Board v. Jones & Laughlin Steel Corp.*, 301 U.S. 1 (1937), upheld 5–4 the application of the National Labor Relations Act of 1935 to resolve labor–management disputes that are directly related to the flow of interstate commerce.

19. *United States v. Darby Lumber Co.*, 312 U.S. 100 (1941), upheld 9–0 the constitutionality of the Fair Labor Standards Act prescribing minimum-wage, maximum-hour and other provisions, declaring that Congress may prohibit the interstate transportation of goods made in substandard working conditions. "The power of Congress over interstate commerce is complete in itself, may be exercised to its utmost extent, and acknowledges no limitations, other than are prescribed by the Constitution." 312 U.S. 114. The Court overruled *Hammer v. Dagenhart*, 247 U.S. 251 (1918), which had voided 5–4 restrictions on child labor. 312 U.S. 116.

20. *Edwards v. California*, 314 U.S. 160 (1941), invalidated 9–0 the state statute, popularly known as the "Okie Law," that prohibited a person from bringing any nonresident indigent person into the state. The Court ruled that the transportation of persons constituted commerce under the clause. No state may isolate itself from the troubles of the Union. 314 U.S. 173.

21. *Wickard v. Filburn*, 317 U.S. 111 (1942), held 9–0 that production quotas under the Agricultural Adjustment Act of 1938 were constitutionally applied to excess wheat that was produced for the farmer's private consumption on his own farm even though it never entered commerce at all, much less interstate commerce. The court reasoned that, if farmers were allowed to consume their own excess wheat outside the quotas, the cumulative affect would be substantial on the interstate market in wheat.

22. *Southern Pacific Company v. Arizona*, 325 U.S. 761 (1945), invalidated 7–2, as applied to interstate trains, a state train limit law making it unlawful to operate within the state a passenger train of more than 14 cars or a freight train of more than 70 cars. The Court, in balancing national and state interests, found that the law was a burden on interstate commerce because it seriously affected transportation efficiency, economy and safety.

23. *Morgan v. Virginia*, 328 U.S. 373 (1946), invalidated 7–1 a state law requiring racial segregation of passengers traveling on interstate buses in the state because the reseating of interstate passengers to comply with varying state laws burdened interstate commerce. *Boynton v. Virginia*, 364

U.S. 454 (1960), held 7–2 that bus terminals serving interstate bus passengers cannot engage in racial discrimination.

24. *Phillips Petroleum Co. v. Wisconsin*, 347 U.S. 672 (1954), upheld 5–3 Federal Power Commission jurisdiction under the Natural Gas Act to regulate the prices which natural gas producers charge when selling gas at the wellhead for later interstate transmission.

25. *Heart of Atlanta Motel v. United States*, 379 U.S. 241 (1964), upheld 9–0 the use of the commerce power to justify the Civil Rights Act of 1964, which forbade racial discrimination in public accommodations, such as hotels and restaurants, that were privately owned, because they affected interstate commerce. The same result was reached in *Katzenbach v. McClung*, 379 U.S. 294 (1964), which forbade 9–0 racial discrimination in privately owned restaurants as a burden on interstate commerce.

26. *Griggs v. Duke Power Company*, 401 U.S. 424 (1971), invalidated 8–0 Duke's hiring and advancement policy, requiring a high school education and passing two aptitude tests, that racially discriminated against a disproportionate number of African American employees. The Court found that the policy violated the Civil Rights Act of 1964 because the test requirements were not related to job performance and had a disparate impact on an ethnic minority.

27. *United States v. Maine*, 420 U.S. 515 (1975), upheld 8–0 federal exclusive control over the seabed beyond the 3-mile limit along state coastal waters pursuant to the Submerged Lands Act of 1953 and the Outer Continental Shelf Lands Act of 1953 which are supported by the federal government's constitutional jurisdiction over foreign commerce, foreign affairs and national defense. 420 U.S. 522.

28. *Complete Auto Transit, Inc. v. Brady*, 430 U.S. 274, 279 (1977), upheld 9–0 a state tax on imported cars under a four-prong test: 1. the activity taxed has a substantial nexus with the taxing state; 2. the tax is fairly apportioned between states; 3. the tax does not discriminate against interstate commerce; and 4. the tax is fairly related to services the state provides to the taxpayer. In *Quill Corporation v. North Dakota*, 504 U.S. 298 (1992), the Supreme Court invalidated 8–1 a North Dakota use tax on sales by an out-of-state mail-order company to state residents because the company had no physical presence in the state and, hence, no substantial nexus.

29. *Philadelphia v. New Jersey*, 437 U.S. 617 (1978), invalidated 7–2 a state law that prohibited the importation of waste into the state from outside its borders as a violation of the Dormant Commerce Clause. A state may not attempt to isolate itself from a problem common to many by erecting a barrier against the movement of interstate trade by imposing on out-of-state commercial interests the full burden of conserving the state's remaining landfill space.

30. *United States v. Lopez*, 514 U.S. 549 (1995), invalidated 5-4 the Gun-Free School Zones Act of 1990 because the possession of a gun near a school is not an economic activity that has a substantial effect on interstate commerce. This was the first time since 1935 that the Court had invalidated a law on the ground that Congress had exceeded its authority under the Commerce Clause.

31. *United States v. Morrison*, 529 U.S. 598 (2000), struck down 5–4 part of the Violence Against Woman Act of 1994, which allowed victims of gender-based violence to sue for damages in federal court, because it did not bear a sufficient relationship to interstate commerce.

32. *Gonzales v. Raich*, 545 U.S. 1 (2005), held 6–3 that Congress under the Controlled Substances Act (CSA) may ban the use of homegrown marijuana for medicinal purposes even where states approve its use. The Court reasoned that consuming one's locally grown marijuana affects the interstate marijuana market and hence Congress may prohibit such consumption. In *Gonzales v. Oregon*, 546 U.S. 243 (2006), the Supreme Court held 6–3 that the CSA does not empower the U.S. Attorney General to prohibit doctors from prescribing drugs for use in physician-assisted suicide of the terminally ill as permitted by state law.

These cases reflect that the Supreme Court affords great latitude to the Congress in the exercise of its jurisdiction over interstate commerce, although on occasion it may exceed constitutional parameters.

INDIAN TRIBES

The Supreme Court in *Worcester v. Georgia*, 31 U.S. 515 (1832), in an opinion by Chief Justice John Marshall, confirmed 5–1 the supremacy of federal authority over the states in regard to the Indians. This case held that the Cherokee Nation was entitled to federal protection from the actions of Georgia which would infringe on tribal sovereignty. The court struck down Georgia's regulation of the Cherokees as unconstitutional under the Commerce and Treaty (Art. II, Sec. 2, Cl. 2) Clauses. President Andrew Jackson (1829–1837) refused to enforce the decision as to Indian sovereignty, supposedly saying: "John Marshall has made his decision, now let him enforce it!" Pursuant to the Indian Removal Act of 1830, supported by President Jackson, about 50,000 eastern Indians were removed to territory west of the Mississippi River to facilitate white settlements in the vacated areas. Under the guns of federal and Georgia troops, the Cherokee tribe made their trek to present-day Oklahoma. It is estimated that between three and four thousand out of fifteen to sixteen thousand Cherokees died en route from the brutal conditions of the "Trail of Tears."

The last treaties between the United States and the Indians were entered into in 1871. In 1924, Congress granted citizenship to all Indians born in the United States who were not otherwise citizens. In 1968, Congress passed the Indian Civil Rights Act that extended constitutional guarantees to Indians in relation to their own tribal governments.

Article I, Section 8, Clause 4. Naturalization; Bankruptcy. [The Congress shall have Power] To establish an uniform Rule of Naturalization, and uniform Laws on the subject of Bankruptcies throughout the United States [...].

NATURALIZATION

Naturalization is the legal process whereby a person acquires a citizenship different from that person's citizenship at birth. The Supreme Court in *Chirac v. Lessee of Chirac*, 15 U.S. 259 (1817), held that the power of naturalization is exclusively in the Congress, notwithstanding any contrary state laws. Accordingly, Congress has the discretion to determine the mode of naturalization, the conditions upon which it will be granted, and the classes of persons to whom the right may be extended. The Supreme Court in *American Insurance Co. v. 356 Bales of Cotton*, 26 U.S. 511 (1828), upheld 7–0 congressional authority to vest citizenship collectively of those residing in the Louisiana Territory and Florida upon acquisition by the United States.

In contrast to naturalization, expatriation is the renunciation of the citizenship acquired by birth or otherwise. The Supreme Court has overturned congressional authority on involuntary expatriation in the following cases: for desertion from the military in wartime, *Trop v. Dulles*, 356 U.S. 86 (1958), 5–4 vote; for service by a dual national in the Japanese army during World War II, *Nishikawa v. Dulles*, 356 U.S. 129 (1958), 7–2 vote; for fleeing the country during wartime to evade military service, *Kennedy v. Mendoza-Martinez*, 372 U.S. 144 (1963), 5–4 vote; and for relocation to a foreign country and voting in its elections, *Afroyim v. Rusk*, 387 U.S. 253 (1967), 5–4 vote.

BANKRUPTCY

In *United States v. Fisher*, 6 U.S. 358 (1805), the Supreme Court upheld 5–0, under the Necessary and Proper Clause (Article I, Section 8, Clause 18) a 1797 statute that gave the United States a preference in bankruptcy over other creditors.

Bankruptcy Law, *U.S. Code*, Title 11, is limited to the adjustment of the debts of debtors and their creditors, and does not extend to the general regulation of debtor-creditor law. States may not regulate bankruptcy although they may pass laws that govern other aspects of the debtor-creditor relationship. Several sections of Title 11 incorporate the debtor-creditor law of individual states. Bankruptcy proceedings are handled in the U.S. bankruptcy courts that are a part of the U.S. district courts. U.S. Trustees handle many of the supervisory and administrative duties of bankruptcy proceedings.

The Supreme Court in *Sturges v. Crowninshield*, 17 U.S. 122 (1819), held 7–0 that a state law which permits a discharge against a debtor is unconstitutional as an impairment of the obligation of a contract. However, a state debtor relief law is constitutional as applied to contracts entered into after the law became effective. *Ogden v. Sanders*, 25 U.S. 213 (1827), 4–3 vote.

Article I, Section 8, Clause 5. Coinage; Weights and Measures. [The Congress shall have Power] To coin Money, regulate the Value thereof, and of foreign Coin, and fix the Standard of Weights and Measures [...].

COINAGE

Legal tender is the kind of money which a creditor is required by law to accept at face value. Congressional power to coin money is exclusive. However, the states, under Article I, Section 10, Clause 1, may make "gold and silver Coin a Tender in Payment of Debts." The Congress enacted the Legal Tender Act of 1862 that allowed the federal government to print paper money (greenbacks) not directly tied to gold and silver reserves. The Act was originally intended only as a strategy to finance the enormously costly Civil War, but it eventually led to the establishment of a national currency. The Supreme Court in *Knox v. Lee*, 79 U.S. 457 (1871), upheld 5–4 the Legal Tender Act of 1862 requiring that paper money be accepted as legal tender for both past and future debts. In *Juilliard v. Greenman*, 110 U.S. 421 (1884), the Supreme Court 8–1 extended *Knox* by upholding the validity of legal tender laws during peacetime.

WEIGHTS AND MEASURES

The purpose of the clause is to empower Congress to facilitate domestic and international commerce by adopting and enforcing national measurement standards. However, Congress has not sought to preempt the field thereby leaving room for state prescriptions. The Metric Conversion Act of 1975, as amended, *U.S. Code*, Title 15, designated the metric system as the preferred system of weights and measures for U.S. trade and commerce.

Article I, Section 8, Clause 6. Counterfeiting. [The Congress shall have Power] To provide for the Punishment of counterfeiting the Securities and current Coin of the United States [...].

In *Fox v. Ohio*, 46 U.S. 410 (1847), the Supreme Court upheld a state law that punished the passing of counterfeit money. The Court reasoned that the act of counterfeiting was a federal offense, whereas passing the counterfeit money was a "private harm" punishable under the state's police power. Federal and state governments possess concurrent power to punish the possession of devices for making counterfeit money. *Baender v. Barnett*, 255 U.S. 224 (1921), 9–0 vote.

Article I, Section 8, Clause 7. Post Office. [The Congress shall have Power] To establish Post Offices and post Roads [...].

Since the postal service is operated under federal authority, vehicles carrying the U.S. mail are exempt from the payment of state tolls for the use of the roads (*Searight v. Stokes*, 44 U.S. 151 [1845], 8–1 vote), and a state may not require a U.S. postal employee to have a state driver's license to operate a postal vehicle (*Johnson v. Maryland*, 254 U.S. 51 [1920], 7–2 vote).

The Supreme Court in *Ex parte Jackson*, 96 U.S. 727 (1878), 9–0 has broadly interpreted congressional power over the mail, including the right to determine what can and cannot be mailed. The Court in *In re Rapier*, 143 U.S. 110 (1892), held 9–0 that Congress has the right to prohibit circulation of materials that are immoral and injurious, such as lottery tickets. *Brennan v. United States Postal Service*, 439 U.S. 1345 (1978), reaffirmed the government's monopoly over the postal system. *United States Postal Service v. Council of Greenburgh Civic Associations*, 453 U.S. 114 (1981), upheld federal law prohibiting the placing of unstamped mail in home mailboxes, while acknowledging that congressional power cannot be exercised in a way that abridges rights protested by the First Amendment.

Article I, Section 8, Clause 8. Patent and Copyright. [The Congress shall have Power] To promote the Progress of Science and useful Arts, by securing for limited Times to Authors and Inventors the exclusive Right to their respective Writings and Discoveries [...].

Copyrights allow creators of literary or artistic works to retain exclusive right to publish or reproduce their work for a term of years. Patents allow inventors the exclusive right to make, use, sell or lease their inventions for a term of years. Upon the expiration of the terms, the product enters the "public domain" for use by all. The protection of this intellectual property is important in encouraging innovation and creativity in American society.

In *Eldred v. Ashcroft*, 537 U.S. 186 (2003), the Supreme Court upheld 7–2 the congressional extension of copyright terms by an additional 20 years beyond those set in the Copyright Act of 1976 for both new and existing works. Congress needed only to set time limits for copyright to comply with the "limited Times" prescribed by the clause. The Court in *Burrow-Giles Lithographic Co. v. Sarony*, 111 U.S. 53 (1884), upheld 9–0 copyright protection for photographs. The Court in *Graham v. John Deere Co.*, 383 U.S. 1 (1966), declared 7–0 that Congress may not grant patents "without regard to the innovation, advancement or social benefit gained thereby" or "whose effects are to remove existent knowledge from the public domain, or to restrict free access to materials already available." 383 U.S. 6. In *Feist Publications, Inc. v. Rural Telephone Service Co.*, 499 U.S. 340 (1991), the Court 9–0 stated that because the clause permits copyright protection only for creative works, facts cannot be copyrighted. In *Sony Corp. of America v. Universal City Studios*, 464 U.S. 417 (1984), the Supreme Court ruled 5–4 that the sale of Betamax video tape recorders to the general public did not constitute contributory infringement of copyrighted public broadcasts, and that the personal use of the devices to record television broadcasts for later viewing constituted fair use. In *MGM Studios v. Grokster*, 545 U.S. 913 (2005), the Supreme Court, in a case involving the marketing of file-sharing software, held 9–0 that "one who distributes a device with the object of promoting its use to infringe copyright, as shown by clear expression or other affirmative steps taken to foster infringement, is liable for the resulting acts of infringements by third parties." 545 U.S. 919.

The Court ruled 9–0 that the clause did not provide authority for federal trademark legislation, *In re Trade-Mark Cases*, 100 U.S. 82 (1879). But that limitation was later circumvented by congressional use of the commerce power as authority for trademark legislation. A trademark is a distinctive name, symbol or other device used by the owner to identify that the product or service originates from a unique source.

Article I, Section 8, Clause 9. Inferior Courts. [The Congress shall have Power] To constitute Tribunals inferior to the supreme Court [...].

The judges of the inferior tribunals established under this clause, called Article I courts, do not have the lifetime tenure and compensation guarantee accorded the judges of the inferior courts that are established under Article III, Section 1. The Article III courts include the Supreme Court, the 13 courts of appeals, and the 94 district courts. The Article I courts include tribunals such as the Court of Appeals for the Armed Forces, the Court of Appeals for Veterans Claims, the Tax Court, bankruptcy courts, armed forces courts-martial, and administrative law adjudicative entities.

Article I, Section 8, Clause 10. Define and Punish. [The Congress shall have Power] To define and punish Piracies and Felonies committed on the high Seas, and Offences against the Law of Nations [...].

The Supreme Court in *United States v. Arjona*, 120 U.S. 479 (1887), 9–0 interpreted the clause broadly not only to permit Congress to punish actual violations of the law of nations, but also to punish offenses that would trigger the international responsibility of the United States if left unpunished. In *Ex parte Quirin*, 317 U.S. 1 (1942), the Court upheld 8–0 congressional "authority to define and punish offenses against the law of nations by sanctioning, within constitutional limitations, the jurisdiction of military commissions to try persons for offenses which, according to rules and precepts of the law of nations, and more particularly the law of war, are cognizable by such tribunals." 317 U.S. 28. The decisions of the military commissions are subject to review by civilian courts.

Article I, Section 8, Clause 11. Declare War; Marque and Reprisal; Captures. [The Congress shall have Power] To declare War, grant Letters of Marque and Reprisal, and make Rules concerning Captures on Land and Water [...].

Clauses 11–14 are collectively referred to as the War Clause.

DECLARE WAR

Under the War Powers Clause the Congress is authorized to declare war, and under Article II, Section 2, Clause 1, the President, as the commander in chief of the armed forces, is authorized to wage war. In *The Prize Cases*, 67 U.S. 635 (1863), involving the constitutionality of President Abraham Lincoln's ordering the blockade of Confederate ports during the Civil War, the Supreme Court held 5–4 that the President has the authority to initiate military action to protect the country without awaiting a congressional declaration of war.

Although the country has been involved in many armed conflicts, the Congress has formally declared war on only five occasions: War of 1812, Mexican-American War of 1846, Spanish-American War of 1898, World War I, and World War II. On some occasions, Congress has authorized hostilities by instruments other than formal declarations.

Advocates of congressional power contend that the President cannot initiate hostilities without congressional authorization. Advocates of presidential power contend that the President has the inherent constitutional authority to engage in hostilities without a formal declaration of war. In 1973, Congress passed the War Powers Resolution, over President Richard Nixon's veto, requiring congressional authorization for engagement in hostilities. Presidents have disputed the constitutionality of the resolution. The Supreme Court has thus far refused to rule on the issue.

In *Hamilton v. Kentucky Distilleries & Warehouse Co.*, 251 U.S. 146 (1919), the Supreme Court upheld 9–0 the War-Time Prohibition Act of 1918 that prohibited liquor traffic as a means of increasing war efficiency as part of the war power of Congress. The Eighteenth Amendment (1919), prohibiting intoxicating liquors, did not repeal the War-Time Prohibition Act. In *Ashwander v. Tennessee Valley Authority*, 297 U.S. 288 (1936), the Supreme Court upheld 8–1 the construction of hydroelectric installations in the Tennessee Valley, and the acquisition by the Tennessee Valley Authority of transmission lines for the distribution and sale of its electric power, as a means to assure abundant electric energy for the manufacture of munitions in the event of war pursuant to congressional war powers under this clause, and to improve river navigation pursuant to congressional commerce powers (Article I, Section 8, Clause 3). The Supreme Court in *Lichter v. United States*, 334 U.S. 742 (1948), upheld 7–2 executive authority under the Renegotiation Act to recover "excessive profits" from private contractors for war goods in time of war. Under the War Powers Clause the Congress may provide for the production of war supplies in the successful conduct of the war, and establish means to eliminate excessive private profits.

MARQUE AND REPRISAL

A letter of marque and reprisal is an authorization granted by a government to the owner of a private vessel to capture enemy vessels and goods on the high seas without being punished for piracy by the grantor government. The signatory powers to the Declaration of Paris in 1856 agreed to stop issuing such authorizations.

CAPTURES

The Captures Clause authorizes Congress to make rules for the confiscation, disposition and distribution of captured enemy property. In *Brown v. United States*, 12 U.S. 110 (1814), the Supreme Court, in interpreting the clause, held 7–0 that the executive lacks inherent constitutional authority to confiscate property owned by subjects of enemy nations, and must seek congressional authorization in order to do so.

Article I, Section 8, Clause 12. Army. [The Congress shall have Power] To raise and support Armies, but no Appropriation of Money to that Use shall be for a longer Term than two Years [...].

This is the only clause related to military affairs that includes a time limit on appropriations due to the founders' concern for historical precedents of standing armies posing threats to liberty.

The Supreme Court in the *Selective Draft Law Cases*, 245 U.S. 366

(1918), upheld 9–0 the compulsory features of the Selective Service Act of 1917. The Court ruled that congressional power to raise and support armies is separate from its power to call the states' militia into federal service; that the power to raise armies includes the power to compel military service; and that compulsory service is an obligation of a citizen to his government. The Act did not violate the Thirteenth Amendment's prohibition of involuntary servitude.

Following Reconstruction, in which the army had been used for law enforcement in the South, the Congress enacted the Posse Comitatus Act of 1878 to prohibit the use of the military to aid civil authorities in enforcing the law or suppressing civil disturbances unless ordered to do so by the President.

Article I, Section 8, Clause 13. Navy. [The Congress shall have Power] To provide and maintain a Navy [...].

This clause does not contain an appropriation limitation as does Clause 12 because the founders considered navies to be less dangerous to liberty than standing armies.

Article I, Section 8, Clause 14. Military Regulations. [The Congress shall have Power] To make Rules for the Government and Regulation of the land and naval Forces [...].

The purpose of this clause is the establishment of a system of military law and justice outside of the ordinary jurisdiction of the civil courts. In 1950, the system was unified among the services by congressional enactment of the Uniform Code of Military Justice, supplemented by the *Manual for Courts-Martial.* Military courts and tribunals established by Congress pursuant to Article I do not have the same protections and independence as Article III courts. The jurisdiction of a court-martial depends solely on the defendant's status as a member of the Armed Forces. *Solorio v. United States,* 483 U.S. 435 (1987), 6–3 vote. However, civilian dependents charged with crimes during peacetime may not be tried by court-martial (*Reid v. Covert,* 354 U.S. 1 [1957], 6–2 vote); not may civilian employees of the military (*Grisham v. Hagan,* 361 U.S. 278 [1960], 7–2 vote).

The Supreme Court in *Ex parte Milligan,* 71 U.S. 2 (1866), held 9–0 that military tribunals may not try civilians for crimes against the military when civil courts are functioning. The Court observed:

> The Constitution of the United States is a law for rulers and people, equally in war and in peace, and covers with the shield of its protection all classes of men, at all times, and under all circumstances. No doctrine,

involving more pernicious consequences, was ever invented by the wit of
man than that any of its provisions can be suspended during any of the
great exigencies of government. Such a doctrine leads directly to anarchy
or despotism, but the theory of necessity on which it is based is false; for
the government, within the Constitution, has all the powers granted to it,
which are necessary to preserve its existence. [71 U.S. 120.]

In *Ex parte Quirin*, 317 U.S. 1 (1942), the Court upheld 8–1 the jurisdiction of a military tribunal over the trial of eight German saboteurs as
unlawful combatants who had entered the United States in secret to commit hostile acts. The saboteurs are not entitled a grand jury process or trial
by jury, but the decisions of the military tribunal are subject to review by
civilian courts. In *Johnson v. Eisentrager*, 339 U.S. 763 (1950), the Supreme
Court held 6–3 that U.S. courts have no jurisdiction over German war criminals held in a U.S. prison in Germany.

Additional cases on this subject are reported under Article I, Section
9, Clause 2, relating to the writ of habeas corpus.

Article I, Section 8, Clause 15. Militia. [The Congress shall have Power]
To provide for calling forth the Militia to execute the Laws of the Union,
suppress Insurrections and repel Invasions [...].

Clauses 15 and 16 are collectively referred to as the Militia Clause.

The militia (now known as the National Guard) is the military force
of a state that is maintained to handle civil and military emergencies within
its borders. It is derived from the ancient doctrine of posse comitatus whereby
the sheriff could summon citizens to assist him in law enforcement. This
clause provides an important means for the President, as empowered by Congress, to supplement the national military in emergencies.

Article I, Section 8, Clause 16. Organizing Militia. [The Congress shall
have Power] To provide for organizing, arming, and disciplining, the Militia, and for governing such Part of them as may be employed in the Service
of the United States, reserving to the States respectively, the Appointment
of the Officers, and the Authority of training the Militia according to the
discipline prescribed by Congress [...].

In *Houston v. Moore*, 18 U.S. 1 (1820), the Supreme Court ruled that
the federal government's power over the militia "may be exercised to any
extent that may be deemed necessary by Congress." In 1916, the Congress
enacted the National Security Act that "federalized" the state militias that
had become known as the National Guard. The Act essentially stripped the
states of all their militia powers by authorizing detailed procedures for the

appointment of officers and training. The Supreme Court upheld the Act by ruling that the plenary power of Congress to raise armies was not restricted by the Militia Clause. *Cox v. Wood*, 247 U.S. 3 (1918). However, state governors continue to have the authority to call up the Guard to quell disturbances and to aid in disaster relief, subject to ultimate federal control.

Article I, Section 8, Clause 17. Enclave. [The Congress shall have Power] To exercise exclusive Legislation in all Cases whatsoever, over such District (not exceeding ten Miles square) as may, by Cession of particular States, and the Acceptance of Congress, become the Seat of the Government of the United States, and to exercise like Authority over all Places purchased by the Consent of the Legislature of the State in which the Same shall be, for the Erection of Forts, Magazines, Arsenals, dock–Yards, and other needful Buildings [...].

After ratification of the Constitution in 1788, there was disagreement as to where the permanent capital should be located. The first capital was located in New York City with the Congress meeting in the City Hall (Federal Hall) from 1788 to 1790. The second capital was in Philadelphia with the Congress meeting in the Philadelphia County Building (Congress Hall) from 1790 to 1800. In 1790, Alexander Hamilton, Secretary of the Treasury, Thomas Jefferson, Secretary of State, and Congressman James Madison reached an agreement locating the permanent capital in the South, at the northernmost point of commercial navigation on the Potomac River at the ports of Georgetown and Alexandria, with cession of lands from Maryland and Virginia. In exchange for the southern capital, Jefferson and Madison agreed to Hamilton's plan for the federal government to assume the states' Revolutionary War debts, which were more burdensome to the North than to the South. Hamilton believed that it was important for the federal government to assume these state debts to achieve national financial stability, which included satisfying the demands of foreign creditors.

Accordingly, Maryland and Virginia ceded "ten Miles square" on their respective sides of the Potomac River, and the government moved to its permanent seat in the District of Columbia in 1800. On September 7, 1846, Congress returned to Virginia its portion of the capital (Old Town Alexandria and Arlington County).

In 1961, the Twenty-third Amendment gave District residents the right to vote in presidential elections by electing the number of electors the District would be entitled to if it were a state, "but in no event more than the least populous State."

The application of federal enclave jurisdiction may extend from individual buildings to vast territories such as military installations and national parks. The state consenting to the acquisition retains no authority over the enclave unless it specifically reserved such authority at the time of consent. Otherwise, state minimum wholesale price regulations for sale of milk in federal enclaves were an unconstitutional burden because they conflicted with federal procurement regulations. *Paul v. United States*, 371 U.S. 245 (1963), 6–3 vote. The Supreme Court in *Evans v. Cornman*, 398 U.S. 419 (1970), held 8–0 that residents of a federal enclave treated as state residents by the adjoining state are entitled to vote in state elections under the Equal Protection Clause of the Fourteenth Amendment.

Article I, Section 8, Clause 18. Necessary and Proper. [The Congress shall have Power] To make all Laws which shall be necessary and proper for carrying into Execution the foregoing Powers, and all other Powers vested by this Constitution in the Government of the United States, or in any Department or Officer thereof.

This clause is the source of many of the implied powers of the Congress. *McCulloch v. Maryland*, 17 U.S. 316 (1819), arose from the refusal of the cashier of the Baltimore branch of the Bank of the United States to pay a state tax on the issuance of bank notes. In striking down the tax, 7–0, as a threat to national supremacy, Chief Justice John Marshall gave the classic exposition of the doctrine of implied powers by declaring: "Let the end be legitimate, let it be within the scope of the constitution, and all means which are appropriate, which are plainly adapted to that end, which are not prohibited, but consist with the letter and spirit of the constitution, are constitutional." 17 U.S. 421. Decisions throughout the Marshall Court (1801–1835) established a broad interpretation of the powers of the national government while the Constitution was still in its infancy.

Practically every power of the federal government has been expanded in some degree by the Necessary and Proper Clause. Under its authority, for example, Congress has adopted laws: defining and punishing crimes; regulating commerce, currency and the national economy; collecting revenue; imposing monetary and fiscal controls; acquiring property through eminent domain; and chartering banks and corporations. Accordingly, this clause has also been called the Basket, Coefficient, Elastic, Necessary and Proper, and Sweeping Clause.

Article I, Section 9, Clause 1. Slave Trade. The Migration or Importation of such Persons as any of the States now existing shall think proper to admit, shall not be prohibited by the Congress prior to the Year one thousand eight hundred and eight, but a Tax or duty may be imposed on such Importation, not exceeding ten dollars for each Person.

Congress passed, and President Thomas Jefferson signed, a law banning the importation of slaves, effective January 1, 1808, the earliest date permitted by the clause. However, the law did not restrict the domestic slave trade.

In *The Amistad v. United States*, 40 U.S. 518 (1841), Portuguese slave traders in 1839 abducted Africans from Sierra Leone and shipped them to Havana, Cuba. Fifty-three of them were purchased by two Spanish planters and placed aboard the Cuban schooner *Amistad* for shipment to a Caribbean plantation. The Africans seized the ship while traveling along the coast of Cuba, killed the captain and the cook, and ordered the planters to return them to Africa. The planters deceived them by sailing east toward the rising sun by day and north in darkness, winding up off the coast of Long Island, New York, where they were captured by the U.S. Navy. The planters were freed and the Africans were imprisoned in New Haven, Connecticut. On appeal, the Supreme Court ruled 7–1 that the Africans were not slaves, but had been kidnapped and were entitled to their freedom because the international slave trade had been banned in the United States and Spain. Thirty-five of them were returned to their homeland. The others died at sea or in prison while awaiting trial. John Quincy Adams, the sixth U.S. President (1825–1829) and then a U.S. Representative from Massachusetts, advocated the cause of the Africans before the Supreme Court. This incident was portrayed by the 1997 movie *Amistad*, directed by Steven Spielberg and starring Morgan Freeman and Anthony Hopkins.

Article I, Section 9, Clause 2. Habeas Corpus. The Privilege of the Writ of Habeas Corpus shall not be suspended, unless when in Cases of Rebellion or Invasion the public Safety may require it.

The writ of habeas corpus is known historically as the "great writ of liberty" because it affords protection against arbitrary imprisonment. When the writ is issued the officer holding a prisoner is required by court order to show cause why the prisoner is being held. If there is no lawful basis for the imprisonment, the court orders the release of the prisoner.

In *Ex parte Merryman*, 17 F Cases 144 (CC MD 1861), Supreme Court Chief Justice Roger Taney, sitting as a circuit judge, held that the privilege of the writ of habeas corpus may be suspended only by Congress, not by the President. President Abraham Lincoln refused to honor Taney's order for the release of John Merryman, a Southern sympathizer, who was confined in a military prison during the Civil War. Eventually, Merryman was handed over to civilian authorities, and Congress gave the President the power, which he had previously drawn to himself, to suspend the privilege of habeas corpus at his discretion during wartime.

The liberal use of the federal habeas corpus relief was narrowed by the Supreme Court in *Stone v. Powell*, 428 U.S. 465 (1976), holding 6–3 that such relief is not available to state prisoners whose Fourth Amendment (Search & Seizure) objections to their convictions had been reviewed and rejected by state appellate courts. Following the Oklahoma City bombing on April 19, 1995, Congress enacted the Antiterrorism and Effective Death Penalty Act of 1996 (AEDPA) that included limitations on federal habeas corpus relief. The Act placed a statute of limitations of one year following conviction for prisoners to seek relief, curbed successive petitions for relief, and limited the power of federal judges to grant relief unless the state court's adjudication of the claim was unreasonable. The constitutionality of limiting habeas corpus relief under the Act was upheld 9–0 in *Felker v. Turpin*, 518 U.S. 651 (1996).

In *Rasul v. Bush*, 542 U.S. 466 (2004), the Court ruled 6–3 that the civil court system has the authority to decide whether foreign nationals (non–U.S. citizens), held by the military in the prison camp at the U.S. Naval Base at Guantanamo Bay, were rightly imprisoned. (The base is on land leased by the United States from Cuba.) In *Hamdi v. Rumsfeld*, 542 U.S. 507 (2004), the Court held 6–3 that enemy combatants who are U.S. citizens have the right to challenge their detention before an impartial judge. In *Hamdan v. Rumsfeld*, 548 U.S. 557 (2006), the Court held 5–3 that military commissions used to try suspected terrorists detained at Guantanamo Bay violate the Uniform Code of Military Justice and the Geneva Conventions, and that the President did not have the authority to establish these commissions without congressional authorization. In response, the Congress enacted the Military Commissions Act (MCA) of 2006. The Supreme Court in *Boumediene v. Bush*, 553 U.S. 723 (2008), held 5–4 that foreign citizens detained at Guantanamo Bay have a constitutional right to challenge their detention in federal district courts, and that the habeas corpus restriction of the MCA violated the Habeas Corpus Suspension Clause.

Article I, Section 9, Clause 3. Bill of Attainder; Ex Post Facto Law. No Bill of Attainder or ex post facto Law shall be passed.

The Constitution prohibits the federal government (in this clause) and the states (in Article I, Section 10, Clause 1) from passing bills of attainder and ex post facto laws.

BILL OF ATTAINDER

Bill of Attainder is a legislative condemnation of a specifically designated person or group without the formality of a judicial trial. In *United States v. Brown*, 381 U.S. 437 (1965), the Supreme Court voided 5–4 as a bill of attainder a statute making it a crime for a member of the Communist Party to serve as an officer or employee of a labor union. While Congress under its commerce power may enact prohibitions generally applicable to any person who commits certain acts or possesses certain characteristics making him likely to initiate harmful deeds and leaving it to the courts to determine guilt or innocence, it may not designate a class of persons (members of the Communist Party) as being forbidden to hold union office. The Court observed that the clause was intended to implement the separation of powers among the three branches of government by guarding against the legislative exercise of judicial power.

In *Selective Service System v. Minnesota Public Interest Research Group*, 468 U.S. 841 (1984), the Supreme Court held 6–2 that the Military Selective Service Act, which denied federal financial assistance to students who had not registered for the draft, did not constitute a bill of attainder because the Act did not single out an identifiable group and does not inflict punishment.

Ex Post Facto Law

Collins v. Youngblood, 497 U.S. 37 (1990), defined 9–0 an expost facto law as "one that (1) punishes as a crime an act previously committed which was innocent when done, (2) makes more burdensome the punishment for a crime after its commission, or (3) deprives one charged with a crime of any defense available according to law at the time when the act was committed." The Ex Post Facto Clause applies solely to criminal cases, not civil cases, *Calder v. Bull*, 3 U.S. 386 (1798), 6–0 vote.

In the *Test Oath Cases* (*Cummings v. Missouri*, 71 U.S. 277 [1867], and *Ex parte Garland*, 71 U.S. 333 [1867]), the Supreme Court held 5–4 that retrospective test or loyalty oaths were invalid as both bills of attainder and ex post facto laws. A test oath is a weapon to punish a person for past conduct, whereas an oath of allegiance concerns future conduct such as allegiance or the faithful discharge of duties. *Cummings* concerned a state law requiring voters and persons in various occupations to swear that they had not aided or sympathized with the rebellion, and *Garland* concerned a federal law compelling attorneys who practiced in federal courts to swear that they had not supported the Confederacy. The Court ruled that, while the laws did not impose fines or imprisonment, they were punitive measures because they prevented former confederates from engaging in their occupations. The laws were bills of attainder because they subjected a designated class to punishment without trial and conviction, and they were ex post facto laws because they inflicted punishment for acts that had not been criminal when committed or inflicted additional punishment for acts that had been criminal.

Article I, Section 9, Clause 4. Direct Taxes. No Capitation, or other direct, Tax shall be laid, unless in Proportion to the Census or Enumeration herein before directed to be taken.

In *Hylton v. United States*, 3 U.S. 171 (1796), the Supreme Court held 3–0 that a federal tax on carriages used as passenger vehicles was an excise tax and not a direct tax requiring apportionment among the states by population. The Court interpreted a direct tax as one that is imposed directly upon property or upon the person (capitation), as distinguished from a tax based on privilege or use. Although upholding the tax, the Court assumed that it had the power to nullify unconstitutional acts of Congress—a power that would be later confirmed in *Marbury v. Madison*, 5 U.S. 137 (1803). The expression of such an assumption is an example of obiter dictum (said in passing) because it was merely a gratuitous non-binding opinion that was entirely unnecessary to the decision in this case which upheld the tax.

In *Pollock v. Farmers' Loan & Trust Co.*, 157 U.S. 429 (1895), the Supreme Court greatly limited congressional authority to levy an un-apportioned income tax, holding 5–4 that a tax on income from real and personal property, such as rent, interest or dividends, should be treated as a tax on the property itself and, therefore, it was a direct tax that required apportionment. *Pollock* made the source of income (such as property or wages) relevant in determining whether the tax was direct or indirect, and thus frustrated the ability of Congress to impose a comprehensive income tax. The *Pollock* decision was overturned and this clause was repealed by the adoption of the Sixteenth Amendment (1913), which permits Congress to levy taxes upon income from whatever source derived without apportionment among the states.

Article I, Section 9, Clause 5. Export Taxation. No Tax or Duty shall be laid on Articles exported from any State.

This prohibition applies only to the imposition of duties on goods by reason of exportation. *Turpin v. Burgess*, 117 U.S. 504, 507 (1886), 9–0 vote. A general tax on all property alike, including that intended for export, is not within the prohibition, if it is not levied on goods in the course of exportation or because of their intended exportation. *Cornell v. Coyne*, 192 U.S. 418, 428 (1904), 6–2 vote. In *United States v. IBM Corp.*, 517 U.S. 843 (1996), the Court 6–2 relied on the clause to strike down a nondiscriminatory federal excise tax on insurance premiums paid for the purpose of insuring goods against loss during exportation. In *United States v. United States Shoe Corp.*, 523 U.S. 360 (1998), the Court 9–0 struck down a harbor maintenance tax applied, on an ad valorem basis, to goods loaded at U.S. ports for export.

Article I, Section 9, Clause 6. Port Preference. No Preference shall be given by any Regulation of Commerce or Revenue to the Ports of one State over those of another; nor shall Vessels bound to, or from, one State, be obliged to enter, clear, or pay Duties in another.

This clause has been narrowly construed by the Supreme Court due to the wide variety of port improvements provided by Congress to the states. *Pennsylvania v. Wheeling & Belmont Bridge Co.*, 59 U.S. 421 (1856), 8–1 vote.

Article I, Section 9, Clause 7. Appropriations. No Money shall be drawn from the Treasury, but in Consequence of Appropriations made by Law; and a regular Statement and Account of the Receipts and Expenditures of all public Money shall be published from time to time.

This clause empowers Congress to control spending by the federal government—the "power of the purse." The Supreme Court in *Cincinnati Soap Co. v. United States*, 301 U.S. 308, 321 (1937), declared 9–0 that the clause "was intended as a restriction upon the disbursing authority of the Executive department," that "no money can be paid out of the Treasury unless it has been appropriated by an act of Congress," and that Congress has wide discretion in prescribing details of expenditures. A court may not order the payment of funds for which there is no appropriation. *Reeside v. Walker*, 52 U.S. 272 (1850), 9–0 vote; *Rochester Pure Water District v. United States Environmental Protection Agency*, 960 F2d 180, 184 (DC Cir 1992). The clause is referred to as the Statement and Account Clause.

Article I, Section 9, Clause 8. Titles of Nobility; Emoluments. No Title of Nobility shall be granted by the United States: And no Person holding any Office of Profit or Trust under them, shall, without the Consent of the Congress, accept of any present, Emolument, Office, or Title, of any kind whatever, from any King, Prince, or foreign State.

The federal government, like the states under Article I, Section 10, Clause 1, is prohibited from granting titles of nobility. The Congress has exercised its power of "Consent" under the clause by enacting the Foreign Gifts and Decorations Act of 1966, which establishes policies and procedures pertaining to the acceptance, use and disposition of gifts or decorations from foreign governments. Emolument refers to the salary, fees or perquisites of an office. The clause is referred to as the Emolument Clause.

Article I, Section 10, Clause 1. State Absolute Prohibitions. No State shall enter into any Treaty, Alliance, or Confederation; grant Letters of Marque and Reprisal; coin Money; emit Bills of Credit; make any Thing but gold and silver Coin a Tender in Payment of Debts; pass any Bill of Attainder, ex post facto Law, or Law impairing the Obligation of Contracts, or grant any Title of Nobility.

The clause is referred to as the Contract, Ex Post Facto, or Obligation of Contracts Clause.

STATE TREATIES, LETTERS OF MARQUE AND REPRISAL

The authority is centralized in the federal government to enter into treaties, alliances or confederations with foreign governments and to grant letters of marque and reprisal for privateers to capture enemy vessels.

STATE COINAGE

The prohibition on the states to create money placed the development of economic policy primarily in the federal government. In *Veazie Bank v. Fenno*, 75 U.S. 533 (1869), the Supreme Court upheld 7–2 a federal tax of 10 percent on the value of notes issued by state banks, thereby driving such notes out of circulation and making the note-issue privilege a monopoly of the then newly created national banks. The Court validated the tax as an exercise of Congress' constitutional power to provide a sound and uniform national currency. Earlier, in *Briscoe v. Bank of Kentucky*, 36 U.S. 257 (1837), the Supreme Court had upheld 6–1 the constitutionality of bank notes issued by a state-chartered bank because they were not formally issued by the state.

STATE BILLS OF ATTAINDER AND EX POST FACTO LAWS

The states, like the Congress under Article I, Section 9, Clause 3, are prohibited from passing bills of attainder and ex post facto laws.

In *Carmell v. Texas*, 529 U.S. 513 (2000), Carmell was convicted of multiple sexual offenses against his stepdaughter from 1991 to 1995, when she was 12 to 16 years old. Texas law in 1993 reduced the evidentiary burden required for conviction by increasing the age from 14 to 18 at which uncorroborated evidence could be received from the victim. The Supreme Court overturned 5–4 the convictions based on the reduced evidence as a violation of the Ex Post Facto Clause. "A law reducing the quantum of evidence required to convict an offender is as grossly unfair as, say, retrospectively eliminating an element of the offense, increasing the punishment for an existing offense, or lowering the burden of proof." 529 U.S. 532.

In *Smith v. Doe*, 538 U.S. 84 (2003), a state law, commonly known as "Megan's Law," required that sex offenders register with a state agency that maintains a central registry and publishes on the Internet information such as the offenders' names, photographs and physical descriptions. The defendants, convicted of aggravated sex offenses prior to the effectiveness of the law, contended that it was invalid as applied to them under the Ex Post Facto Clause. The Supreme Court held 6–3 that the retroactive application of the law does not violate the clause because the law is a civil, non-punitive means of identifying previous offenders for the protection of the public.

OBLIGATION OF CONTRACT

This clause is directed at state action alone. *New York v. United States,* 257 U.S. 591 (1922). It is not a limitation on the power of Congress, which may pass laws impairing the obligations of contracts, subject to the guarantees of the Fifth Amendment that no person shall be deprived of property without due process of law. *Sinking Fund Cases,* 99 U.S. 700 (1878); *Mitchell v. Clark,* 110 U.S. 633 (1884).

Fletcher v. Peck, 10 U.S. 87 (1810), arose from the Yazoo Land Fraud and an attempt by the Georgia legislature to repeal a land grant corruptly made by the preceding legislature. The Supreme Court held 6–1 that the action of one legislature rescinding a former grant was void because, although legislative acts may be repealed, rights vested under prior acts cannot be divested. The original grant was in the nature of a contract the obligation of which, under the Constitution, cannot be impaired. In *Green v. Biddle,* 21 U.S. 1 (1823), the Supreme Court held 4–0 that the Contract Clause applied to contracts between two states (Virginia–Kentucky compact) as well as those between private persons.

Dartmouth College was established in 1769 under a perpetual charter from King George III of England. The New Hampshire legislature amended the charter, making it a state university, enlarging the number of trustees, and revising its educational purpose. Dartmouth protested and was represented by Daniel Webster. The Supreme Court in *Dartmouth College v. Woodward,* 17 U.S. 518 (1819), held 6–1 that the act of the New Hampshire legislature unilaterally altering the charter of Dartmouth College was an unconstitutional impairment of the obligation of contract.

However, in *Charles River Bridge v. Warren Bridge,* 36 U.S. 420 (1837), the state had granted a charter in 1785 to Charles River Bridge Company to construct and operate a toll bridge between Boston and Charlestown. In 1828, the state authorized the Warren Bridge Company to construct a competing bridge across the Charles River. The first company sued, claiming that its charter was a contract granting it a monopoly on such traffic. The Supreme Court denied this claim 5–2, narrowly construing the original charter by holding that it had not specifically granted a monopoly, and that the state was entitled to exercise its police power to promote the general welfare by the opening of a second bridge.

In *Stone v. Mississippi*, 101 U.S. 814 (1880), the state in 1867 had granted Stone's corporation a 25 year charter to conduct a lottery. The following year the state adopted a new constitution prohibiting lottery activity. On appeal, the Supreme Court overturned the charter, holding 8–0 that the state could not contract away its inalienable police power to protect public morals

The police power is an exercise of the sovereign right of government to protect the lives, health, morals, comfort and general welfare of the people and is paramount to any rights under contracts between individuals or between the state and individuals. *Manigault v. Springs*, 199 U.S. 473 (1905), 9–0 vote; *Butchers Union Slaughter-House Co. v. Crescent City Slaughter-House Co.*, 111 U.S. 746 (1884), 9–0 vote. A charter for sale of liquor must yield to subsequent state prohibition legislation. *Boston Beer Co. v. Massachusetts*, 97 U.S. 25 (1877), 9–0 vote. The states have a right to regulate or abolish imprisonment for debt as a part of the remedy for enforcing the performance of contracts. *Mason v. Haile*, 25 U.S. 370 (1827), 6–1 vote. In *Home Building & Loan Association v. Blaisdell*, 290 U.S. 398 (1934), the Supreme Court upheld 5–4 a state mortgage moratorium law, enacted during the Great Depression, that extended the time that borrowers could pay their indebtedness on property to lenders. The court observed "that the question is no longer merely that of one party to a contract as against another, but of the use of reasonable means to safeguard the economic structure upon which the good of all depends." 290 U.S. 442.

Another exception to the rule against the impairment of contracts is the state's exercise of the power of eminent domain, which is the paramount right of the sovereign to acquire private property for a public purpose and on payment of just compensation. *West River Bridge Co. v. Dix*, 47 U.S. 507 (1848), 7–1 vote; *Illinois Central Railroad Co. v. Illinois*, 146 U.S. 387 (1892). A contract by a state to refrain from opening streets through the grounds of a hospital without the latter's consent is subject to the right of eminent domain. *Pennsylvania Hospital v. Philadelphia*, 245 U.S. 20 (1917). And where a city has contracted with a water company for the supply of water to the city for a term of years, it may subsequently condemn the company's property and franchise. *Long Island Water Supply Co. v. Brooklyn*, 166 U.S. 685 (1897).

STATE TITLE OF NOBILITY

This prohibition on state titles of nobility matches the prohibition on federal titles of nobility in Article I, Section 9, Clause 8.

Article I, Section 10, Clause 2. Import-Export. No State shall, without the Consent of the Congress, lay any Imposts or Duties on Imports or Exports, except what may be absolutely necessary for executing its inspection Laws; and the net Produce of all Duties and Imposts, laid by any State on Imports or Exports, shall be for the Use of the Treasury of the United States; and all such Laws shall be subject to the Revision and Controul of the Congress.

The Export or Import-Export Clause prohibits states, without congressional approval, from taxing imports and exports, except for inspection laws.

In *Brown v. Maryland*, 25 U.S. 419 (1827), the Supreme Court announced the "original package doctrine" by holding 6–1 that imported goods which became "incorporated and mixed up with the mass of property in the country" were subject to state taxation, but those that remained "in the original form or package" were still imports subject to congressional regulation. However, *Brown* was diluted by *Michelin Tire Corp. v. Wages*, 423 U.S. 276 (1976), where Michelin operated a warehouse in Georgia in which goods imported from foreign countries were stored for later distribution. The county levied a nondiscriminatory ad valorem property tax on the goods that was not based on their origin. Michelin contended that the goods were exempt from county taxation under the Import-Export Clause because they were in their original containers. The county replied that goods were subject to tax because they had been sorted and arranged for sale. The Supreme Court upheld 8–0 the tax because it did not interfere with the federal government's regulation of foreign commerce; deprive the federal government of its exclusive right to revenues from imposts and duties on imports; and interfere with the flow of goods between the states.

Article I, Section 10, Clause 3. Compact. No State shall, without the Consent of Congress, lay any Duty of Tonnage, keep Troops, or Ships of War in time of Peace, enter into any Agreement or Compact with another State, or with a foreign Power, or engage in War, unless actually invaded, or in such imminent Danger as will not admit of delay.

Tonnage duty is a tax on ships based on weight of goods carried or cubic capacity.

Two adjacent states may fix and settle their boundaries by compact or agreement with congressional consent. Compacts or agreements increasing the power of a state would also require congressional consent. But there are some matters upon which different states may agree that can in no way concern the United States, and therefore congressional consent is unnecessary. *Virginia v. Tennessee*, 148 U.S. 503 (1893), 9–0 vote. *Bode v. Barrett*, 344 U.S. 583 (1953), involved an Illinois tax on the gross weight of vehicles of motor carriers for the use of the public highways. Illinois residents were required to pay the tax, whereas nonresidents were exempt if the states of their residence reciprocated and granted like exemptions to Illinois residents. The

Supreme Court held that such a reciprocal arrangement does not violate the Compact Clause. In *United States Steel Corp. v. Multistate Tax Commission*, 434 U.S. 452 (1978), 21 states were members of the Multistate Tax Compact, a body formed by states, without congressional approval, to assist them in administering tax law relating to multistate businesses. The Supreme Court held 7–2 that state compacts require congressional approval only if they encroach upon the supremacy of the United States.

Article II
The Executive Branch

Article II, Section 1. Executive Vesting; Electoral College; Eligibility; Succession. [Section 1 is here presented in its current form as amended by the ratification of the Twelfth Amendment (1804), the Twentieth Amendment (1933), and the Twenty-fifth Amendment (1967). The italicized subtitles are added for ease of reference. The variations in spelling, capitalization and punctuation are due to different authors.]

[*Executive Power.*] The executive Power shall be vested in a President of the United States of America. He shall hold his Office during the Term of four Years, and, together with the Vice President, chosen for the same Term, be elected, as follows: [Original text]

[*Presidential Electors.*] Each State shall appoint, in such Manner as the Legislature thereof may direct, a Number of Electors, equal to the whole Number of Senators and Representatives to which the State may be entitled in the Congress: but no Senator or Representative, or Person holding an Office of Trust or Profit under the United States, shall be appointed an Elector. [Original text]

[*Electoral College.*] The Electors shall meet in their respective states, and vote by ballot for President and Vice-President, one of whom, at least, shall not be an inhabitant of the same state with themselves; they shall name in their ballots the person voted for as President, and in distinct ballots the person voted for as Vice-President, and they shall make distinct lists of all persons voted for as President, and of all persons voted for as Vice-President, and of the number of votes for each, which lists they shall sign and certify, and transmit sealed to the seat of government of the United States, directed to the President of the Senate;—The President of the Senate shall, in the presence of the Senate and House of Representatives, open all the certificates and the votes shall then be counted;—The person having the greatest number of votes for President, shall be the President, if such number be a majority of the whole number of Electors appointed; and if no person have such majority, then from the persons having the highest numbers not exceeding three on the list of those voted for as President, the House of Representatives shall choose immediately, by ballot, the President. But in choosing the President, the votes shall be taken by states, the representation from each state having one vote; a quorum for this purpose shall consist of a member or members from two-thirds of the states, and a majority of all the states shall be necessary to a choice. [As changed by Twelfth Amendment]

The person having the greatest number of votes as Vice-President, shall be the Vice-President, if such number be a majority of the whole number of Electors appointed, and if no person have a majority, then from the two highest numbers on the list, the Senate shall choose the Vice-President; a quorum for the purpose shall consist of two-thirds of the whole number of Senators, and a majority of the whole number shall be necessary to a choice. But no person constitutionally ineligible to the office of President shall be eligible to that of Vice-President of the United States. [As changed by Twelfth Amendment]

[*Presidential Elector Vote.*] The Congress may determine the Time of chusing the Electors, and the Day on which they shall give their Votes; which Day shall be the same throughout the United States. [Original text]

[*Presidential Eligibility.*] No Person except a natural born Citizen, or a Citizen of the United States, at the time of the Adoption of this Constitution, shall be eligible to the Office of President; neither shall any Person be eligible to that Office who shall not have attained to the Age of thirty five Years, and been fourteen Years a Resident within the United States. [Original text]

[*Presidential Succession.*] If, at the time fixed for the beginning of the term of the President, the President elect shall have died, the Vice President elect shall become President. If a President shall not have been chosen before the time fixed for the beginning of his term, or if the President elect shall have failed to qualify, then the Vice President elect shall act as President until a President shall have qualified; and the Congress may by law provide for the case wherein neither a President elect nor a Vice President elect shall have qualified, declaring who shall then act as President, or the manner in which one who is to act shall be selected, and such person shall act accordingly until a President or Vice President shall have qualified. [As changed by Twentieth Amendment, Section 3]

[*Congressional Role in Presidential Succession.*] The Congress may by law provide for the case of the death of any of the persons from whom the House of Representatives may choose a President whenever the right of choice shall have devolved upon them, and for the case of the death of any of the persons from whom the Senate may choose a Vice President whenever the right of choice shall have devolved upon them. [As added by the Twentieth Amendment, Section 4.]

Presidential Vacancy. In case of the removal of the President from office or of his death or resignation, the Vice President shall become President. [Twenty-fifth Amendment, Section 1]

Vice Presidential Vacancy. Whenever there is a vacancy in the office of the Vice President, the President shall nominate a Vice President who shall take office upon confirmation by a majority vote of both Houses of Congress. [Twenty-fifth Amendment, Section 2]

Voluntary Declaration of Presidential Incapacity. Whenever the President transmits to the President pro tempore of the Senate and the Speaker of the House of Representatives his written declaration that he is unable to discharge the powers and duties of his office, and until he transmits to them a written declaration to the contrary, such powers and duties shall be discharged by the Vice President as Acting President. [Twenty-fifth Amendment, Section 3]

Involuntary Declaration of Presidential Incapacity. Whenever the Vice President and a majority of either the principal officers of the executive departments or of such other body as Congress may by law provide, transmit to the President pro tempore of the Senate and the Speaker of the House of Representatives their written declaration that the President is unable to discharge the powers and duties of his office, the Vice President shall immediately assume the powers and duties of the office as Acting President. [Twenty-fifth Amendment, Section 4, Paragraph 1]

Thereafter, when the President transmits to the President pro tempore of the Senate and the Speaker of the House of Representatives his written declaration that no inability exists, he shall resume the powers and duties of his office unless the Vice President and a majority of either the principal officers of the executive department or of such other body as Congress may by law provide, transmit within four days to the President pro tempore of the Senate and the Speaker of the House of Representatives their written declaration that the President is unable to discharge the powers and duties of his office. Thereupon Congress shall decide the issue, assembling within forty-eight hours for that purpose if not in session. If the Congress, within twenty-one days after receipt of the latter written declaration, or, if Congress is not in session, within twenty-one days after Congress is required to assemble, determines by two-thirds vote of both Houses that the President is unable to discharge the powers and duties of his office, the Vice President shall continue to discharge the same as Acting President; otherwise, the President shall resume the powers and duties of his office. [Twenty-fifth Amendment, Section 4, Paragraph 2]

[*Presidential Compensation.*] The President shall, at stated Times, receive for his Services, a Compensation, which shall neither be increased nor diminished during the Period for which he shall have been elected, and he shall not receive within that Period any other Emolument from the United States, or any of them. [Original text]

[*Oath of Office.*] Before he enter on the Execution of his Office, he shall take the following Oath or Affirmation:—"I do solemnly swear (or affirm) that I will faithfully execute the Office of President of the United States, and will to the best of my Ability, preserve, protect and defend the Constitution of the United States." [Original text]

[*Term.*] The terms of the President and Vice President shall end at noon on the 20th day of January, and the terms of Senators and Representatives at noon on the 3d day of January, of the years in which such terms would have ended if this article had not been ratified; and the terms of their successors shall then begin. [Twentieth Amendment, Section 1]

Article II, Section 1, Clause 1.
Executive Power.

The chief duty of the President is to enforce the laws of the United States. The Supreme Court in *Nixon v. Fitzgerald*, 457 U.S. 731 (1982), cited this clause as a source of three powers: law enforcement, foreign affairs, and a supervisory power over the executive branch.

In *Myers v. United States*, 272 U.S. 52 (1926), the Supreme Court held 6–3 that the President has the power to remove officers appointed with the consent of the Senate because of the general grant of executive power and as a necessary adjunct to his duty to "take care that the laws are faithfully executed." However, in *Humphrey's Executor v. United States*, 295 U.S. 602 (1935), the Court held 9–0 that the President's power to remove principal officers of the government at pleasure, as recognized in *Myers*, does not extend to the removal of members of independent administrative agencies such as the Federal Trade Commission created by Congress to exercise quasi-legislative and quasi-judicial powers, or to officers not performing an "executive" function. Non-executive officers may only be removed by procedures in accord with statutory standards enacted by Congress. Also, in *Morrison v. Olson*, 487 U.S. 654 (1988), the Supreme Court held 7–1 that the removal of an independent counsel under the Ethics in Government Act of 1978 for good cause, rather than at will, did not impermissibly limit executive authority.

The President is empowered, by virtue of his office, to conduct foreign affairs not otherwise granted to Congress or shared with the Senate. *American Insurance Association v. Garamendi*, 539 U.S. 396 (2003), 5–4 vote. In *United States v. Curtiss–Wright Export Corp.*, 299 U.S. 304 (1936), a joint resolution of Congress delegated to the President the authority to embargo arms and munitions shipments to Bolivia and Paraguay in their border dispute over Chaco territory. The Supreme Court held 7–1 that the Congress had properly delegated legislative power to the President, and that the general conferral of executive power by Article II afforded "plenary" authority for the President to act in foreign affairs.

In *United States v. Nixon*, 418 U.S. 683 (1974), the Supreme Court held 8–0 that the President's need for complete candor and objectivity from advisors calls for great deference from the courts, but that executive privilege may not be used to withhold evidence that is "demonstrably relevant in a criminal case." Accordingly, the President is not immune to subpoenas for evidence in a federal criminal trial such as tape recordings of his White House conversations for use in the Watergate prosecution. (The decision was issued on July 24, 1974. President Richard Nixon resigned on August 9.) And in *Clinton v. Jones*, 520 U.S. 681 (1997), the Court held 9–0 that the Constitution does not protect the President, while in office, from civil litigation involving actions committed before he entered office. However, in *Nixon v. Fitzgerald*, 457 U.S. 731 (1982), the Court held 5–4 that the President "is entitled to absolute immunity from damages liability predicated on his official acts." 457 U.S. 749.

In *Butz v. Economou*, 438 U.S. 478 (1978), the Supreme Court held 5–4 that executive officials exercising discretionary functions are entitled to qualified good faith immunity for error so long as they acted without malice or knowledge of illegality and reasonably believed that their actions were lawful. This rule was reiterated in *Harlow v. Fitzgerald*, 457 U.S. 800 (1982), where the Supreme Court held 8–1 "that government officials performing discretionary functions, generally are shielded from liability for civil damages insofar as their conduct does not violate clearly established statutory or constitutional rights of which a reasonable person would have known." 457 U.S. 818.

The original Constitution did not limit the number of times that a President could be reelected. George Washington established the tradition of serving only two terms. However, this precedent was broken by President Franklin D. Roosevelt in 1940 when he was reelected for his third term, and in 1944 when he was reelected for his fourth term. The Twenty-second Amendment, ratified in 1951, provided that no person shall be elected to the office of President more than twice; and that no person who has held the office for more than two years of a term to which another was elected as President shall be elected to the office of President more than once.

The role of the Vice President has acquired much greater prominence in recent times. Earlier, Vice President John Adams (1789–1797) called the job "the most insignificant office that ever the invention of man contrived or his imagination conceived." When President Zachary Taylor (1849–1850) offered the vice presidency to Daniel Webster he replied. "I do not intend to be buried until I am dead." Vice President Thomas Marshall (1913–1921) recalled that "once there were two brothers, one went away to sea and the other was elected vice president, and nothing was heard of either one of them again." Vice President John Nance Garner (1933–1941) described the job as "not worth a bucket of warm spit."

Article II, Section 1, Clause 2.
Presidential Electors

The Constitution provides that each state legislature shall select electors, equal to the number of its congressional delegation (electoral college). Accordingly, the smaller states in population preserve the same advantage in the composition of the electoral college that they have in the Senate. The framers created the electoral college on the assumption that in a nation as large as America the citizens would not be able to make an informed choice and that, therefore, the state legislatures would select the electors on their behalf. In order to ensure the independence of the process no federal official may serve as an elector. The Twenty-third Amendment (1961) provides for the District of Columbia to appoint three presidential electors as though it were the least populous state.

Article II, Section 1, Clause 3,
Electoral College

The Constitution provided that all electors shall meet at the same time in their respective capitals and vote for the President and Vice President. No elector may cast votes for presidential and vice-presidential candidates who both inhabit the same state as that elector. (The presidential and vice-presidential candidates can come from the same state, but, if so, an elector of that state can only vote for one of them.) If a candidate for President did not receive the majority of electoral votes, the House of Representatives would choose the President with each state entitled to cast one vote and an absolute majority needed to win. Similarly, if a candidate for Vice President did not receive the majority of electoral votes, the Senate would make the choice.

Originally, the Constitution provided that the person receiving the highest number of electoral votes would be elected President and the person receiving the second highest number would be elected Vice President.

This worked well for the first two terms of President George Washington (1789–1797), who was the only President to be elected unanimously and the only one who did not represent a political party. John Adams was elected as the Vice President for these two terms. However, in the election of 1796, John Adams, Federalist, was elected President, and his political opponent, Thomas Jefferson, Democratic-Republican, was elected Vice President. In the election of 1800, both political parties offered a slate of two candidates, but because the electoral vote did not distinguish between President and Vice President, the result was a tie. Thomas Jefferson and his running mate, Aaron Burr, received the same number of electoral votes, requiring the House of Representatives to choose the President. On the 36th ballot, the House elected Jefferson as President on February 17, 1801, and he was inaugurated 15 days later on March 4. Before the next election, the Twelfth Amendment was ratified (June 15, 1804) to provide for the separate balloting procedures for the President and Vice President.

Political parties soon took over the nomination process by offering their own slates of electors in the general election, pledged to vote for the party's candidates for President and Vice President. By 1880, all states provided for the popular election of electors. Many states today list on the ballots only the names of the party's presidential and vice presidential candidates, but a vote for them is actually a vote the for their party's electors. States may also require electors to pledge, if chosen, to vote for their party's candidate. *Ray v. Blair*, 343 U.S. 214 (1952), 5–2 vote.

All states except Maine and Nebraska award all of the electoral votes to the candidate slate winning the statewide election. In Maine and Nebraska, the votes are awarded by congressional district, with the two additional votes awarded to the statewide winner. However, a state legislature may take back the power to appoint presidential electors. *Bush v. Gore*, 531 U.S. 98, 104 (2000), 5–4 vote.

The Electoral College, in affording the states two electoral votes for Senate representation beyond what their respective populations would otherwise require, has resulted in three presidents' being elected by winning the electoral vote while losing a plurality of the national popular vote. In 1876, Republican Rutherford B. Hayes defeated Democrat Samuel J. Tilden; in 1888, Republican Benjamin Harrison defeated Democrat Grover Cleveland; and in 2000, Republican George W. Bush defeated Democrat Albert Gore, Jr.

A state legislature, in directing the manner of choosing electors, is exercising its federal constitutional power under the Electoral College Clause and, therefore, is not constrained by state constitutional requirements, such as presenting its decision to the governor for possible veto. *McPherson v. Blacker*, 146 U.S. 1 (1892). However, the exercise of this power must be consistent with other provisions of the U.S. Constitution such as the First and

Fourteenth Amendments. *Williams v. Rhodes*, 393 U.S. 23 (1968), 6–3 vote; *Anderson v. Celebrezze*, 460 U.S. 780 (1983), 5–4 vote.

In the 2000 presidential election, the outcome hung on the popular vote in Florida. Republican presidential candidate George W. Bush held a slim lead. Democratic presidential candidate Albert Gore, Jr., challenged the decisions of the Florida Secretary of State to certify the electoral vote, and to ignore the outcome of manual vote recounts that were underway in four Florida counties. The Florida Supreme Court upheld Gore's challenges. On appeal, the U.S. Supreme Court in *Bush v. Palm Beach County Canvassing Board*, 531 U.S. 70 (12/4/2000), overruled 9–0 the Florida court for failing to recognize that Florida law may not circumscribe the plenary power of the Florida legislature in determining electoral votes pursuant to the Electoral College Clause. Eight days later, the U.S. Supreme Court in *Bush v. Gore*, 531 U.S. 98 (12/12/2000), in a lengthy per curiam decision, voided 7–2 the statewide manual recount of ballots ordered by the Florida court four days earlier, on the ground that there was no uniform standard for election officials to apply in the recount, thereby violating the Equal Protection and Due Process Clauses of the Fourteenth Amendment. The Court further held 5–4 that no alternative method could be established within the time limits established by Florida election law. The decision resulted in Florida's 25 electoral votes going to Bush, giving him a total of 271 votes, defeating Gore with 266 electoral votes. One D.C. elector had abstained from voting. In order to limit the precedential value of the decision, the Court stated: "Our consideration is limited to the present circumstances, for the problem of equal protection in election processes generally presents many complexities." 531 U.S. 109.

Article II, Section 1, Clause 4.
Presidential Elector Vote

The Congress has determined that electors shall be chosen on the Tuesday after the first Monday in November of each presidential election year, but if the state's election "has failed to make a choice" on that day, then the state legislature may afterward appoint electors in such manner as it deems appropriate. On the first Monday after the second Wednesday in December, the electors assemble in their state capitals and cast separate ballots for the next President and Vice President. The votes are sent to Congress where they are counted by the President of the Senate on January 6, unless it falls on a Sunday, in which case they are counted on the following day. An absolute majority is required for election as President and Vice President. With 538 electoral votes, a candidate must receive at least 270 votes for election. The President-elect and the Vice President-elect are inaugurated on January 20. 2 USC, Chapter 1.

Article II, Section 1, Clause 5.
Presidential Eligibility

The Natural Born Citizen Clause specifies three eligibility requirements for the presidency concerning age (35 years), residency (14 years) and citizenship (U.S.). The last sentence of the Twelfth Amendment (1804) made the qualifications the same for the vice presidency. The citizenship requirement refers to a "natural born Citizen." The Immigration and Naturalization Act, 8 USC Section 1401, defines eight categories of "citizens of the United States at birth" that includes anyone born outside the U.S. whose parents are U.S. citizens and as long as one parent has lived in the U.S..

Article II, Section 1, Clause 6.
Presidential Succession

Under this clause as originally framed, it was unclear whether the Vice President actually became President when a predecessor died, or merely acted as President until another President was elected. When President William Henry Harrison died in 1841, Vice President John Tyler asserted that he became the President. This precedent was followed thereafter in the successions of Zachary Taylor by Millard Fillmore in 1850; Abraham Lincoln by Andrew Johnson in 1865; James A. Garfield by Chester A. Arthur in 1881; William McKinley by Theodore Roosevelt in 1901; Warren G. Harding by Calvin Coolidge in 1923; Franklin D. Roosevelt by Harry S. Truman in 1945; and John F. Kennedy by Lyndon B. Johnson in 1963.

Pursuant to the authorization of Clause 6, the Congress enacted the Presidential Succession Act of 1792, declaring that, in the event of the removal, resignation, death or disability of the President and the Vice President, the President Pro Tempore of the Senate was next in line of succession, followed by the Speaker of the House of Representatives. The 1792 Act was superseded by the Presidential Succession Act of 1886, which replaced the President Pro Tempore and the Speaker with the heads of the cabinet departments in the order of their establishment beginning with the Secretary of State. This Act was superseded by the Presidential Succession Act of 1947, which revised the line of succession beginning with the Speaker of the House, the President Pro Tempore of the Senate, the Secretaries of State, the Treasury, and Defense, the Attorney General, the Postmaster General, and the Secretaries of the Interior, Agriculture, Commerce and Labor. The 1947 Act has been amended several times with the addition of new cabinet positions.

The Twentieth (1933) and Twenty-fifth (1967) Amendments establish procedures for the Vice President to assume the office of the President in the event of the President's temporary or permanent disability. In the event of a temporary disability, the Vice President serves as Acting President until the President recovers. The President may declare the beginning and ending of his own disability, such as a medical operation where anesthesia is administered. But, if the President appears disabled and fails to acknowledge his disability, the Vice President and a majority of the presidential cabinet, or such "other body as Congress may by law provide," may determine that the President is disabled, and the Vice President immediately becomes the Acting President. If the President challenges this determination, Congress must promptly decide the issue. If each House determines by a two-thirds vote that the President is disabled, he remains as President, but is stripped of his authority, and the Vice President continues to serve as the Acting President. Otherwise, the President resumes the office with full authority.

The Twenty-fifth Amendment also provides for filling a vacancy in the office of Vice President by the President's nominating a person to fill the vacancy. That person must be confirmed by a majority vote of both Houses of Congress. Accordingly, when Vice President Spiro Agnew resigned in 1973, President Richard Nixon nominated Gerald R. Ford to fill the vacancy and he was confirmed. Upon President Nixon's resignation in 1974, Vice President Ford became President; Ford nominated Nelson Rockefeller for Vice President, and he was confirmed.

In the event of the simultaneous death, resignation, removal or disability of the President and Vice President, the Presidential Succession Act of 1947, as amended, 3 USC, Sec. 19, prescribes the following succession of officials to assume the presidency (conditioned on each one's meeting the three eligibility requirements for President): Speaker of the House, President Pro Tempore of the Senate, Secretaries of State, the Treasury, and Defense, Attorney General, Secretaries of the Interior, Agriculture, Commerce, Labor, Health and Human Services, Housing and Urban Development, Transportation, Energy, Education, Veterans' Affairs, and Homeland Security.

When the President and his successors are scheduled to attend an event, such as the State of the Union address, one of them remains in seclusion elsewhere. This "designated successor" would become the Acting President in case the others were disabled or killed in a catastrophic accident or attack.

Article II, Section 1, Clause 7.
Presidential Compensation

The president's compensation must remain constant throughout the term of office. The President may not receive other compensation from either the federal or state governments.

Article II, Section 1, Clause 8.
Oath of Office

In taking his oath, George Washington added the words "so help me God" and started the practice of swearing the oath on a bible, although it is not required. Chester A. Arthur in 1881 and Theodore Roosevelt in 1901 did not use a bible while Lyndon B. Johnson in 1963 used a Roman Catholic missal (guide for celebrating Mass) because there was no bible on Air Force One. Usually, the Chief Justice of the United States administers the oath of office.

Article II, Section 2, Clause 1. Commander in Chief; Opinions; Reprieves and Pardons. The President shall be Commander in Chief of the Army and Navy of the United States, and of the Militia of the several States, when called into the actual Service of the United States; he may require the Opinion, in writing, of the principal Officer in each of the executive Departments, upon any Subject relating to the Duties of their respective Offices, and he shall have Power to grant Reprieves and Pardons for Offences against the United States, except in Cases of Impeachment.

COMMANDER IN CHIEF

Under the Constitution, the war powers are divided between the Congress and the President. The Congress has the power to declare war and raise and support the armed forces under Article I, Section 8, Clauses 11–13, while the President is the commander in chief of the armed forces under Article II, Section 2, Clause 1. The congressional advocates contend that, because of Congress' authority to declare war and provide military funding, the President cannot initiate hostilities without prior congressional authorization. The presidential advocates contend that, because of the President's broad executive authority and command of the armed forces, the President has the exclusive authority to commit military forces in hostilities, and that the congressional power to declare war is only a power to alter international legal relationships. Although the United States has engaged in numerous foreign military conflicts over the years, the Congress has issued formal declarations of war only for the War of 1812, the Mexican-American War, the Spanish-American War, and World Wars I and II.

During the Vietnam War, Congress sought to exert its authority by the enactment of the War Powers Resolution of 1973 over the veto of President Richard Nixon, who challenged its constitutionality. The main purpose of the resolution was to circumscribe the President's authority to use armed forces in foreign hostilities without a declaration of war or other congressional authorization, yet provide flexibility for the President to quickly respond to an attack or other emergency. The validity and effectiveness of the resolution remain a matter of debate. Courts have avoided ruling on the constitutionality of the resolution on a variety of procedural grounds or as posing nonjusticiable political questions.

With respect to the state militias (now called national guards), Article I, Section 8, Clause 15, empowers Congress to "provide for calling forth the Militia to execute the Laws of the Union, suppress Insurrections and repel Invasions" and Article II, Section 2, Clause 1, authorizes the President to assume command of the militia "when called into the actual Service of the United States." Beginning in 1792, Congress has enacted legislation authorizing the President to call forth the militia. In *Martin v. Mott*, 25 U.S. 19 (1827), the Supreme Court held 7–0 that the Constitution authorizes the President alone to determine when to call out the militia against actual or imminent invasion, in which case his decision is final. This decision established the President's power to federalize state national guards and to integrate them within the regular armed forces. In *Perpich v. Department of Defense*, 496 U.S. 334 (1990), the Court held 9–0 that Congress may authorize national guard members to be ordered to active federal duty for purposes of training outside the U.S. without either the consent of a state governor under the Second Militia Clause (Article I, Section 8, Clause 16) or the declaration of a national emergency.

OPINIONS

The Opinion Clause reinforces the authority of the President to demand written reports from executive officers regarding the performance of their duties.

REPRIEVES AND PARDONS

Under this Clause, the President's authority to issue reprieves and pardons is limited to offenses against the United States, and does not apply to impeachment and civil cases. The President's power to grant reprieves and pardons is absolute and may not be infringed by the congressional or judicial branches. *United States v. Klein*, 80 U.S. 128 (1871), 7–2 vote. A reprieve reduces the severity of a punishment without removing the guilt of the person. A pardon avoids or removes both punishment and guilt. It may be issued anytime after an offense is committed so as to either avoid prosecution or to erase the legal effects of a conviction. *Ex parte Garland*, 71 U.S. 333 (1867), 5–4 vote. A pardon may be imposed without the prisoner's consent. *Biddle v. Perovich*, 274 U.S. 480 (1927). However, a pardon cannot be granted before an offense has been committed, which would give the President the power to waive the laws.

The President can make a pardon conditional; for example, by vacating a conviction but leaving paid fines in place, or by making the payment of a fine a prerequisite before a pardon takes effect. *Schick v. Reed*, 419 U.S. 256 (1974), 6–3 vote. A pardon can also be granted to a class of people: President George Washington pardoned leaders of the Whiskey Rebellion; President Andrew Johnson pardoned Confederate soldiers after the Civil War; and President Jimmy Carter pardoned those who had evaded military service in the Vietnam War.

Article II, Section 2, Clause 2. Treaties; Appointments. He shall have Power, by and with the Advice and Consent of the Senate, to make Treaties, provided two thirds of the Senators present concur; and he shall nominate, and by and with the Advice and Consent of the Senate, shall appoint Ambassadors, other public Ministers and Consuls, Judges of the supreme Court, and all other Officers of the United States, whose Appointments are not herein otherwise provided for, and which shall be established by Law: but the Congress may by Law vest the Appointment of such inferior Officers, as they think proper, in the President alone, in the Courts of Law, or in the Heads of Departments.

This Clause is referred to as the Advice and Consent, Appointments, or Treaty Clause.

TREATIES

The President has the responsibility for negotiating treaties with foreign governments, but such treaties do not become binding on the United States without the advice and consent of the Senate and by the concurrence of two-thirds of the senators with a quorum present. Under the Supremacy Clause (Article VI, Clause 2), both statutes and treaties are declared to be the "supreme Law of the Land"; both share equal status and both must comply with the Constitution. If a statute and a treaty are inconsistent, the one later in time will control, "provided the stipulation of the treaty on the subject is self-executing." *Whitney v. Robertson*, 124 U.S. 190, 194 (1888). The scope of the treaty-making power is not restricted to specific Article I powers of Congress, but may address local matters such as the hunting of migratory birds. *Missouri v. Holland*, 252 U.S. 416 (1920), 7–2 vote.

In *Medellin v. Texas*, 552 U.S. 491 (2008), the Supreme Court held 6–3 that an international treaty is not binding on state courts unless it is "self-executing" or the Congress has enacted implementing legislation. Thus the decision of the International Court of Justice to review a death penalty case involving a foreign national is not binding on the Texas courts, and the President lacks the power to enforce the treaty and the decisions of the International Court of Justice.

U.S. law distinguishes Clause 2 treaties, requiring a two-thirds vote by the Senate, from congressional-executive agreements, passed by majorities of both Houses, and executive agreements made by the President alone. All three classes are considered treaties under international law.

Congressional-executive agreements often address trade-related matters that Congress has clear constitutional authority to regulate. Executive agreements generally cover matters that are solely within the President's power, or are made pursuant to a treaty or appropriate congressional legislation. *United States v. Belmont*, 301 U.S. 324 (1937), 9–0 vote. Examples of executive agreements are the 1945 Yalta agreement dividing Germany among allied nations, the 1980 agreement with Iran to end the hostage crisis, and status-of-forces agreements with foreign governments.

As to the termination of treaties, *Goldwater v. Carter*, 444 U.S. 996 (1979), involved a challenge to the constitutionality of President Jimmy Carter's unilaterally terminating the United States–Taiwan Mutual Defense Treaty. The Supreme Court dismissed the case, ruling 8–1 that the issue "was essentially a political question and could not be reviewed by the court, as Congress had not issued a formal opposition."

APPOINTMENTS

The three stages in appointments by the President with the advice and consent of the Senate are: (1) nomination of the candidate by the President alone; (2) the consent of the Senate by majority vote to the candidate's appointment; and (3) the final appointment and commissioning of the appointee by the President. However, after the Senate grants advice and consent, the President is under no obligation to commission the officer.

Since the power of nomination belongs to the President alone, the Senate may not attach conditions to its consent of an appointment. Its role is confined to affirmation or rejection of the nominations, and such nominations fail whenever it rejects them. In *Myers v. United States*, 272 U.S. 52 (1926), an 1876 law provided that postmasters of the first, second and third classes shall be appointed and may be removed by the President with the advice and consent of the Senate. President Woodrow Wilson removed Myers, a postmaster first class, without seeking Senate approval. The Supreme Court ruled 6–3 the law unconstitutionally restricted the President's power to remove appointed officials. Otherwise, the President would not be allowed to "discharge his own constitutional duty of seeing that the laws be faithfully executed." 272 U.S. 135.

Congress has often prescribed qualifications for those who can serve in the offices it has created, thereby limiting the President's discretion in selecting nominees. In *Myers*, the Court recognized the congressional power to establish offices, determine their functions and jurisdiction, fix the terms of office, and prescribe reasonable and relevant qualifications and rules of eligibility, provided "that the qualifications do not so limit selection and so trench upon executive choice as to be in effect legislative designation."

In *Wiener v. United States*, 357 U.S. 349 (1958), the Supreme Court held 9–0 that the President had no power to remove a member of the War Claims Commission created by Congress to adjudicate claims for compensating internees, prisoners of war and religious organizations who suffered losses at the hands of the enemy in World War II. The Commission's determinations were final and not subject to review by any executive official or court. The commissioners were appointed by the President and confirmed by the Senate for terms to expire with the end of the Commission. There was no provision for removal of a commissioner.

In *Buckley v. Valeo*, 424 U.S. 1 (1976), the Supreme Court held that the method of appointing the six commissioners of the Federal Election Commission under the 1974 Amendments to the 1971 Federal Election Campaign Act (FECA), two by the President, two by the Speaker of the House, and two by the President Pro Tempore, violated the principle of separation of powers because the commissioners exercised executive powers. Accordingly, under the 1976 FECA Amendments, the Commission was reconstituted with the President appointing the six commissioners, subject to Senate confirmation.

In the case of "inferior Officers" (as distinguished from principal officers above), the Congress has the discretion to vest their appointment "in the President alone, in the Courts of Law, or in the Heads of Departments." The Supreme Court in *Edmund v. United States*, 520 U.S. 651, 662 (1997), 9–0, defined inferior officers as those "whose work is directed and supervised at some level by others who were appointed by Presidential nomination with the advice and consent of the Senate." Constituting a third category, below inferior officers, are employees who are lesser functionaries subordinate to officers of the United States. *Auffmordt v. Hedden*, 137 U.S. 310, 327 (1890).

The Supreme Court in *Morrison v. Olson*, 487 U.S. 654 (1988), addressed the Ethics in Government Act of 1978 providing for appointment of an independent counsel, by a special court upon application of the Attorney General, to investigate and prosecute criminal conduct by senior executive officials. An independent counsel, so appointed, is subject to removal by the Attorney General only for good cause, unlike regular federal prosecutors who may be removed at will. The Court held 7–1 that the independent counsel is an "inferior officer" who may be appointed by a court of law under the Appointments

Clause, and that the removal limitation did not impermissibly limit executive authority, or violate the separation of powers doctrine.

Article II, Section 2, Clause 3. Recess Appointments. The President shall have Power to fill up all Vacancies that may happen during the Recess of the Senate, by granting Commissions which shall expire at the End of their next Session.

A recess appointment occurs when the President fills a vacancy with respect to an officer of the United States during a recess of the Senate. The commission or appointment must be approved by the Senate by the end of the next session, or the office becomes vacant again. Since Congress is almost continuously in session, a recess appointment could well last until near the end of the next calendar year.

Presidents have made both intersession (between sessions) and intrasession (during a recess within a session) recess appointments. Accordingly, an intrasession appointment would last longer than an intersession appointment because the former would include the balance of the session in which it was made plus the succeeding session. In *Evans v. Stephens*, 387 F 3d 1220 (11th Cir, 2004), cert. denied, 544 U.S. 942 (2005), Judge William Pryor received a recess appointment to the court of appeals on the seventh day of a 10-day intrasession recess. Several criminal defendants, whose appeals were denied by panels that included Judge Pryor, contended that the decisions on their appeals were invalid because Pryor was not constitutionally empowered to participate. The Court denied the challenge to Pryor's appointment, holding that "Recess of the Senate" includes an intrasession recess, and that vacancies need not arise during the recess in order to "happen during the Recess."

On occasion, the Senate has thwarted presidential recess appointments by keeping the Senate in session by holding pro forma sessions every three days.

Article II, Section 3. State of the Union; Convening and Adjourning Congress; Receiving Ambassadors; Faithful Execution; Commissioning Officers. He shall from time to time give to the Congress Information of the State of the Union, and recommend to their Consideration such Measures as he shall judge necessary and expedient; he may, on extraordinary Occasions, convene both Houses, or either of them, and in Case of Disagreement between them, with Respect to the Time of Adjournment, he may adjourn them to such Time as he shall think proper; he shall receive Ambassadors and other public Ministers; he shall take Care that the Laws be faithfully executed, and shall Commission all the Officers of the United States.

STATE OF THE UNION

The State of the Union address is traditionally delivered by the President to a joint session of Congress assembled in the House of Representatives Chamber in the Capitol after Congress convenes each January. The address focuses on the President's views on current conditions, foreign affairs, national priorities and legislative needs.

The first address was orally delivered by President George Washington (1789–1797) on January 8, 1790. President Thomas Jefferson (1801–1809) believed that such a speech resembled those delivered by British monarchs to Parliament and chose instead to send written messages to Congress. This practice of written submissions continued for 112 years until President Woodrow Wilson (1913–1921) orally delivered his address to the Congress on December 2, 1913. Washington's example, revived by Wilson, has been followed ever since.

CONVENING AND ADJOURNING CONGRESS

The President may call extraordinary sessions of one or both Houses of Congress. If the two Houses cannot agree on a date for adjournment, the President may adjourn both Houses to such a time as he thinks proper. On 27 occasions, Presidents have called both Houses into extraordinary session to deal with urgent matters of war and economic crisis. The most recent was in July 1948 when President Harry Truman, a Democrat, called Congress back into session to pass laws to ensure civil rights, extend Social Security coverage and establish a national health-care program. The Republican-controlled Congress refused to enact any legislation. Truman's castigation of the "Do-nothing Eightieth Congress" contributed to his surprise reelection as President the following November.

Today, there is little need for the President to call extraordinary sessions since Congress remains in session year around.

RECEIVING AMBASSADORS

The President is required to receive ambassadors and other public ministers and, accordingly, the Constitution empowers the President to recognize foreign governments and establish diplomatic relations. Such actions are not subject to judicial review. *In re Baiz*, 135 U.S. 403 (1890), 9–0 vote.

FAITHFUL EXECUTION

The Faithful Execution Clause, also known as the Take Care Clause, requires the President to see that the laws are faithfully executed. As a practical matter, the President has wide discretion in deciding the extent to which laws are enforced. In the case of congressionally created independent agencies, which operate as a fourth branch of government in administering various regulatory laws, the President does not have the authority to oversee their faithful execution of the laws.

In *Mississippi v. Johnson*, 71 U.S. 475 (1867), the Supreme Court denied 9–0 injunctive relief sought by Mississippi to prohibit President Andrew Johnson from enforcing the allegedly unconstitutional Military Reconstruction Act of 1867. The Court held that while courts can command an executive official to perform ministerial duties, which involve no discretion, they cannot command the performance of executive duties that involve broad discretion and the exercise of political judgment. However, actions taken in performing duties are subject to judicial review.

In re Neagle, 135 U.S. 1 (1890), involved the Attorney General's appointment of U.S. Marshall Neagle to serve as a bodyguard to U.S. Supreme Court Justice Stephen J. Field while he rode circuit in California. After shooting and killing a person assaulting the Justice, Neagle was arrested and charged with murder under California law. He petitioned in federal court for his release by a writ of habeas corpus. On appeal, the Supreme Court held 6–2 that the appointment of a bodyguard for Justice Field assured that the nation's laws would be faithfully executed and, hence, the federal court could determine the issue of justifiable homicide and thereby preempt the operation of California law.

In *Youngstown Sheet & Tube Co. v. Sawyer*, 343 U.S. 579 (1952), the *Steel Seizure Case*, President Harry Truman, during the Korean War, ordered that the government seize and operate the nation's private steel mills in order to avoid an expected strike that would interrupt military supply. The Supreme Court held 6–3 that the President did not have the constitutional or statutory authority to issue such an order on several grounds, one of which was that "the President's power to see that the laws are faithfully executed refutes the idea that he is to be a lawmaker." 343 U.S. 587.

On occasion the President has asserted the discretion to impound funds appropriated by Congress for various purposes. However, in *Train v. City of New York*, 420 U.S. 35 (1975), the Supreme Court ruled 9–0 that an impoundment was unconstitutional where President Richard Nixon had directed the Environmental Protection Agency to reduce the monies to be distributed to states as required by the Federal Water Pollution Control Act Amendments of 1972.

President Ronald Reagan and his successors have made extensive use of so-called signing statements, which are written pronouncements issued by the executive upon signing bills into law. These statements are published in the *Federal Register*. A statement may contend that constitutional defects in a law should guide executive officials in limiting its implementation, or may provide interpretations of the law to guide implementation. The American Bar Association in August 2006 said that the use of signing statements to modify the meaning of duly enacted laws is "contrary to the rule of law and our constitutional system of separation of powers." The Supreme Court has not yet specifically addressed this issue. To the extent that a signing statement seeks to nullify part or all of a law, it may be invalidated as a line-item veto in violation of bicameralism and presentment under Article I, Section 7, Clause 2. *Clinton v. City of New York*, 524 U.S. 417 (1998), 6–3 vote.

COMMISSIONING OFFICERS

The President is obligated to "Commission all the Officers of the United States," which includes judges, ambassadors, ministers, consuls, and civil and military officers. In *Marbury v Madison*, 5 U.S. 137, 160–162 (1803), the Supreme Court held 6–0 "that when a commission has been signed by the president, the appointment is made; and that the commission is complete when the seal of the United States has been affixed to it by the secretary of state." Delivery of the commission is not necessary to effectuate the appointment. However, William Marbury, a wealthy supporter of President John Adams, never occupied the office of justice of the peace pursuant to his appointment. Apparently, his primary interest was in challenging the authority of President Thomas Jefferson.

Article II, Section 4, Impeachment. The President, Vice President and all civil Officers of the United States, shall be removed from Office on Impeachment for, and Conviction of, Treason, Bribery, or other high Crimes and Misdemeanors.

The House of Representatives has the sole power of impeachment under Article I, Section 2, Clause 5. Impeachment is tried by the Senate under Article I, Section 3, Clause 6. Under Clause 6, the Chief Justice resides over a presidential impeachment trial in the Senate to avoid the possible conflict of interest of a Vice President presiding over a trial in which conviction of the President would result in the Vice President's assuming the office. Under Clause 7, a person convicted of impeachment is removed from office and barred from holding any "Office of honor, Trust or Profit under the United States." No other punishment may be inflicted pursuant to a conviction on impeachment, but the convicted party remains liable to trial and punishment in the courts for civil and criminal charges. The President may not pardon a person who has been impeached. Article II, Section 2, Clause 1.

This Section 4 applies only to executive branch officials and judges. Under Article I, Section 5, Clause 2, each House of Congress may expel a member for disorderly behavior upon a two–thirds vote.

The term "high Crimes and Misdemeanors" is quite vague and, accordingly, it is a political question for Congress to determine what constitutes an impeachable offense. In *Nixon v. United States*, 506 U.S. 224 (1993), the Supreme Court held 9–0 that the question of whether the Senate had properly tried the impeachment of Judge Walter Nixon was a political one that could not be judicially resolved.

Article III
The Judicial Branch

Article III, Section 1. Judicial Vesting; Good Behavior; Compensation.
The judicial Power of the United States shall be vested in one supreme Court, and in such inferior Courts as the Congress may from time to time ordain and establish. The Judges, both of the supreme and inferior Courts, shall hold their Offices during good Behaviour, and shall, at stated Times, receive for their Services, a Compensation, which shall not be diminished during their Continuance in Office.

JUDICIAL VESTING

In *Hayburn's Case*, 2 U.S. 409 (1792), the Supreme Court held 5–0 that the Constitution established three separate and independent branches of government (legislative, executive and judicial), and that neither Congress nor the Executive could assign non-judicial duties to the Judiciary. Congress had enacted legislation requiring federal courts to hear disability claims by veterans of the Revolutionary War and certify their findings to the Secretary of War (an executive branch officer) who could revise or deny the findings. The Court characterized the duties assigned to the federal courts as administrative, rather than judicial, because the issue had not been presented as a case or controversy (Article III, Section 2, Clause 1) and the judicial decisions would not be final, but subject to executive or congressional review.

In *Kilbourn v. Thompson*, 103 U.S. 168 (1881), a committee of the House of Representatives held Kilbourne in contempt for failure to produce evidence regarding a bankrupt real estate venture in which the government was a creditor. The Supreme Court invalidated 9–0 the contempt order because the Congress had conducted an improper investigation into a private matter, and not for the purpose of gathering information for future legislation. The House committee had attempted to assume a judicial role which could be exercised only by the courts under the separation of powers prescribed by the Constitution.

The Supreme Court is the only court established by the Constitution. All other federal courts are created by Congress. The Judiciary Act of 1789 established a three-tiered federal judicial system composed of the Supreme Court with six justices, the circuit courts of appeals, and the district courts. In the beginning, the circuit courts were composed of district court judges and Supreme Court justices who had to travel ("riding circuit") across the country to hear cases. The circuit riding ended with the Judiciary Act of 1891 that established nine courts of appeals composed of three judges each. The biographies of federal judges since 1789 are reported in the Federal Judicial Center website, *www.fjc.gov*. The Supreme Court justices, 1789 to the present, are listed in Appendix A.

The Constitution does not prescribe qualifications for a Supreme Court justice. The Chief Justice is the only judicial officer named in the Constitution as the official to preside over the impeachment trial of the President under Article I, Section 3, Clause 6.

The Constitution does not specify the size of the Supreme Court, but leaves it to Congress to fix the number of justices. The Court began in 1789 with six members and was increased to seven in 1807, to nine in 1837, and to ten in 1863. In 1866, the membership was reduced to eight to prevent President Andrew Johnson from filling any vacancies. Since 1869, the membership has been fixed at nine members. When the Court invalidated New Deal legislation in the 1930s, President Franklin D. Roosevelt sought to raise the membership to fifteen. However, his "court-packing" proposal failed because it was deemed a direct attack on the independence of the judiciary.

Chief Justice William Howard Taft (1857–1930), who had served as the 27th U.S. President (1909–1913), viewed the Constitution as the "Ark of the Covenant," and the judiciary as a priestly class guarding its sacred principles. Taft, as Chief Justice (1921–1930), persuaded Congress to authorize the construction of the Supreme Court Building, which was completed in 1935. This is the first permanent home of the Court since it convened for its first session on February 1, 1790. During the intervening years, it met in a variety of locations, and ended up occupying space in the Capitol Building.

The Supreme Court now hears and decides about 100 cases a term, out of thousands submitted. The term begins by statute on the first Monday in October and usually ends in late June. When the Court is in session, the justices sit according to seniority of service, by order of appointment, with the Chief Justice in the center. The eight associate justices alternate by seniority between the two sides of the bench with the most senior justice seated to the immediate right of the Chief Justice, and the most junior justice seated at the end of the bench to the left of the Chief Justice. During oral arguments each side (petitioners and respondents) is usually allotted 30 minutes. Interested third parties, with the Court's permission, may submit amicus curiae (friend of the court) briefs advocating their views. The audio recordings of many of the arguments and decisions since October 1955 are reported at the Oyez Project website, *www.oyez.org*.

Each justice usually hires four law clerks, who are recent graduates from prestigious law schools, to serve for one-year terms. They assist in the screening of the writs of certiorari, and perform legal research and drafting. Certiorari is a Latin term meaning "to be informed of" and now refers to an appellate proceeding for re-examination of the action of an inferior tribunal.

In formulating decisions, the Court deliberates in secret with only the justices present. They speak and vote in order of seniority of service, beginning with the Chief Justice and ending with the most junior justice, who also performs any menial tasks of the meeting, such as answering the door of the conference room. Usually, no justice may speak a second time until all have had an opportunity to speak. Each justice has one vote, and a majority of five or more votes decides the issue. If the Chief Justice is in the majority, he assigns the writing of the majority opinion to himself or another justice in the majority. If the Chief Justice is in the minority, the senior justice in the majority makes the assignment. Other justices may write concurring or dissenting opinions. Sometimes a per curiam (by the court) decision, usually in a non-controversial matter, is issued by the Court, without identifying a justice as the author. If the justices divide evenly on a case due to recusals or vacancies, the decision of the lower court is affirmed, but no binding precedent is established thereby. When the Chief Justice is unable to perform his duties because of disability, or the office is vacant, the senior associate justice performs the duties of the Chief Justice until the disability or vacancy ends.

The Reporter of Decisions prepares a synopsis of the facts and law decided (syllabus) that precedes the decision, but is not a part of it. The decisions are published on the Court's website, *www.supremecourtus.gov*, in slip opinion pamphlets, and eventually in bound volumes.

In the classic case, with the all-star cast, of *Marbury v. Madison*, 5 U.S. 137 (1803), Chief Justice John Marshall wrote the opinion in which the Supreme Court declared 6–0 that it had the authority to determine the constitutionality of a statute enacted by Congress. President John Adams, a Federalist, in the closing days of his administration that ended on March 4, 1801, made a series of so-called "midnight appointments" to fill as many government offices as possible with members of his party. Among these was

William Marbury's appointment on March 2 as a justice of the peace for the District of Columbia. However, President Thomas Jefferson, a Democratic-Republican and a political foe of Adams, assumed the presidency before Marbury received his commission as justice of the peace. Jefferson directed his Secretary of State, James Madison (who would become the fourth President), to withhold the commission. Marbury applied directly to the Supreme Court, as provided by Section 13 of the Judiciary Act of 1789, for a writ of mandamus to compel Madison to deliver the commission. The Court ruled that Marbury was entitled to his commission, but that that part of Section 13 was unconstitutional because it sought to add the power to issue the writ of mandamus to the original jurisdiction of the Court in violation of Article III, Section 2, Clause 2; and that "It is emphatically the province and duty of the judicial department to say what the law is." 5 U.S. 177. While the decision confirmed judicial supremacy over constitutional interpretation, it also avoided a conflict with President Jefferson by denying the mandamus.

Interestingly, President Adams had nominated Marshall as the fourth Chief Justice of the United States on January 20, 1801. He was unanimously confirmed by the Senate on February 4. However, Marshall continued to serve as Secretary of State until Adams' term expired on March 4, 1801, when Thomas Jefferson assumed the presidency. Some have questioned whether Marshall should have disqualified himself from participating in the *Marbury* case since his office of Secretary of State had failed to issue the commission in question.

Starting with *Marbury*, the Supreme Court confirmed its power to finally resolve constitutional issues, although it had "neither the purse or the sword." In the beginning, this doctrine of judicial supremacy was opposed by Presidents Thomas Jefferson and Andrew Jackson, who advocated the departmental theory of constitutional interpretation, under which each branch (congressional or executive) could determine for itself the constitutional matters before it without interference by the Supreme Court.

John Marshall (1755–1835) served as Chief Justice for more than 34 years (1801–1835), the longest tenure of any Chief Justice. He participated in more than 1,000 decisions and authored over 500 opinions. Four of his most important decisions were *Marbury v. Madison*; *McCulloch v. Maryland*, 17 U.S. 316 (1819), holding 7–0 that the doctrine of implied powers permitted the Congress to create a bank as a "necessary and proper" means to carry out its financial and other powers; *Cohens v. Virginia*, 19 U.S. 264 (1821), holding 7–0 that state courts are subject to federal appellate jurisdiction in cases involving federal laws, treaties and the Constitution; and *Gibbons v. Ogden*, 22 U.S. 1 (1824), holding 7–0 that congressional power to regulate foreign and interstate commerce embraced every species of commercial intercourse between the United States and foreign nations and every commercial transaction that was not wholly carried on within a single state, and that the power did not stop at the boundary of a state but was applicable within its interior. Marshall remains the single most important figure on constitutional law.

In the beginning, the Supreme Court followed the practice of justices writing seriatim opinions, whereby each one presented a separate judgment on a case. Under Chief Justice John Marshall, this practice was changed in *Talbot v. Seeman*, 5 U.S. 1 (1801), by issuing a single opinion, styled the opinion of the court. However, justices continued to often write concurring or dissenting opinions.

The inferior courts under Article III include the 13 courts of appeals and the 94 district courts. As with the Supreme Court, the judges of these courts have lifetime appointments with undiminished compensation. Most cases in the courts of appeals are heard by panels of three judges. A losing party before a three-judge panel can ask for a full-court, or en banc, review by all members of the court of appeals. However, en banc hearings are not favored and will be granted only for compelling reasons.

A second category of inferior courts are the courts or tribunals established by Congress under Article I, Section 8, Clause 9, such as the Court of Appeals for the Armed Forces, the Court of Appeals for Veterans Claims, the Tax Court, the Court of Federal Claims, the Merit Systems Protection Board, bankruptcy courts, armed forces courts-martial, and other adjudicative bodies. These tribunals have differing levels of independence from the executive and legislative branches, and their judges do not have lifetime tenure or compensation guarantees. The Supreme Court in *Northern Pipeline Construction Co. v. Marathon Pipe Line Co.*, 458 U.S. 50 (1982), held 6–3 that Article III jurisdiction could not be conferred on non–Article III courts because they lack the independence and protection given to Article III judges.

The third category of adjudicators covers employees of the executive branch engaged in determining the rights of individuals in the administration of regulatory programs.

GOOD BEHAVIOR

This phrase is interpreted to refer to life tenure rather than to a standard for removal which would be by conviction on impeachment for "Treason, Bribery, or other high Crimes and Misdemeanors" under Article II, Section 4.

In *Stump v. Sparkman*, 435 U.S. 349 (1978), a mother petitioned a state judge to have her 15-year-old daughter sterilized, alleging that she was "somewhat retarded" and associating with men. The judge granted the petition without holding an evidentiary hearing or appointing an attorney to represent the daughter's interest. The daughter was unaware of the sterilization, having been told that she was undergoing surgery for the removal of her appendix. The Supreme Court held 5–3 that "the scope of the judge's jurisdiction must be construed broadly where the issue is the immunity of the judge. A judge will not be deprived of immunity because the action he took was in error, was done maliciously, or was in excess of his authority; rather he will be subject to liability only when he acted in the clear absence of all jurisdiction." 435 U.S. 356. The Court observed that this immunity is justified because judges decide great controversies involving pecuniary interests and the liberty and character of parties that excite the deepest emotions over conflicts in evidence and legal interpretation. 435 U.S. 364.

COMPENSATION

Under the Compensation Clause, it is clear that salaries cannot be reduced. However, questions arise as to taxes and cost-of-living increases that are begun and then cancelled. In *United States v. Will*, 449 U.S. 200 (1980), Congress had enacted automatic annual cost-of-living pay increases for federal employees, including judges. Subsequently, Congress interrupted such raises that were scheduled to occur. The Supreme Court held 8–1 that revoking these automatic pay increases amounted to salary reduction for judges and violated the Compensation Clause. In *United States v. Hatter*, 532 U.S. 557 (2001), the Court held 6–1 that the clause prevents the collection of Social Security taxes from federal judges who held office before Congress extended those taxes to federal employees. However, the collection of the Medicare taxes was upheld 5–2 as the imposition of generally applicable, nondiscriminatory taxes that are not forbidden by the clause.

Regarding the citation of Supreme Court cases, from 1790 to 1874, the cases were cited by the names of the reporters of the decisions: Alexander J. Dallas, 1790–1800 (Dallas 1–4 equals 1–4 US); William Cranch, 1801–1815 (Cranch 1–9 equals 5–13 US); Henry Wheaton, 1816–1827 (Wheat. 1–12 equals 14–25 US); Richard Peters, 1828–1842 (Peters 1–24 equals 26–41 US); Benjamin Chew Howard, 1843–1860 (Howard 1–24 equals 42–65 US); Jeremiah Sullivan Black, 1861–1862 (Black 1–2 equals 66–67 US); and John William Wallace, 1863–1874 (Wall. 1–23 equals 68–90 US). Today, this old system of citation is seldom used because the *U.S. Reports* citations are shorter and readily found in the popular unofficial reports in the *Lawyer's Cooperative Edition* and *Supreme Court Reporter*. Sometimes the old and new systems are combined, such as *Marbury v. Madison*, 5 US (1 Cranch) 137 (1803).

Article III, Section 2, Clause 1, Judicial Power. The judicial Power shall extend to all Cases, in Law and Equity, arising under this Constitution, the Laws of the United States, and Treaties made, or which shall be made, under their Authority;—to all Cases affecting Ambassadors, other public Ministers and Consuls;—to all Cases of admiralty and maritime Jurisdiction;—to Controversies to which the United States shall be a Party;—to Controversies between two or more States;—[between a State and Citizens of another State;]—between Citizens of different States;—between Citizens of the same State claiming Lands under Grants of different States—[and between a State, or the Citizens thereof, and foreign States, Citizens or Subjects]. [The bracketed provisions were amended by the Eleventh Amendment, ratified January 8, 1798, which provides that. "[t]he Judicial power of the United States shall not be construed to extend to any suit in law or equity, commenced or prosecuted against one of the United States by Citizens of another State, or by Citizens or Subjects of any Foreign State."]

CASES AND CONTROVERSIES

The exercise of judicial power is limited to cases and controversies that confine "the business of federal courts to questions presented in an adversary context and in a form historically viewed as capable of resolution through the judicial process." *Flast v. Cohen*, 392 U.S. 83, 95 (1968). These terms imply the existence of adverse parties whose contentions are submitted to the court for adjudication. *Muskrat v. United States*, 219 U.S. 346 (1911), 9–0. Therefore, an action is not a case or controversy if the federal court is called upon to determine moot questions or to render advisory opinions which are unenforceable by its decree or on matters of law not involved in actual litigation. *Keller v. Potomac Electric Power Company*, 261 U.S. 428 (1923).

FEDERAL QUESTION

This clause defines the subject matter jurisdiction of the federal courts. A case arises under federal law if the decision depends in some way on federal law. In *Osborn v. Bank of the United States*, 22 U.S. 738 (1824), the bank chartered by Congress sued in federal court to restrain collection of a state tax. The Supreme Court held 6–1 that federal jurisdiction attaches because the bank's rights depended on its federally granted charter. The fact that other principles of state law are also involved in the case does not defeat federal jurisdiction.

In *Cohens v. Virginia*, 19 U.S. 264 (1821), the Supreme Court held 7–0 that it had jurisdiction to review state criminal proceedings involving federal law issues, and that state laws and constitutions, when repugnant to the Constitution and federal laws, are "absolutely void."

TREATIES

In *Martin v. Hunter's Lessee*, 14 U.S. 304 (1816), Denny Martin, a British subject, inherited Virginia land from Lord Fairfax, a Loyalist, who had fled to England during the Revolution. The Virginia legislature confiscated the Fairfax land and conveyed part of it to David Hunter. Martin claimed that he was entitled to the land under the Jay Treaty of 1794 between the United States and Great Britain which forbade the confiscation of Loyalist property. In overruling the Virginia court's denial of the claim, the Supreme Court declared 6–0 that it had the power to exercise appellate jurisdiction over state courts whenever cases in such courts come within the scope of the judicial power of the United States. 14 U.S. 340.

A federal statute and a properly executed treaty have equal status in law, the latter in time taking precedence.

AMBASSADORS

The Supreme Court relies on the certification of the executive with respect to the status of a person claiming to be a public minister. *In re Baiz*, 135 U.S. 403, 432 (1890). Federal jurisdiction under this clause does not apply to U.S. diplomats, but only to persons accredited to the United States by foreign governments. *Ex parte Gruber*, 269 U.S. 302 (1925).

ADMIRALTY

The federal district courts have exclusive jurisdiction over admiralty and maritime cases. In *Glass v. The Sloop Betsey*, 3 U.S. 6 (1794), the Supreme Court upheld 6–0 federal jurisdiction over the prize dispute involving the French capture of a Swedish ship that was brought into a U.S. port. While under the laws of England at the time of framing the Constitution, distinctions were made between admiralty and maritime jurisdiction; in federal law the terms are used interchangeably to apply to cases arising upon domestic navigable waterways and the high seas. The grants of power under the Commerce Clause (Article I, Section 8, Clause 3) and the Admiralty Clause are entirely separate. The former extends to only navigable waters which are highways of foreign or interstate commerce, while the latter extends to all navigable waters of the United States irrespective of any interstate feature. *The Daniel Ball*, 77 U.S. 557 (1870).

FEDERAL PARTY

The federal courts have exclusive jurisdiction over any case in which the United States is a party. The United States as a legal entity has the inherent right to initiate litigation. *Dugan v. United States*, 16 U.S. 172 (1818). Sovereign immunity shields the United States from being sued unless it has waived its immunity or consented to suit. *Cohens v. Virginia*, 19 U.S. 264 (1821). Consent has been given under such statutes as the Federal Tort

Claims Act (1946) that permit private parties to sue the United States for most torts committed by persons acting on behalf of the United States.

DISPUTES BETWEEN STATES

The federal courts have exclusive jurisdiction over disputes between two or more states. The subject of such disputes often involves territorial claims, water rights and financial conflicts. *Louisiana v. Mississippi*, 466 U.S. 96 (1984).

DIVERSITY

The extension of federal judicial power to controversies between a state and citizens of another state was interpreted as impairing state sovereign immunity in *Chisholm v. Georgia*, 2 U.S. 419 (1793). This case involved a suit by a South Carolina citizen to collect Revolutionary War debts owed by Georgia. Georgia claimed sovereign immunity, but the Supreme Court upheld 4–1 federal jurisdiction and ordered Georgia to pay Chisholm the money damages he sought. The *Chisholm* decision was overturned by the ratification of the Eleventh Amendment on February 7, 1795, providing that: "[t]he Judicial power of the United States shall not be construed to extend to any suit in law or equity, commenced or prosecuted against one of the United States by Citizens of another State, or by Citizens or Subjects of any Foreign State."

Although the Eleventh Amendment does not expressly forbid suits in federal court against a state by its own citizens, it has been held that such suits are prohibited by the Amendment and the doctrine of sovereign immunity. *Hans v. Louisiana*, 134 U.S. 1 (1890), 9–0 vote. However, suit may lie against a state officer who has acted in excess of his authority, or under the authority of an invalid law. *Tindal v. Wesley*, 167 U.S. 204 (1897).

The extension of federal judicial power to controversies between citizens of different states was intended to protect out-of-state litigants from local bias in state courts. A corporation is treated as a citizen of the state in which it is incorporated. Congress has limited the exercise of diversity jurisdiction by specifying the minimum amount of money that parties must be seeking in the litigation. In *Erie Railroad Co. v. Tompkins*, 304 U.S. 64 (1938), the Supreme Court held 6–2 that a federal district court in a diversity jurisdiction case must apply the law of the state in which it sits, including the judicial doctrine of the state's highest court, where it does not conflict with federal law.

Diversity and federal question issues constitute the two primary sources of subject matter jurisdiction in the federal courts.

ABSTENTION DOCTRINE

This is a doctrine of federalism and intergovernmental comity based on the recognition that state courts should be permitted to decide federal constitutional issues free from interference by federal courts until the conclusion of the state judicial process, except in extraordinary circumstances, such as when the danger of irreparable injury is substantial and imminent. In *Railroad Commission of Texas v. Pullman Co.*, 312 U.S. 496 (1941), involving allegations of equal protection violations by black sleeping car porters, the Supreme Court held 8–0 that the federal courts should abstain from adjudicating the constitutionality of state enactments fairly open to interpretation until the state courts have been afforded a reasonable opportunity to decide them. In *Younger v. Harris*, 401 U.S. 37 (1971), involving alleged violation of the freedom of speech guarantee, the Supreme Court held 8–1 that the challenged unconstitutionality of a state statute is not grounds for a federal court to enjoin state court criminal proceedings. However, the Court noted these exceptions to the application of the abstention doctrine by a federal court: (1) where "expressly authorized by Act of Congress"; (2) "where necessary in aid of its jurisdiction"; (3) where necessary "to protect or effectuate its judgments"; and (4) where those subject to state prosecution will "suffer irreparable damages." 401 U.S. 43.

Article III, Section 2, Clause 2. Original and Appellate Jurisdiction. In all Cases affecting Ambassadors, other public Ministers and Consuls, and those in which a State shall be Party, the supreme Court shall have original Jurisdiction. In all the other Cases before mentioned, the supreme Court shall have appellate Jurisdiction, both as to Law and Fact, with such Exceptions, and under such Regulations as the Congress shall make.

ORIGINAL JURISDICTION

The original jurisdiction defines the cases that the Supreme Court can hear directly, and not through appeals from lower courts. This jurisdiction may only be changed by constitutional amendment. *Marbury v. Madison*, 5 U.S. 137 (1803). On the other hand, the appellate jurisdiction of the Supreme Court may be changed by Congress.

A major aspect of original jurisdiction is state cases involving such matters as boundary disputes (*Virginia v. Tennessee*, 148 U.S. 503 [1893]), property ownership disputes over coastal waters (*United States v. Texas*, 339 U.S. 707 [1950]), and interstate conflicts over the exercise of economic, regulatory or tax powers. These cases are not heard as of right before the Supreme Court even though its jurisdiction is exclusive. Original cases are commenced by petition for leave to file a complaint. Upon the granting of a complaint, the court usually appoints a special master to make factual and legal recommendations. The master may hold hearings and take testimony, including receiving briefs, arguments and proposed recommendations from the parties. The final report of the special master may be appealed by the parties to the Supreme Court where the case may be briefed and argued before the Court as in other cases.

APPELLATE JURISDICTION

The vast majority of cases appealed to the Supreme Court under the Appellate Jurisdiction Clause are by petitions for a writ of certiorari filed by parties in federal and state courts in which a federal question of law is presented. This appeal process is discretionary on the part of the Supreme Court, and depends on at least four justices agreeing to issue the writ of certiorari for the case to be heard by the Court. The writ is issued only for "compelling reasons" such as to resolve a conflict among lower courts in the interpretation of federal law, correct an egregious departure from the usual course of judicial proceedings, resolve an important federal issue, or review a lower court decision in direct conflict with a prior decision of the Court. A denial of the writ of certiorari is not a judgment on the merits of the case, and results in the decision of the lower court standing as the final ruling in the case.

The 13 federal circuits are divided among the nine Supreme Court justices in order to permit the justice assigned to the circuit to consider applications for emergency relief such as granting a stay of a lower court ruling in the circuit.

Justice Louis Brandeis, in his concurring opinion in *Ashwander v. Tennessee Valley Authority*, 297 U.S. 288, 346 (1936), formulated the following avoidance doctrine of seven rules to minimize the decision of constitutional issues and thereby avoid encroachment on the domain of the other branches of government under the separation of powers principle: 1. The Court will not decide the constitutionality of legislation in a non-adversarial proceeding. 2. The Court will not anticipate a question of constitutional law in advance of the necessity of deciding it. 3. The Court will not formulate a rule of constitutional law broader than what is required by the facts to which it is applied. 4. The Court will not rule on a constitutional question if there is another ground upon which the case may be disposed of. 5. The Court will not rule on the validity of legislation unless the plaintiff has been injured by its operation. 6. The Court will not rule on the constitutionality of legislation at the request of one who has benefitted from it. 7. The Court will always ascertain whether any reasonable construction of the legislation may avoid constitutional interpretation.

While the Supreme Court has upheld congressional withdrawal of jurisdiction over habeas corpus appeals from the Court under the Appellate Jurisdiction Clause in *Ex parte McCardle*, 74 U.S. 506 (1869), 8–0 vote, it is questionable how far the Congress may go in reducing the Court's appellate jurisdiction under the Exceptions Clause. In contrast to *McCardle*, the

Supreme Court in *United States v. Klein*, 80 U.S. 128 (1871), denied congressional authority to restrict the element of proof in judicial proceedings. In *Boumediene v. Bush*, 553 U.S. 723 (2008), the Supreme Court held 5–4 that foreign citizens detained at Guantanamo Bay have a constitutional right to challenge their detention in federal district courts, and that the habeas corpus restriction of the Military Commissions Act (MCA) of 2006 violated the Habeas Corpus Suspension Clause, Article I, Section 9, Clause 2. The majority ruled that to "hold that the political branches may switch the Constitution on or off at will would lead to a regime in which they, not this Court, say 'what the law is.' *Marbury v. Madison*."

Article III, Section 2, Clause 3, Criminal Trials. The Trial of all Crimes, except in Cases of Impeachment, shall be by Jury; and such Trial shall be held in the State where the said Crimes shall have been committed; but when not committed within any State, the Trial shall be at such Place or Places as the Congress may by Law have directed.

The basic right to a trial by jury of one's peers traces its lineage back to the Magna Carta, and is one of the few individual rights protected in the original Constitution (1788). Further requirements for jury trials are specified three additional times in the Bill of Rights (1791): grand jury indictments in the Fifth Amendment; jury trials for criminal prosecutions in the Sixth Amendment; and jury trials for common law cases in the Seventh Amendment.

Originally, under the Constitution, juries decided both law and fact. However, in *Sparf v. United States*, 156 U.S. 51 (1895), the Supreme Court held 5–4 that federal judges were not required to inform jurors of their right to decide both the facts and the law in reaching a verdict. Since then judges have asserted the authority to instruct juries that they must accept the judges' interpretation of the law. However, as a practical matter a jury in delivering a non-reviewable verdict of acquittal may ignore legal interpretations that it deems inappropriate.

Also, irrespective of the use of the mandatory "shall," a defendant may waive a jury trial with the consent of the prosecution and the sanction of the court. *Patton v. United States*, 281 U.S. 276 (1930).

Article III, Section 3, Clause 1. Treason. Treason against the United States, shall consist only in levying War against them, or in adhering to their Enemies, giving them Aid and Comfort. No Person shall be convicted of Treason unless on the Testimony of two Witnesses to the same overt Act, or on Confession in open Court.

Two early judicial interpretations of treason arose from the alleged Burr Conspiracy. Aaron Burr (1756–1836), while serving as Vice President in the Jefferson Administration, challenged and mortally wounded Alexander Hamilton in a duel at Weehawken, New Jersey, on July 11, 1804. This, along with political indiscretions, placed Burr in general disrepute. Upon leaving the vice presidency, Burr allegedly planned to betray the United States by establishing a separate country in the Southwest to be headed by him. He was accused of organizing an assemblage of men in Ohio to carry out this expedition, although Burr was not present.

In *Ex parte Bollman*, 8 U.S. 75 (1807), involving two of Burr's confederates, Chief Justice John Marshall, speaking for himself and three other Justices, confined the meaning of levying war to the actual waging of war. "To conspire to levy war, and actually to levy war, are distinct offences." Conspiracy short of the actual levying of war is insufficient. On the basis of this interpretation and the fact that no part of the alleged crime had been committed in the District of Columbia, the Court held that the two confederates could not be tried in the District and ordered their discharge.

Shortly thereafter, Chief Justice Marshall went to Richmond, VA, to preside as a circuit judge over the trial of Aaron Burr himself. (In those days, justices spent time on circuit duty when there was insufficient business before the Supreme Court.) Marshall held that Burr, if not physically present in an assemblage of men, could still be convicted of treason on the testimony of two witnesses that he actively supported such an assembly for the levying of war. In the absence of such testimony, Burr was acquitted. *United States v. Burr*, 8 U.S. 469, 25 F Cases 55, CC VA (1807).

The *Bollman* and *Burr* decisions made it extremely difficult to convict one of levying war against the United States without personal participation in actual hostilities.

In *Haup v. United States*, 330 U.S. 631 (1947), the Supreme Court held 8–1 that the testimony of two witnesses to overt acts might be supported by other evidence as to the accuser's treasonable intent, including out-of-court confessions and admissions.

Subversive acts may also be prosecuted under laws such as the Espionage Act of 1917. U.S. citizens Julius and Ethel Rosenberg were executed on June 19, 1953, under this Act after having been found guilty of conspiracy to commit espionage in passing secret information on the American atomic bomb to the Soviet Union. *Rosenberg v. United States*, 346 U.S. 273 (1953), 6–3 vote.

Article III, Section 3, Clause 2, Punishment of Treason. The Congress shall have Power to declare the Punishment of Treason, but no Attainder of Treason shall work Corruption of Blood, or Forfeiture except during the Life of the Person attainted.

Under early English law, attainder meant the elimination of all civil rights and privileges, including forfeiture of property, resulting from a conviction for treason. Corruption of blood meant that a person attained lost all capacity to inherit or transmit property to his or her descendents. Accordingly, under Clause 2, while Congress could provide for a traitor to be deprived of his property, it could not punish the heirs of a traitor by revoking their inheritance if there was any property left to inherit.

A bill of attainder is a legislative condemnation of a specifically designated person or group without the formality of a judicial trial, and is prohibited by Article I, Section 9, Clause 3, of the Constitution.

Article IV
State Relations

Article IV, Section 1, Full Faith and Credit. Full Faith and Credit shall be given in each State to the public Acts, Records, and judicial Proceedings of every other State. And the Congress may by general Laws prescribe the Manner in which such Acts, Records and Proceedings shall be proved, and the Effect thereof.

This Full Faith and Credit Clause is an essential mechanism for creating a union of multiple sovereigns by requiring a state to recognize and give effect to the legislative acts, public records and judicial decisions of other states when attested according to the forms prescribed by Congress. The clause makes it unnecessary for a person who has established rights in one state in such matters as judgments, contracts, deeds and wills to have to re-establish them in other states where necessary to protect his legal interests. However, in *Williams v. North Carolina*, 325 U.S. 226 (1945), the Supreme Court held 6–3 that judgments of courts in divorce cases are not binding upon other states unless one of the parties had a bona fide domicile in the state in which the divorce was granted. Jurisdiction to grant a divorce is founded on domicile.

As a result of the same-sex marriage controversy, Congress enacted the Defense of Marriage Act (DOMA) in 1996 providing that no state need treat a relationship between persons of the same sex as a marriage, even if the relationship is considered a marriage in another state, and that the federal government may not treat same-sex relationships as marriages for any purpose, even if recognized by one of the states. Critics contend that DOMA violates the Due Process and Equal Protection clauses of the Fourteenth Amendment because it unlawfully discriminates between heterosexual and homosexual relationships. The Supreme Court has thus far declined to address this issue.

Aside from DOMA, federal courts have been reluctant to apply the law of one state to another state in contravention of the latter's own public policy. This public policy exception has been applied in cases of marriages involving polygamy or incest.

The Full Faith and Credit Clause does not apply to occupational licensing; a doctor, lawyer or other practitioner licensed to practice in one state is not automatically licensed in another. However, the rights of ministers and journalists to pursue their work are protected by the First Amendment.

Article IV, Section 2, Clause 1. Privileges and Immunities. The Citizens of each State shall be entitled to all Privileges and Immunities of Citizens in the several States.

The purpose of the Privileges and Immunities Clause, or Comity Clause, is to prevent arbitrary discriminations by one state in favor of its own citizens and against the citizens of other states. It places the citizens of each state upon the same footing with citizens of other states, as far as the advantages resulting from citizenship in those states are concerned. Accordingly, a state may not levy a higher license fee on non-residents than on residents, *Ward v. Maryland*, 79 U.S. 418 (1870), 9–0 vote; a state may not tax property of non-residents at a higher rate than that applied to its residents, *Chalker v. Birmingham & Northwestern Ry. Co.*, 249 U.S. 522 (1919), 9–0 vote; a state may not limit jobs on its oil pipeline to state residents, *Hicklin v. Orbeck*, 437 U.S. 518 (1978), 9–0 vote; and a state may not deny nonresidents admission to the bar to practice law, *Supreme Court of New Hampshire v. Piper*, 470 U.S. 274 (1985), 8–1 vote. However, a state may charge higher tuition to out-of-state students because local citizens have paid taxes to support public universities. *Vlandis v. Kline*, 412 U.S. 441 (1973), 6–3 vote.

Citizens have the right to travel freely from state to state. *Griffin v. Breckenridge*, 403 U.S. 88, 105 (1971), 9–0 vote.

The Fourteenth Amendment (1868), Section 1, also contains a "privileges or immunities" clause applicable to state action. Accordingly, the decisions cited there are relevant here.

Article IV, Section 2, Clause 2. Interstate Extradition (Rendition). A Person charged in any State with Treason, Felony, or other Crime, who shall flee from Justice, and be found in another State, shall on Demand of the executive Authority of the State from which he fled, be delivered up, to be removed to the State having jurisdiction of the Crime.

This Extradition Clause provides for the delivery of fugitives from justice by the authorities of the state where such fugitives have sought asylum to the authorities of the state from which they fled. A fugitive must have been actually, and not constructively, in the demanding state at the time of the commission of the alleged offense. The fact that he subsequently enters and leaves the state does not make him a fugitive. *Hyatt v. New York*, 188 U.S. 691 (1903). It is not necessary that the person charged should have left the state after indictment, or for the purpose of avoiding a prosecution. *Roberts v. Reilly*, 116 U.S. 80 (1885). It is enough that he left the state where the alleged crime was committed. The motive which prompted him to leave, or the fact that he did not believe he had committed a crime, is not material. *Appleyard v. Massachusetts*, 203 U.S. 222 (1906).

The governor of the asylum state may determine only whether the person sought is charged with a crime under the demanding state's law, and whether the person was in the demanding state when the alleged offense occurred. *Munsey v. Clough*, 196 U.S. 364 (1905). Other questions, such as guilt or innocence, sufficiency of evidence, interpretation of state law, or adequacy of justice in the demanding state, are litigable only in the demanding state. *New Mexico ex rel. Ortiz v. Reed*, 524 U.S. 151 (1998), 9–0 vote. Federal courts may compel governors to render fugitives properly demanded. *Puerto Rico v. Branstad*, 483 U.S. 219 (1987), 9–0 vote.

Article IV, Section 2, Clause 3. Fugitive Slaves. No Person held to Service or Labour in one State, under the Laws thereof, escaping into another, shall, in Consequence of any Law or Regulation therein, be discharged from such Service or Labour, but shall be delivered up on Claim of the Party to whom such Service or Labour may be due.

This Fugitive Slave Clause, requiring the return of interstate runaway slaves to their masters, was overturned by the Thirteenth Amendment (1865) prohibiting slavery.

In 1857, the Supreme Court in *Dred Scott v. Sandford*, 60 U.S. 393, held 7–2 that slaves were not citizens, but property, and that under this clause, "the States pledge themselves to each other to maintain the right of property of the master, by delivering up to him any slave who may have escaped from his service, and be found within their respective territories." 60 U.S. 411. Dred Scott (1799–1858) and his wife Harriet, were slaves, but had lived in Illinois and territories where slavery was illegal. They argued that they were free under the doctrine of "once free, always free." Nevertheless, the Court rejected their claim of citizenship and confirmed their status as private property.

The Supreme Court further held that Congress did not have the authority to forbid slavery in the territories, and that those provisions of the

Missouri Compromise of 1820 were unconstitutional. The Missouri Compromise was an agreement between members of Congress, representing 11 free and 11 slave states, under which (1) Maine was admitted as a free state, (2) Missouri was admitted as a slave state, and (3) slavery would be thereafter prohibited in the region north of the parallel 36° 30' (Missouri's southern border), except within the boundaries of the proposed state of Missouri.

Article IV, Section 3, Clause 1. New States. New States may be admitted by the Congress into this Union; but no new State shall be formed or erected within the Jurisdiction of any other State; nor any State be formed by the Junction of two or more States, or Parts of States, without the Consent of the Legislatures of the States concerned as well as of the Congress.

New states are admitted into the Union on an equal basis with the states that are already in the Union. *Pollard's Lessee v. Hagan*, 44 U.S. 212 (1845). Except for Maine (1820), Vermont (1791), Kentucky (1792), Texas (1845), California (1850) and West Virginia (1863), all new states have been elevated from territorial status. The procedure usually followed is a petition of the territory for statehood, the passing by Congress of an enabling act which authorizes the inhabitants to draft a constitution, and the passing of an act of admission following the acceptance of the constitution. Congress may not admit new states formed out of the area of an existing state or combining two existing states without the consent of the legislatures of the states affected.

In *Coyle v. Smith*, 221 U.S. 559 (1911), Oklahoma was admitted as a state in 1907, with the state capital located at Guthrie. The state constitution, as accepted by Congress, provided that the state capital could not be changed prior to 1913, but could be changed thereafter by a vote of the electorate. In 1910, the state legislature enacted a statute moving the capital from Guthrie to Oklahoma City. The Supreme Court upheld 7–2 the change in the location of the capital. Congress, in admitting a new state, cannot impose conditions in the enabling act, the acceptance of which will deprive the state when admitted of any attribute of power essential to its equality with the other states.

Article IV, Section 3, Clause 2, Territory, Property. The Congress shall have Power to dispose of and make all needful Rules and Regulations respecting the Territory or other Property belonging to the United States; and nothing in this Constitution shall be so construed as to Prejudice any Claims of the United States, or of any particular State.

The Disposing Clause empowers the Congress to manage and control the vast lands of the United States. In *Kleppe v. New Mexico*, 426 U.S. 529

(1976), the Supreme Court held 9–0 that the complete power that Congress has over federal lands under this clause necessarily includes the power to regulate and protect wildlife living there, state law notwithstanding.

In *Ashwander v. Tennessee Valley Authority*, 297 U.S. 288 (1936), the Supreme Court upheld 8–1 the construction of hydroelectric installations in the Tennessee Valley, and the acquisition by the Tennessee Valley Authority of transmission lines for the distribution and sale of its electric power, pursuant to congressional commerce and war powers (Art. I, Sec. 8, CL. 3, 11). The Court upheld the sale of the surplus electric power pursuant to the congressional right of disposal under this clause.

Under the Enclave Clause, Article I, Section 8, Clause 17, Congress is granted sovereign authority over the District of Columbia and over other places purchased with state consent.

In 1898, the United States annexed Hawaii and, pursuant to the Treaty of Paris of 1898, ending the Spanish-American War, acquired Cuba, Guam, the Philippines, and Puerto Rico. The issue arose as to whether the "Constitution follows the flag." In the ten Insular Cases decided 1901 to 1904, the Supreme Court held that the constitutional guarantees of private rights are applicable to territories which have been made a part of the United States by congressional action, but are not applicable to unincorporated territories. In *Downes v. Bidwell*, 182 U.S. 244 (1901), the Supreme Court held 5–4 that the Constitution does not automatically apply to the people of an annexed territory, nor confer upon them all the privileges of U.S. citizenship, but that it was up to Congress to extend constitutional guarantees to them as it saw fit. The Supreme Court relied on the Insular Cases in *United States v. Verdugo-Urquidez*, 494 U.S. 259, 269 (1990), by holding 6–3 that the Fourth Amendment does not apply to the search and seizure by U.S. agents of property owned by a nonresident alien and located in a foreign country.

Article IV, Section 4, Guarantee of Republican Government. The United States shall guarantee to every State in this Union a Republican Form of Government, and shall protect each of them against Invasion; and on Application of the Legislature, or of the Executive (when the Legislature cannot be convened), against domestic Violence.

Under the Guarantee Clause, or Republican Form Clause, a republican form of government is one that is administered under the rule of law by responsible officers chosen directly or indirectly by the electorate. In *Luther v. Borden*, 48 U.S. 1 (1849), the Supreme Court, in refusing to decide which of two competing governments in Rhode Island was legitimately elected, declared that enforcement of the clause was a political question for Congress and the President, and not a justiciable issue for the courts. In *Pacific States*

Telephone and Telegraph Company v. Oregon, 223 U.S. 118 (1912), the company sought to invalidate a state tax that had been imposed by an initiative voted into law directly by the electorate, rather than through representatives. The company contended that direct citizen lawmaking by initiative violated the republican form of government which the clause guaranteed to each state. The Court refused jurisdiction, holding that the issue was a political question to be addressed to Congress.

Article V
The Amendment Process

Article V, Amendments. The Congress, whenever two thirds of both Houses shall deem it necessary, shall propose Amendments to this Constitution, or, on the Application of the Legislatures of two thirds of the several States, shall call a Convention for proposing Amendments, which, in either Case, shall be valid to all Intents and Purposes, as Part of this Constitution, when ratified by the Legislatures of three fourths of the several States, or by Conventions in three fourths thereof, as the one or the other Mode of Ratification may be proposed by the Congress; Provided that no Amendment which may be made prior to the Year One thousand eight hundred and eight shall in any Manner affect the first and fourth Clauses in the Ninth Section of the first Article; and that no State, without its Consent, shall be deprived of its equal Suffrage in the Senate.

This Article provides two methods of proposing amendments to the Constitution: (1) by a two-thirds vote of both houses of Congress; or (2) by a convention called by Congress upon the application of two-thirds of state legislatures. (The latter proposal method has never occurred.) Amendments proposed by Congress need not be submitted to the President according to the Presentment Clause (Article I, Section 7, Clause 2). *Hollingsworth v. Virginia*, 3 U.S. 378 (1798). The "two thirds of both Houses" requirement applies to a present quorum, not to the total membership of each body. *National Prohibition Cases*, 253 U.S. 350 (1920). Congress, when proposing an amendment, may set a reasonable time limit for ratification by the states; and the date of ratification, not its proclamation, determines the effectiveness of the amendment. *Dillon v. Gloss*, 256 U.S. 368 (1921), 9–0 vote.

Amendments so proposed may be ratified either by the legislatures or conventions of three-fourths of the states. Regardless of how an amendment is proposed, Congress has the authority to direct the mode of ratification, either by state legislatures or by conventions. *United States v. Sprague*, 282 U.S. 716 (1931), 8–0 vote. A state may not make ratification of a constitutional amendment subject to vote of the people because Article V specifically provides for ratification by state legislatures or conventions. *Hawke v. Smith*, 253 U.S. 221 (1920). Constitutional amendments are considered pending before the states indefinitely unless Congress establishes a deadline within which the states must act. Congress, and not the courts, is responsible for deciding if an amendment has been validly ratified. *Coleman v. Miller*, 307 U.S. 433 (1939), 7–2 vote.

The proviso at the end of Article V prohibits any constitutional amendment prior to 1808 that would affect Article I, Section 9, Clause 1, relating to slave trade, and Clause 4, relating to capitation or other direct taxes based on census figures. These prohibitions became moot in 1808. The subject matter of the former was prohibited by the ratification of the Thirteenth Amendment abolishing slavery, and the subject matter of the latter was repealed by the Sixteenth Amendment authorizing the federal income tax without regard to census figures.

The latter part of the proviso of Article V provides that no state, without its consent, shall be denied equal representation in the Senate. This provision underscores the sanctity of the Great Compromise reflected in Article I, Sections 2 and 3, whereby small states are equally represented in the Senate and large states are represented in the House according to population. The states are a part of a perpetual and indestructible union, and any effort to secede during the Civil War was a nullity because states retain their membership in the union. *Texas v. White*, 74 U.S. 700 (1869), 5–3 vote.

Article VI
The Supremacy of
the Constitution

Article VI, Clause 1, Debt Assumption. All Debts contracted and Engagements entered into, before the Adoption of this Constitution, shall be as valid against the United States under this Constitution, as under the Confederation.

This Debt Assumption Clause confirmed the obligation of the United States to pay the substantial debts incurred by the Continental Congress under the Articles of Confederation, chief among which was the cost of waging the War for Independence. This clause is now obsolete.

Article VI, Clause 2, Supreme Law of the Land. This Constitution, and the Laws of the United States which shall be made in Pursuance thereof; and all Treaties made, or which shall be made, under the Authority of the United States, shall be the supreme Law of the Land; and the Judges in every State shall be bound thereby, any Thing in the Constitution or Laws of any State to the Contrary notwithstanding.

The Supremacy or Preemption Clause declares that the Constitution is the supreme law of the land, and that federal laws and treaties, and state constitutions and laws, in conflict with it, are void. Also, state constitutions and laws are void if they are in conflict with federal laws made pursuant to the Constitution or treaties made under U.S. authority. A federal law and treaty have equal status, and if there is a conflict between them, the one adopted later in time controls.

In *Ware v. Hylton*, 3 U.S. 199 (1796), the Treaty of Paris of 1783, ending the Revolutionary War with Great Britain, stated that British creditors could recover pre war debts owed by Americans. Virginia law provided for the confiscation of such debts on the ground that they were owed to alien enemies. The Supreme Court invalidated 6–0 the Virginia law, establishing the supremacy of national treaties over conflicting state laws.

In *Graves v. New York Ex Rel. O'Keefe*, 306 U.S. 466 (1939), the Supreme Court held 7–2 that there was no implied constitutional immunity from non-discriminating state taxation on the salaries of federal and state employees because a tax on employee income is not a tax on its source.

In *Pennsylvania v. Nelson*, 350 U.S. 497 (1956), the Supreme Court developed criteria for assessing whether federal law preempts state action when Congress has not specifically stated its intent. These criteria include whether the scheme of federal regulation is so pervasive as to infer that Congress left no room for the states to supplement it, whether the federal interest is so dominant that the federal system must be assumed to preclude enforcement of state laws on the same subject, or whether the enforcement of a state law presents a serious danger of conflict with the administration of the federal program. In this case, the Court held 6–3 that a state anti-subversion law was unconstitutional because the scheme of federal regulation of the subject was "pervasive" and "left no room for the States to supplement it." 350 U.S. 502.

In *Crosby v. National Foreign Trade Council*, 530 U.S. 363 (2000), Massachusetts in 1996 passed a law barring state entities from buying goods and services from companies doing business with Myanmar (Burma). Subsequently, Congress imposed sanctions on Myanmar, and authorized the President to impose further sanctions or lift them as warranted. The Supreme Court held 9–0 that the state law was preempted as an obstacle to the goals of the federal law, despite the lack of an express preemption clause.

The treaty-making power of the President is broader than the law-making power of the Congress. The Supreme Court in *Missouri v. Holland*, 252 U.S. 416 (1920), ruled 7–2 that pursuant to the Migratory Bird Treaty with Britain, the President, with the approval of the Senate, could regulate the hunting of migratory birds, even though Congress had no independent authority to pass such legislation. However, the Supreme Court in *Reid v. Covert*, 354 U.S. 1 (1957), ruled 6–2 that treaties cannot create obligations that violate constitutional guarantees such as those found in the Bill of Rights.

Article VI, Clause 3, Loyalty. The Senators and Representatives before mentioned, and the Members of the several State Legislatures, and all executive and judicial Officers, both of the United States and of the several States, shall be bound by Oath or Affirmation, to support this Constitution; but no religious Test shall ever be required as a Qualification to any Office or public Trust under the United States.

In order to unify the national and state governments, the Loyalty Clause, or Oath or Affirmation Clause, requires that all federal and state officials take an oath or affirmation to support the Constitution. The clause prohibits the federal and state governments from requiring any kind of religious test for public office. *Torcaso v. Watkins*, 367 U.S. 488 (1961), 9–0 vote.

Article VII
The Ratification Process

Article VII, Clause 1. Ratification. The Ratification of the Conventions of nine States, shall be sufficient for the Establishment of this Constitution between the States so ratifying the Same.

The need for only nine states to ratify the Constitution for its establishment was questionable because the Constitution was actually a revision of the Articles of Confederation (1781), Article XIII of which stated that it could be amended only by the unanimous vote of all states. Following the signing of the Constitution on September 17, 1787, the signed document was delivered to the Congress in New York City. The Congress on September 28 transmitted the Constitution to the state legislatures with the recommendation that the issue of ratification be considered by special state conventions, instead of state legislatures, in order to demonstrate that the action thereon was the will of the people rather than a compact among the states.

After extensive debate in the state conventions on the issue of conferring additional powers on the national government, Delaware became the first state to ratify the new Constitution on December 7, 1787, followed by Pennsylvania (12/12/1787), New Jersey (12/18/1787), Georgia (1/2/1788), Connecticut (1/9/1788), Massachusetts (2/6/1788), Maryland (4/28/1788), South Carolina (5/23/1788), New Hampshire (6/21/1788), Virginia (6/25/1788), New York (7/26/1788), North Carolina (11/21/1789), and Rhode Island (5/29/1790).

After the ratification of the Constitution by New Hampshire as the ninth state, Congress on September 13, 1788, fixed the City of New York as the capital of the new government. (The capital was moved to Philadelphia in 1790, and to Washington, DC, in 1800.) Congress set January 7, 1789, as the day for choosing presidential electors, and February 4 for the meeting of electors to select a President and Vice President. On April 6, the new Congress began regular sessions, counted the electoral ballots and declared George Washington elected as President and John Adams elected as Vice President. Adams was sworn in on April 21, and Washington was sworn in on April 30.

In *Owings v. Speed*, 18 U.S. 420 (1820), the Supreme Court held that the Constitution did not replace the Articles of Confederation until Wednesday, March 4, 1789, since there was a need for a transitional period following the ratification by New Hampshire as the ninth state on June 21, 1788.

The Twentieth Amendment (1933) changed the quadrennial inauguration date from March 4 to January 20, with Franklin D. Roosevelt being the first President to be inaugurated thereunder on January 20, 1937.

Article VII, Clause 2, Subscription. Done in Convention by the Unanimous Consent of the States present the Seventeenth Day of September in the Year of our Lord one thousand seven hundred and Eighty seven and of the Independence of the United States of America the Twelfth In witness whereof We have hereunto subscribed our Names. [*The signatures are reported at pages 256–257.*]

As proposed by Benjamin Franklin, the Constitution was signed by the delegates as individual witnesses of "the Unanimous consent of the States present" as to what was "Done in Convention." Accordingly, the delegates could sign the document as witnesses to the action of the Convention as a whole, despite any individual objections they might have. Franklin stated:

"I confess that there are several parts of this constitution which I do not at present approve, but I am not sure I shall never approve them: For having lived long, I have experienced many instances of being obliged by better information, or fuller consideration, to change opinions even on important subjects, which I once thought right, but found to be otherwise.... On the whole, Sir, I can not help expressing a wish that every member of the Convention who may still have objections to it, would with me, on this occasion doubt a little of his own infallibility, and to make manifest our unanimity, put his name to this instrument."

Amendments to the Constitution

The 27 amendments to the Constitution do not address specific provisions of the original Constitution, such as by striking and adding language, but are stated independently thereby requiring interpretation to determine the modification of the earlier text.

The first ten amendments are collectively known as the Bill of Rights. Many of the delegates to the Constitutional Convention did not believe that it was appropriate to include a bill of rights in the Constitution because the federal government would have only the powers delegated to it by the Constitution and, hence, no power to infringe on the freedoms and rights of the people. Also, the people already possessed these rights as reflected in several of the state constitutions. However, it became clear during the constitutional ratification process that there was strong support for the adoption of a bill of rights as a part of the Constitution. Accordingly, James Madison, as a member of the Virginia delegation of the 1st Congress, drafted the Bill of Rights and submitted it for congressional consideration on June 8, 1789. (Madison had based his Bill of Rights on the Virginia Declaration of Rights drafted by George Mason and adopted by the Virginia Convention on June 12, 1776.) Congress on September 25, 1789, submitted the Bill of Rights to the states as a proposed amendment to the Constitution, and it was ratified on December 15, 1791, as the first ten amendments.

While the Bill of Rights originally applied only to federal action (*Barron v. Baltimore*, 32 U.S. 243 [1833]), the Supreme Court, after the ratification of the Fourteenth Amendment (1868), began to apply many of these rights to state action through their "incorporation" in the Due Process Clause of the Fourteenth Amendment, thereby making them enforceable against state and local governments. The guarantees of the Bill of Rights restrict only government action, not action by private parties or other non-governmental entities.

In *West Virginia State Board of Education v. Barnette*, 319 U.S. 624 (1943), Supreme Court Justice Robert H. Jackson, writing for the majority, stated, "The very purpose of a Bill of Rights was to withdraw certain subjects from the vicissitudes of political controversy, to place them beyond the reach of majorities and officials and to establish them as legal principles to be applied by the courts. One's right to life, liberty, and property, to free speech, a free press, freedom of worship and assembly, and other fundamental rights may not be submitted to vote; they depend on the outcome of no elections." 319 U.S. 638.

Amendment I
The Five Freedoms of Religion, Speech, Press, Assembly and Petition

Ratified December 15, 1791

Congress shall make no law respecting an establishment of religion, or prohibiting the free exercise thereof; or abridging the freedom of speech, or of the press; or the right of the people peaceably to assemble, and to petition the Government for a redress of grievances.

ESTABLISHMENT OF RELIGION CLAUSE

This clause prohibits the government from creating an official or established church, preferring one religion over another, or preferring believers over nonbelievers. In *Everson v. Board of Education of Ewing Township*, 330 U.S. 1 (1947), the Supreme Court upheld 5–4 a state statute funding student transportation to schools, whether parochial or not. Justice Hugo Black, in delivering the majority opinion for the Court, stated:

> Neither a state nor the Federal Government can set up a church. Neither can pass laws which aid one religion, aid all religions, or prefer one religion over another. Neither can force nor influence a person to go to or to remain away from church against his will or force him to profess a belief or disbelief in any religion. No person can be punished for entertaining or professing religious beliefs of disbeliefs, for church attendance or non-attendance. No tax in any amount, large or small, can be levied to support any religious activities or institutions, whatever they may be called, or whatever form they may adopt to teach or practice religion. Neither a state nor the Federal Government can, openly or secretly, participate in the affairs of any religious organizations or groups and vice versa.

In the words of Jefferson, the clause against establishment of religion by law was intended to erect "a wall of separation between Church and State" [380 U.S. 15].

The statute was upheld because of its general application for the benefit of all parents, without regard to religious belief, in facilitating school transportation for their children. The same result was reached in *Board of Education v. Allen*, 392 U.S. 236 (1968), where the Supreme Court upheld 6–3 a state law requiring public school boards to lend textbooks free of charge to students enrolled in public, private and parochial schools. The Court reasoned that the financial benefit is to parents and children, not to schools.

Similarly, the Court in *Zelman v. Simmons-Harris*, 536 U.S. 639 (2002), upheld 5–4 a municipal voucher program that allowed parents to pay tuition at private schools using public funds, reasoning that the "program is entirely neutral with respect to religion. It provides benefits directly to a wide spectrum of individuals, defined only by financial need and residence in a particular school district. It permits such individuals to exercise genuine choice among options public and private, secular and religious. The program is therefore a program of true private choice." 536 U.S. 662. In *Board of Education of Westside Community Schools v. Mergens*, 496 U.S. 226 (1990), the Court upheld 8–1 the federal Equal Access Act of 1984 that required public high schools receiving federal funds to provide "equal access" to student groups seeking to express "religious, political, philosophical, or other content" messages. The Court reasoned that the Act served an overriding secular purpose by prohibiting discrimination on the basis of speech content. If other non-curricular student groups are allowed to meet on school premises, then access may not be denied to a Christian Bible study club. Earlier, the Supreme Court in *Widmar v. Vincent*, 454 U.S. 263 (1981), held 8–1 that the refusal of equal access to use of public university facilities to a Christian student group violated the fundamental principle that state regulation of speech should be content-neutral. The state was not assumed to be in support of all messages that were communicated in its facilities.

The Supreme Court in interpreting the Establishment of Religion Clause has:

1. Enjoined a state from compelling education in public schools because of irreparable harm to schools operated by religious organizations and denial of parental choice. *Pierce v. Society of the Sisters of the Holy Names of Jesus and Mary*, 268 U.S. 510 (1925), 9–0 vote.

2. Upheld a state law that provided state funds for the purchasing of textbooks for both religious and public school students since the intent was to benefit school children and not religious schools. *Cochran v. Louisiana State Board of Education*, 281 U.S. 370 (1930).

3. Enjoined the practice of allowing religious education to take place in public school classrooms during the school day. *McCollum v. Board of Education, School District 71*, 333 U.S. 203 (1948), 8–1 vote.

4. Permitted "released time" for public school students to travel to parochial schools to receive religious education. *Zorach v. Clauson*, 343 U.S. 306 (1952), 6–3 vote.

5. Enjoined state reimbursement of nonpublic (mostly religious) schools for teachers' salaries, textbooks and instructional materials for secular subjects, *Lemon v. Kurtzman*, 403 U.S. 602 (1971), 8–0 vote. Here the Court established the three-part "Lemon Test." The violation of any part of this test would be deemed a conflict with the Establishment Clause. According to this test, the government's action (1) must have a secular legislative purpose; (2) must not have the primary effect of either advancing or inhibiting religion; and (3) must not foster an excessive government entanglement with religion. 403 U.S. 612.

6. Upheld grants under the Federal Higher Education Facility Act of 1963 to church-sponsored higher education institutes for construction of non-religious school facilities, but invalidating the provision that after 20 years the school could use the facilities for whatever purpose it chose. *Tilton v. Richardson*, 403 U.S. 672 (1971), 5–4 vote.

7. Upheld state property tax exemptions for churches because they are not aimed at establishing or supporting religion, and for over two centuries they have helped guarantee the free exercise of all forms of religious belief. *Walz v. Tax Commission of the City of New York*, 397 U.S. 664 (1970), 7–1 vote.

8. Enjoined state grants for maintenance of school facilities to religious schools serving low-income students, and tuition reimbursements or tax deductions for their low-income parents in order to avoid overcrowding of public schools, the Court holding that this program has the effect of furthering religion. *Committee for Public Education v. Nyquist*, 413 U.S. 756 (1973), 6–3 vote.

9. Enjoined state tuition reimbursement program for parents sending their children to parochial and other nonpublic schools. *Sloan v. Lemon*, 413 U.S. 825 (1973), 6–3 vote.

10. Upheld annual state grants to private colleges, including religious ones, to be used only for non-religious purposes. The primary effect of the law is to promote secular education, and it neither advances or inhibits religion *Roemer v. Maryland Public Works Board*, 426 U.S. 736 (1976), 5–4 vote.

11. Invalidated a state law allowing schools and churches to prevent the issuance of liquor licenses to establishments within 500 feet of the school or church objecting to the license application because the law substituted the decision making of the church for that of a public legislative body. *Larkin v. Grendel's Den*, 459 U.S. 116 (1982), 8–1 vote.

12. Upheld state law allowing parents income tax deductions for school tuition, textbooks and transportation for their children in attending public and religious schools, reasoning that the secular purpose of an educated populace is advanced, and any benefit to religious schools is indirect since parents had the ultimate decision. *Mueller v. Allen*, 463 U.S. 388 (1983), 5–4 vote.

13. Enjoined two public school programs, Shared Time and Community Education, that used public funds to support the teaching of courses offered by religious schools. *Grand Rapids School District v. Ball*, 473 U.S. 373 (1985), 7–2 vote.

14. Upheld aid under the state vocational rehabilitation program to finance a student's training at a Christian college because the aid went directly to the student who then transmits it to the educational institution of his choice. *Witters v. Washington Department of Services for the Blind*, 474 U.S. 481 (1986), 9–0 vote.

15. Required a public school district to continue to provide a sign-language interpreter to a deaf child on transfer from a public to a religious school, reasoning that the service is part of a general government program that provides benefits neutrally to handicapped children. *Zobrest v. Catalina Foothills School District*, 509 U.S. 1 (1993), 5–4 vote.

16. Upheld a state education initiative to allow public school teachers to instruct in religious schools, so long as the material was secular and neutral in nature and no "excessive entanglement" between government and religion was apparent, *Agostini v. Felton*, 521 U.S. 203 (1997), 5–4 vote.

17. Upheld federal funding of loans of educational materials and equipment, such as library and media materials and computer software and hardware, to public and private elementary and secondary schools to implement secular programs, ruling that "[i]f the religious, irreligious, and areligious are all alike eligible for governmental aid, no one would conclude that any indoctrination that any particular recipient conducts has been done at the behest of the government." *Mitchell v. Helms*, 530 U.S. 793, 809 (2000).

The Supreme Court has banned in public schools: nondenominational prayer ("Almighty God, we acknowledge our dependence upon Thee, and we beg Thy blessings upon us, our parents, our teachers, and our Country"), *Engel v. Vitale*, 370 U.S. 421 (1962), 6–1 vote; reading of Bible verses, *Abington School District v. Schempp*, 374 U.S. 203 (1963), 8–1 vote; posting of the Ten Commandments, *Stone v. Graham*, 449 U.S. 39 (1980), 5–4 vote; daily observance of one minute of silence for private meditation or voluntary prayer, *Wallace v. Jaffree*, 472 U.S. 38 (1985), 6–3 vote; prayers by clergy at graduation ceremonies, *Lee v. Weisman*, 505 U.S. 577 (1992), 5–4 vote; and student-led prayer prior to school events, *Santa Fe Independent School*

District v. Doe, 530 U.S. 290 (2000), 6–3 vote. The Court has struck down state laws banning the teaching of evolution, *Epperson v. Arkansas*, 393 U.S. 97 (1968), 9–0 vote, and requiring the teaching of biblical creationism or intelligent design whenever evolution is taught, *Edwards v. Aguillard*, 482 U.S. 578 (1987), 7–2 vote.

Epperson and *Edwards* resolved the issue in the famous 1925 Scopes Monkey Trial in Dayton, Tennessee, in which high school teacher John Scopes was convicted of violating a state law prohibiting the teaching of evolution. William Jennings Bryan assisted the prosecution, and Clarence Darrow assisted the defense. On appeal, the conviction was overturned on a legal technicality [*Scopes v. Tennessee*, 154 Tenn. 105, 289 SW 363 (1927)], and the prosecution decided not to seek a retrial. The 1960 movie *Inherit the Wind*, starring Frederic March and Spencer Tracy, was loosely based on the trial.

In *Lynch v. Donnelly*, 465 U.S. 668 (1984), the Supreme Court upheld 5–4 a municipal Christmas display in a shopping district that included a Santa Claus house, a Christmas tree, and a nativity scene. The Court found that the display was not a purposeful effort to advocate a particular religious message, but merely depicted the historical origins of the holiday and had "legitimate secular purposes." In *County of Allegheny v. American Civil Liberties Union, Greater Pittsburgh Chapter*, 492 U.S. 573 (1989), the Supreme Court considered the constitutionality of two holiday displays located on public property in downtown Pittsburgh. The first, a nativity scene (crèche), was placed on the grand staircase of the Allegheny County Courthouse. The second was an 18-foot menorah, which was placed just outside the City-County Building next to the city's 45-foot Christmas tree. The Supreme Court ruled 5–4 that the nativity scene inside the courthouse violated the Establishment Clause because it unmistakably promoted Christianity. As to the menorah, the Court ruled 6–3 that its display did not violate the clause because of its combined display with the Christmas tree. The Court found that the display simply recognized that both Christmas and Hanukkah are part of the same holiday season that has attained a secular status in U.S. society.

In *Van Orden v. Perry*, 545 U.S. 677 (2005), the Court upheld 5–4 the display of the Ten Commandments on a monument, among numerous other monuments and historical markers, on the grounds of a state capitol building, reasoning that the monument served a valid secular purpose and would not appear to a reasonable observer to represent a government endorsement of religion. At the same time, the Court decided *McCreary County v. American Civil liberties Union of Kentucky*, 545 U.S. 844 (2005), reaching a different conclusion, 5–4, with Justice Stephen Breyer being the "swing vote" between the two cases. In this case the Court found impermissible the display of the Ten Commandments in county courthouses because they were not integrated with a secular display, and thus considered to have a religious purpose.

In *Waltz v. Tax Commission of the City of New* York, 397 U.S. 664 (1970), the Court upheld 8–1 the tax exemption of churches as a part of the same privilege given to other nonprofit organizations that are beneficial to society. In *Marsh v. Chambers*, 463 U.S. 783 (1983), the Court held 6–3 that the practice of beginning the legislative session with a prayer by a publicly funded chaplain was constitutional because of historical custom. However, a state may not exempt religious publications from sales tax when other publications are taxed. *Texas Monthly Inc. v. Bullock*, 489 U.S. 1 (1989), 6–3 vote. In *McGowan v. Maryland*, 366 U.S. 420 (1961), the Court upheld 8–1 Sunday closing laws because they serve the secular purpose of providing a Sunday atmosphere of recreation, cheerfulness, repose and enjoyment. However, a state may not provide that no employee could be forced to work on his Sabbath day because the endorsement of such a specific religious practice is impermissible. *Estate of Thornton v. Calder, Inc.*, 472 U.S. 703 (1985), 8–1 vote.

Interestingly, the Supreme Court Building, completed in 1935, depicts Moses in two locations, and Muhammad in one. The friezes on the south and north walls of the courtroom depict the following eighteen influential lawgivers, listed chronologically. South wall: Menes, Egypt; Hammurabi, Babylon; Moses, Israel; Solomon, Israel; Lycurgus, Sparta; Solon, Athens; Draco, Athens; Confucius, China; and Octavian, Rome. North wall: Justinian, Byzantine Empire; Muhammad, Arabia; Charlemagne, Western Europe; King John, England; Louis IX, France; Hugo Grotius, Dutch; Sir William Blackstone, England; John Marshall, United States; and Napoleon, France. In addition, Moses, flanked by Confucius and Solon, representing three great civilizations, are depicted in the center of the pediment over the east (back) entrance to the building. The depictions of Moses and Muhammad are in accord with *Lynch v. Donnelly*, above, holding that the inclusion of religious symbols in public displays is constitutionally permissible so long as those symbols are part of a larger work that serves a secular purpose.

FREE EXERCISE OF RELIGION CLAUSE

While the Establishment of Religion Clause prohibits government actions that unduly aid religion, the Free Exercise of Religion Clause prohibits government actions that unduly limit the free exercise of religion. The clause embraces the concept of freedom to believe and freedom to act. The first of these freedoms is absolute, but the second remains subject to regulation for the protection of society. Cases involving the free exercise of religion are sometimes brought and decided under the Freedom of Speech Clause which includes speech concerning religion.

In *Reynolds v. United States*, 98 U.S. 145 (1878), federal law prohibited polygamy in the Utah Territory. Reynolds, a Mormon who had been convicted of polygamy, claimed that the law interfered with the free exercise of his religion. The Supreme Court upheld 9–0 the conviction, ruling that permitting a certain class of people to willfully defy the law without repercussion in the name of religious liberty would lead to chaos. While the law cannot interfere with religious beliefs, it can interfere with religious practices that violate public order or public morals.

In *Cantwell v. Connecticut*, 310 U.S. 296 (1940), three Jehovah's Witnesses were seeking converts in a predominantly Catholic neighborhood by distributing religious messages door-to-door and approaching people on the street. They were arrested for failing to obtain a license for those soliciting for religious or charitable purposes. The Supreme Court ruled 9–0 that the statute requiring a license to solicit for religious purposes was a prior restraint that vested the state with excessive power in determining which causes were religious and which ones were not. Also, the Jehovah's Witnesses did not pose a threat to public order by spreading their message. The Supreme Court in *Murdock v. Pennsylvania*, 319 U.S. 105 (1943), invalidated 5–4 a municipal licensing tax on Jehovah's Witnesses selling religious literature door-to-door. The Court distinguished between commercial and religious sales activities.

In *Prince v. Massachusetts*, 321 U.S. 158 (1944), a Jehovah's Witness was convicted of violating child labor laws by having her nine-year-old ward distribute religious literature on the streets in exchange for voluntary contributions. The Supreme Court upheld 5–4 the conviction, ruling that religious liberty is not absolute, but may be restricted to protect child welfare. Justice Frank Murphy in dissenting stated, "The sidewalk, no less than the cathedral or the evangelist's tent, is a proper place, under the Constitution, for the orderly worship of God." 321 U.S. 174.

In *United States v. Ballard*, 322 U.S. 78 (1944), a religious leader was convicted of fraudulently using the mails to seek and collect donations on the basis of religious claims that he could heal people. The prosecution asserted that he well knew these claims were false and used them to defraud others. The Supreme Court ruled 5–4 that the question of whether Ballard believed his religious claims should not have been submitted to the jury. Determining the truth or falsity of religious views, regardless of how incredible they may seem to others, violates the Free Exercise of Religion Clause.

Subsequently, the Supreme Court has applied the Free Exercise of Religion Clause in a variety of cases.

1. *Sherbert v. Verner*, 374 U.S. 398 (1963), overturned 7–2 the state denial of unemployment compensation to a Seventh-Day Adventist who was fired from her job for refusing to work on Saturday, the Sabbath Day of her faith. The court ruled that the denial imposed a significant burden on her

ability to freely exercise her faith, and that there was no compelling state interest that justified the denial.

2. *United States v. Seeger*, 380 U.S. 163 (1965), held 9–0 that the exemption from the military draft for conscientious objectors could not be reserved only for those professing conformity with the moral directives of a supreme being, but that it also applied to believers in nontraditional variances of monotheism. In *Welsh v. United States*, 398 U.S. 333 (1970), the Supreme Court held 5–3 that Welsh was entitled to conscientious objector status even though his objection to war was not based on religious convictions. The Court reasoned that the objector status applies to "all those whose consciences, spurred by deeply held moral, ethical, or religious beliefs, would give them no rest or peace if they allowed themselves to become a part of an instrument of war." 398 U.S. 344.

3. *Wisconsin v. Yoder*, 406 U.S. 205 (1972), held 7–0 that a state requirement that Amish children attend school beyond the eighth grade interfered with the right of parents to direct the religious upbringing of their children.

4. *Cruz v. Beto*, 405 U.S. 319 (1972), held 8–1 that a prisoner must be given a reasonable opportunity to pursue his Buddhist faith comparable to that offered other prisoners adhering to conventional religious precepts.

5. *United States v. Lee*, 455 U.S. 252 (1982), held 9–0 that Amish employers may not avoid Social Security taxes on religious grounds. So long as government can demonstrate a compelling interest, it may limit religious liberty.

6. *Bob Jones University v. United States*, 461 U.S. 574 (1983), held 8–1 that the Internal Revenue Service may revoke the tax exempt status of an organization that operates contrary to established public policy. The university, based on its interpretation of the Bible, denied admission to applicants engaged in, or who advocated, interracial dating or marriage.

7. *Goldman v. Weinberger*, 475 U.S. 503 (1986), upheld 5–4 an Air Force rule prohibiting non-regulation headgear, despite a Jewish officer's request to wear a yarmulke while on duty. Military regulations are examined with less scrutiny than similar challenges from civilian society because of the need for military cohesiveness. In 1987, Congress enacted legislation allowing members of the armed forces to wear religious apparel in a "neat and conservative" manner.

8. *Employment Division, Oregon Department of Human Resources v. Smith*, 494 U.S. 872 (1990), upheld 6–3 the firing of two Native Americans, who worked as counselors for a private drug rehabilitation organization, for ingesting peyote, a powerful hallucinogen, as part of their religious ceremonies as members of the Native American Church. This decision upheld legislation that incidentally prohibited religiously mandatory activities as long as the ban was generally applicable to all citizens, thereby discarding

the "compelling interest" standard of *Sherbert v. Verner* and *Wisconsin v. Yoder*. Congress sought to retain the "compelling interest" standard by the enactment of the Religious Freedom Restoration Act (RFRA) of 1993, but the Supreme Court ruled it invalid as to state application for usurping the Court's role in interpreting the Constitution, thus leaving the *Smith* test in place. *City of Boerne v. Flores*, 521 U.S. 507 (1997), 6–2 vote.

9. *Church of the Lukumi Babalu Aye v. City of Hialeah*, 508 U.S. 520 (1993), invalidated 9–0 a municipal ordinance forbidding animal sacrifice as a form of worship as practiced by the Santeria religion. The ordinance specifically exempted state-licensed activities. The Court ruled that the ordinance was neither neutral nor generally applicable, but targeted religious behavior.

10. *Cutter v. Wilkinson*, 544 U.S. 709 (2005), held 9–0 that under the Religious Land Use and Institutionalized Persons Act (RLUIPA), prisoners in facilities that accept federal funds cannot be denied accommodations necessary to engage in the practice of their own religious beliefs. The case was brought by Ohio prisoners including two adherents of Asatru, a minister of the white supremacist Church of Jesus Christ Christian, a Wiccan and a Satanist.

FREEDOM OF SPEECH CLAUSE

The freedom of speech guaranteed by the clause is the liberty to express opinions and ideas, and embraces written and electronic publication as well as oral delivery. It also includes expressive conduct such as picketing, refusal to salute the flag, and flag burning. The freedom of association is an essential part of the freedom of speech in cases where people can engage in effective speech only when they join with others. The free exchange of ideas is an essential ingredient of democracy and resistance to tyranny, and an important means for progress. However, the guarantee is not absolute and is limited by such acts as defamation, obscenity, threats, perjury, contempt of court, fighting words, hate speech, copyright infringement, disclosure of trade secrets or classified security information, and treason.

In *Schenck v. United States*, 249 U.S. 47 (1919), Charles Schenck, a Socialist Party official, distributed circulars opposing the draft in World War I, and was charged with conspiracy to violate the Espionage Act of 1917 by attempting to cause insubordination in the military and to obstruct recruitment. In upholding 9–0 his conviction, the Supreme Court, in an opinion written by Justice Oliver Wendell Holmes, Jr., stated that: "the character of every act depends upon the circumstances in which it is done. The most stringent protection of free speech would not protect a man in falsely shouting fire in a theatre and causing a panic.... The question in every case is whether the words used are used in such circumstances and are of such a nature as to create a clear and present danger that they will bring about the substantive evils that Congress has a right to prevent." 249 U.S. 52. *Schenck* was followed in *Debs v. United States*, 249 U.S. 211 (1919), in which the Supreme Court upheld 9–0 the conviction of Eugene V. Debs for violation of the Espionage Act. Debs was a labor leader and five-time candidate of the Socialist Party for election as U.S. President.

In *Gitlow v. New York*, 268 U.S. 652 (1925), Benjamin Gitlow was convicted under a state criminal anarchy law for distributing copies of the Left-Wing Manifesto advocating the establishment of socialism through massive strikes and class action in any form. The Supreme Court upheld 7–2 the conviction on the basis that the state may forbid speech and publication that have a tendency to result in action dangerous to public safety. "The State cannot reasonably be required to measure the danger from every such utterance in the nice balance of a jeweler's scale. A single revolutionary spark may kindle a fire that, smoldering for a time, may burst into a sweeping and destructive conflagration." 268 U.S. 669. This rationale has been called the "dangerous tendency test." Justice Holmes, in a dissent joined in by Justice Louis D. Brandeis, declared, "The only difference between the expression of an opinion and an excitement in the narrower sense is the speaker's enthusiasm for the result. Eloquence may set fire to reason. But whatever may be thought of the redundant discourse before us, it had no chance of starting a present conflagration." 268 U.S. 673.

In *Dennis v. United States*, 341 U.S. 494 (1951), the Supreme Court upheld 6–2 the conviction of Eugene Dennis and other American Communist Party leaders under the Smith Act that made it unlawful to knowingly conspire to teach and advocate the violent overthrow or destruction of the U.S. government by force. In finding no violation of free speech, the Court stated that there was a distinction between the mere teaching of communist philosophies, and the active advocacy of those ideas that create a "clear and present danger" to the government. Justice Felix Frankfurter, in concurring, stated: "History teaches that the independence of the judiciary is jeopardized when courts become embroiled in the passions of the day and assume primary responsibility in choosing between competing political, economic and social pressures." 341 U.S. 525.

In *Yates v. United States*, 354 U.S. 298 (1957), the Court overturned 6–1 the conviction of Communist Party leaders under the Smith Act, holding that there is a distinction between the "advocacy and teaching of forcible overthrow as an abstract principle," which is protected free speech, and the "advocacy and teaching of concrete action for the forcible overthrow of the Government."

Schenck was later limited by *Brandenburg v. Ohio*, 395 U.S. 444 (1969), in which the Supreme Court overturned Brandenburg's conviction and held

8–0 "that the constitutional guarantees of free speech and free press do not permit a State to forbid or proscribe advocacy of the use of force or of law violation except where advocacy is directed to inciting or producing imminent lawless action and is likely to incite or produce such action." 395 U.S. 447. In this case, Brandenburg, a Ku Klux Klan leader, spoke at a Klan rally disparaging African Americans and Jews, advocating white supremacy, and vaguely threatening vengeance in the future. *Brandenburg* overruled *Abrams v. United States*, 250 U.S. 616 (1919), which upheld 7–2 the convictions of several Russian immigrants for distributing pamphlets denouncing U.S. efforts to impede the Russian Revolution and advocating resistance to the war effort and curtailment of the production of war material. Justices Oliver Wendell Holmes and Louis Brandeis dissented in *Abrams*, finding no clear and present danger. *Brandenburg*, in effect, adopted the rationale of Holmes' dissent, concurred in by Brandeis, stating in part that "when men have realized that time has upset many fighting faiths, they may come to believe even more than they believe the very foundations of their own conduct that the ultimate good desired is better reached by free trade in ideas—that the best test of truth is the power of the thought to get itself accepted in the competition of the market, and that truth is the only ground upon which their wishes safely can be carried out. That at any rate is the theory of our Constitution. It is an experiment, as all life is an experiment." 250 U.S. 630.

In *West Virginia State Board of Education v. Barnette*, 319 U.S. 624 (1943), the Supreme Court held 6–3, in a case brought by Jehovah's Witnesses, that the compulsory flag salute for public school children violated the Freedom of Speech Clause. The Court majority, in an opinion by Justice Robert H. Jackson, stated: "If there is any fixed star in our constitutional constellation, it is that no official, high or petty, can prescribe what shall be orthodox in politics, nationalism, religion, or other matters of opinion or force citizens to confess by word or act their faith therein." 319 U.S. 642. The Court overruled *Minersville School District v. Gobitis*, 310 U.S. 586 (1940), 8–1 vote, which reached a contrary conclusion. The Supreme Court in *Taylor v. Mississippi*, 319 U.S. 583 (1943), overturned 9–0 the convictions of three Jehovah's Witnesses for urging others to refuse to salute the flag.

In *Terminiello v. Chicago*, 337 U.S. 1 (1949), the Supreme Court overturned 5–4 the disorderly conduct conviction of a priest whose anti–Semitic, pro–Nazi speech at a rally had incited a riot. The majority stated that the "vitality of civil and political institutions in our society depends on free discussion," and that speech could be restricted only in the event that it was "likely to produce a clear and present danger of a serious substantive evil that rises far above public inconvenience, annoyance, or unrest." Justice Robert H. Jackson in his dissent wrote: "The choice is not between order and liberty. It is between liberty with order and anarchy without either.

There is a danger that, if the Court does not temper its doctrinaire logic with a little practical wisdom, it will convert the constitutional Bill of Rights into a suicide pact." 337 U.S. 36.

The Supreme Court has applied the Freedom of Speech Clause in a variety of other cases as well.

1. In *Thornhill v. Alabama*, 310 U.S. 88 (1940), the Supreme Court reversed the conviction of a local labor leader who was peacefully picketing in violation of a state statute that prohibited labor picketing. The Court ruled 8–1 that free discussion of labor issues is indispensable to the functioning of popular government, and that peaceful picketing is protected by the Freedom of Speech Clause.

2. In *Chaplinsky v. New Hampshire*, 315 U.S. 568 (1942), the Supreme Court articulated 9–0 the "fighting words" doctrine by upholding the conviction of Chaplinsky, a Jehovah's Witness, for breaching the peace by calling a town marshal a "damned racketeer" and "damned Fascist." Insulting or "fighting" words which by "their very utterance inflict injury or tend to incite an immediate breach of the peace" are not protected by the free speech guarantee. 315 U.S. 572. While *Chaplinsky* has not been overruled, it is the last case in which the Supreme Court has upheld a conviction for "fighting words" directed at a public official.

3. In *Marsh v. Alabama*, 326 U.S. 501 (1946), the Supreme Court upheld 5–3 the right of a Jehovah's Witness to distribute religious literature on the sidewalk in the town of Chickasaw, Alabama, which was a company town owned and operated by the Gulf Shipbuilding Corporation, rather than a public municipality. The Court found that the company-owned town was freely accessible and used by the public, and that there was no significant difference between Chickasaw and public municipalities.

4. In *Kovacs v. Cooper*, 336 U.S. 77 (1949), the Supreme Court held 5–4 that a municipality may prohibit "loud and raucous" loudspeakers on the public streets as a reasonable regulation of time, place and manner of speech.

5. In *Joseph Burstyn, Inc. v. Wilson*, 343 U.S. 495 (1952), the state had denied a license for the showing of Roberto Rossellini's movie *The Miracle* for being sacrilegious. The Supreme Court held 9–0 that the denial was a violation of the Freedom of Speech Clause, reasoning: "It is not the business of government in our nation to suppress real or imagined attacks upon a particular religious doctrine, whether they appear in publications, speeches, or motion pictures." 343 U.S. 505. In *Kingsley International Pictures Corp. v. Regents of the University of New York*, 360 U.S. 684 (1959), the Regents had denied a license for the motion picture *Lady Chatterley's Lover* because it "alluringly portrays adultery as proper behavior." The Supreme Court

held 9–0 that the denial of the license based on the film's portrayal of immorality was arbitrary and infringed on the freedom to advocate ideas as guaranteed by the First Amendment.

6. In *National Association for the Advancement of Colored People (NAACP) v. Alabama*, 357 U.S. 449 (1958), Alabama ordered the NAACP to disclose its membership lists during the bitter civil rights struggle—a disclosure that could subject members to harassment and violence. The Supreme Court ruled 9–0 that compelling such disclosure would violate the constitutionally guaranteed freedom of association among NAACP members. The Court in *Brown v. Socialists Workers '74 Campaign Committee*, 459 U.S. 87 (1982), reached 6–3 the same result. In *NAACP v. Button*, 371 U.S. 415 (1963), the Supreme Court invalidated 6–3 a state anti-solicitation law intended to foreclose the NAACP from providing legal services to assist its members in the assertion of their rights. The Court ruled that such activities are "modes of expression and association protected by the First and Fourteenth Amendments." 371 U.S. 428.

7. In *Barenblatt v. United States*, 360 U.S. 109 (1959), the Supreme Court upheld 5–4 a university professor's conviction for contempt of Congress for refusing to answer questions concerning his political and religious beliefs along with his communist associational activities. The Court found that the government's interest in protecting national security outweighed the professor's First Amendment rights. However, in *DeGregory v. New Hampshire*, 383 U.S. 825 (1966), the Court held 6–3 that the state's interest in protecting itself against subversion is too remote to override appellant's First Amendment right to political and associational privacy.

8. In *Elfbrandt v. Russell*, 384 U.S. 11 (1966), the Supreme Court invalidated 5–4 a loyalty oath requiring state employees to declare they were not members of the Communist Party or any other organization espousing the violent overthrow of the state government. The Court held that the loyalty oath could not be used to penalize a member of an organization that had both legal and illegal purposes even though the member did not subscribe to the illegal purposes and, therefore, the oath violated the freedom of association guaranteed by the First Amendment. Similarly, the Supreme Court in *United States v. Robel*, 389 U.S. 258 (1967), invalidated 6–2 part of the Subversive Activities Control Act that prohibited any member of the Communist Party from working in a defense facility. The Court held that this was an abridgement of the right of association guaranteed by the First Amendment because the statute established guilt by association without proof that the member posed a threat to national defense.

9. In *United States v. O'Brien*, 391 U.S. 367 (1968), the Supreme Court upheld 7–1 the conviction of a Vietnam War protester under a federal law that made the destruction or mutilation of draft cards a crime. The Court

ruled that the law was content neutral, unrelated to the suppression of free expression, and narrowly tailored to achieve the government's interest in the efficient functioning of the Selective Service System. "We cannot accept the view that an apparently limitless variety of conduct can be labeled 'speech' whenever the person engaging in the conduct intends thereby to express an idea." 391 U.S. 376.

10. In *Cohen v. California*, 403 U.S. 15 (1971), a teenager expressed his opposition to the draft and the Vietnam War by wearing inside the Los Angeles Courthouse a jacket emblazoned with a message that contained a four-letter expletive. He was convicted under a state law that prohibited maliciously and willfully disturbing the peace and quiet of any neighborhood or person by offensive conduct. The Supreme Court overturned the conviction, ruling 5–4 that the expletive, while provocative, was not directed toward anyone in particular, and that there was no evidence that people would be provoked into physical action by the message on the jacket; "one man's vulgarity is another's lyric." 403 U.S. 25.

11. In *Healy v. James*, 408 U.S. 169 (1972), involving a public college's denial of recognition of a local chapter of Students for a Democratic Society, the Supreme Court held 9–0 that college students' First Amendment rights of free speech and association apply with the same force on a college campus as in the larger community.

12. In *Rosario v. Rockefeller*, 410 U.S. 752 (1973), state law required a voter to enroll in the party of his choice at least 30 days before a general election in order to vote in the next party primary, resulting in an enrollment cutoff date of about eight months before a presidential, and 11 months before a nonpresidential, primary. The Supreme Court held 5–4 that the law does not deprive voters of their First Amendment right to associate with the party of their choice or to change parties so long as the time limit is observed, and that the law is not arbitrary because of the legitimate state purpose of avoiding party "raiding," in which voters of one party enroll in the opposite party in order to influence the outcome of that party's primary.

13. In *Lehman v. City of Shaker Heights*, 418 U.S. 298 (1974), the Supreme Court held 5–4 that city policy prohibiting political advertising on its streetcars, while permitting advertisements by businesses and public service groups, does not violate the Free Speech Clause. The Court found: "The city consciously has limited access to its transit system advertising space in order to minimize chances of abuse, the appearance of favoritism, and the risk of imposing upon a captive audience. These are reasonable legislative objectives advanced by the city in a proprietary capacity." 418 U.S. 304.

14. In *Greer v. Spock*, 424 U.S. 828 (1976), the Supreme Court upheld 6–3 army post regulations banning speeches and demonstrations of a partisan political nature and the distribution of literature without prior approval

of post headquarters. Military posts are not public forums like municipal streets and parks. The military may indiscriminately ban partisan political campaigns and the distribution of literature on post that might endanger troop discipline.

15. In *Virginia State Pharmacy Board v. Virginia Citizens Consumer Council*, 425 U.S. 748 (1976), the Supreme Court invalidated 7–1 a state law that prohibited the advertisement of prescription drug prices as commercial speech protected by the First Amendment. The same result was reached in *Bates v. State Bar of Arizona*, 433 U.S. 350 (1977), when the Supreme Court ruled 5–4 that lawyer advertising is protected commercial speech. However, in *Florida Bar v. Went For It, Inc.*, 515 U.S. 618 (1995), the Supreme Court upheld 5–4 state bar rules prohibiting lawyers from direct-mail solicitation of potential clients within 30 days of an accident or disaster. The Court reasoned that such restriction of commercial speech was justified by the bar's substantial interest in the subject and was narrowly drawn to advance that interest.

16. In *Young v. American Mini Theatres, Inc.*, 427 U.S. 50 (1976), the Supreme Court upheld 5–4 a Detroit zoning ordinance to prevent the concentration of adult sexually oriented businesses by requiring their dispersal in the city. Since there was no prohibition of the material, the Court found no violation of the guarantee of free speech. In *City of Renton v. Playtime Theatres, Inc.*, 475 U.S. 41 (1986), the Court upheld 7–2 a zoning ordinance that prohibited adult motion picture theaters within 1,000 feet of any residence, church, park or school. The Court ruled that "content-neutral time, place, and manner regulations are acceptable so long as they are designed to serve a substantial governmental interest and do not unreasonably limit alternative avenues of communication." 475 U.S. 47. In *City of Erie v. Pap's AM*, 529 U.S. 277 (2000), the Court upheld 6–3 a city ordinance prohibiting nude appearances in public and required the use of G-strings and pasties in nude dancing. "So long as a regulation is unrelated to the suppression of expression, the government generally has a freer hand in restricting expressive conduct than it has in restricting the written or spoken word." 529 U.S. 299. The *Erie* case followed *Barnes v. Glen Theatre, Inc.*, 501 U.S. 560 (1991), upholding 5–4 a similar state prohibition against nudity in public places as furthering a substantial government interest in protecting the morality and order of society.

17. In *Wooley v. Maynard*, 430 U.S. 705 (1977), New Hampshire law required all noncommercial vehicles to display plates containing the state motto "Live Free or Die." Maynard, a Jehovah's Witness, found the motto to be contrary to his religious and political beliefs and cut the words "or Die" off his plates. He was convicted of violating the law. The Supreme Court overturned the conviction, ruling 6–3 that the state may not require indi-

viduals to "use their private property as a 'mobile billboard' for the State's ideological message." 430 U.S. 715. The state's interest in requiring the display of the motto did not outweigh the free speech principles under the First Amendment.

18. In *Federal Communications Commission v. Pacifica Foundation*, 438 U.S. 726 (1978), a New York radio station, in the mid-afternoon, broadcast George Carlin's "Filthy Words" monologue entitled "Seven Words You Can Never Say on Television." The Supreme Court held 5-4 that the FCC was justified in concluding that Carlin's monologue was indecent and subject to sanction. Due to its pervasive nature, broadcasting has less First Amendment protection than other means of communication. The case became known as the "Seven Dirty Words Case."

19. In *Central Hudson Gas & Electric Corp. v. Public Service Commission*, 447 U.S. 557 (1980), the Supreme Court held 8-1 that the PSC regulation banning the use of promotional advertising by the utility was a restraint of commercial speech in violation of the First Amendment. However, in *Board of Trustees of State University of New York v. Fox*, 492 U.S. 469 (1989), the Court upheld 6-3 a state prohibition against private commercial enterprises (Tupperware parties) being conducted in dormitories on college campuses because the restriction on commercial speech was narrowly tailored in light of the dormitories' purpose.

20. In *Board of Education, Island Trees School District v. Pico*, 457 U.S. 853 (1982), the Board of Education ordered the removal from school libraries of certain books it found to be "anti–American, anti–Christian, and anti–Semitic, and just plain filthy." The Supreme Court overruled the board 5-4, holding that it could not restrict the availability of library books because it disagreed with their idea content. The "discretion of the States and local school boards in matters of education must be exercised in a manner that comports with the transcendent imperatives of the First Amendment." 457 U.S. 864.

21. In *Clark v. Community for Creative Non-Violence (CCNV)*, 468 U.S. 288 (1984), the National Park Service denied a CCNV request to conduct a demonstration in Lafayette Park (across from the White House) to call attention to the plight of the homeless by erecting a symbolic tent city for camping overnight. The Supreme Court held 7-2 that the denial of the sleeping activities did not infringe on CCNV's right to expressive conduct under the First Amendment. The Park Service regulation forbidding sleeping is a reasonable means for preserving park property, and there are ample alternatives for communicating the message regarding the plight of the homeless.

22. In *Roberts v. United States Jaycees*, 468 U.S. 609 (1984), the Supreme Court upheld 7-0 a state antidiscrimination law prohibiting a private organization from excluding a person based on sex because the state had a com-

pelling interest in prohibiting gender discrimination which outweighed the Jaycees' right of freedom of association under the First Amendment. The Court held that the state law "requires no change in the Jaycees' creed of promoting the interests of young men, and it imposes no restrictions on the organization's ability to exclude individuals with ideologies or philosophies different from those of its existing members." 468 U.S. 627. Consistent with *Roberts*, the Supreme Court upheld state and local laws prohibiting gender discrimination in private organizations when applied to a Rotary club (*Rotary International v. Rotary Club of Duarte*, 481 U.S. 587 [1987], 7-0 vote); and private clubs with more than 400 members (*New York State Club Association v. City of New York*, 487 U.S. 1 [1988], 9-0 vote).

23. In *Bethel School District v. Fraser*, 478 U.S. 675 (1986), the Supreme Court ruled 7-2 that school officials could discipline a student for delivering a speech to a high school assembly filled with sexual references and innuendoes but not obscenities. The Court held that the "First Amendment does not prevent school officials from determining that to permit a vulgar and lewd speech such as respondent's would undermine the school's basic educational mission. A high school assembly or classroom is no place for a sexually explicit monologue directed towards an unsuspecting audience of teenage students." 478 U.S. 686.

24. In *Turner v. Safley*, 482 U.S. 78 (1987), the Supreme Court upheld 5-4 a state prison regulation restricting inmate-to-inmate correspondence as justified by prison security needs. However, the Court invalidated 9-0 a prison regulation prohibiting inmates from marrying without the permission of the warden as a violation of their constitutional right to marry and as not related to any legitimate penal concern. See also *Loving v. Virginia*, 388 U.S. 1 (1967).

25. In *Airport Commissioners of Los Angeles v. Jews for Jesus*, 482 U.S. 569 (1987), the Supreme Court invalidated 9-0 the airport's resolution banning all First Amendment activities in the central terminal area. The resolution was overbroad because it prohibited all protected expression such as talking, distributing literature or the wearing of campaign buttons or symbolic clothing, and was not limited to addressing problems such as congestion or the disruption of airport user activities. However, in *International Society for Krishna Conscientious (ISKCON) v. Lee*, 505 U.S. 672 (1992), the Court upheld 6-3 a ban on solicitation of funds in the New York metropolitan airports (Kennedy, LaGuardia and Newark) because an airport terminal is a non-public forum and thus the ban is reasonable in reducing the disruptive effect on airport travelers. In the companion case of *Lee v. ISKCON*, 505 U.S. 830 (1992), the Court voided 5-4 the ban on the distribution and sale of Krishna literature in the terminals as an unreasonable restriction because leafleting is a lesser impediment to travelers than solicitation.

26. In *Texas v. Johnson*, 491 U.S. 397 (1989), the Supreme Court held 5-4 that the desecration of an American flag, by burning or otherwise, is a symbolic form of speech protected by the Freedom of Speech Clause. The Court stated: "If there is a bedrock principle underlying the First Amendment, it is that the government may not prohibit the expression of an idea simply because society finds the idea itself offensive or disagreeable." 491 U.S. 414. In *United States v. Eichman*, 496 U.S. 310 (1990), the Court invalidated 5-4 the 1989 Flag Protection Act (passed by Congress in response to *Texas v. Johnson*), ruling that that the government's interest in preserving the flag as a symbol did not outweigh the individual's right to disparage that symbol through expressive conduct. These decisions are supported by precedents such as *Stromberg v. California*, 283 U.S. 359 (1931), 7-2 vote (displaying red flag as speech); *Tinker v. Des Moines Independent Community School District*, 393 U.S. 503 (1969), 7-2 vote (wearing of black anti-war armband as speech); and *Spence v. Washington*, 418 U.S. 405 (1974), 6-3 vote (displaying U.S. flag upside down with peace symbol attached). In *Tinker*, the Court ruled that students do not "shed their constitutional rights to freedom of speech or expression at the schoolhouse gate." 393 U.S. 506.

27. In *Rutan v. Republican Party of Illinois*, 497 U.S. 62 (1990), the Supreme Court held 5-4 that hiring, promotion, transfer, recall and dismissal decisions involving low-level public employees may not be based on party affiliation or support because the First Amendment guarantees the freedom of association. Such employees are not required to compromise their political beliefs or alter their associations to ensure favorable treatment in the government workplace. The ruling applies only to low-level employees, and recognizes the need for an administration to choose higher-ranking officials based on political loyalty. This principle was applied earlier in *Elrod v. Burns*, 427 U.S. 347 (1976), where the Court held 5-3 that non-policy making employees may not be dismissed because of patronage by a newly elected sheriff. In *O'Hare Truck Service v. City of Northlake*, 528 U.S. 712 (1996), the Supreme Court held 7-2 that the removal of the truck service from the city's list of independent contractors, because the owner supported an opposition candidate in the mayor's reelection campaign, abridged the truck service's freedom of association. Independent contractors are entitled to the same First Amendment safeguards of political association as are afforded to government employees.

28. *Simon & Schuster v. New York State Crime Victims Board*, 502 U.S. 105 (1991), involved David Berkowitz (Son of Sam), who committed a series of murders in New York City, 1976-1977. After being apprehended, he decided to sell his story for publication. New York passed the so-called Son of Sam law (1977) that required anyone who published a criminal's story to pay the proceeds to the Crime Victims Board instead of to the criminal. The

board would hold the money to pay victims who successfully sued the criminal for damages. If no lawsuits were filed for five years, the money would accrue to the benefit of the criminal. In 1987, the board ordered Henry Hill, a former gangster who sold his story to Simon & Schuster, to turn over his proceeds from a book deal. The Supreme Court ruled 8-0 that the law violated the free speech guarantee because it "singled out speech on a particular subject for a financial burden that it places on no other speech and no other income." 105 U.S. 123. Except in rare cases, laws that limit speech based on its content violate the First Amendment.

29. In *Burson v. Freeman*, 504 U.S. 191 (1992), the Supreme Court upheld 5-3 a state law forbidding the solicitation of votes and the display or distribution of campaign materials within 100 feet of entrances to polling places. "A long history, a substantial consensus, and simple common sense show that some restricted zone around polling places is necessary to protect that fundamental right." 504 U.S. 211. In *Hill v. Colorado*, 530 U.S. 703 (2000), the Supreme Court upheld 6-3 a state law prohibiting persons within 100 feet of the entrance of a health care facility (such as an abortion clinic) to approach within eight feet of another person, without consent, for the purpose of speaking, displaying signs or distributing literature on a public sidewalk. The Court found that the speech restriction was content neutral and narrowly tailored to serve a compelling state interest.

30. In *RAV v. City of St. Paul*, 505 U.S. 377 (1992), a white teenager, Robert A. Viktora (referred to in court documents as RAV), burned a cross on the lawn of an African American family, and was convicted for violating a municipal ordinance which prohibited the display of a symbol that "arouses anger, alarm or resentment in others on the basis of race, color, creed, religion or gender." The Supreme Court ruled 9-0 that the ordinance violated the free speech clause because it was overbroad, proscribing both "fighting words" and protected speech, and because the regulation was "content based," proscribing only activities based on race, religion or gender and omitting hostility based on other subjects such as political affiliation, union membership, and homosexuality. In *Virginia v. Black*, 538 U.S. 343 (2003), the Supreme Court invalidated 7-2 that part of a state law placing the burden of proof on the defendant to show that he did not intend the cross burning as an act of intimidation, but upheld the banning of cross burning carried out with the intent to intimidate. In *Wisconsin v. Mitchell*, 508 U.S. 476 (1993), the Supreme Court held 9-0 that enhanced sentencing for hate motivated crimes does not violate a defendant's First Amendment rights.

31. In *McIntyre v. Ohio Elections Commission*, 514 U.S. 334 (1995), McIntyre distributed leaflets at a public meeting expressing her opposition to a proposed school tax. The leaflets were authored anonymously as views of "Concerned Parents and Tax Payers," in violation of state law that pro-

hibited the distribution of campaign literature without the name and address of the issuer. The Supreme Court ruled 7-2 that the publication of anonymous campaign literature is protected by the freedom of speech guarantee.

32. In *Hurley v. Irish-American Gay, Lesbian, and Bisexual Group of Boston (GLIB)*, 515 U.S. 557 (1995), the City of Boston had authorized the South Boston Allied War Veterans Council, a private nonprofit group, to conduct the St. Patrick's Day parade. The council denied a request by GLIB to participate in the parade to publicize its sexual orientation. On appeal, the Supreme Court held 9-0 that private citizens organizing a public demonstration, such as the council, may not be compelled by the state to include groups who impart a message the organizers do not want to be included in their demonstration. A fundamental rule of protection under the First Amendment is "that a speaker has the autonomy to choose the content of his own message," and also to decide "what not to say."

33. In *Rosenberger v. University of Virginia*, 515 U.S. 819 (1995), the university collected mandatory student activity fees which paid off-campus businesses to print student secular publications. The university denied payment for the publication of a Christian magazine. The Supreme Court ruled 5-4 that denying funds available to other student publications, but not to a religious publication, violated the freedom of speech guarantee. There was no violation of the Establishment Clause because the funds were apportioned neutrally among the student publications. This decision follows *Lamb's Chapel v. Center Moriches School District*, 508 U.S. 384 (1993), in which the Court held 9-0 that excluding a religious organization from the after-hour use of school facilities, while at the same time allowing other organizations to use the facilities for social, civic and recreational purposes, was a violation of the First Amendment.

34. In *44 Liquormart, Inc. v. Rhode Island*, 517 U.S. 484 (1996), the Court invalidated 9-0 a state law banning the advertisement of retail liquor prices in newspapers and other media as an infringement of the sellers' freedom of commercial speech under the First Amendment. The Court concluded that "a state legislature does not have the broad discretion to suppress truthful, nonmisleading information for paternalistic purposes." 517 U.S. 510. Similar results were reached in the following cases: *Rubin v. Coors Brewing Co.*, 514 U.S. 476 (1995), voiding 9-0 a federal law prohibiting the advertisement of alcohol content of beer to suppress the threat of "strength wars" among brewers, while irrationally permitting the advertisement of alcohol content in other situations; *Greater New Orleans Broadcasting Association v. United States*, 527 U.S. 173 (1999), overturning 9-0 federal prohibition against advertising of lawful casino gambling; *Lorillard Tobacco Co. v. Reilly*, 533 U.S. 525 (2001), overturning 5-4 state restrictions on the advertising of tobacco products; and *Thompson v. Western States Medical Center*, 535 U.S.

357 (2002), overturning 5-4 federal prohibition against advertising and soliciting prescriptions for compounded drugs.

35. In *Arkansas Educational Television Commission v. Forbes*, 523 U.S. 666 (1998), the Supreme Court ruled 6-3 that a state-owned public television broadcaster did not violate Forbes' right to freedom of speech by excluding him from a debate between the major party candidates in a congressional race. Forbes was an independent candidate with little popular support. The broadcaster, so long as the debates were not designed as "public forums," could selectively exclude participants based on objective indications of their support and not their viewpoints.

36. In *National Endowment of the Arts v. Finley*, 524 U.S. 569 (1998), the Supreme Court held 8-1 that a law requiring the National Endowment to consider "general standards of decency and respect for the diverse beliefs and values of the American public" before awarding grants to artistic projects was not overly vague and impermissibly discriminatory in violation of the First Amendment's freedom of expression guarantee. When the Congress is acting as a patron, rather than engaging in speech regulation, it has wide latitude in setting spending priorities which may affect various forms of expression. Denying government funding does not infringe upon an artist's freedom of expression.

37. In *Boy Scouts of America v. Dale*, 530 U.S. 640 (2000), the Supreme Court upheld 5-4 the Boy Scouts' First Amendment right of freedom of association to bar homosexuals from serving as scout leaders, irrespective of state antidiscrimination laws. The Court recognized that homosexual conduct is inconsistent with the values the Boy Scouts seek to instill. Similarly, in *Clingman v. Beaver*, 544 U.S. 581 (2005), the Supreme Court upheld 6-3 Oklahoma's semi-closed primary law in which a party could invite only its own members and independents to vote in its primary. The Libertarian Party had contended that the law violated its First Amendment freedoms of expression and association by preventing members of other parties from voting in its primary elections. The Court stated that Oklahoma's primary law advanced a number of state interests, including the preservation of parties as viable and identifiable interest groups.

38. In *Bartnicki v. Vopper*, 532 U.S. 514 (2001), an unidentified person illegally recorded a phone call between union officials during collective-bargaining negotiations, and the recording was broadcast by a radio commentator. The Supreme Court held 6-3 that the broadcaster cannot be held liable for broadcasting the recording illegally procured by an unknown third party. A "stranger's illegal conduct does not suffice to remove the First Amendment shield from speech about a matter of public concern." 532 U.S. 535.

39. In *Republican Party of Minnesota v. White*, 536 U.S. 765 (2002), the Supreme Court invalidated 5-4 the state supreme court's judicial canon

prohibiting candidates for popular election to judicial office from announcing their views on disputed legal and political issues that could come before them if elected. The prohibition burdens a category of speech that is at the core of First Amendment freedoms.

40. In *Johanns v. Livestock Marketing Association*, 544 U.S. 550 (2005), the Supreme Court held 6-3 that a program under the Beef Promotion and Research Act of 1985 that compelled beef producers to subsidize generic beef advertisements with which they disagreed does not violate their First Amendment right to free speech. This government speech doctrine is justified by the need for the government to communicate with the public even if some citizens disagree with the message. Compelled funding of private speech may violate the First Amendment, but compelled funding of government speech does not.

41. In *Rumsfeld v. Forum for Academic and Institutional Rights, Inc. (FAIR)*, 547 U.S. 47 (2006), the Supreme Court held 8-0 that the Solomon Amendment, withholding federal funds from colleges and universities that restrict student access by military recruiters, does not violate schools' First Amendment rights to free speech and association by requiring them to assist in military recruitment. The Court reasoned that Congress may attach reasonable conditions on the receipt of federal funding that educational institutions are not obligated to accept. The Amendment neither limits what they may say nor requires them to say anything.

42. In *Garcetti v. Ceballos*, 547 U.S. 410 (2006), a deputy district attorney, declaring that a sheriff misrepresented facts in obtaining a search warrant involved in a prosecution by his office, claimed that his superior, the district attorney, retaliated against him in violation to his free speech guarantee. The Supreme Court held 5-4 that statements made by a public employee pursuant to his official duties, rather than as a private citizen, are not protected by the First Amendment from employer discipline.

43. In *Morse v. Frederick*, 551 U.S. 393 (2007), high school student Joseph Frederick displayed a sign saying "Bong Hits 4 Jesus," across the street from his school, at an Olympic torch relay rally supervised by his school. He was suspended for eight days for violating the school's anti-drug policy. The Supreme Court upheld 5-4 the suspension because the school reasonably concluded that the sign advocated the use of illegal drugs, and that the school had a compelling interest in deterring student drug use.

44. In *New York State Board of Elections v. Torres*, 552 U.S. 196 (2008), the Supreme Court held 9-0 that a political party has the First Amendment right of association to limit its membership as it wishes and to choose the process for the selection of its candidates for election.

On the issue of *campaign finance* laws, the Supreme Court in *Buckley v. Valeo*, 424 U.S. 1 (1976), held that the restrictions of the 1971 Federal

Election Campaign Act (FECA), as amended in 1974, on individual contributions to candidates and political campaigns ("hard money") did not violate the First Amendment because the restrictions enhance the "integrity of our system of representative democracy" by guarding against unscrupulous practices. However, the Court voided the restriction on independent campaign expenditures by individuals and groups, and on expenditures by candidates from their own personal or family resources because these restrictions do not enhance the potential for corruption as do restrictions on individual contributions to candidates. Accordingly, these restrictions violated protected free expression and association, yet lacked any compelling countervailing government interest necessary to sustain them.

While FECA continued the prohibition against corporations and labor unions contributing directly to candidates in federal elections, it authorized the establishment of political action committees (PACs) to solicit contributions for use in political campaigns from executives and shareholders of corporations, and members of labor unions.

The Supreme Court in *Colorado Republican Federal Campaign Committee v. Federal Election Commission*, 518 U.S. 604 (1996), held 7-2 that the FECA campaign finance limits on the amount of money that a political party may spend independently of a candidate's campaign violate the First Amendment.

In *Randall v. Sorrell*, 548 U.S. 230 (2006), a Vermont campaign finance law imposed limits on expenditures by candidates seeking public office, such as $300,000 for governor, $100,000 for lieutenant governor, and $45,000 for other statewide offices. The law also imposed contribution limits of $200 to $400 per candidate for individuals and political groups. The Supreme Court held 6-3 that such strict limits violate the free speech guarantees of the First Amendment because they prevented candidates from campaigning effectively.

In *Austin v. Michigan Chamber of Commerce*, 494 U.S. 652 (1990), the Supreme Court upheld 6-3 the Michigan Campaign Finance Act that barred corporations from using their general funds to support or oppose candidates for election to state offices. The court found that the Act was narrowly drawn to achieve the important goal of maintaining integrity in the political process. However, the Act permitted corporations to make such expenditures from segregated funds used solely for political purposes because the contributors to such funds understood that their money would be used for such purposes.

In *McConnell v. Federal Election Commission*, 540 U.S. 93 (2003), the Supreme Court upheld 5-4 much of the Bipartisan Campaign Reform Act (BCRA) of 2002, also known as the McCain-Feingold Act, which amended the FECA. The Act (1) banned donations not designated for a particular candidate ("soft money") from being contributed to political parties; (2)

banned the use of soft money from corporations and labor unions for the broadcasting of express advocacy advertisements supporting or opposing candidates, and political issue advertisements, referring to a candidate (but not endorsing or opposing him) with regard to a particular issue, in the 30 days prior to a primary or caucus, or 60 days prior to an election; (3) doubled the contribution limit for hard money from $1,000 to $2,000 with an inflation escalator; and (4) required candidates to announce approval of their broadcast campaign ads, known as "stand by your ad." However, a further challenge in *Federal Election Commission v. Wisconsin Right to Life, Inc.*, 551 U.S. 449 (2007), resulted in parts of *McConnell* being reversed. The Court invalidated 5-4 the ban on the use of corporate and labor union funds for the broadcast of political issue advertisements, referring to a candidate (but not endorsing or opposing him) with regard to a particular issue in the 30 days prior to a primary or caucus, or 60 days prior to an election, as an infringement of First Amendment rights. Neither the interest of government in preventing corruption nor the goal of limiting the distorting effects of corporate wealth is sufficient to override the right of a corporation to speak through ads on public issues.

In *Davis v. Federal Election Commission*, 554 U.S.___ (2008), the Supreme Court voided 5-4 the so-called "Millionaire's Amendment" (part of the BCRA) which provided that when a candidate's personal expenditures exceeded certain thresholds, the candidate's opponents could receive contributions from individuals at an increased level and also benefit from enhanced coordinated party expenditures. The Court reasoned that the Amendment imposed different financing restraints on candidates competing against each other, and thereby infringed the political speech of self-financed candidates who may give unlimited amounts of money to their own campaigns since they cannot be corrupted by their own money.

In *Citizens United v. Federal Election Commission*, 558 U.S. ___ (2010), the Supreme Court sharply departed from prior precedents in overturning 5-4 the ban on the broadcasting of a 90-minute documentary called *Hillary: The Movie* that attacked the candidacy of Senator Hillary Clinton in the 2008 presidential campaign. The Court invalidated the prohibitions on corporations (and labor unions by inference) from using their money for the broadcasting of express advocacy advertisements supporting or opposing candidates in the 30 days prior to a primary or caucus, or 60 days prior to an election. The Court retained the prohibition on corporations (and labor unions by inference) contributing directly to candidates in federal elections, and upheld the requirements for sponsor identification and disclosure of contributors. PACs were not disturbed. Accordingly, the Court overruled *Austin v. Michigan Chamber of Commerce*, 494 U.S. 652 (1990), partially overruled *McConnell v. Federal Election Commission*, 540 U.S. 93 (2003), and invalidated part of the BCRA. "If the First Amendment has any force, it prohibits Congress from fining or jailing citizens, or associations of citizens, for simply engaging in political speech."

Among the limitations on free speech, *obscenity* was addressed by the Supreme Court in *Miller v. California*, 413 U.S. 15 (1973), involving a mass mailing by Miller advertising the sale of illustrated books primarily consisting of pictures explicitly depicting men and women in groups of two or more engaging in a variety of sexual activities, with genitals often prominently displayed. In defining the test for obscenity not protected by the First Amendment, the Supreme Court held 5-4 that: (1) the average person, applying contemporary community standards (not national standards), would find the work, taken as a whole, appeals to prurient interest; (2) the work depicts or describes, in a patently offensive way, sexual conduct or excretory functions specifically defined by applicable state law; and (3) the work, taken as a whole, lacks serious literary, artistic, political or scientific value. The Court in *Miller* modified the test for obscenity established in *Roth v. United States*, 354 U.S. 476 (1957), 6-3 vote, and *Memoirs v. Massachusetts*, 383 U.S. 413 (1966), 6-3 vote, which held as unprotected only that which is patently offensive and utterly without redeeming social value to the average person applying contemporary community standards. In *Jacobellis v. Ohio*, 378 U.S. 184 (1964), the Supreme Court overturned 6-3 the conviction of a theater manager for showing the 1958 French movie *The Lovers (Les Amants)*, starring Jeanne Moreau, finding that the movie was not obscene. Justice Potter Stewart, in his concurrence, admitted difficulty in defining obscenity, stating, "But I know it when I see it, and the motion picture involved in this case is not that." 378 U.S. 197.

In *Stanley v. Georgia*, 394 U.S. 557 (1969), police, with a warrant, searched Stanley's home for alleged bookmaking activities, but instead found obscene film. The Supreme Court overturned his conviction for possession of obscene material, holding 9-0 that the First Amendment prohibits making the mere private possession of obscene material a crime. Justice Thurgood Marshall stated, "If the First Amendment means anything, it means that a State has no business telling a man, sitting alone in his own house, what books he may read or what films he may watch. Our whole constitutional heritage rebels at the thought of giving government the power to control men's minds." 394 U.S. 565. In *Jenkins v. Georgia*, 418 U.S. 153 (1974), the Supreme Court overturned 9-0 the conviction of a theater manager for showing the 1971 movie *Carnal Knowledge*, starring Jack Nicholson, Candice Bergen and Ann-Margret. The Court ruled that the movie did not "depict sexual conduct in a patently offensive way," and that the *Miller* obscenity test had been misapplied because it did not give juries "unbridled discretion" to determine obscenity. 418 U.S. 160, 161.

In *New York v. Ferber*, 458 U.S. 747 (1982), the Supreme Court upheld 9-0 a state child pornography law prohibiting persons from knowingly promoting sexual performances by children by distributing descriptive material. The state's interest in protecting children allows such laws even where the content does not meet the obscenity tests under *Miller v. California*. However, in *Sable Communications of California v. Federal Communications Commission*, 492 U.S. 115 (1989), the Supreme Court invalidated 9-0 the Communications Act's ban on indecent commercial telephone messages (dial-a-porn) because the denial of adult access to such messages far exceeds that which is necessary to serve the compelling interest of preventing minors from being exposed to the messages. "Sexual expression which is indecent but not obscene is protected by the First Amendment." 492 U.S. 126. In *Reno v. American Civil Liberties Union*, 521 U.S. 844 (1997), the Supreme Court invalidated 9-0 anti-indecency provisions of the Communications Decency Act (CDA) of 1996 that sought to protect minors from explicit material on the Internet by criminalizing the knowing transmission to them of obscene and indecent messages. The Court ruled that the provisions were so overly broad and vague as to amount to a content-based blanket restriction of free speech; and that the Internet is entitled to the same full protection of free speech as that given to the print media. In *United States v. Playboy Entertainment Group*, 529 U.S. 803 (2000), the Supreme Court invalidated 5-4 part of the CDA which required cable television operators, offering channels with sexually explicit content, to either restrict such material to late-night hours or scramble or block it. If "a statute regulates speech based on its content, it must be narrowly tailored to promote a compelling Government interest. If a less restrictive alternative would serve the Government's purpose, the legislature must use that alternative." 529 U.S. 813.

In *Ashcroft v. Free Speech Coalition*, 535 U.S. 234 (2002), the Court struck down 6-3 two overbroad provisions of the Child Pornography Prevention Act (CPPA) of 1996 which made it illegal to produce or possess "virtual" child pornography that is created by computer images but does not involve real children, and thereby abridged "the freedom to engage in a substantial amount of lawful speech." The CPPA fails the *Miller* tests because it lacks the required link between its prohibitions and the affront to community standards, and is unsupported by *Ferber* because the CPPA's prohibited speech does not involve real children and therefore creates no victims. In *Ashcroft v. American Civil Liberties Union*, 542 U.S. 656 (2004), the Supreme Court ruled 5-4 that the requirement of the Child Online Protection Act (COPA) of 1998 that online publishers prevent children from "accessing material that is harmful to minors" was too restrictive of protected speech and that other methods were more effective in protecting minors.

In *United States v. American Library Association*, 539 U.S. 194 (2003), the Supreme Court held 6-3 that Congress had the authority under the Children's Internet Protection Act of 2000 to require public schools and libraries to censor obscene Internet content on their computers in order to receive federal funding. In *United States v. Williams*, 553 U.S. 285 (2008), the Supreme Court upheld 7-2 the federal PROTECT Act of 2003 criminalizing the pandering (promoting) of child pornography, finding that the Act was not overly broad or impermissibly vague. PROTECT is the acronym for "Prosecutorial Remedies and Other Tools to end the Exploitation of Children Today."

FREEDOM OF THE PRESS CLAUSE

Freedom of the press, like freedom of speech, is subject to restrictions such as defamation, although proof of actual malice is required in cases against publishers. Prior restraint on publication is generally prohibited.

In *Lovell v. City of Griffin*, 303 U.S. 444 (1938), the Supreme Court held 8-0 that an ordinance requiring the city manager's prior written permission for distribution of circulars, leaflets, magazines, pamphlets or other literature amounted to censorship and violated the Freedom of the Press Clause. The clause is not confined to newspapers and periodicals, but also embraces pamphlets and leaflets. The freedom of publication includes distribution. In *Schneider v. State of New Jersey*, 308 U.S. 147 (1939), the Court held 8-1 that the purpose to keep the streets clean and neat is insufficient to justify an ordinance which prohibits a person rightfully on a public street from handing literature to one willing to receive it. Any burden imposed on the city in cleaning and caring for the streets as an indirect consequence of such distribution results from the constitutional protection of the freedom of speech and press.

In *Associated Press v. National Labor Relations Board*, 301 U.S. 103 (1937), the Supreme Court held 5-4 that the freedom of the press was not abridged by the Associated Press (AP) being required by the NLRB to rehire an editorial employee discharged for union activities in violation of the National Labor Relations Act. The Act does not compel the AP to employ anyone, or to retain an incompetent editor. The AP may discharge an employee for any cause save only the forbidden reasons of union activities and advocacy of collective bargaining.

In *Winters v. New York*, 333 U.S. 507 (1948), the Supreme Court held 6-3 that a state law, prohibiting the distribution of a magazine principally made up of criminal news, police reports, or pictures, and stories of deeds of bloodshed, lust or crime, was so vague and indefinite as to violate the guarantee of free speech and press.

In *Smith v. California*, 361 U.S. 147 (1959), a bookseller was convicted of violating a city ordinance that made him criminally liable for the sales of books later determined to be obscene even if he did not know the contents of the books. The Supreme Court voided 5-4 the ordinance because it is unreasonable to require booksellers to know the contents of every book they sell. The enforcement of such an ordinance would sharply curtail the sale of books to only those read by the booksellers. The free publication and dissemination of books are within constitutionally protected freedom of the press.

In *New York Times v. Sullivan*, 376 U.S. 254 (1964), the *Times* had published an advertisement stating that officials in Montgomery, Alabama, had violently suppressed the protests of African Americans during the civil rights movement. Sullivan, a city commissioner, won a libel action in state court against the newspaper and others on the basis that the ad contained factual errors. The Supreme Court, in overturning the state decision, ruled 9-0 that the First Amendment protects the publication of statements, even false ones, about the conduct of public officials, except when the statements are made with "actual malice"—meaning that the statement was made with knowledge of its falsity or with reckless disregard of whether it was true or false. To ensure that citizens have the right to freely criticize public officials, the Court reasoned "[t]hat erroneous statement is inevitable in free debate, and that it must be protected if the freedoms of expression are to have the 'breathing space' that they 'need ... to survive.'" 376 U.S. 271. In *Monitor Patriot Co. v. Roy*, 401 U.S. 265 (1971), the Supreme Court held 7-2 that publications concerning candidates for public office must be accorded at least as much protection under the First Amendment as those concerning occupants of public office. In *Herbert v. Lando*, 441 U.S. 153 (1979), the Supreme Court held 7-2 that a plaintiff in a libel suit may inquire into the editorial process in order to meet the burden of proving "actual malice."

The actual malice standard also applies to public figures, including celebrities, as illustrated by *Hustler Magazine v. Falwell*, 485 U.S. 46 (1988), in which the magazine featured a "parody" of an advertisement claiming that Falwell, a minister and political leader, had a drunken incestuous relationship with his mother in an outhouse. Falwell sued and recovered damages for libel. On appeal, the Supreme Court ruled 8-0 that public figures, such as Falwell, may not recover damages without showing that the offending publication contained a false statement of fact that was made with "actual malice." Since the parody could not be reasonably interpreted to state actual facts about Falwell, it was protected. However, in *Masson v. New Yorker Magazine*, 501 U.S. 496 (1991), the Supreme Court held 7-2 that the deliberate alteration of a public figure's statement constituted knowledge of falsity if it "results in a material change in the meaning conveyed by the statement."

501 U.S. 517. Accordingly, the contested passages created issues of fact for the jury as to truth or falsity.

Unlike public officials or figures, private individuals do not need to prove actual malice in order to receive damages for defamation. *Gertz v. Robert Welch, Inc.*, 418 U.S. 323 (1974), 5-4 vote. However, the private plaintiff must bear the burden of proof in showing that defamatory statements by the press are false. *Philadelphia Newspapers, Inc., v. Hepps*, 475 U.S. 767 (1986), 5-4 vote.

In *Greenbelt Cooperative Publishing Association, Inc. v. Bresler*, 398 U.S. 6 (1970), a newspaper article quoted a visitor at a city council meeting who accused Bresler, a real estate developer and state legislator, of "blackmail" for his aggressive negotiations with the city. The Supreme Court ruled that the accusation was not libelous because it was unreasonable to believe that anyone was claiming that Bresler had actually committed a crime and, hence, the accusation was essentially hyperbole.

In *Miami Herald Publishing Co. v. Tornillo*, 418 U.S. 241 (1974), the Supreme Court overturned 9-0 a state "right to reply" law requiring a newspaper to allow a political candidate the right to equal space to reply to attacks by the newspaper on the candidate's character or official record, such as reflected in editorials and endorsements. "The choice of material to go into a newspaper, and the decisions made as to limitations on the size and content of the paper, and treatment of public issues and public officials—whether fair or unfair—constitute the exercise of editorial control and judgment." 418 U.S. 258. In contrast, the Supreme Court in *Red Lion Broadcasting Co. v. Federal Communications Commission*, 395 U.S. 367 (1969), upheld 8-0 the constitutionality of the FCC's Fairness Doctrine requiring that the holders of broadcast licenses present controversial issues of public importance in a fair and balanced manner. The results in *Tornillo* and *Red Lion* are reconciled by newspapers being unlicensed and facing numerous competitors, whereas broadcast licensees are granted the use of scarce radio spectrum by the FCC. Accordingly, the government may require a licensee to share its frequency with others for the benefit of viewers and listeners. In 1987, the FCC abolished the Fairness Doctrine.

In *Bigelow v. Virginia*, 421 U.S. 809 (1975), the Supreme Court held 7-2 that a newspaper editor may not be punished for publishing an advertisement for an abortion referral service in violation of a state statute criminalizing the publication of information for the procurement of abortions. The court reasoned that the advertisement merited First Amendment protection because it conveyed truthful information about a matter of significant public interest.

In *Milkovich v. Lorain Journal Co.*, 497 U.S. 1 (1990), a sportswriter wrote a newspaper article expressing an opinion that a high school wrestling coach had lied under oath in a judicial proceeding about a brawl occurring after a wrestling match. The Supreme Court, while recognizing the constitutional protections afforded the press, held 7-2 that labeling a statement as "opinion" does not automatically exempt the news media from defamation laws, and sent the case back for a trial on the merits. The Court pointed out that the statement "'In my opinion Jones is a liar,' can cause as much damage to reputation as the statement, 'Jones is a liar.'" 497 U.S. 19.

In *City of Cincinnati v. Discovery Network*, 507 U.S. 410 (1993), the Supreme Court held 6-3 that the city may not constitutionally ban news racks for the dissemination of publications that are comprised primarily of advertisements.

The *prior restraint* or censorship issue was addressed by the Supreme Court in *Near v. Minnesota ex rel. Olson*, 283 U.S. 697 (1931). Near, the publisher of a scandal sheet attacking the integrity of public officials, was enjoined from further publication under a state law providing for such relief against those publishing "malicious, scandalous and defamatory newspapers." The Court ruled 5-4 that the law constituted a prior restraint in violation of the First Amendment. The Court established the doctrine that, with some narrow restraints, the government could not censor or otherwise prohibit a publication in advance, even though the communication might be subject to civil damages or criminal punishment after publication.

The *Near* decision was followed in *New York Times v. United States*, 403 U.S. 713 (1971), in which the Nixon Administration attempted to prevent the *Times* and *Washington Post* from publishing the so-called "Pentagon Papers" on the ground that prior restraint was necessary to protect national security. The Supreme Court ruled 6-3 that the government did not present sufficient evidence that the publication would cause "grave and irreparable" danger and, therefore, did not overcome the "heavy presumption against" prior restraint of the press in this case. The Pentagon Papers were the 47-volume top-secret U.S. Department of Defense history of the country's political and military involvement in Vietnam from 1945-1967.

The Supreme Court has limited the ability of the press to use the First Amendment as a shield against the disclosure of confidential information in testimony before grand juries as shown in *Branzburg v. Hayes*, 408 U.S. 665 (1972). In this case, newspaper reporters were summoned to testify before a grand jury regarding the witnessing of people manufacturing and using hashish, and interviewing leaders of the Black Panthers. The Court ruled 5-4 that requiring reporters to disclose confidential information to grand juries regarding criminal acts served a "compelling" and "paramount" state interest and did not violate the First Amendment.

In *Nebraska Press Association v. Stuart*, 427 U.S. 539 (1976), a state trial judge issued an order ("gag rule") prohibiting the news media from publishing or broadcasting accounts of the confessions made by the accused in a sensational murder case. The Supreme Court overturned 9-0 the order because "prior restraints on speech and publication are the most serious and the least tolerable infringement on First Amendment rights." 427 U.S. 559. The Court reached its decision after weighing the rights of the free press under the First Amendment against the right of the accused to a fair trial under the Sixth Amendment. The Supreme Court has upheld the right of the news media to identify victims or defendants, contrary to state law, where the information is lawfully obtained about a matter of public significance and the government has failed to demonstrate that such prohibition was narrowly tailored to serve "a state interest of the highest order." *Cox Broadcasting Corp. v. Cohn*, 420 U.S. 469 (1975), 8-0 vote, 17-year old-rape-murder victim; *Oklahoma Publishing Co. v. District Court*, 430 U.S. 308 (1977), *per curiam*, 11-year-old defendant accused of murder; *Smith v. Daily Mail Publishing Co.*, 443 U.S. 97 (1979), 8-0 vote, juvenile offender; and *Florida Star v. BJF*, 491 U.S. 524, 534 (1989), 6-3 vote, rape victim.

With respect to student newspapers, *Hazelwood School District v. Kuhlmeier*, 484 U.S. 260 (1988), involved a school-sponsored newspaper, written and edited by students. The school principal found two upcoming articles on student pregnancy and parental divorce to be inappropriate and ordered them withheld from publication. On appeal, the Supreme Court ruled 5-3 in favor of the principal, holding that schools are entitled to set high standards for student speech disseminated under their auspices, and may refuse to sponsor speech that is inconsistent with "legitimate pedagogical goals." Public school curricular student newspapers are subject to a lower level of First Amendment protection than independent newspapers established as forums for student expression. The censored articles were later published by the *St. Louis Post-Dispatch*, thus affording them much wider coverage than they would have received in the student newspaper. Earlier, in *Papish v. Board of Curators of the University of Missouri*, 410 U.S. 667 (1973), the Supreme Court held 6-3 that a public university could not punish a graduate student for her on-campus distribution of an underground newspaper for indecent or offensive speech that did not disrupt campus order.

FREEDOM OF ASSEMBLY CLAUSE

The right to assemble peaceably for the discussion of public or other questions is an attribute of citizenship under a free government.

The Supreme Court in *United States v. Cruikshank*, 92 U.S. 542 (1876), held 9-0 that the "right of the people peaceably to assemble for the purpose of petitioning Congress for a redress of grievances, or for any thing else connected with the powers or duties of the national government, is an attribute of national citizenship, and, as such, under the protection of, and guaranteed by, the United States." 92 U.S. 552.

In *Hague v. Committee for Industrial Organization*, 307 U.S. 496 (1939), Mayor Hague used a city ordinance to prevent labor meetings in public places and to stop the distribution of literature promoting the labor cause. The Supreme Court ruled 5-2 that Hague's ban on political meetings violated the Freedom of Assembly Clause. In *Cox v. New Hampshire*, 312 U.S. 569 (1941), the Supreme Court held 8-0 that although government cannot regulate speech content, it can place reasonable time, place and conduct restrictions on assemblies for public convenience and safety, and charge reasonable licensing fees to cover the cost of policing and overseeing parades.

In *Edwards v. South Carolina*, 372 U.S. 229 (1963), the Supreme Court held 8-1 that the First Amendment forbids state police from forcing civil rights protesters to disperse when they are otherwise legally marching on the state house grounds. A state cannot "make criminal the peaceful expression of unpopular views." 372 U.S. 327. In *Cox v. Louisiana, I & II*, 379 U.S. 536, 559 (1965), the Supreme Court held that breach of the peace and obstruction of public passageway laws may not be used to punish unpopular speech in a peaceable civil rights demonstration that may potentially incite violence. The Court noted, however, that the state has the right to impose reasonable nondiscriminatory restrictions on travel on city streets and assembly in public places. In *Grayned v. City of Rockford*, 408 U.S. 104 (1972), the Supreme Court upheld 8-1 an anti-noise ordinance prohibiting picketing near a school as narrowly tailored to further a significant government interest.

The Supreme Court in *Lloyd Corp. v. Tanner*, 407 U.S. 551 (1972), held 5-4 that the owner of large shopping center may prohibit the distribution of anti-war handbills in the interior mall area where the handbilling was unrelated to any activity within the center and where the distributors had adequate alternative means of communication, such as the public streets and sidewalks adjacent to the center.

PETITION CLAUSE

The right to petition public authorities for the redress of grievances is an attribute of citizenship under a free government. This right is exemplified by the Declaration of Independence that explained the reasons for the colonists' decision to declare their independence from Great Britain.

The *Noerr-Pennington* doctrine was set forth by the Supreme Court in a pair of cases which held that under the First Amendment it is not a violation of the antitrust laws for competitors to lobby the government to change the law so as to reduce or eliminate competition. *Eastern Railroad Presidents Conference v. Noerr Motor Freight, Inc.*, 365 U.S. 127 (1961), 9-0 vote; and *United Mine Workers v. Pennington*, 381 U.S. 657 (1965), 9-0 vote. The doctrine thus protects those who petition government entities, including the judiciary, to further private ends.

In *McDonald v. Smith*, 472 U.S. 479 (1985), involving letters to the President opposing Smith's appointment as a United States attorney, the Supreme Court held 8-0 that the Petition Clause does not provide absolute immunity to defendants charged with expressing libelous and damaging falsehoods in petitions to government officials, and is subject to the same restrictions as freedom of speech rights.

Amendment II
Right to Bear Arms

Ratified December 15, 1791

A well regulated Militia, being necessary to the security of a free State, the right of the people to keep and bear Arms, shall not be infringed.

The Second Amendment is awkwardly worded because the first clause seems to say that the right to keep and bear arms is only through militia service, whereas the second clause seems to recognize an individual right to keep and bear arms.

Prior to a definitive Supreme Court decision, two competing interpretations emerged. Some argued that the right of the people to bear arms is only as a part of a "well regulated militia," which today has become the National Guard as the successor to the colonial minutemen. Others argued that it protects an individual right to possess a firearm unconnected with service in a militia, and to use that arm for traditionally lawful purposes, such as self-defense within the home.

The Supreme Court resolved this issue in *District of Columbia v. Heller*, 554 U.S. __ (2008) , by ruling 5-4 that the Second Amendment protects an individual's right to possess a firearm, unconnected with militia service, and to use the firearm for traditionally lawful purposes, such as self-defense in the home. The Court held that the first clause is prefatory and does not limit or expand the scope of the second clause which is operative. However, the Court stated that the majority decision does not impair "longstanding prohibitions" on gun possession such as by "felons and the mentally ill, or laws forbidding the carrying of firearms in sensitive places such as schools and government buildings, or laws imposing conditions and qualifications on the commercial sale of arms." This ruling is consistent with: *United States v. Miller*, 307 U.S. 174 (1939), upholding 8-0 the National Firearms Act of 1934 that regulates the interstate transportation of machine guns and short-barreled shotguns, and *United States v. Hayes*, 555 U.S. ___ (2009), upholding 7-2 the Federal Gun Control Act of 1968 that bars convicted felons, and those convicted of misdemeanors involving domestic violence, from possessing firearms.

Amendment III
Quartering of Soldiers

Ratified December 15, 1791

No Soldier shall, in time of peace be quartered in any house, without the consent of the Owner, nor in time of war, but in a manner to be prescribed by law.

The Third Amendment is among the least cited provisions of the Constitution because its relevance has greatly declined since the Revolutionary War.

Griswold v. Connecticut, 381 U.S. 479 (1965), was a landmark case in which the Supreme Court, relying in part on the Third Amendment, held that the Constitution protected a right of privacy. Griswold was convicted under a state law which criminalized the provision of counseling, and other medical treatment, to married persons for purposes of preventing conception. The Court, in overturning the law, ruled 7-2 that the First, Third, Fourth, Fifth and Ninth Amendments create penumbras or zones that establish a right to privacy in marital relations. The right to privacy established by *Griswold* was applied by the Supreme Court in *Roe v. Wade*, 410 U.S. 113 (1973), holding 7-2 that a woman's choice to terminate her pregnancy by abortion was within her constitutional right to privacy. However, in *Roe* the Court relied instead on the Due Process Clause of the Fourteenth Amendment.

Engblom v. Carey, 677 F2d 957 (USCA 2d Cir 1982), involved a 1979 strike by New York State correction officers. While on strike, the correction officers were evicted from their rented prison facility residences which were then occupied by National Guardsmen who had temporarily taken their place as prison guards. The Court of Appeals for the Second Circuit held that the National Guardsmen qualified as soldiers under the Third Amendment, and that New York violated the Amendment when it took over the strikers' residences and housed the Guardsmen in their place. The protection of the Amendment was extended beyond home owners to include tenants, such as the strikers.

Amendment IV
Search and Seizure; Warrants

Ratified December 15, 1791

The right of the people to be secure in their persons, houses, papers, and effects, against unreasonable searches and seizures, shall not be violated, and no Warrants shall issue, but upon probable cause, supported by Oath or affirmation, and particularly describing the place to be searched, and the persons or things to be seized.

The Amendment's twin commands (Search and Seizure Clause; Warrant Clause) must be read in tandem: When people have a reasonable expectation of privacy in their persons or effects, all searches and seizures by public officials must be based on probable cause and specific information, and supported by a warrant, unless they fall into one of the exceptions where officials may dispense with securing a warrant when their conduct is otherwise objectively reasonable. The reasonableness of a search is judged by balancing the intrusion on the individual's Fourth Amendment rights against the promotion of legitimate governmental interests. Under the exclusionary rule adopted as a means to deter illegal police conduct, evidence obtained in violation of the Amendment is generally inadmissible by the prosecution during the defendant's criminal trial.

In *Stanford v. Texas*, 379 U.S. 476 (1965), a state judge issued a warrant authorizing the search of Stanford's home and the seizure there of "books, records, pamphlets, cards, receipts, lists, memoranda, pictures, recordings and other written instruments concerning the Communist Party of Texas." The police conducted a search of over four hours and seized more than 2,000 items, including Stanford's business and personal records, but no records of the Communist Party. On appeal, the Supreme Court held 9-0 that a state may not constitutionally issue general warrants that do not describe with particularity the things to be seized, which is a requirement of the most scrupulous exactitude where the seizure also impinges upon First Amendment freedoms.

In the ill-fated case of *Olmstead v. United States*, 277 U.S. 438 (1928), the Supreme Court held 5-4 that the evidence obtained in the use of wiretapped private telephone conversations by federal agents, without judicial approval, did not violate Olmstead's rights under the Search and Seizure Clause of the Fourth Amendment and the Self-Incrimination Clause of the Fifth Amendment. The majority ruled that that wiretapping does not constitute a search and seizure because there was no actual physical examination of one's person, personal property or home; and that self-incrimination was not compelled because the conversations were voluntary. In dissent, Associate Justice Louis Brandeis wrote that the framers of the Constitution sought "to protect Americans in their beliefs, their thoughts, their emotions, and their sensations." It is for this reason that they "conferred, as against the government, the right to be let alone—the most comprehensive of rights and the right most valued by civilized man." 277 U.S. 478.

Olmstead was reversed 7-1 by the Supreme Court in *Katz v. United States*, 389 U.S. 347 (1967), when it adopted the rationale of Justice Louis Brandeis' dissent. The Court held that the Fourth Amendment required the police to obtain a search warrant in order to wiretap Katz's conversation in a public telephone booth. The Court ruled, "No less than an individual in a business office, in a friend's apartment, or in a taxicab, a person in a telephone booth may rely upon the protection of the Fourth Amendment." 389 U.S. 352. The rights of a person may not be violated, regardless of whether there is a physical intrusion of any space. The Fourth Amendment protects people, not places. In *United States v. U.S. District Court*, 407 U.S. 297 (1972), the Supreme Court held 8-0 that government officials were obligated to obtain a warrant before engaging in electronic surveillance even in the case of threats to domestic security as identified by the President. "Security surveillances are especially sensitive because of the inherent vagueness of the domestic security concept, the necessarily broad and continuing nature of intelligence gathering, and the temptation to utilize such surveillances to oversee political dissent." 407 U.S. 320.

In *Kyllo v. United States*, 533 U.S. 27 (2001), a federal agent used a thermal imaging device to penetrate the exterior of Kyllo's home to determine if the amount of heat emanating from the home was consistent with the high-intensity lamps typically used for indoor marijuana growth. Based upon the heat radiation recorded, a warrant was issued for the search of the home which revealed the marijuana. The Supreme Court held 5-4 that the thermal imaging of a home constituted a "search" under the Fourth Amendment and may be performed only with a warrant issued before the thermal imaging, not afterwards.

In *Wilson v. Arkansas*, 514 U.S. 927 (1995), police officers, with a warrant, found the main door of defendant's home open. Without knocking, they opened the unlocked screen door, entered the home and found narcotics, a gun and ammunition. On appeal, the Supreme Court held 9-0 that the Fourth Amendment's protection against unreasonable searches and seizures included the common law "knock and announce" rule. However, police may dispense with "knock and announce" to prevent the destruction of evidence, endangerment of police officers, and suspect escape. *Richards v. Wisconsin*, 520 U.S. 385 (1997), 9-0 vote; *United States v. Ramirez*, 523 U.S. 65 (1998), 9-0 vote.

In *Wilson v. Layne*, 526 U.S. 603 (1999), the Supreme Court held 9-0 that allowing news media reporters and photographers on a "ride-along" to observe and record the execution of an arrest warrant by law enforcement officers in a private residence violated the Fourth Amendment rights of the residents.

While the "reasonable expectation of privacy" test would cover a home and its curtilage, or immediate surrounding area, a warrantless search and seizure would be upheld for garbage placed curbside outside the home for pickup because there was no reasonable expectation of privacy for trash on public streets "readily accessible to animals, children, scavengers, snoops, and other members of the public." *California v. Greenwood*, 486 U.S. 35, 40 (1988),

6-2 vote. In *Florida v. Riley*, 488 U.S. 445 (1989), the Supreme Court held 5-4 that surveillance of the interior of a partially covered greenhouse in a residential backyard from a helicopter 400 feet above the greenhouse did not constitute a search requiring a warrant under the Fourth Amendment.

In *Bivens v. Six Unknown Named Agents*, 403 U.S. 388 (1971), agents of the Federal Bureau of Narcotics, without probable cause, made a warrantless entry of Bivens' apartment, searched it, arrested him on narcotics charges, and later dropped the charges and released him. The Supreme Court held 6-3 that Bivens had an implied private right of action for monetary damages against the agents where no other federal remedy is provided for the vindication of his interests protected by the Fourth Amendment.

The concept of "probable cause" is central to the meaning of the Warrant Clause. The Supreme Court held in *Brinegar v. United States*, 338 U.S. 160 (1949), that probable cause exists where the facts and circumstances within the officers' knowledge, and of which they have reasonably trustworthy information, are sufficient in themselves to warrant a belief by a man of reasonable caution that a crime is being committed. In *Illinois v. Gates*, 462 U.S. 213 (1983), the Supreme Court adopted 6-3 the "totality of the circumstances" approach to probable cause, meaning that there is no single deciding factor, but that one must consider all the facts as well as the context, and conclude from the whole picture whether there is probable cause. The phrase means more than a mere possibility, but less than a near certainty.

In *Tennessee v. Garner*, 471 U.S. 1 (1985), a police officer, pursuant to state law, shot and killed a fleeing criminal suspect, after ordering him to stop. The Supreme Court held 6-3 that the state law is unconstitutional insofar as it authorizes the use of deadly force against an apparently unarmed, non-dangerous fleeing suspect, and that such force may be used only when necessary to prevent the escape and when the officer has probable cause to believe that the suspect poses a significant threat of death or serious physical injury to the officer or others. Apprehension by the use of deadly force is a seizure subject to the Fourth Amendment. In *Winston v. Lee*, 470 U.S. 753 (1985), the Supreme Court held 9-0 that it is unconstitutional for a state to compel surgery under general anesthesia on a person to retrieve a bullet as evidence for a criminal prosecution.

In *Ferguson v. City of Charleston*, 532 U.S. 67 (2001), a state hospital, in an effort to reduce the number of "crack babies" and amount of cocaine use among pregnant women receiving prenatal care, conducted diagnostic tests of the patients and turned over any evidence of illicit drug use to police. The Supreme Court held 6-3 that the hospital's revealing of the incriminating test results to police without the patient's consent violated her reasonable expectation of privacy as guaranteed by the Fourth Amendment.

In *Georgia v. Randolph*, 547 U.S. 103 (2006), Randolph's estranged wife consented to the police search of the residence without a warrant, while Randolph objected to the search and the resulting evidentiary seizure. The Supreme Court held 5-3 that when two co-occupants are present, and one consents to a warrantless search and the other refuses, the search is unconstitutional as to the latter.

In *Arizona v. Gant*, 556 U.S. ___ (2009), state police arrested Gant for driving with a suspended driver's license. After he left his vehicle, they handcuffed him and placed him in a patrol car. Police then searched his vehicle, found a handgun and cocaine, and charged him with illicit narcotic possession. The Supreme Court held 5-4 that the search of the vehicle was a violation of Gant's constitutional guarantee against unreasonable search and seizure. A warrantless vehicular search incident to an arrest can only be justified by an actual and continuing threat to the safety of police officers, or a need to preserve evidence of the crime for which the arrest is made (an element not relevant to driving with a suspended driver's license). The decision sharply curtailed *New York v. Belton*, 453 U.S. 454 (1981), which held 6-3 that when a police officer has made a lawful custodial arrest of the occupant of an automobile, the officer may, as a contemporaneous incident of the arrest, conduct a warrantless search of the passenger compartment of the automobile.

In *Florida v. Bostick*, 501 U.S. 429 (1991), the police, because of the growing illicit drug traffic, randomly searched buses, asking passengers for identification and permission to search their luggage. Bostick consented to such a search, after being told he could refuse, and the police found cocaine in his luggage. The Supreme Court held 6-3 that this was not per se ("by itself") an illegal seizure because he was free to decline the officer's request or otherwise terminate the encounter. In *Ohio v. Robinette*, 519 U.S. 33 (1996), a police officer stopped Robinette for speeding and, after issuing him a verbal warning, asked if he had any illegal drugs or weapons in his vehicle. Robinette answered no, but consented to the search of his vehicle in which the officer found illegal drugs. The Supreme Court held 8-1 that the Fourth Amendment does not require a police officer to inform a motorist at the end of a traffic stop that he is "free to go" before seeking permission to search his vehicle.

The following cases depict situations where warrantless searches and seizures do not require probable cause to be reasonable.

• STOP AND FRISK. In *Terry v. Ohio*, 392 U.S. 1 (1968), a policeman observed Terry and others continually reconnoitering a store as though they were "casing" it for robbery. The Supreme Court ruled 8-1 that the police may stop and frisk someone for weapons if they have a reasonable suspicion that a crime has occurred or is about to occur. In *United States v. Hensley*, 469 U.S. 221 (1985), police issued a "wanted flyer" based on information provided by an informant that the defendant was the getaway driver in a robbery. Police officers, aware of the flyer, recognized the defendant, pulled him over to investigate, discovered guns in his vehicle, and arrested him. The Supreme Court upheld 9-0 the warrantless arrest because the flyer provided the police with reasonable suspicion to justify the stop. In *Minnesota v. Dickerson*, 508 U.S. 366 (1993), the Supreme Court upheld 9-0 the stop-and-frisk for weapons under *Terry*, but found the seizure of cocaine in a pat-down search to be unconstitutional because the contraband was revealed by touch and was not in "plain view."

   • PLAIN VIEW. In *Horton v. California*, 496 U.S. 128 (1990), police officers, in executing a search warrant for stolen property in Horton's home, did not find the stolen property, but did find the weapons used in the robbery in plain view and seized them. The Supreme Court upheld 7-2 the seizure of the weapons because the officers were lawfully present, and the incriminating evidence was in plain view.

   • OPEN FIELDS. In *Oliver v. United States*, 466 U.S. 170 (1984), police entered the defendant's land, continued past his house, ignored a "no trespassing" sign at a gate, and went nearly a mile beyond to find a large marijuana crop. The Supreme Court held 7-3 that there was no Fourth Amendment violation because there was no privacy expectation regarding an open field. In *California v. Ciraolo*, 476 U.S. 207 (1986), the Supreme Court held 5-4 that the warrantless aerial observation of a person's backyard did not violate the Fourth Amendment.

   • SEARCHES INCIDENT TO LAWFUL ARREST. In *United States v. Rabinowitz*, 339 U.S. 56 (1950), police lawfully arrested Rabinowitz in his one-room office for allegedly selling and possessing forged government stamps. The police then searched his office without a search warrant and seized the stamps that were used as evidence against him. The Supreme Court ruled 5-3 that the Fourth Amendment permits, as incident to a lawful arrest, a warrantless search of the area within the immediate control of the arrestee. A similar result was reached in *United States v. Robinson*, 414 U.S. 218 (1973), 6-3 vote, where a police officer arrested Robinson for driving with a revoked driver's license, and discovered heroin during a pat-down of his clothing. However, in *Chimel v. California*, 395 U.S. 752 (1969), police apprehended Chimel in his home with a warrant authorizing his arrest for burglary. The police then conducted a comprehensive search of his home without a search warrant and found incriminating evidence. The Supreme Court ruled 7-2 that the police may search only the area "within the immediate control" of the arrestee from which he might obtain a weapon or destroy evidence. Any further search of the home would require a second warrant pursuant to the

Fourth Amendment. In *Illinois v. Lafayette*, 462 U.S. 640 (1983), involving the arrest of a theatergoer for disturbing the peace, the Supreme Court held 9-0 that, consistent with the Fourth Amendment, it is reasonable for police to search the personal effects of a person under lawful arrest as part of the routine administrative procedure at a police station incident to booking and jailing the suspect.

• AUTOMOBILE EXCEPTION (Carroll Doctrine). In *Carroll v. United States*, 267 U.S. 132 (1925), the police, on suspicion that Carroll was transporting liquor in an automobile in violation of the Volstead Act, stopped him, made a warrantless search of his automobile, and found the liquor. The Supreme Court upheld 6-2 the warrantless search because probable cause existed and the mobility of the automobile made it impracticable to obtain a search warrant, and there is also less of an expectation of privacy in automobiles. The Supreme Court has applied the Carroll Doctrine to uphold the warrantless search of an automobile after impoundment at the police station, *Chambers v. Maroney*, 399 U.S. 42 (1970), 7-1 vote; and a mobile motor home, *California v. Carney*, 471 U.S. 386 (1985), 6-3 vote.

• AIRPORT SEARCHES. In *United States v. Hartwell*, 436 F 3d 174 (3rd Cir 2006), Hartwell set off a metal detector at a security checkpoint in an airport. The Transportation Security Administration (TSA) agents then used a magnetic wand to pinpoint any metal on his person and detected a solid object in his pocket. When Hartwell refused to empty his pocket, the agent reached into the pocket and withdrew a package of crack cocaine. In denying the Fourth Amendment claim, the court held that the search and seizure was permissible under the consensual administrative search doctrine. Air passengers are given advance notice that the search will be conducted, and they can avoid the search by deciding not to board the aircraft.

• BORDER SEARCHES. In *United States v. Flores-Montano*, 541 U.S. 149 (2004), the Supreme Court held 9-0 that the Fourth Amendment does not require reasonable suspicion for custom officers to remove the gas tank from a vehicle entering the United States in order to check for contraband. The Court stated that the search was "justified by the Government's paramount interest in protecting the border." Also, under *United States v. Arnold*, 533 F 3d 1003 (9th Cir 2008), custom officers at the border may search any laptop computer or other electronic device randomly, without any suspicion, and without any First Amendment restrictions as to content.

• SOBRIETY CHECKPOINTS. In *Michigan Department of State Police v. Sitz*, 496 U.S. 444 (1990), the Supreme Court ruled 6-3 that a sobriety checkpoint program aimed at reducing drunk driving did not offend the Fourth Amendment. The Court found that the magnitude of the drunken driving problem justified the slight intrusion on motorists briefly stopped at the checkpoints.

• OTHER CHECKPOINTS. However, in *Delaware v. Prouse*, 440 U.S. 648 (1979), the Supreme Court held 8-1 that random spot checks of drivers' licenses and vehicle registrations, in the absence of traffic violations or suspicious conduct, violated the Fourth Amendment. Otherwise, drivers would be subject to "unfettered government intrusion." *City of Indianapolis v. Edmond*, 531 U.S. 32 (2000), involved the conduct of highway checkpoints to discover and interdict illegal narcotics without reasonable suspicion or probable cause. The Supreme Court ruled 6-3 that the primary purpose of these checkpoints was indistinguishable from the general interest in crime control, stating: "We cannot sanction stops justified only by the generalized and ever-present possibility that interrogation and inspection may reveal that any given motorist has committed some crime." 531 U.S. 44. Warrantless checkpoints must have a more specific purpose such as keeping roadways safe from impaired drivers or enforcing border security.

• STUDENT SEARCHES. In *New Jersey v. TLO*, 469 U.S. 325 (1985), TLO was a 14-year-old freshman who was accused of smoking in the bathroom in violation of high school regulations. A school official searched her purse and found a bag of marijuana and other drug paraphernalia. The Supreme Court ruled 6-3 that school officials may search without a warrant based upon a reasonable suspicion of a violation of disciplinary rules, which is a lower standard than that of probable cause. In *Safford Unified School District No. 1 v. Redding*, 557 U.S. ___ (2009), the Supreme Court ruled 8-1 that school officials violated the constitutional right to privacy of a 13-year-old student when they strip-searched her on suspicion that she was hiding relatively harmless ibuprofen in her underwear contrary to the school's policy for eradicating drug abuse. The school had reasonable suspicion for searching her backpack and outer clothing, but violated her Fourth Amendment protection against unreasonable search and seizure in the strip search without the threat of a clear danger to other students. However, the Court held 7-2 that school officials were not personally liable for damages for such a search because of qualified immunity.

• DRUG TESTING. In *Vernonia School District v. Acton*, 515 U.S. 646 (1995), the Supreme Court upheld 6-3 the random urinalysis drug testing of student athletes who are under state supervision during school hours and subject to greater control than non-student adults. Government concern over the safety of minors under its supervision overrides the minimal intrusion in their privacy. The Court reached a similar result in *Board of Education v. Earls*, 536 U.S. 822 (2002), upholding 5-4 urinalysis drug testing for all students who participate in competitive extracurricular activities. However, in *Chandler v. Miller*, 520 U.S. 305 (1997), the Supreme Court invalidated 8-1 a Georgia statute requiring all candidates for elected state office to pass a urinalysis drug test. The Court found that the state failed to show why its desire to avoid drug users in state office should outweigh the candidates' privacy rights.

• PAROLEE SEARCHES. In *Samson v. California*, 547 U.S. 843 (2006), the Supreme Court upheld 6-3 the warrantless search of a person subject to a parole search condition where there was no suspicion of criminal wrongdoing. Parole allows convicted criminals to leave prison before their sentence is completed; therefore, parolees remain in legal custody with significantly reduced privacy rights.

• PRISON SEARCHES. In *Hudson v. Palmer*, 468 U.S. 517 (1984), the Supreme Court held 5-4 that prison inmates do not have a right of privacy in their prison cells that would entitle them to Fourth Amendment protection against unreasonable searches.

• SOCIAL SERVICE HOME VISITATIONS. In *Wyman v. James*, 400 U.S. 309 (1971), the Supreme Court held 6-3 that, under a voluntary state program to aid families with dependent children, home visitations by caseworkers to determine compliance with the law are a reasonable administrative tool and are not searches in the traditional criminal law context of the Fourth Amendment.

• REGULATORY SEARCHES. In *Donovan v. Dewey*, 452 U.S. 594 (1981), the Supreme Court upheld 8-1 warrantless searches of mines by federal inspectors under the Federal Mine Safety and Health Act of 1977 because Congress has reasonably determined that a system of warrantless inspections is necessary to further a regulatory scheme to improve the health and safety conditions of mines. Similarly, the Supreme Court in *United States v. Biswell*, 406 U.S. 311 (1972), upheld 8-1 warrantless searches of the premises of federally licensed gun dealers under the Federal Gun Control Act of 1968.

• SPECIAL GOVERNMENT NEEDS. In *Skinner v. Railway Labor Executives Association*, 489 U.S. 602 (1989), the Federal Railroad Administration had adopted regulations requiring blood and urine tests of railroad employees involved in major train accidents, and breath and urine tests of employees involved in safety rule violations. The Supreme Court upheld 7-2 the regulations because the government's interest in ensuring safety presented a "special need" that made the program reasonable, thereby eliminating the constitutional requirements of a warrant, probable cause and suspicion of individual wrongdoing. The doctrine of special needs justifies the random drug testing of public employees in safety sensitive positions. In *National Treasury Employees Union v. Von Raab*, 489 U.S. 656 (1989), the Court upheld 5-4 the drug testing program of the U.S. Customs Service for employees involved in drug interdiction, carrying firearms, or having access to classified information. The Court reasoned that such employees have a "diminished expectation of privacy," and that the government has a compelling interest in their "fitness and probity."

• EXIGENT CIRCUMSTANCES. This doctrine applies in emergency situations requiring swift action. Police are allowed to enter a structure without a warrant to prevent imminent danger to life or serious property damage, or to forestall the imminent escape of a suspect or the destruction or removal of evidence. *Michigan v. Tyler*, 436 U.S. 499, 509 (1978); *Brigham City v. Stuart*, 547 U.S. 398 (2006), 9-0 vote.

The *"exclusionary rule"* has been adopted by the courts as a means to enforce the rights guaranteed by the Fourth Amendment. The rule was announced in *Weeks v. United States*, 232 U.S. 383 (1914), when the Supreme Court held 9-0 that the warrantless seizure of documents from a private home violated the Fourth Amendment and that evidence obtained thereby must be excluded from use in criminal trials. In *Silverthorne Lumber Co. v. United States*, 251 U.S. 385 (1920), federal agents seeking evidence of tax evasion conducted a warrantless search of the lumber company and seized its books. The books were subsequently returned because of the illegal search. In the trial, the prosecution produced photocopies of the books which resulted in the conviction of Silverthorne. The Supreme Court 7-2 overturned the conviction under the "fruit of the poisonous tree doctrine," ruling that evidence derived from that obtained in illegal seizures cannot be used by the prosecution. The doctrine was again applied in *Nardone v. United States*, 308 U.S. 338 (1939), where the Supreme Court held 7-2 that evidence procured by illicit wiretaps is inadmissible, which applies not only to the intercepted conversations themselves, but also to the evidence procured through the knowledge gained from such conversations. In *Mapp v. Ohio*, 367 U.S. 643 (1961), the Supreme Court held 6-3 that evidence of possessing obscene materials, discovered in a warrantless search of Mapp's home, must be excluded in her trial. In *Kaupp v. Texas*, 538 U.S. 626 (2003), the Supreme Court held 9-0 that a confession "obtained by exploitation of an illegal arrest" may not be used against a criminal defendant.

Exceptions to the exclusionary rule have been recognized. In *Nix v. Williams*, 467 U.S. 431 (1984), the Supreme Court applied the "inevitable discovery doctrine" as an exception to the exclusionary rule by holding 7-2 that unlawfully obtained evidence is admissible if it would inevitably have been discovered lawfully. In *United States v. Leon*, 468 U.S. 897 (1984), the Supreme Court created the "good faith" exception to the rule by holding 6-3 that evidence obtained in good faith by police relying on a search warrant subsequently found to be deficient may be used in a criminal trial. The purpose of the exclusionary rule is not to provide a right to the defendant, but to deter illegal police conduct. The "good faith" exception was extended by the Supreme Court in *Illinois v. Krull*, 480 U.S. 340 (1987), holding 5-4 that it covered searches conducted in good faith reliance on a state statute later determined to be invalid; and in *Arizona v. Evans*, 514 U.S. 1 (1995), holding 6-3 that it covered evidence obtained by good faith reliance on a warrant that contained a clerical error. In *Hudson v. Michigan*, 547 U.S. 586 (2006), the Supreme Court held 5-4 that the failure of police to abide by the "knock and announce" rule, by abruptly entering a private residence with a warrant, does not require exclusion of the evidence obtained in the ensuing search. The purpose of the rule is to provide notice and prevent violence and property damage, and not to prevent police from conducting a search covered by the warrant.

Amendment V
The Five Rights of Grand Jury, Protection from Double Jeopardy, Protection from Self-Incrimination, Due Process, and Just Compensation

Ratified December 15, 1791

No person shall be held to answer for a capital, or otherwise infamous crime, unless on a presentment or indictment of a Grand Jury, except in cases arising in the land or naval forces, or in the Militia, when in actual service in time of War or public danger; nor shall any person be subject for the same offence to be twice put in jeopardy of life or limb; nor shall be compelled in any criminal case to be a witness against himself, nor be deprived of life, liberty, or property, without due process of law; nor shall private property be taken for public use, without just compensation.

GRAND JURY CLAUSE

Under this requirement for grand jury presentment or indictment, a capital crime is one that may be punishable by death. Like a capital crime, an "infamous" crime depends upon its punishment rather than the character of the criminal act. The courts have ruled that any crime that may be punished by more than one year of imprisonment in a penitentiary or at hard labor is an infamous crime. *Green v. United States*, 356 U.S. 165, 183 (1958); *United States v. Russell*, 585 F 2d 368, 370 (8th Cir 1978). Since all federal felonies are subject to such punishment they are infamous crimes. A defendant may waive his right to be indicted by a grand jury in non-capital cases. *Smith v. United States*, 360 U.S. 1 at 9 (1959).

A grand jury, composed of an impartial panel of ordinary citizens, determines whether there is sufficient evidence ("probable cause" instead of "beyond reasonable doubt") for a criminal trial. Instead of a judge presiding, a prosecutor leads the proceeding. A grand jury examines the evidence presented to it by a prosecutor and issues indictments, or investigates alleged crimes and issues presentments independent of a prosecutor. A grand jury, usually 23 members, is traditionally larger than a petit jury, usually 6 to 12 members, which is used during a trial to determine the guilt or innocence of a defendant. In the case of a federal grand jury with 23 members, 16 constitute a quorum for the transaction of business, and 12 must vote in favor of issuing an indictment. Grand jurors are typically drawn from the same pool of citizens as a petit jury, and serve for a specific term, usually considering several different cases during the term. The selection of grand jury members must be on a racially non-discriminatory basis. *Alexander v. Louisiana*, 405 U.S. 625 (1972). Government cannot, consistent with due process, subject an accused to indictment by a grand jury that has been selected in an arbitrary and discriminatory manner contrary to constitutional and statutory requirements, and regardless of any showing of actual bias. *Peters v. Kiff*, 407 U.S. 493 (1972).

The grand jury requirement is intended as an independent check on the authority of a prosecutor by preventing a case from going to trial on his word alone. A prosecutor must convince the grand jury that there exists sufficient evidence to prove the commission of a crime. The grand jury deliberates in secret. *United States v. Procter & Gamble Co.*, 356 U.S. 677 (1958). It is an institution separate from the courts, over whose functioning the courts do not preside. The grand jury has broad subpoena power to summon witnesses and documents, and the accused and his counsel are generally not present for the testimony of other witnesses. Unlike petit jurors, who sit quietly during the trial, grand jurors are allowed to directly question witnesses. In *Costello v. United States*, 350 U.S. 359 (1956), the Supreme Court ruled 7-0 that a grand jury may rely on hearsay evidence in issuing an indictment even though such evidence would not be admissible in a later trial. And in *United States v. Williams*, 504 U.S. 36 (1992), the Supreme Court ruled 5-4 that a trial court may not dismiss an otherwise valid indictment because the government failed to disclose to the grand jury "substantial exculpatory evidence" in its possession. The Court reasoned that "requiring the prosecutor to present exculpatory as well as inculpatory evidence would alter the grand jury's historical role, transforming it from an accusatory body that sits to assess whether there is adequate basis for bringing a criminal charge into an adjudicatory body that sits to determine guilt or innocence."

In *Hurtado v. California*, 110 U.S. 516 (1884), Hurtado had been convicted in state court of murdering his wife's paramour, based upon the pre-trial examination of evidence by a magistrate and not by grand jury indictment. The Supreme Court ruled 8-1 that Hurtado's due process right under the Fourteenth Amendment was not violated by denial of a grand jury hearing in a state criminal trial, and that the grand jury requirement of the Fifth Amendment was not incorporated under the Fourteenth Amendment as applicable to the states as were many other provisions of the Bill of Rights. Accordingly, many states have replaced the grand jury indictment with a preliminary hearing where the prosecutor and accused present their evidence to a judge who determines if a sufficient case has been presented to go to trial.

With respect to the military exception to the grand jury requirement, the Supreme Court ruled 7-2 in *Burns v. Wilson*, 346 U.S. 137, at 142 (1953), that military courts have the same responsibilities as federal civil courts in protecting a person from a violation of his constitutional rights. Although the Uniform Code of Military Justice provides that determinations of military tribunals, after all military remedies have been exhausted, are final and binding on all courts, this does not displace civil courts' jurisdiction over an application for habeas corpus from the military prisoner.

DOUBLE JEOPARDY CLAUSE

The clause providing that no person shall "be subject for the same offence to be twice put in jeopardy of life or limb" protects against being retried for the same crime after an acquittal or conviction, and against multiple punishments for the same offense. A mistrial or a "hung jury" does not bar a new trial. *Richardson v. United States*, 468 U.S. 317 (1984). Also, retrials, following reversal of convictions on appeal, are not generally barred. The "jeopardy of life or limb" is not read literally, but is interpreted to apply to any person charged with any criminal penalty, whether felony or misdemeanor, punishable with death, imprisonment or fine.

As to what constitutes separate offenses, the Supreme Court in *Blockburger v. United States*, 284 U.S. 299 (1932), held 9-0 that two sales of morphine in or from the original stamped package, the second having been initiated after the first was completed, were separate and distinct offenses under the Harrison Narcotics Tax Act, although the buyer and seller were the same in both cases and but little time had elapsed between the two transactions. In *Gavieres v. United States*, 220 U.S. 338 (1911), the Court held 8-1 that a person convicted and punished under one ordinance prohibiting drunkenness and rude and boisterous language was not put in second jeopardy by being subsequently tried under another ordinance for insulting a public officer, although the latter charge was based on the same conduct and language as the former. They were separate offenses, and required separate proof to convict.

The following decisions illustrate the application of the Double Jeopardy Clause.

1. In *North Carolina v. Pearce*, 395 U.S. 711 (1969), involving retrial and resentencing after the original conviction was set aside for error, the Supreme Court held 7-2 that the guarantee against double jeopardy does not prevent a more severe sentence upon reconviction when justified by the

record. Any punishment already exacted for an offense, such as time-served, must be credited in imposing a new sentence for the same offense.

2. In *Ashe v. Swenson*, 397 U.S. 436 (1970), involving three or four men robbing six poker players, Ashe was separately charged with robbing one of the players, and was acquitted. In a second state prosecution for robbing another player, the Supreme Court held 7-1 that the Double Jeopardy Clause prevents the state from rc-litigating a question already decided in favor of Ashe at the previous trial on the same robbery. The same result was reached in *Harris v. Washington*, 404 U.S. 55 (1971), involving the explosion of a mail bomb that killed a man and his infant son and injured his wife. Following the acquittal of the defendant in the previous trial for the man's death, the Supreme Court ruled 7-2 that a second trial, prosecuting the defendant for the death of the man's son and injury of his wife, was barred because it would require re-litigation of the same ultimate fact.

3. In *Price v. Georgia*, 398 U.S. 323 (1970), Price was tried for murder, but was found guilty of the lesser included offense of voluntary manslaughter. Following reversal of that conviction on appeal, the Supreme Court ruled 8-0 that under the Double Jeopardy Clause Price could be retried for voluntary manslaughter, but not for murder, of which he had been implicitly acquitted when the jury returned a verdict on the lesser included offense of voluntary manslaughter.

4. In *Breed v. Jones*, 421 U.S. 519 (1975), the Supreme Court held 9-0 that the prosecution of a juvenile in adult court, after an adjudicatory finding in juvenile court that he had violated a criminal law, violated the Double Jeopardy Clause. Although he never faced the risk of more than one punishment, the clause applies to potential or risk of trial and conviction, not punishment.

5. In *Brown v. Ohio*, 432 U.S. 161 (1977), the Supreme Court held 6-3 that the Double Jeopardy Clause barred prosecution for the crime of stealing an automobile following prosecution for the lesser included offense of operating the same vehicle without the owner's consent. The same result was reached in *Thigpen v. Roberts*, 468 U.S. 27 (1984), where the Supreme Court held 6-3 that a manslaughter prosecution of Roberts was barred after he had been convicted earlier of four misdemeanor charges for the same automobile accident.

6. In *Missouri v. Hunter*, 459 U.S. 359 (1983), the Supreme Court held 7-2 that the Double Jeopardy Clause does not prohibit in a single trial multiple punishments for two crimes (robbery and armed criminal action) committed in the same event.

7. In *Smalis v. Pennsylvania*, 476 U.S. 140 (1986), the Supreme Court held 9-0 that the trial court's dismissal of a criminal action for insufficient evidence was an acquittal under the Double Jeopardy Clause that barred fur-

ther prosecution. The Supreme Court in *Crist v. Bretz*, 437 U.S. 28 (1978), ruled 6-3 that jeopardy attaches in a jury trial when the jury is empanelled and sworn.

8. In *Kansas v. Hendricks*, 521 U.S. 346 (1997), Kansas sought to commit Hendricks indefinitely for mental abnormality under its Sexually Violent Predator Act upon his release from prison for conviction for child sexual molestation. The Supreme Court, in rejecting Hendricks' claim of double jeopardy, held 5-4 that the involuntary civil commitment in a mental hospital was not punishment but a form of treatment.

Under the doctrine of *dual sovereignty*, the federal and state governments each have the independent sovereignty to punish for offenses against their laws on the basis of the same offense and evidence (*United States v. Lanza*, 260 U.S. 377 [1922], 9-0 vote), and one state may prosecute and punish a person for an act that he had already been convicted and sentenced for in another state (*Heath v. Alabama*, 474 U.S. 82 [1985], 7-2 vote). Conviction by a sovereign tribal court will not preclude prosecution in federal court for the same incident. *United States v. Wheeler*, 435 U.S. 313 (1978), 8-0 vote. However, the state and its local governments are not separate sovereign entities entitled to impose separate punishment for the same alleged crime. Therefore, a second trial in a state court for the identical offense for which a person was tried in a municipal court constitutes double jeopardy. *Waller v. Florida*, 397 U.S. 387 (1970), 9-0 vote.

The right against double jeopardy precludes only subsequent criminal prosecutions. It does not preclude civil proceedings against a person who has already been prosecuted for the same act or omission. Nor is prosecution barred by double jeopardy if it is preceded by a final civil determination on the same issue. Criminal and civil proceedings operate in separate spheres and the outcome of one does not control the other. A plaintiff's civil case may succeed based on "a preponderance of the evidence" standard, whereas a criminal prosecution for the same event may fail based on "beyond a reasonable doubt" standard. In civil cases, the rule of res judicata (a matter already judged, may not be raised again) is similar to that of double jeopardy, providing that a final judgment by a court of competent jurisdiction is conclusive upon the parties in any subsequent litigation involving the same cause of action.

Self-Incrimination Clause

The right against self-incrimination, known as "pleading the Fifth," forbids the government from compelling any person to give testimonial evidence that would likely incriminate him during a subsequent criminal case. As the Supreme Court ruled 9-0 in *Lefkowitz v. Turley*, 414 U.S. 70 (1973), the Fifth "Amendment not only protects the individual against being involuntarily called as a witness against himself in a criminal proceeding but also privileges him not to answer official questions put to him in any other proceeding, civil or criminal, formal or informal, where the answers might incriminate him in future criminal proceedings." Since the privilege against self-incrimination is for the benefit of the witness, he may not refuse to testify solely for the purpose of protecting another from punishment. *Rogers v. United States*, 340 U.S. 367 (1951). The right against self-incrimination may only be asserted by persons and does not protect artificial entities such as corporations. *Doe v. United States*, 487 U.S. 201 (1988).

The right against self-incrimination applies only to testimonial evidence, and does not prevent the defendant from having to produce physical evidence, for identification purposes, such as fingerprints, blood, tissue, DNA or hair samples, dental impressions, handwriting or voice exemplars, private papers and other physical evidence; or from being compelled to stand in a police lineup or to perform physical sobriety or breathalyzer tests. Nor does the right against self-incrimination permit a suspect to refuse to provide the police with booking information such as name, address and birthday. *Pennsylvania v. Muniz*, 496 U.S. 582 (1990), 8-1 vote. While the acquisition of such evidence does not constitute Fifth Amendment self-incrimination, it must comply with the Fourth Amendment search and seizure requirements.

In *Hiibel v. Sixth Judicial District Court of Nevada, Humboldt County*, 542 U.S. 177 (2004), the Supreme Court upheld 5-4 a state "stop-and-identify" law, requiring suspects to identify themselves during investigative stops by law enforcement officers, as not violating Hiibel's Fourth Amendment rights or the Fifth Amendment prohibition on self-incrimination. Here there was a minimal intrusion on his privacy, and a legitimate need for officers to investigate criminal activity. "Answering a request to disclose a name is likely to be so insignificant in the scheme of things as to be incriminating only in unusual circumstances." 542 U.S. 191.

The right against self-incrimination may be voluntarily waived when freely and intelligently made. Confessions are inadmissible when obtained by police torture (*Brown v. Mississippi*, 297 U.S. 278 [1936], 9-0 vote); after five days of prolonged police questioning with the defendant held incommunicado (*Chambers v. Florida*, 309 U.S. 227, 237 [1940], 9-0 vote: "The rack, the thumbscrew, the wheel, solitary confinement, protracted questioning and cross questioning, and other ingenious forms of entrapment of the helpless or unpopular had left their wake of mutilated bodies and shattered minds along the way to the cross, the guillotine, the stake and the hangman's noose"); by 36 hours of continuous police questioning under electric lights (*Ashcraft v. Tennessee*, 322 U.S. 143 [1944], 6-3 vote); under the influence of a truth serum (*Townsend v. Sain*, 372 U.S. 293 [1963], 6-3 vote); and by 16 hours of police questioning with the defendant held incommunicado (*Haynes v. Washington*, 373 U.S. 503 [1963], 5-4 vote).

Coerced or compelled confessions also may be shown by economic pressures such as threatened loss of jobs or contracts. A guilty plea must be voluntarily and understandingly entered into after the defendant has been informed of his constitutional rights. *Boykin v. Alabama*, 395 U.S. 238 (1969), 6-2 vote. The prosecution may not infer guilt from the silence of the defendant in a criminal trial. *Griffin v. California*, 380 U.S. 609 (1965), 7-2 vote. A criminal defendant who elects to testify waives the right with respect to questions asked on cross-examination that are related to the direct examination. *Jenkins v. Anderson*, 447 U.S. 231 (1980), 7-2 vote.

In *Miranda v. Arizona*, 384 U.S. 436 (1966), the Supreme Court ruled 5-4 that the privilege against self-incrimination requires law enforcement officers to advise a suspect interrogated in custody of his rights, which are typically stated as follows: "You have the right to remain silent. Anything you say can and will be used against you in a court of law. You have the right to have an attorney present during questioning. If you cannot afford an attorney, one will be appointed for you." (In the jargon of law enforcement, a suspect thus advised has been "Mirandized.") Although this warning is widely heard in movies and on television, the Court did not specify the exact wording to be used when informing a suspect of his rights. While the rights do not have to be read in any particular order, and there are variations in the wording used by law enforcement agencies, the rights must be adequately and fully conveyed to the suspect in custody. *California v. Prysock*, 453 U.S. 355 (1981). Any statements made by a defendant prior to receiving the *Miranda* warning are inadmissible, and any evidence derived solely from such statements are also inadmissible under the "fruit of the poisonous tree" doctrine. Of course, other evidence may be used by the prosecution.

Prior to *Miranda*, the Supreme Court had held that indigent criminal defendants have a right to be provided counsel at trial (*Gideon v. Wainwright*, 372 U.S. 335 [1963], 9-0 vote); and that criminal suspects have a right to an attorney during police interrogations (*Escobedo v. Illinois*, 378 U.S. 478 [1964], 5-4 vote).

For *Miranda* to apply, the evidence must have been obtained while the suspect was in custody, which means either that the suspect was under arrest or that his freedom of movement was restrained to an extent "associated with a formal arrest." *New York v. Quarles*, 467 U.S. 649, 655 (1984).

In *Edwards v. Arizona*, 451 U.S. 477 (1981), Edwards was arrested on a state criminal charge and Mirandized; police questioning ended when he requested an attorney. The next day police visited him in jail, again Mirandized him, questioned him without counsel present, and obtained his confession. The Supreme Court held 9-0 that the confession was inadmissible for suspicion of coercion. When an accused has invoked his right to have counsel present during custodial interrogation, a valid waiver of that right cannot be established by showing only that he responded to police-initiated interrogation after being advised of his rights. In *Maryland v. Shatzer*, 559 U.S. ___ (2010), the Court held 9-0 that an initial request for counsel does not mean that police can never reinitiate questioning, provided that the suspect has been released from custody at least 14 days in the meantime. "That provides plenty of time for the suspect to get reacclimated to his normal life, to consult with friends and counsel, and to shake off any residual coercive effects of his prior custody." In other words, a suspect may be arrested, Mirandized, and provided counsel at his request. If he is released from custody, he may be rearrested after 14 days, Mirandized again, and if he does not invoke his right to counsel, it is deemed waived during police questioning.

Miranda has been limited in several cases:

1. In *Harris v. New York*, 401 U.S. 222 (1971), the Supreme Court held 5-4 that a defendant's statements made prior to the *Miranda* warning, and hence inadmissible in the prosecution's direct case, may be used to attack his credibility on the witness stand when he changes his statements. A defendant has the privilege to testify in his own defense, but that does not include the right to commit perjury.

2. In *Beckwith v. United States*, 425 U.S. 341 (1976), the Supreme Court held 7-1 that statements made by the petitioner taxpayer to Internal Revenue agents in his home during a noncustodial interview in a criminal tax investigation were admissible against him in the ensuing prosecution even though he was not given his *Miranda* warning. The taxpayer interview was not the equivalent of that required by *Miranda* for "questioning initiated by law enforcement officers after a person has been taken into custody or otherwise deprived of his freedom of action in any significant way." 425 U.S. 347.

3. In *Rhode Island v. Innis*, 446 U.S. 291 (1980), Innis was arrested as a suspect in an armed robbery and advised of his *Miranda* rights, after which he requested to speak with a lawyer. While escorting him in an automobile to the police station, two police officers discussed the need to find the shotgun used in the robbery because children in the area might find it and injure themselves. Innis interrupted the conversation, and led them to where the shotgun was hidden. The Supreme Court held 6-3 that the conversation between the two police officers within the presence of Innis did not constitute an interrogation in violation of his *Miranda* rights.

4. In *New York v. Quarles*, 467 U.S. 649 (1984), a police officer, after

receiving the description of Quarles as an alleged assailant, stopped and frisked him, found an empty shoulder holster, and asked Quarles where the gun was. Upon acquiring the gun, the police officer arrested Quarles and read him his *Miranda* warning. The Supreme Court held 5-4 that there is a "public safety" exception to the *Miranda* requirement because here there was an immediate need to locate the gun for the safety of the officers and other bystanders.

5. In *Illinois v. Perkins*, 496 U.S. 292 (1990), the Supreme Court held 8-1 that a *Miranda* warning is not required when a jailed suspect has freely confessed to committing a murder to a police officer posing as an inmate. Such a confession was not done in a "police-dominated atmosphere" where compulsion to confess is present. "It is the premise of *Miranda* that the danger of coercion results from the interaction of custody and official interrogation."

In 1968, Congress enacted a law that purported to overrule *Miranda* by directing federal trial judges to admit statements of criminal defendants if made voluntarily, without regard as to whether they had received *Miranda* warnings. In *Dickerson v. United States*, 530 U.S. 428 (2000), the Supreme Court struck down the law, holding 7-2 that *Miranda* announced a constitutional rule that Congress may not supersede legislatively.

Self-incriminating evidence may be compelled by the government granting the witness "transactional immunity" or "use immunity," and if such immunity is refused, the witness may be punished by being held in contempt. Transactional immunity bars any subsequent action against the immunized person relating to his testimony, regardless of the source of the evidence against that person. This kind of immunity is much like a full pardon for the offense; once it is granted, one may not be prosecuted. Use immunity protects the witness only against the government's use of his immunized testimony in a prosecution against him. A witness with use immunity may still be prosecuted, but only based on evidence not derived from the protected testimony. *United States v. Harvey*, 900 F 2d 1253, 1257 (8th Cir 1990). An immunized witness may not refuse to testify because of personal humiliation or public opprobrium. *Ullman v. United States*, 350 U.S. 422, 430 (1956), 7-2 vote.

Although the federal and state governments are separate sovereigns, a witness granted immunity from prosecution under the law of one sovereign may not be compelled to give testimony on the same subject which may incriminate him under the law of the other sovereign. *Murphy v. Waterfront Commission*, 378 U.S. 52 (1964), 9-0 vote.

DUE PROCESS CLAUSE

The Fifth Amendment (applicable to the federal government), like the Fourteenth Amendment (applicable to state government), provides that no person shall be deprived of life, liberty or property without due process of law. The bulk of the case law on this subject is developed under the Due Process Clause of the Fourteenth Amendment.

Due process is divided into procedural and substantive categories. Procedural due process requires the application of fair methods for obtaining rights under the law. Daniel Webster defined the procedure as "a law, which hears before it condemns; which proceeds upon inquiry, and renders judgment only after trial." *Dartmouth College v. Woodward*, 17 U.S. 518, 581 (1819). Substantive due process requires that the content of the law must be free from arbitrary and unjust provisions.

In *Snyder v. Massachusetts*, 291 U.S. 97, 105 (1934), the Supreme Court ruled that procedural due process is violated if it "offends some principle of justice so rooted in the traditions and conscience of our people as to be ranked as fundamental." In his dissent in *Snyder*, Associate Justice Owen Roberts further elaborated on this doctrine by stating at 137: "Procedural due process has to do with the manner of the trial; dictates that, in the conduct of judicial inquiry certain fundamental rules of fairness be observed; forbids the disregard of those rules; and is not satisfied, though the result is just, if the hearing was unfair."

In *Brady v. United States*, 397 U.S. 742 (1970), the petitioner pleaded not guilty to kidnapping, but switched his plea to guilty for a lesser sentence when his codefendant confessed and planned to testify against him. The petitioner later claimed that his plea bargain was coerced. The Supreme Court held 8-0 that a guilty plea is not invalidated merely because it was entered to avoid the death penalty where, as here, the plea was made voluntarily and upon the advice of competent counsel.

In *Mathews v. Eldridge*, 424 U.S. 319 (1976), the Social Security Administration terminated Eldridge's disability benefits after notice, but without an evidentiary hearing for him to argue for the continuation of the benefits. He sued for a violation of his due process rights under the Fifth Amendment, although he had not exhausted his post-termination administrative remedies. The Supreme Court held 6-2 that the termination of benefits without a hearing did not violate the Fifth Amendment because due process "is flexible and calls for such procedural protections as the particular situation demands." Here, there were numerous safeguards to prevent errors in making such termination decisions. "Requiring an evidentiary hearing upon demand in all cases prior to the termination of disability benefits would entail fiscal and administrative burdens out of proportion to any countervailing benefits."

With respect to substantive due process, the Supreme Court in *United States v. Carolene Products*, 304 U.S. 144 (1938), upheld 6-1 a federal law banning the interstate shipment of "filled milk" (skim milk with vegetable oils added as a substitute for butter fat) as essentially a legislative judgment and in accord with congressional authority under the Commerce Clause (Article I, Section 8, Clause 3) and Due Process under the Fifth Amendment. Associate Justice Harlan Fiske Stone, in footnote four of the majority opinion, applied minimal scrutiny to the economic regulation in this case (rational basis test), but suggested strict scrutiny for legislation that violates specifically enumerated constitutional rights or makes it more difficult to achieve change through normal political processes, or is aimed at "discrete and insular minorities," who lack the usual protections of the political process. This rationale has greatly influenced equal protection jurisprudence under the Fourteenth Amendment.

In *Hirabayashi v. United States*, 320 U.S. 81 (1943), the Supreme Court upheld 9-0 congressionally ratified presidential executive orders authorizing the curfew and exclusion of Japanese Americans from "military areas" on the West Coast following the Japanese attack on Pearl Harbor. Although the Court recognized that racial discrimination was usually unconstitutional, it deferred, in the urgency of war, to the judgment of military authorities that such action was necessary for national security. In *Korematsu v. United States*, 323 U.S. 214 (1944), the Supreme Court again upheld (although this time 6-3) the constitutionality of the exclusion order authorizing the internment of Japanese Americans.

In *Federal Power Commission v. Hope Natural Gas Company*, 320 U.S. 591 (1944), the Supreme Court upheld 5-3 the broad power of regulatory agencies to choose appropriate methods to evaluate property for ratemaking purposes under the Natural Gas Act of 1938. The "Commission was not bound to the use of any single formula or combination of formulae in determining rates.... If the total effect of the rate order cannot be said to be unjust and unreasonable, judicial inquiry under the Act is at an end." 320 U.S. 602. (In 1977, the Federal Power Commission [FPC] was renamed the Federal Energy Regulatory Commission [FERC]). The *Hope* case overruled *Smyth v. Ames*, 169 U.S. 466 (1898), in which the Supreme Court invalidated 9-0 railroad rates prescribed by Nebraska. The Court held that a regulated industry under the Due Process Clause of the Fourteenth Amendment was entitled to earn a "fair return" on the "fair value" of the property being used by it in serving the public ("rate base"). In *Hope*, the Court decided that the *Smyth* ratemaking formula was unduly burdensome for administrative proceedings.

The Supreme Court in *Bolling v. Sharpe*, 347 U.S. 497 (1954), ruled 9-0 that racial segregation in the public schools of the District of Columbia denied blacks due process of law as guaranteed by the Fifth Amendment. In the companion case of *Brown v. Board of Education of Topeka*, 347 U.S. 483 (1954), the Court ruled 9-0 that state laws establishing separate public schools for black and white students denied black students equal protection of the law as guaranteed by the Fourteenth Amendment. In *Bolling*, the Court recognized that, while the Fifth Amendment did not contain an equal protection clause like the Fourteenth Amendment, "the concepts of equal protection and due process, both stemming from our American ideal of fairness, are not mutually exclusive." In effect, the Court made a "reverse incorporation" of the equal protection clause of the Fourteenth Amendment into the Fifth Amendment. The equal protection component of the Fifth Amendment's Due Process Clause was applied by the Court in *Washington v. Davis*, 426 U.S. 229 (1976), holding 7-2 that personnel tests administered to two black applicants for employment by the D.C. police department were not racially discriminatory because, although they may have had a racially disproportionate impact, the applicants failed to prove a racially discriminatory motivation on the part of the police department. Also, in *Rostker v. Goldberg*, 453 U.S. 57 (1981), the Court held 6-3 that the exemption of females from registration under the Military Selective Service Act does not violate the equal protection principle contained in the Fifth Amendment's Due Process Clause.

In *Federal Communications Commission v. Beach Communications, Inc.*, 508 U.S. 307 (1993), involving a dispute over the classification of satellite master antenna television systems for regulatory purposes, the Supreme Court upheld the FCC 9-0, ruling that, in areas of social and economic policy, a statutory classification that neither proceeds along suspect lines nor infringes fundamental constitutional rights must be upheld against an equal protection challenge under the Fifth Amendment's Due Process Clause if any reasonable conceivable state of facts could provide a rational basis for the classification.

In *Sell v. United States*, 539 U.S. 166 (2003), the Supreme Court upheld 6-3 the authority of the Federal Government to administer antipsychotic drugs to a mentally ill defendant, against his will, to render him competent to stand trial on serious criminal charges if the treatment is medically appropriate, is substantially unlikely to produce side effects that may undermine the trial's fairness, and, in the absence of less intrusive alternatives, is necessary to further important governmental trial-related interests.

JUST COMPENSATION OR TAKINGS CLAUSE

The clause defines the government's power of eminent domain by providing that private property shall not be taken for public use without the payment of just compensation. The courts have shown substantial deference to legislative determinations as to what constitutes "public use."

In *Kelo v. City of New London*, 545 U.S. 469 (2005), the City established a private entity economic development corporation to act as the City's agent to acquire by eminent domain the residential properties of Kelo and others to redevelop an economically depressed neighborhood in order to encourage new economic activities to increase the City's tax base and job growth. Kelo contended that the City had misused its eminent domain power because the transfer of residential property to a private corporation did not qualify as a public use. On appeal, the Supreme Court ruled 5-4 in favor of the City, finding it was appropriate to defer to the City's decision that the development plan has a public purpose, saying that the "City has carefully formulated an economic development plan that it believes will provide appreciable benefits to the community, including—but by no means limited to—new jobs and increased tax revenue." 545 U.S. 483. The Court also held that the Fifth Amendment does not require "literal" public use, but the "broader and more natural interpretation of public use as 'public purpose.'" 545 U.S. 480. *Kelo* followed *Berman v. Parker*, 348 U.S. 26 (1954), which held 8-0 that the condemnation of blighted property for economic redevelopment is a public purpose and may be taken with the payment of just compensation.

Governments that are dissatisfied with the *Kelo* decision may avoid its consequences by prohibiting the exercise of eminent domain powers for economic development purposes.

In *Hawaii Housing Authority v. Midkiff*, 467 U.S. 229 (1984), the Hawaii legislature, having determined that the state and federal governments owned nearly 49 percent of the land in the state and that another 47 percent was owned by 72 private parties, concluded that this concentration of land ownership was "skewing the State's residential fee simple market, inflating land prices, and injuring the public tranquility and welfare." Accordingly, the legislature adopted the Land Reform Act of 1967 to provide a method of redistribution in which title in land could be transferred from lessors to lessees with just compensation. On appeal, the Supreme Court upheld 8-0 the redistribution as a rational approach to correcting a market failure and satisfying the public use doctrine. Land did not have to be put into actual public use in order to use eminent domain because here the taking's purpose was to provide an overall market benefit to the public.

While courts have upheld zoning and historic preservation laws that regulate property without compensation, the Supreme Court in *Lucas v. South Carolina Coastal Council*, 505 U.S. 1003 (1992), held 6-2 that a state construction ban that deprived Lucas of all economically beneficial use of his property amounted to a "taking" requiring "just compensation." Lucas had purchased beachfront residential lots on a barrier island for the construction of single-family homes, and the state subsequently banned the construction of permanent habitable structures on such land to protect erosion and destruction of barrier islands. The doctrine of regulatory taking was announced earlier in *Pennsylvania Coal Co. v. Mahon*, 260 U.S. 393 (1922), where the Supreme Court held 8-1 that a state law restricting coal mining to avoid subsidence amounted to the taking of a coal company's preexisting right to mine an underground stratum of coal.

Similarly, the following "takings" were found to require just compensation: installation of military firing range causing noise disruption of land owner, *Portsmouth Harbor Land & Hotel Co. v. United States*, 260 U.S. 327 (1922); air traffic destruction of farmer's use of chicken farm, *United States v. Causby*, 328 U.S. 256 (1946), 7-2 vote; destruction of the value of liens by government's acquisition of uncompleted boats due to shipbuilder's default, *Armstrong v. United States*, 364 U.S. 40 (1960), 6-3 vote; land-use regulation temporally denying owner use of property, *First Lutheran Church v. Los Angeles County*, 482 U.S. 304 (1987), 6-3 vote; owners of beachfront property seeking building permit required to maintain a pathway on their property for public access, *Nollan v. California Coastal Commission*, 483 U.S. 825 (1987), 5-4 vote; and owner seeking a permit to expand her store and pave her parking lot required to dedicate part of her land for a greenway along nearby creek to alleviate runoff from the pavement and a pedestrian/bicycle path to relieve traffic congestion, *Dolan v. City of Tigard*, 512 U.S. 374 (1994), 5-4 vote. For the government to win it must show an "essential nexus" between a legitimate government interest and the permit requirements.

In *Loretto v. Teleprompter Manhattan CATV Corp.*, 458 U.S. 419 (1982), Teleprompter placed television cables and transmission boxes on Loretto's apartment building pursuant to a state law requiring property owners to permit the installation and maintenance of such equipment on their property. The Supreme Court held 6-3 that the application of the law constituted a "regulatory taking," requiring compensation, because of the permanent physical occupation of property, regardless of whether the action achieves an important public benefit or has a minimal economic impact on the owner.

In *Penn Central Transportation Co. v. New York City*, 438 U.S. 104 (1978), the New York City Landmarks Law was enacted in 1965 to protect culturally significant structures following the demolition of the Pennsylvania Station in 1963. The City denied the proposal of Penn Central to build a 50-plus story office building over Grand Central Terminal (1913). Penn Central sued, contending that the denial was a "regulatory taking" and that it was entitled to "just compensation" under the Fifth and Fourteenth Amendments. The Supreme Court held 6-3 that the City's denial was a reasonable restriction substantially related to the municipal general welfare. The denial does not interfere with Penn Central's present uses of the terminal and continuance to profit from its investment therein.

In *Tahoe-Sierra Preservation Council, Inc. v. Tahoe Regional Planning*

Agency, 535 U.S. 302 (2002), the Supreme Court held 6-3 that moratoria on development imposed during the process of devising a comprehensive land-use plan does not constitute a per se ("by itself") taking of landowners' property requiring compensation under the Takings Clause.

In *Bennis v. Michigan*, 516 U.S. 442 (1996), Bennis was a joint owner, with her husband, of an automobile in which her husband engaged in sexual activity with a prostitute. The automobile was forfeited as a public nuisance under the state statutory abatement scheme. On appeal, the Supreme Court held 5-4 that the forfeiture did not violate the Takings Clause because Bennis' innocence or lack of knowledge concerning her husband's illegal use of the automobile could not serve as an "innocent owner" defense against its forfeiture. Similar issues are also addressed under the Excessive Fines Clause of the Eighth Amendment.

Amendment VI
Seven Rights of the Accused:
Criminal Court Procedures

Ratified December 15, 1791

In all criminal prosecutions, the accused shall enjoy the right to a speedy and public trial, by an impartial jury of the State and district wherein the crime shall have been committed, which district shall have been previously ascertained by law, and to be informed of the nature and cause of the accusation; to be confronted with the witnesses against him; to have compulsory process for obtaining witnesses in his favor, and to have the Assistance of Counsel for his defence.

1. SPEEDY TRIAL CLAUSE

This clause guarantees that the accused shall have the right to a speedy trial in criminal prosecutions. The Supreme Court stated in *Klopfer v. North Carolina*, 386 U.S. 213 (1967), "that the right to a speedy trial is as fundamental as any of the rights secured by the Sixth Amendment," and that the "right has its roots at the very foundation of our English law heritage," tracing it back to the Magna Carta (1215). In this case, Klopfer's trial for criminal trespass had ended in a mistrial when the jury failed to reach a verdict. After the case was postponed for two terms, the prosecutor was granted a nolle prosequi with leave, a procedural device whereby the accused is discharged from custody but remains subject to prosecution in the future at the discretion of the prosecutor. On appeal, the Supreme Court held 6-3 that, by indefinitely postponing the prosecution over Klopfer's objection and without stated justification, the state had denied him a speedy trial as guaranteed by the Sixth Amendment.

In *Barker v. Wingo*, 407 U.S. 514 (1972), the Supreme Court held 9-0 that determinations of whether or not the constitutional right to a speedy trial for defendants in criminal cases has been denied must be made on a case-by-case basis according to the conduct of the prosecution and the defense, weighing such factors as (1) the length of the delay, although no time limit was set; (2) the reason for the delay; (3) the defendant's timely assertion of rights (if the defendant has acquiesced in the delay for his benefit, he cannot later claim undue delay); and (4) the degree of prejudice to the defendant which the delay has caused. In *Strunk v. United States*, 412 U.S. 434 (1973), the Supreme Court held 9-0 that the dismissal of a criminal case on speedy trial grounds means that no further prosecution for the alleged offense can take place. The Court distinguished this result from the protection of other guarantees by observing that a "failure to afford a public trial, an impartial jury, notice of charges, or compulsory service can ordinarily be cured by providing those guaranteed rights in a new trial."

The Speedy Trial Act of 1974 generally requires that a federal criminal trial begin within 70 days of the filing of information or an indictment or the initial appearance of the defendant in court, but provides for a list of acceptable delays which do not count toward the 70-day period. If the trial does not begin on time, the defendant may move for dismissal, which the court must grant under most circumstances. The Supreme Court in *Zedner v. United States*, 547 U.S. 489 (2006), ruled 9-0 that a defendant cannot prospectively waive the protection of the Act, because its purpose is not only to protect his rights, but also to protect the public's interest in a speedy trial.

2. PUBLIC TRIAL CLAUSE

As the Supreme Court stated in *In re Oliver*, 333 U.S. 257, 270 (1948), the guarantee of a public trial "has always been recognized as a safeguard against any attempt to employ our courts as instruments of persecution. The knowledge that every criminal trial is subject to contemporaneous review in the forum of public opinion is an effective restraint on possible abuse of judicial power." The defendant's right to a public trial under the Sixth Amendment is related to the freedoms of speech and the press under the First Amendment.

In *Richmond Newspapers Inc. v. Virginia*, 448 U.S. 555 (1980), the judge, after a series of mistrials in a murder case, closed the trial to the public and the news media, at the request of defense counsel and without objection from the prosecution. On appeal, the Supreme Court ruled 7-1 that the right to attend criminal trials was implicit in the guarantees of the First Amendment, which encompasses not only the right to speak but also the freedom to listen and to receive information and ideas. In *Globe Newspaper Co. v. Superior Court*, 457 U.S. 596 (1982), the Court voided 6-3 a state law that required the public and the press to be excluded from the courtroom whenever a minor testifies about being the victim of a sexual attack. The judge should be permitted to initially determine if compelling circumstances require the closure. Also, in *Press-Enterprise Co. v. Superior Court*, 478 U.S. 1 (1986), the Court held 7-2 that the First Amendment right of access to criminal proceedings applies to preliminary hearings unless there is a "substantial probability" that the defendant will be prejudiced by publicity that closure would prevent.

However, in *Sheppard v. Maxwell*, 384 U.S. 333 (1966), Dr. Sam Sheppard, after his conviction of second-degree murder for the bludgeoning death of his pregnant wife, challenged the verdict as a denial of his constitutional right to a fair trial because of the trial judge's failure to protect him from the massive, pervasive and prejudicial publicity that attended his prosecution. On appeal, the Supreme Court held 8-1 that Sheppard had not received a fair trial because of the blatant and hostile coverage by the news media. Although freedom of expression should be given great latitude, it must not be so broad as to divert the trial from its primary purpose of adjudicating matters in an objective, calm and solemn courtroom setting. The Court concluded that the trial judge should have either postponed the case or transferred it to a different venue. (Many believe that the television series, *The Fugitive*, 1963-67, starring David Janssen, and the 1993 movie of the same name starring Harrison Ford and Tommy Lee Jones, were based on this murder case, but this has been denied by the creators.)

In *Rideau v. Louisiana*, 373 U.S. 723 (1963), the Supreme Court held 7-2 that it was a denial of due process of law for the trial judge to refuse the request for a change of venue after the people of the parish had been exposed repeatedly and in depth to the spectacle of Rideau confessing in detail to the crimes with which he was later to be charged. In *Groppi v. Wisconsin*, 400 U.S. 505 (1971), the Supreme Court held 8-1 that a change of venue even in a misdemeanor case may be required because of local prejudice against the defendant.

In *Chandler v. Florida*, 449 U.S. 560 (1981), involving the trial of two Miami Beach police officers for burglary, the Supreme Court upheld 8-0 the use of electronic media and still photography coverage of judicial proceedings, subject to the control of the presiding judge to protect the fundamental right of the accused in a criminal case to a fair trial.

Closure of a hearing to prevent the disclosure of sensitive information must meet the following tests: "the party seeking to close the hearing must advance an overriding interest that is likely to be prejudiced; the closure must be no broader than necessary to protect that interest; the trial court must consider reasonable alternatives to closing the hearing; and it must make findings adequate to support the closure." *Waller v. Georgia*, 467 U.S. 39 (1984), 9-0 vote.

3. JURY TRIAL CLAUSE

The right of trial by jury in criminal prosecutions is secured by this clause and also by Article III, Section 2, Clause 3, which provides for a jury in the trial of all crimes, except in cases of impeachment, and by the Seventh Amendment which provides for jury trials in common law cases. In a jury trial, the judge presides and rules on the law, and the jury determines the facts. Government cannot, consistent with due process, subject a defendant to trial by a jury that has been selected in an arbitrary and discriminatory manner contrary to constitutional and statutory requirements, and regardless of any showing of actual bias. *Peters v. Kiff*, 407 U.S. 493 (1972). Defendants are entitled to a jury in any trial in which the possible sentence is more than six months of imprisonment. *Baldwin v. New York*, 399 U.S. 66 (1970), 7-2 vote.

• JURY POOL. The first step in jury selection is the establishment of the jury pool (venire) composed of those persons from whom jurors are to be chosen for jury duty. Prospective jurors are usually drawn randomly from lists of registered voters, licensed drivers or other broad-based lists of residents in the community, or a combination of such lists, to compile a master jury list. As the Supreme Court held in *Taylor v. Louisiana*, 419 U.S. 522 (1975), juries must be selected from a representative cross-section of the community. Some classes of persons may be exempted from jury service such as government officials, lawyers, firefighters, police and others engaged in the criminal justice system. Courts may also excuse persons from jury service on grounds of medical or financial hardship or extreme inconvenience.

• VOIR DIRE. Next, prospective jurors for a particular trial are examined by the prosecution (or plaintiff in a civil case) and the defense, or sometimes by the trial judge, in a process known as *voir dire* to determine their competence and impartiality and, hence, their suitability to serve on the jury in the trial and render a verdict. General questions may be asked of the prospective jurors, answered by a show of hands, or individual questions may be asked by calling for a verbal answer. Challenges for cause may be used to exclude unsuitable jurors with the approval of the trial judge on grounds, such as knowing one of the parties or exhibiting prejudicial opinions. In a capital felony murder case, a prospective juror may be removed who is adamantly opposed to capital punishment. *Lockhart v. McCree*, 476 U.S. 162 (1986), 6-3 vote.

Also, the prosecution and the defense have a specific number of unconditional peremptory challenges to exclude jurors without stated justifications. However, in *Batson v. Kentucky*, 476 U.S. 79 (1986), the Supreme Court held 7-2 that a prosecutor's use of peremptory challenges to exclude four black prospective jurors from the trial of a black defendant, without stating a valid reason for doing so, violated the Equal Protection Clause of the Fourteenth Amendment. While a defendant has no right to a jury composed in whole or in part of persons of his own race, the Equal Protection Clause guarantees him that the state will not exclude members of his race from the jury venire on account of race. Later, the Supreme Court extended the *Batson* rule prohibiting race-based use of peremptory challenges to civil trials, *Edmonson v. Leesville Concrete Company*, 500 U.S. 614 (1991), 6–3 vote; and further extended the *Batson* rule to prohibit sex-based peremptory challenges, *J.E.B. v. Alabama ex rel. T.B.*, 511 U.S. 127 (1994), 6–3 vote.

• JURY DELIBERATIONS. Upon the completion of the *voir dire*, the jury for the trial is selected (impaneled). Often, alternate jurors are also selected to replace those that fail to complete the trial for ill health or other reasons. An alternate hears the case, but does not participate in deciding the verdict unless filling a vacancy on the jury. The trial judge must take care to see that the impartiality of jurors is not affected, before or during the trial, by extraneous sources such as the news media or contacts by friends or family. Parties, lawyers and witnesses are not allowed to speak with a juror. The participation of a juror tainted by partiality may constitute reversible error. In order to avoid undue influence, a jury may be sequestered (placed in seclusion) for its deliberations or for the entire trial. Also, jurors are forbidden to begin deliberations until all of the evidence has been introduced, the attorneys have made their closing arguments, and the judge has instructed the jury. Otherwise, premature deliberations could prejudice the verdict by jurors developing initial opinions that might not be altered by subsequent developments in the case.

• JURY NULLIFICATION. In general, the role of the jury is to decide issues of fact presented to it, and the role of the judge is to interpret the relevant law and instruct the jury accordingly, with the result that the jury renders its verdict in the case. However, as a practical matter, the jury may "nullify" the application of a law that it believes to be unjust, or unjustly applied, by refusing to find the defendant guilty, in spite of the evidence and the judge's instructions. Once a jury returns a verdict of "not guilty," the Double Jeopardy Clause of the Fifth Amendment prohibits a retrial on the same charge. Nonetheless, the Supreme Court ruled 5–4 in *Sparf v. United States*, 156 U.S. 51 (1895), that a trial judge has no responsibility to inform the jury of its power to nullify laws.

• ENHANCED PENALTY. In *Apprendi v. New Jersey*, 530 U.S. 466 (2000), the defendant, after firing several shots into the home of a black family, was convicted by the jury, on evidence proved beyond a reasonable doubt, of the crime of unlawful possession of a firearm which carried a prison term of 5–10 years. The trial judge, as authorized by the state hate-crime statute, imposed an enhanced sentence of 12 years after finding, by a preponderance of the evidence, that the crime was racially motivated. On appeal, the Supreme Court held 5–4 that the Sixth Amendment prohibited judges from enhancing criminal sentences beyond statutory maximums based on facts other than those decided by the jury. In *Ring v. Arizona*, 536 U.S. 584 (2002), the Supreme Court held 7–2 that a defendant has the right to have a jury, rather than a judge, decide on the existence of an aggravating factor that makes the defendant eligible for the death penalty. Following *Apprendi*, the Supreme Court in *Blakely v. Washington*, 542 U.S. 296 (2004), held 5–4 that facts increasing the penalty for a crime beyond the prescribed statutory maximum must be submitted to a jury and proved beyond a reasonable doubt. In *United States v. Booker*, 543 U.S. 220 (2005), the Supreme Court held 5–4 that *Blakely* applies to the federal sentencing guidelines and, therefore, all facts that increase a defendant's punishment beyond the guidelines' range must be proved to a jury beyond a reasonable doubt. The Court invalidated the mandatory features of the guidelines, and required the trial courts instead to focus on a broader range of factors in imposing sentences and appellate courts to review the reasonableness of the sentences. In *Gall v. United States*, 552 U.S. 38 (2007), the Supreme Court reiterated 7–2 that the Guidelines are advisory only, and that the federal courts may set any reasonable sentence as long as they explain their justification.

• JURY SIZE. The Supreme Court in *Patton v. United States*, 281 U.S. 276, 288 (1930), held 8–0 that trial by jury followed the precedent of the English common law that required a jury of 12 persons who must reach a unanimous verdict. However, in *Williams v. Florida*, 399 U.S. 78 (1970), the Supreme Court held 6–2 that six-member state criminal juries in noncapital cases were functionally equivalent to twelve-member juries, and did not violate the Sixth Amendment. The majority reasoned that a six-member jury is "large enough to promote group deliberation, free from outside attempts at intimidation, and to provide a fair possibility for obtaining a cross-section of the community." The Supreme Court reached the same conclusion in *Colgrove v. Battin*, 413 U.S. 149 (1973), which upheld 5–4 six-member juries in civil cases in federal courts. Conversely, the Court ruled 9–0 in *Ballew v. Georgia*, 435 U.S. 223 (1977), that a five-member jury was constitutionally inadequate because small juries foster poor group deliberation.

• NON-UNANIMOUS VOTE. Also, there is no Sixth Amendment right to a unanimous jury. In *Johnson v. Louisiana*, 406 U.S. 356 (1972), Johnson was convicted of armed robbery by a jury vote of 9–3. The Supreme Court held 5–4 that this non-unanimous vote did not violate the reasonable doubt standard of the Due Process Clause of the Fourteenth Amendment because a minority opposing the conviction does not prevent the other jurors from reaching their decisions beyond a reasonable doubt. In the companion case of *Apodaca v. Oregon*, 406 U.S. 404 (1972), three defendants were convicted separately of assault, burglary and grand larceny by three juries, two of whom voted 11–1, and the other 10–2, for conviction. The Supreme Court upheld the convictions 5–4, reasoning that the majorities were sufficient to provide "commonsense judgment" in evaluating the respective arguments of accused and accuser. However, in *Burch v. Louisiana*, 441 U.S. 130 (1979), the Supreme Court held 9–0 that a conviction in a state criminal trial for a non-petty offense by a verdict by five of six jurors violated the Sixth and Fourteenth Amendments. The state interest in reducing the time and expense in administering its criminal justice system is insufficient justification for its use of non-unanimous six-member juries.

• PETTY OFFENSES. The right to a jury trial is reserved for defendants accused of serious offenses and does not extend to "petty" offenses, *Duncan v. Louisiana*, 391 U.S. 145, 159 (1968), 7–2 vote. A "petty" offense is defined as a crime where the maximum authorized prison term is six months or less, *Blanton v. North Las Vegas*, 489 U.S. 538 (1989), 9–0 vote. A defendant who is prosecuted in a single proceeding for multiple petty offenses (none of which individually exceeds a maximum authorized prison term of six months) does not have a right to a jury trial even though the aggregate prison term authorized for the offenses exceeds six months, *Lewis v. United States*, 518 U.S. 322 (1996), 7–2 vote.

4. NOTICE OF ACCUSATION CLAUSE

The Sixth Amendment guarantees the defendant the right to be informed of the nature and cause of the accusation against him so that he may prepare his defense. Therefore, the accusation must allege all the elements of a crime with specificity. The Supreme Court held in *United States v. Carll*, 105 U.S. 611 (1881), that an indictment tracking the statutory language defining the offense was insufficient because of the failure to allege that the defendant knew that the instruments he issued were forged or counterfeited. The Court stated: "It is not sufficient to set forth the offense in the words of the statute, unless the words of themselves fully, directly, and expressly, without any uncertainty or ambiguity, set forth the elements necessary to constitute the offense intended to be punished."

If a defendant is convicted with a material variance between the formal charge and the proof offered at trial, the court will vacate the verdict and sentence. In *Stirone v. United States*, 361 U.S. 212 (1960), the Supreme Court reversed a conviction for a material variance between an indictment charging the defendant with illegal importation of sand whereas the trial evidence showed that he had engaged in illegal exportation of steel.

5. CONFRONTATION CLAUSE

The right granted to the accused by the Sixth Amendment to confront the witnesses against him, which includes the right to cross-examine them under oath to test their credibility as witnesses, is a fundamental right essential to a fair trial. *Pointer v. Texas*, 380 U.S. 400 (1965), 9–0 vote. The accused has the right to be present during the critical stages of his trial, allowing him to hear the evidence offered by the prosecution, consult with his attorney, and otherwise participate in his defense. However, a defendant may lose this right of confrontation by being removed from the courtroom for repeated disruptive behavior and the use of vile and abusive language, notwithstanding admonishment by the trial judge. In *Illinois v. Allen*, 397 U.S. 337 (1970), the Supreme Court identified at least three constitutionally permissible approaches for the court's handling of an obstreperous defendant: (1) bind and gag him as a last resort, thereby keeping him present; (2) cite him for criminal or civil contempt; or (3) remove him from the courtroom, while the trial continues, until he promises to conduct himself properly.

Hearsay evidence is generally not permitted since it is not subject to cross-examination. Hearsay evidence is an oral or written statement, or gesture, made out of court that is offered in court as evidence to prove the truth of the matter asserted; or, stated differently, testimony of a witness as to statements made by another individual who is not present in the courtroom to testify. However, there are many exceptions to the hearsay rule that permit the introduction of evidence where there are indicia of reliability, such as excited utterances; medical histories; recorded recollections; business, public, religious or family records; commercial or educational publications; statements against interest; and dying declarations. *Federal Rules of Evidence*, Rules 803, 804, 807.

In *Crawford v. Washington*, 541 U.S. 36 (2004), Crawford stabbed Lee for allegedly trying to rape his wife. Crawford claimed that he had acted in self-defense because he believed Lee had picked up a weapon. However, during a tape-recorded police interrogation of Crawford's wife, when there was no ongoing emergency, she said that Lee was not holding a weapon (meaning that her husband had no reasonable belief that he was endangered by Lee). Under the state marital privilege law, she could not testify in court without Crawford's consent. Over Crawford's objection that his wife's tape-recorded statement was hearsay that violated his Sixth Amendment rights, the prosecution introduced it in evidence, and he was convicted of assault. On appeal, the Supreme Court reversed 9–0 the conviction, holding that the Amendment guarantees the defendant the right to confront witnesses and cross-examine their testimony and, accordingly, prohibits the use out-of-court testimony as evidence against the defendant. The Supreme Court reached the same conclusion in

Hammon v. Indiana, 547 U.S. 813 (2006), holding 8–1 that the witness's statement was testimonial in character because it was given when there was no ongoing emergency and the police interrogation was part of an investigation into past criminal conduct. Thus, the defendant was entitled to cross-examine the witness at trial as required by the Confrontation Clause.

In *Maryland v. Craig*, 497 U.S. 836 (1990), an allegedly sexually abused six-year-old child, in order to avoid suffering serious emotional distress, was permitted to testify against the accused by one-way closed circuit television. The child, prosecutor and defense counsel withdrew to a room outside the courtroom where the child was examined and cross-examined. The judge, jury and defendant remained in the courtroom where the testimony was displayed. The Supreme Court upheld 5–4 the closed circuit television testimony because the Confrontation Clause does not guarantee defendants an absolute right to a face-to-face meeting with adverse witnesses. Here, the state was justified in adopting a special procedure to avoid traumatizing a child witness while preserving the rigorous adversarial testing of the testimony.

In *Melendez-Diaz v. Massachusetts*, 557 U.S. ___ (2009), the Supreme Court ruled 5–4 that a state forensic analyst's laboratory report prepared for use in a criminal prosecution is "testimonial" evidence subject to the requirement of the Confrontation Clause and, accordingly, the defendant has the right to question the analyst.

As to non-testimonial evidence, the Supreme Court in *Davis v. Washington*, 547 U.S. 813 (2006), held 9–0 that hearsay statements made in a 911 call asking for aid were not "testimonial" in nature and thus their introduction at trial did not violate the Sixth Amendment. The Court reasoned that the Amendment does not apply to "non-testimonial" statements which were not intended to be used in a future criminal prosecution. Although the caller identified her attacker to the 911 operator, she provided the information to help the police to resolve an "ongoing emergency," not to testify to a crime. The caller was not acting as a "witness," the 911 transcript was not "testimony" and, therefore, she was not required to appear at trial and be cross-examined. The *Davis* and *Hammon* cases were decided together by the Supreme Court. 547 U.S. 813.

Generally, the rule against hearsay is applicable only to court proceedings. Hearsay is admissible in evidence in many other proceedings, such as grand jury deliberations, probation hearings, and proceedings before administrative and legislative bodies.

6. COMPULSORY PROCESS CLAUSE

The Sixth Amendment guarantees defendants the right to use the compulsory process of the court to subpoena witnesses to force them to testify or produce physical evidence favorable to the defense. The Amendment permits, but does not require, a defendant to testify on his behalf. In the case of an indigent defendant, judicial resources must be used to produce the witness or other evidence. *United States v. Webster*, 750 F 2d 307 (5th Cir 1984). In *Webb v. Texas*, 409 U.S. 95 (1972), the Supreme Court held that a trial judge's extended admonition to a petitioner's witness to refrain from lying, coupled with threats of dire consequences if the witness did lie, effectively discouraged the testimony and, thereby, denied the petitioner due process of law.

In *Washington v. Texas*, 388 U.S. 14 (1967), the Supreme Court overturned 9–0 a state statute prohibiting criminal accomplices from testifying for each other, on the ground that the petitioner was denied the right to have compulsory process for obtaining favorable testimony from his accomplice. However, in *Taylor v. Illinois*, 484 U.S. 400 (1988), the Supreme Court ruled 5–3 that the trial judge may exclude the testimony of a witness favorable to the defendant when defense counsel violated discovery rules, requiring advance disclosure of the witness, in order to obtain a tactical advantage over the prosecution. Nor can a defendant have the results of his polygraph examination admitted in evidence, because such evidence is deemed unreliable by federal and state courts. *United States v. Scheffer*, 523 U.S. 303 (1998), 8–1 vote.

In *Holmes v. South Carolina*, 547 U.S. 319 (2006), the Supreme Court held 9–0 that the evidence of third-party guilt brought by the defense in a rape and murder trial could not be excluded on the basis of the strength of the prosecution's case. The defendant has the right to present a complete defense as guaranteed by the Compulsory Process Clause.

7. RIGHT TO COUNSEL CLAUSE

The Sixth Amendment guarantees defendants the right to counsel to assist in their defense. The right to counsel attaches when the government initiates any adversary criminal proceeding (whether by way of formal charge, preliminary hearing, indictment, information or arraignment), but it does not arise at the moment of arrest. *Kirby v. Illinois*, 406 U.S. 682 (1972), 5–4 vote. However, the defendant may assert a Fifth Amendment right to consult with counsel during a custodial interrogation by police, even though no formal charges have been made. *Miranda v. Arizona*, 384 U.S. 436 (1966).

In *Powell v. Alabama*, 287 U.S. 45 (1932), police stopped a freight train heading through Alabama from Chattanooga, Tennessee, and arrested Powell and eight other illiterate black youths (later known as the "Scottsboro Boys") for the alleged rape of two white women, also on the train, and incarcerated them in Scottsboro, Alabama. The defendants were rapidly convicted and all but one received the death penalty. They were given access to their two court-appointed lawyers immediately prior to trial, leaving little or no time to plan the defense. On appeal, the Supreme Court overturned the convictions and held 7–2 that the right of the accused in a capital case to have the aid of counsel for his defense, which includes the right to have sufficient time to consult with counsel and to prepare a defense, is one of the fundamental rights guaranteed by due process under the Fourteenth Amendment.

The Supreme Court in *Gideon v. Wainwright*, 372 U.S. 335 (1963), held 9-0 that indigent criminal defendants have a right to be provided counsel at trial. (The *Gideon* case was portrayed in *Gideon's Trumpet*, a 1964 book by Anthony Lewis and a 1980 movie starring Henry Fonda.) The Supreme Court in *Escobedo v. Illinois*, 378 U.S. 478 (1964), held 5-4 that criminal suspects have a right to counsel during police interrogations. The right of an indigent defendant to receive court-appointed counsel applies not only to felony offenses, but also to other cases in which the defendant may be punished by imprisonment, regardless of whether the crime is categorized as a misdemeanor or petty offense. *Argersinger v. Hamlin*, 407 U.S. 25 (1972), 9-0 vote. However, if the indigent defendant is not sentenced to imprisonment, even though allowed by the applicable statute, the state is not required to provide counsel. *Scott v. Illinois*, 440 U.S. 367 (1979), 5-4 vote.

The selection of counsel to represent an indigent defendant is within the discretion of the trial judge, and is not controlled by the desires of the defendant. The court-appointed counsel must be a competent member of the bar in good standing who gives the client a loyal and good faith defense. As to counsel competency, the Supreme Court in *Strickland v. Washington*, 466 U.S. 668 (1984), established 8-1 a two-part test for resolving a claim of ineffective assistance of counsel: a criminal defendant may not obtain relief unless he can show that counsel's performance fell below an objective standard of reasonableness, and that counsel's performance gives rise to a reasonable probability that, if counsel had performed adequately, the result of the proceeding would have been different.

The Supreme Court in *Nix v. Whiteside*, 475 U.S. 157 (1986), held 9-0 that the Sixth Amendment right of a criminal defendant to assistance of counsel is not violated when his attorney refuses to cooperate with him in presenting perjured testimony at his trial. In *Jones v. Barnes*, 463 U.S. 745 (1983), the Supreme Court held 7-2 that defense counsel assigned to appeal a criminal conviction does not have a constitutional duty to raise every nonfrivolous issue requested by his client, if counsel, as a matter of professional judgment, decides not to present the points.

As to self-representation (*pro se*), the Supreme Court held 6-3 in *Faretta v. California*, 422 U.S. 806 (1975), that a defendant in a criminal trial has the constitutional right to refuse appointed counsel and to represent himself when he voluntarily and intelligently elects to do so. Justice Harry Blackmun, in concluding his dissent, stated: "If there is any truth to the old proverb that 'one who is his own lawyer has a fool for a client,' the Court by its opinion today now bestows a constitutional right on one to make a fool of himself." In *McKaskle v. Wiggins*, 465 U.S. 168 (1984), the Supreme Court held 6–3 that Wiggins' right to represent himself was not violated by the trial judge appointing standby counsel to assist Wiggins in routine legal matters when the counsel did not interfere with Wiggins' control over his defense or undermine his appearance of self-representation before the jury. In *Godinez v. Moran*, 509 U.S. 389 (1993), the Supreme Court held 7–2 that if a defendant is competent to stand trial he is also competent to plead guilty and to waive the right to appointed counsel. However, in *Martinez v. Court of Appeals of California*, 528 U.S. 152 (2000), the Supreme Court held 9–0 that a criminal defendant does not have a constitutional right to self-representation on a direct appeal of his conviction because the Sixth Amendment applies only to the trial itself and not to any appellate review.

The Supreme Court in *Johnson v. Avery*, 393 U.S. 483 (1969), upheld 7–2 the right of state prisoners to receive the assistance of fellow prisoners (jailhouse lawyers) in the preparation of writs of habeas corpus. The state had sought to prohibit such assistance, but the Court ordered that it be permitted or else that alternative legal assistance be provided for prisoners seeking post-conviction review. In *Bounds v. Smith*, 430 U.S. 817 (1977), the Supreme Court held 6–3 that the fundamental constitutional right to access to the courts requires prison authorities to assist inmates in the preparation and filing of meaningful legal papers by providing them with adequate law libraries or adequate assistance from persons trained in the law.

In *Montejo v. Louisiana*, 556 U.S. ___ (2009), Montejo, a murder suspect, was appointed counsel for his representation. Subsequently, he gave incriminating evidence in response to police questioning, in the absence of his counsel, which resulted in his conviction for murder. On appeal, the Supreme Court held 5–4 that the defendant may validly waive his right to counsel during police interrogation, even if the police initiated the interrogation in the absence of his counsel. The Court overruled *Michigan v. Jackson*, 475 U.S. 625 (1986), which had held 6–3 that, once a defendant had invoked the right of counsel, police could not initiate interrogation of him without his counsel being present.

Amendment VII
Trial by Jury in Common Law Cases

Ratified December 15, 1791

In Suits at common law, where the value in controversy shall exceed twenty dollars, the right of trial by jury shall be preserved, and no fact tried by a jury, shall be otherwise re-examined in any Court of the United States, than according to the rules of the common law.

TRIAL BY JURY CLAUSE

The right of a jury trial under the Seventh Amendment applies to cases arising under the common law, as distinguished from statutory laws enacted by a legislature. The common law originated over the centuries from decisions of English judges based on prevailing customs, broadened as needed to address new issues, and preserved by the following of judicial precedents, "the fruit of reason ripened by experience." The common law was implanted in the New World by the English settlers. The specification of the common law in the Amendment reflects the framers' intent to restrict jury trials to actions seeking monetary relief, and to distinguish them from actions seeking equitable relief (non-monetary relief such as injunctions) that were decided by judges without juries. *Baltimore & Carolina Line, Inc. v. Redman,* 295 U.S. 654 (1935). Although the *Federal Rules of Civil Procedure* merged the law and equity jurisdictions in 1938, the Supreme Court has held that where both law and equity issues are joined in the same case, the jury must first decide the legal issues, followed by a determination of the equitable issues by the judge. *Beacon Theatres v. Westover,* 359 U.S. 500 (1959), 5–3 vote.

While twelve-member juries have been traditional, the Supreme Court has held that a local federal court rule providing for a six-member jury for civil cases comports with the Seventh Amendment. *Colgrove v. Battin,* 413 U.S. 149 (1973), 5–4 vote. The Supreme Court has not made the Seventh Amendment applicable to civil trials in state courts through "incorporation" in the Due Process Clause of the Fourteenth Amendment. *Minneapolis & St. Louis R. Co. v. Bombolis,* 241 U.S. 211 (1916).

The right to trial by jury is also guaranteed by Article III, Section 2, Clause 3, and the Sixth Amendment relating to criminal cases.

REEXAMINATION CLAUSE

The Clause prohibits reviewing courts from reexamining any fact tried by a jury in any manner other than according to the common law. Reviewing courts may only examine errors of law, and may not retry issues settled by a jury trial. However, jury awards for damages may be modified if found to be excessive or inadequate by the court, without conflict with the Seventh Amendment. *Gasperini v. Center for Humanities Inc.,* 518 U.S. 415 (1996), 5–4 vote. Also, in *Weisgram v. Marley Co.,* 528 U.S. 440 (2000), the Supreme Court upheld 9–0 an appeals court order directing entry of judgment for the defendant upon determining that as a matter of law a plaintiff's expert testimony was unreliable and should have been excluded at trial, and that the remaining evidence was insufficient to support the jury verdict.

Amendment VIII
Cruel and Unusual Punishment

Ratified December 15, 1791

Excessive bail shall not be required, nor excessive fines imposed, nor cruel and unusual punishments inflicted.

EXCESSIVE BAIL CLAUSE

Bail (money or property) is given to procure the release of a person from legal custody with the assurance that he shall appear at the proper time and submit himself to the jurisdiction of the court. Bail, by allowing a defendant to remain free pending trial, is based on the assumption that a person is innocent until proven guilty. Bail set at a figure higher than an amount reasonably calculated to fulfill the purpose of assuring the presence of the defendant is "excessive." *Stack v. Boyle*, 342 U.S. 1 (1951). The Supreme Court in *United States v. Salerno*, 481 U.S. 739 (1987), involving La Cosa Nostra figures, upheld 6–3 preventive detention without bail where the government's interest in protecting the community outweighs individual liberty.

Although the Supreme Court has not yet expressly applied the prohibitions on excessive bail to the states through the Due Process Clause of the Fourteenth Amendment, Justice Harry Blackmun, in writing for the majority in *Schilb v. Kuebel*, 404 U.S. 357 (1971), stated that "the Eighth Amendment's proscription of excessive bail has been assumed to have application to the States through the Fourteenth Amendment." 404 U.S. 365.

EXCESSIVE FINES CLAUSE

A fine is the pecuniary or forfeiture punishment imposed by a court upon a person convicted of a crime. In *Austin v. United States*, 509 U.S. 602 (1993), involving the seizure of a mobile home and auto body shop for the owner's illicit drug trade, the Supreme Court held 9–0 that the clause applies to civil actions of forfeiture and that the amount of property a defendant is required to forfeit must be in proportion to the seriousness of the crime. In *United States v. Bajakajian*, 524 U.S. 321 (1989), the Supreme Court held 5–4 that a forfeiture of $357,144, for failure to report the international movement of currency of over $10,000, violated the Excessive Fines Clause as grossly disproportional to the gravity of the offense. Similar issues are also addressed under the Just Compensation or Takings Clause of the Fifth Amendment.

CRUEL AND UNUSUAL PUNISHMENT CLAUSE

Some punishments are forbidden entirely, such as drawing and quartering, dissecting, disemboweling, beheading, burning alive, torture, lingering death and "all others in the same line of unnecessary cruelty." *Wilkerson v. Utah*, 99 U.S. 130 (1878). Also, punishments are forbidden as excessive where they are "grossly disproportionate" to the seriousness of the crime committed or to the competence of the perpetrator, such as the death penalty for the rapist of an adult woman (*Coker v. Georgia*, 433 U.S. 584 [1977], 7–2 vote); a mentally retarded offender [*Atkins v. Virginia*, 536 U.S. 304 [2002], 6–3 vote); an insane prisoner (*Ford v. Wainwright*, 477 U.S. 399 [1986], 5–4 vote); a juvenile offender (*Roper v. Simmons*, 543 U.S. 551 [2005], 5–4 vote); and the driver of a getaway car who had no intent to participate in the murder of robbery victims (*Enmund v. Florida*, 458 U.S. 782 [1982], 5–4 vote). However, in *Tison v. Arizona*, 481 U.S. 138 (1987), the Supreme Court held 5–4 that the death penalty may be imposed on a felony-murder defendant (but not a killer) who was a major participant in the underlying felony and exhibited reckless indifference to human life. *Tison* was distinguished from *Enmund* by the proportionality principle where Tison was a major participant in the felony, and Enmund was a minor participant. The felony-murder rule provides that if a killing occurs during the commission of a felony (major crime), a person participating in the felony may be charged with murder even though the killing was done by another participant.

The Supreme Court has held that the ban on cruel and unusual punishment does not prohibit execution by public shooting (*Wilkerson*, above); electrocution (*In re Kemmler*, 136 U.S. 436 [1890], 9–0 vote); and lethal injection, if administered to avoid unnecessary pain, *Baze v. Rees*, 553 U.S. 35 (2008), 7–2 vote.

In *Trop v. Dulles*, 356 U.S. 86 (1958), the Supreme Court held 5–4 that the denationalization of a citizen, resulting from his court-martial conviction for desertion, was unconstitutional as being "more primitive than torture" and involving "the total destruction of the individual's status in organized society." The majority opinion, by Chief Justice Earl Warren, stated that the Eighth Amendment "must draw its meaning from the evolving standards of decency that mark the progress of a maturing society." 356 U.S. 101. In accordance with these "evolving standards" the majority in *Kennedy v. Louisiana*, 554 U.S.___ (2008), found 5–4 a national consensus and invalidated the death penalty for the crime of raping a child, when the victim does not die and death was not intended.

In *Furman v. Georgia*, 408 U.S. 238 (1972), the Supreme Court, in a 5–4 decision, as reflected in a one-paragraph *per curiam* (by the court) opinion and in 230 pages of concurrences and dissents, held that the death penalty based on the unguided discretion of juries offends the Cruel and Unusual Punishment Clause because it permits juries to impose the death penalty on some convicted defendants while other juries impose imprisonment on large numbers of similarly situated defendants convicted of the same crime. Accordingly, the decision forced Georgia and many other states and the Congress to revise their statutes for capital offenses to assure that the death penalty would not be administered in a capricious or discriminatory manner. The Constitution recognizes the death penalty by referring to "capital" crime in the Fifth Amendment, and to deprivation of "life" in the Fourteenth Amendment, Section 1.

In *Gregg v. Georgia*, 428 U.S. 153 (1976), the Supreme Court upheld 7–2 the imposition of the death penalty for murder where the state statute assures a judicious and careful use of the death penalty by requiring a bifurcated trial in which guilt and sentence are determined separately, with specific findings as to the severity of the crime and the character and record of the defendant, followed by state appellate review comparing each death sentence "with the sentences imposed on similarly situated defendants to ensure that the sentence of death in a particular case is not disproportionate." Accordingly, a state statute that imposes a mandatory death penalty for all convicted first-degree murderers is unconstitutional because it removes the discretion from the judge or jury to make an individual determination in each case. *Woodson v. North Carolina*, 428 U.S. 280 (1976), 5–4 vote. In *Ring v. Arizona*, 536 U.S. 584 (2002), the Supreme Court held 7–2 that a defendant has the right to have a jury, rather than a judge, decide on the existence of an aggravating factor that makes the defendant eligible for the death penalty.

The Supreme Court has ruled in the following cases that the punishment is disproportionate to the crime and therefore violates the Eighth Amendment.

1. Weems, convicted of falsifying records resulting in the government being defrauded of 612 pesos, was sentenced to 15 years incarceration at hard labor, while being chained from wrist to ankle, and fined 4,000 pesetas. *Weems v. United States*, 217 U.S. 349 (1910), 4–2 vote.

2. Robinson, convicted of violating a state law criminalizing addiction to the use of narcotics, was sentenced to 90 days imprisonment for his illness. *Robinson v. California*, 370 U.S. 660 (1962), 6–2 vote. (The law was not aimed at the purchase, sale or possession of illegal drugs.)

3. Helm, convicted of writing a bogus check for $100, his seventh nonviolent felony conviction in South Dakota since 1964, was sentenced to life in prison with no parole. *Solem v. Helm*, 463 U.S. 277 (1983), 5–4 vote.

However, in the following cases the Supreme Court has ruled that the punishment is not disproportionate to the crime.

1. In *Rummel v. Estelle*, 445 U.S. 263 (1980), the Supreme Court upheld 5–4 Rummel's mandatory life sentence (with possibility of parole) under the Texas recidivist (criminal tendency) statute for a third felony, although the three felonies for theft were non-violent and totaled $229.11. The majority reasoned that Texas had a significant interest in dealing "in a harsher manner with those who by repeated criminal acts have shown that they are simply incapable of conforming to the norms of society."

2. In *Harmelin v. Michigan*, 501 U.S. 957 (1991), the Supreme Court upheld 5–4 Harmelin's mandatory life without parole sentence for conviction of possessing 672 grams of cocaine. The majority said: "Severe, mandatory penalties may be cruel, but they are not unusual in the constitutional sense, having been employed in various forms throughout our Nation's history."

3. In *Lockyer v. Andrade*, 538 U.S. 63 (2003), the Supreme Court upheld 5–4 two consecutive terms of 25 years to life sentences, with possibility of parole, under California's three-strikes law (aimed at habitual criminals) for Andrade's conviction of shoplifting about $150 of video tapes (third strike). While admitting that its precedents were not a "model of clarity," the majority said that the "gross disproportionality principle is applicable to sentences for terms of years," but that the "precise contours" of this principle were unclear and applied only in the "exceedingly rare and extreme case."

4. In *Ewing v. California*, 538 U.S. 11 (2003), the companion case to *Lockyer*, the Supreme Court upheld 5–4 the 25 years to life sentence under California's three-strikes law for Ewing's "third strike" conviction for stealing three golf clubs worth $399 each. The majority found that "California has a reasonable basis for believing that dramatically enhanced sentences for habitual felons advance the goals of its criminal justice system in any substantial way."

As to prisoners, the Supreme Court in *Estelle v. Gamble*, 429 U.S. 97 (1976), held 8–1 that deliberate indifference by prison personnel to a prisoner's serious illness or injury would constitute cruel and unusual punishment. Also, the use of excessive physical force against a prisoner may constitute cruel and unusual punishment even though the prisoner does not suffer serious injury. *Hudson v. McMillian*, 503 U.S. 1 (1992), 7–2 vote.

As to the paddling of public school students, the Supreme Court held 5–4 in *Ingraham v. Wright*, 430 U.S. 651 (1977), that the ban on cruel and unusual punishment applied to convicted criminals, and does not apply in non-criminal contexts, such as school discipline. Of course, other remedies are available for excessive corporal punishment.

Amendment IX
Retention of Unenumerated Rights by the People

Ratified December 15, 1791

The enumeration in the Constitution, of certain rights, shall not be construed to deny or disparage others retained by the people.

In contrast to the previous eight amendments, the Ninth Amendment does not specifically identify any individual rights. Instead, it sets forth a rule of construction, clarifying that the enumeration of rights elsewhere in the Constitution is only a partial listing of all the rights retained by the people against governmental infringement. In other words, just because a certain right is not listed in the Constitution does not mean it does not exist. When the Ninth and Tenth Amendments are read together, it is clear that the people and the states retain all powers not delegated to the United States by the Constitution.

In *Griswold v. Connecticut*, 381 U.S. 479 (1965), the Supreme Court invalidated 7–2 a state law prohibiting the use of contraceptives on the ground that it violated the "right of marital privacy." The Court found that this right of privacy was established by guarantees of the First, Third, Fourth, Fifth and Ninth Amendments. Associate Justice Arthur J. Goldberg, in his concurring opinion, stated: "To hold that a right so basic and fundamental and so deep-rooted in our society as the right of privacy in marriage may be infringed because that right is not guaranteed in so many words by the first eight amendments to the Constitution is to ignore the Ninth Amendment and to give it no effect whatsoever." 381 U.S. 491.

However, in applying this right of privacy in *Roe v. Wade*, 410 U.S. 113 (1973), 7–2 vote (upholding a woman's right to abort her pregnancy), and in *Lawrence v. Texas*, 539 U.S. 558 (2003), 6–3 vote (upholding same-sex couples' right to sexual intimacy), the Supreme Court relied instead on the Due Process Clause of the Fourteenth Amendment. Accordingly, the Supreme Court generally recognizes an unenumerated right under the Due Process Clause when the Court determines that such a right is so fundamental as to warrant protection by substantive due process.

According to most courts' interpretation the Ninth Amendment does not confer substantive rights in addition to those conferred by other laws, but was added to the Bill of Rights to ensure that fundamental rights would not be later denied because they were not specifically enumerated in the Constitution. *Gibson v. Matthews*, 926 F 2d 532, 537 (6th Cir 1991). Under that interpretation, courts have found that the Ninth Amendment does not afford the right to resist the draft (*United States v. Uhl*, 436 F 2d 773, 774 [9th Cir 1970]); possess an unregistered submachine gun (*United States v.*

Warin, 530 F 2d 103, 108 [6th Cir 1976]); use mind-altering drugs such as marijuana (*United States v. Fry*, 787 F 2d 903, 905 [4th Cir 1986]); or be guaranteed a radiation-free environment (*Concerned Citizens of Nebraska v. United States Nuclear Regulatory Commission*, 970 F 2d 421, 426 [8th Cir 1992]).

Amendment X
Power Reserved to States or People

Ratified December 15, 1791

The powers not delegated to the United States by the Constitution, nor prohibited by it to the States, are reserved to the States respectively, or to the people.

The Reserved Power Amendment declares that the federal government possesses only the powers delegated to it by the Constitution, and that the Constitution reserves all other powers, not so delegated or denied the states, to the states or to the people. "The amendment states but a truism that all is retained which has not been surrendered." *United States v. Darby Lumber Co.*, 312 U.S. 100, 124 (1941). However, broad interpretations of federal authority under the Constitution have resulted in a corresponding reduction in state authority.

The federal government may not compel states to enforce federal statutes. A statute requiring states that refuse federal monetary incentives to take title to any radioactive waste within their borders and making them liable for all damages directly related to the waste was deemed unconstitutional. *New York v. United States*, 505 U.S. 144 (1992), 6–3 vote. Nor may the federal government require state and local law enforcement officers to conduct background checks on persons seeking to purchase handguns because this is forcing them to participate in the administration of a federal program. *Printz v. United States*, 521 U.S. 898 (1997), 5–4 vote. However, the Supreme Court in *Garcia v. San Antonio Metropolitan Transit Authority*, 469 U.S. 528 (1985), upheld 5–4 the application to municipal employees of the minimum-wage and overtime requirements of the Fair Labor Standards Act. The Court found nothing in the general applicability of the Act "that is destructive of state sovereignty or violative of any constitutional provision." 469 U.S. 554.

The Congress, in the exercise of its constitutional powers, often encourages states to implement national policy by conditioning the allocation of federal funding on state conformity with federal guidelines. For example, the Supreme Court in *South Dakota v. Dole*, 483 U.S. 203 (1987), upheld 7–2 congressional legislation ordering the Secretary of Transportation to withhold 5 percent of federal highway funds from states that did not adopt a 21-year-old minimum drinking age. The Supreme Court in *Hodel v. Virginia Surface Mining & Reclamation Association*, 452 U.S. 264, 290–291 (1981), upheld 9–0 the authority of Congress, in the exercise of its commerce power, to either preempt state regulation over surface coal mining operations, or to permit continued state regulation in accordance with federal standards. The state had the option to voluntarily participate in the federal program or withdraw from the field. In another commerce power case, the Court in *Federal Energy Regulatory Commission v. Mississippi*, 456 U.S. 742, 765 (1982), upheld 5–4 the command of the Public Utility Regulatory Policies Act that a state consider federal standards because the Act did not compel the state to enact a regulatory program, but simply established requirements for continued state activity in an otherwise preemptible field.

Amendment XI
Suits Against a State

Ratified February 7, 1795

The Judicial power of the United States shall not be construed to extend to any suit in law or equity, commenced or prosecuted against one of the United States by Citizens of another State, or by Citizens or Subjects of any Foreign State.

The Eleventh Amendment was adopted to nullify *Chisholm v. Georgia*, 2 U.S. 419 (1793), in which the Supreme Court held 4–1 that pursuant to Article III, Section 2, federal courts had jurisdiction over a suit against a state brought by a citizen of another state, despite the traditional notions of state sovereign immunity. A suit in law seeks monetary damages, and a suit in equity seeks relief such as injunction or specific performance. The Amendment confirms a state's sovereign immunity from being sued in federal court by a citizen of another state or country. However, other states and the United States may still sue a state in federal court. The Amendment does not bestow sovereign immunity on municipalities or other political subdivisions of a state unless they are acting on behalf of the state as distinguished from acting in a municipal or other local government role. A state may choose to waive its sovereign immunity.

Although the Amendment does not expressly refer to a citizen suing his own state, the Supreme Court in *Hans v. Louisiana*, 134 U.S. 1 (1890), ruled 9–0 that the Amendment reflects a broader principle of sovereign immunity that prohibits federal courts from exercising jurisdiction over a suit by a citizen against his own state to recover money damages.

In *Osborn v. Bank of the United States*, 22 U.S. 738 (1824), the Supreme Court held 6–1 that the Eleventh Amendment is inapplicable to suits in which a state is not a party of record, even when a party is acting as a state official. Under the "stripping doctrine," a state official who has used his office to act illegally may be sued in his individual capacity under the theory that his illegal conduct has stripped him of his status as a state official with sovereign immunity. In *Ex parte Young*, 209 U.S. 123 (1908), the Supreme Court held 8–1 that a suit for injunctive relief against a state official did not violate state sovereign immunity because the state official was not acting on behalf of the state when he sought to enforce an unconstitutional law. However, in *Edelman v. Jordan*, 415 U.S. 651 (1974), the Supreme Court ruled 5–4 that in a suit by private parties against state officials in federal court retroactive monetary damages could not be awarded because they would be paid from state funds in violation of state sovereign immunity under the Eleventh Amendment. Monetary damages for past conduct are distinguished from injunctive relief against future conduct.

In *Scheuer v. Rhodes*, 416 U.S. 232 (1974), the Supreme Court held 8–0 that state officials could be sued for damages resulting from national guard troops killing four students protesting the Vietnam War. The Court ruled that the immunity of state officers for their acts is not absolute, but qualified, depending upon the scope of their discretion and responsibilities at the time of the incident. In *Wood v. Strickland*, 420 U.S. 308 (1975), the Supreme Court held 5–4 that public school board members are not immune from liability for damages for unreasonable conduct that violates the constitutional rights of their students. However, the good faith fulfillment of their responsibilities within the bounds of reason will not be punished. *Monell v. City of New York Department of Social Services*, 436 U.S. 658 (1978), established 7–2 local government accountability for unconstitutional acts and the right to obtain damages for such acts.

In *Fitzpatrick v. Bitzer*, 427 U.S. 445 (1976), Congress had enacted legislation allowing persons to sue state governments for money damages for racial, religious or sexual discrimination pursuant to the guarantees of the Fourteenth Amendment. The Supreme Court ruled 9–0 that Congress, under its enforcement power provided by Section 5 of the Fourteenth Amendment, could abrogate state sovereign immunity to enforce the guarantees of the Amendment against the states. However, Congress, in using its Fourteenth Amendment power to abrogate the Eleventh Amendment bar to suits against states, must express its intention in unmistakable language in the statute itself. A general authorization for suit in federal court is not sufficient for abrogation. *Atascadero State Hospital v. Scanlon*, 473 U.S. 234, 242 (1985), 5–4 vote. The relationship between state sovereign immunity under the Eleventh Amendment and congressional enforcement authority under Section 5 of the Fourteenth Amendment is further addressed in the later treatment of the Fourteenth Amendment.

In *Seminole Tribe v. Florida*, 517 U.S. 44 (1996), the tribe sued Florida in federal court for failing to negotiate in good faith as required by the Indian Gaming Regulatory Act of 1988. The Supreme Court ruled 5–4 that Florida had sovereign immunity from the suit under the Eleventh Amendment, and that Congress did not have the authority to abrogate the immunity under the Commerce Clause (Article I, Section 8, Clause 3). The same result was reached in *Alden v. Maine*, 527 U.S. 706 (1999), where the Supreme Court ruled 5–4 that Maine had sovereign immunity from federal suit by its employees who alleged violation of the overtime provisions of the Fair Labor Standards Act of 1938. However, in *Central Virginia Community College v. Katz*, 546 U.S. 356 (2006), the Supreme Court ruled 5–4 that the Bankruptcy Clause (Article I, Section 8, Clause 4) authorized Congress to enact uniform bankruptcy laws with the power to subordinate state sovereignty.

Other cases interpreting the Eleventh Amendment are reported under the Enforcement Clause (Section 5) of the Fourteenth Amendment.

Amendment XII
Electoral College

Ratified June 15, 1804

The Electors shall meet in their respective states, and vote by ballot for President and Vice-President, one of whom, at least, shall not be an inhabitant of the same state with themselves; they shall name in their ballots the person voted for as President, and in distinct ballots the person voted for as Vice-President, and they shall make distinct lists of all persons voted for as President, and of all persons voted for as Vice-President, and of the number of votes for each, which lists they shall sign and certify, and transmit sealed to the seat of the government of the United States, directed to the President of the Senate;—The President of the Senate shall, in the presence of the Senate and House of Representatives, open all the certificates and the votes shall then be counted;—The person having the greatest number of votes for President, shall be the President, if such number be a majority of the whole number of Electors appointed; and if no person have such majority, then from the persons having the highest numbers not exceeding three on the list of those voted for as President, the House of Representatives shall choose immediately, by ballot, the President. But in choosing the President, the votes shall be taken by states, the representation from each state having one vote; a quorum for this purpose shall consist of a member or members from two-thirds of the states, and a majority of all the states shall be necessary to a choice. [And if the House of Representatives shall not choose a President whenever the right of choice shall devolve upon them, before the fourth day of March next following, then the Vice-President shall act as

President, as in case of the death or other constitutional disability of the President.—] The person having the greatest number of votes as Vice-President, shall be the Vice-President, if such number be a majority of the whole number of Electors appointed, and if no person have a majority, then from the two highest numbers on the list, the Senate shall choose the Vice-President; a quorum for the purpose shall consist of two-thirds of the whole number of Senators, and a majority of the whole number shall be necessary to a choice. But no person constitutionally ineligible to the office of President shall be eligible to that of Vice-President of the United States. [The bracketed language was superseded by the Twentieth Amendment, Sections 1 and 3, including the change of the presidential inauguration from March 4 to January 20.]

The Twelfth Amendment revised Article II, Section 1, Clause 3, which originally provided that the electoral college electors would each vote for two candidates, without specifying the President and Vice-President. The candidate receiving the most votes, if a majority, would become President, and the candidate receiving the next most votes would become Vice-President. This process quickly proved impractical with the departure of George Washington as President. In the election of 1796, John Adams, a Federalist, received the majority of votes and became President, while his political opponent, Thomas Jefferson, a Democratic-Republican, received the second highest number of votes and became Vice-President. In the election of 1800, the two Democratic-Republican candidates, Thomas Jefferson for President and Aaron Burr for Vice-President, each received the same number of votes. When Burr refused to withdraw in favor of Jefferson, the election was determined by the House of Representatives, with Jefferson winning after 35 ballots.

The Twelfth Amendment remedied this situation by requiring that separate ballots be cast for the President and Vice President; that candidates receiving a majority of the votes for each office shall be elected thereto;that if a majority is lacking for the presidency, the House of Representatives shall choose the President by voting by state from among the three candidates receiving the highest numbers of electoral votes; that if a majority is lacking for the vice presidency, the Senate shall choose the Vice President by voting on the two candidates receiving the highest numbers of electoral votes. The Amendment also requires that the Vice President possess the same constitutional qualifications as the President.

The Eleventh and Twelfth Amendments were the last amendments adopted by the founders' generation for the correction of defects in the original Constitution.

Amendment XIII
Slavery Abolition

Ratified December 6, 1865

Section 1. Neither slavery nor involuntary servitude, except as a punishment for crime whereof the party shall have been duly convicted, shall exist within the United States, or any place subject to their jurisdiction.

Section 2. Congress shall have power to enforce this article by appropriate legislation.

The language of Section 1 of the Slavery Amendment is patterned after the prohibition of slavery as stated in Article 6 of the Northwest Ordinance of July 13, 1787, which led to the eventual admission into the United States of Illinois, Indiana, Michigan, Minnesota, Ohio and Wisconsin.

Congress enacted the Civil Rights Act of 1866 declaring that all persons born in the United States (except Indians not taxed) were now citizens, without regard to race, color or previous condition of involuntary servitude. As citizens they could make and enforce contracts, sue and be sued, give evidence in court, and inherit, purchase, lease, sell, hold and convey real estate and personal property. Criminal penalties were prescribed for those who denied these rights to former slaves.

The Supreme Court in *Clyatt v. United* States, 197 U.S. 207 (1905), ruled 9–0 that peonage is a condition of compulsory service based upon the indebtedness of the peon to the master. The service is enforced unless the debt is paid, and however created, it is involuntary servitude within the prohibition of the Thirteenth Amendment. In *Bailey v. Alabama*, 219 U.S. 219 (1911), Bailey had agreed to work on a farm for one year at $12 per month. He received a $15 advance. He stopped working after about a month, and did not refund any money. He was convicted and sentenced to 136 days of hard labor under the Alabama peonage law providing punishment for indebtedness. The Supreme Court overturned the law, ruling 7–2 that adjudging a person criminally liable for work not performed was akin to indentured servitude, in violation of the Thirteenth Amendment. In *Taylor v. Georgia*, 315 U.S. 25 (1942), the Georgia statute stated that a person who had received an advance on a contract to render certain services, and failed to do so, could be compelled, under threat of penal sanction, to remain at his employment until the debt was satisfied. The Supreme Court ruled 8–0 that such coerced labor is peonage in violation of the Amendment. And in *Pollock v. Williams*, 322 U.S. 4 (1944), the Supreme Court ruled 7–2 that the Thirteenth Amendment prohibited all legislation that would compel a person to perform labor because of a debt.

The Supreme Court in *Butler v. Perry*, 240 U.S. 328 (1916), rejected 9–0 a challenge by a Florida man convicted under a state law that required all able-bodied men between 21 and 45, when called upon, to work for up to 60 hours on maintaining public roads. The Court observed that from "Colonial days to the present time conscripted labor has been much relied on for the construction and maintenance of roads," and that "involuntary servitude" under the Thirteenth Amendment "was intended to cover those forms of compulsory labor akin to African slavery which, in practical operation, would tend to produce like undesirable results."

In *Jones v. Alfred H. Mayer Co.*, 392 U.S. 409 (1968), the Supreme Court, in banning racial discrimination in the sale of housing, held 7–2 that the Civil Rights Act of 1866 prohibited both private and state-backed discrimination and that the Thirteenth Amendment authorized Congress to prohibit private acts of discrimination as among "the badges and incidents of slavery." However, the Supreme Court in *Palmer v. Thompson*, 403 U.S. 217 (1971), ruled 5–4 the city's action in closing the swimming pools to all persons, instead of keeping them open on an integrated basis, did not create a "badge or incident" of slavery in violation of the Thirteenth Amendment. In *Memphis v. Greene*, 451 U.S. 100 (1981), the Supreme Court ruled 5–4 that that the closing of a road separating an all-white neighborhood from a predominantly black neighborhood was not a violation of the Thirteenth Amendment or the 1866 Act, finding that the modest inconvenience and speculative loss in property value to black residents was insufficient to show such a violation.

In *United States v. Kozminski*, 487 U.S. 931 (1988), employers forced two mentally retarded men to labor on a farm in poor health and in squalid conditions, seven days a week and often 17 hours a day, at first at $15 per week and eventually at no pay. The Supreme Court found 9–0 a violation of the Thirteenth Amendment because such labor constituted involuntary servitude by the use of physical restraint or injury, or by the use or threat of coercion through legal process. However, the majority declared that the Thirteenth Amendment does not prohibit compulsion of servitude through psychological coercion, reasoning that a person's state of mind was too nebulous a standard.

The congressional enforcement power, stated in Section 2 of the Thirteenth Amendment, is repeated in the Fourteenth Amendment, Section 5; Fifteenth Amendment, Section 2; Eighteenth Amendment, Section 2; Nineteenth Amendment, Clause 2; Twenty-third Amendment, Section 2; Twenty-fourth Amendment, Section 2; and Twenty-sixth Amendment, Section 2.

Amendment XIV
Citizenship; Privileges or Immunities;
Due Process; Equal Protection

Ratified July 9, 1868

Section 1. All persons born or naturalized in the United States, and subject to the jurisdiction thereof, are citizens of the United States and of the State
wherein they reside. No State shall make or enforce any law which shall abridge
the privileges or immunities of citizens of the United States; nor shall any State
deprive any person of life, liberty, or property, without due process of law; nor
deny to any person within its jurisdiction the equal protection of the laws.

Section 2. Representatives shall be apportioned among the several States
according to their respective numbers, counting the whole number of persons in each State, excluding Indians not taxed. But when the right to vote
at any election for the choice of electors for President and Vice-President of
the United States, Representatives in Congress, the Executive and Judicial
officers of a State, or the members of the Legislature thereof, is denied to
any of the male inhabitants of such State, being [twenty-one years]* of age,
and citizens of the United States, or in any way abridged, except for participation in rebellion, or other crime, the basis of representation therein shall
be reduced in the proportion which the number of such male citizens shall
bear to the whole number of male citizens twenty-one years of age in such
State. (*Reduced to eighteen years by Twenty-sixth Amendment, Section 1)

Section 3. No person shall be a Senator or Representative in Congress,
or elector of President and Vice-President, or hold any office, civil or military, under the United States, or under any State, who, having previously
taken an oath, as a member of Congress, or as an officer of the United States,
or as a member of any State legislature, or as an executive or judicial officer
of any State, to support the Constitution of the United States, shall have
engaged in insurrection or rebellion against the same, or given aid or comfort to the enemies thereof. But Congress may by a vote of two-thirds of
each House, remove such disability.

Section 4. The validity of the public debt of the United States, authorized by law, including debts incurred for payment of pensions and bounties
for services in suppressing insurrection or rebellion, shall not be questioned.
But neither the United States nor any State shall assume or pay any debt or
obligation incurred in aid of insurrection or rebellion against the United
States, or any claim for the loss or emancipation of any slave; but all such
debts, obligations and claims shall be held illegal and void.

Section 5. The Congress shall have power to enforce, by appropriate
legislation, the provisions of this article.

The Fourteenth Amendment, adopted soon after the Civil War to protect newly freed slaves from discriminatory state laws, greatly expanded the reach of the Constitution by imposing on the states obligations to protect persons with respect to such broad concepts as "due process of law" and "equal protection of the laws." Ironically, this application applied not only to those states who engaged in the rebellion, but to the others as well. Also, the Supreme Court has used the Due Process Clause of the Amendment to require that the states abide by most of the guarantees in the Bill of Rights through the doctrine of selective incorporation. Aside from the structural provisions of the original Constitution, the Fourteenth Amendment stands as the most significant part of our legal system. Section 1 of the Amendment is known as the Liberty or Naturalization Clause.

The Citizenship and Privileges or Immunities Clauses apply to "citizens," whereas the Due Process and Equal Protection Clauses apply to the broader class of "persons."

CITIZENSHIP CLAUSE

Section 1 defined citizenship for the first time in the Constitution by declaring: "All persons born or naturalized in the United States, and subject to the jurisdiction thereof, are citizens of the United States and of the State wherein they reside." (Naturalization is the process by which an alien becomes a citizen.) The Citizenship Clause overturned *Dred Scott v. Sandford*, 60 U.S. 393 (1857), which had held that slaves were not citizens, but property.

In *Elk v. Wilkins*, 112 U.S. 94 (1884), the Supreme Court denied U.S. citizenship to a Native American born on an Indian reservation, who moved to Omaha, Nebraska, renounced his tribal allegiance, and claimed citizenship under the Citizenship Clause. The Court ruled that Native American tribes were independent political powers with no allegiance to the United States and, hence, were not "subject to the jurisdiction" of the United States. Subsequently, American Indians were granted U.S. citizenship under the Indian Citizenship Act of 1924. In *United States v. Wong Kim Ark*, 169 U.S. 649 (1898), the Supreme Court upheld 6–2 U.S. citizenship for a man born in the United States to Chinese citizens who were lawfully residing in the United States, and who were not employed in a diplomatic or other official capacity by a foreign government.

As to the retention of citizenship, *Afroyim v. Rusk*, 387 U.S. 253 (1967), involved a naturalized U.S. citizen who moved to Israel and voted in an Israeli election in 1951. Later, the U.S. Department of State denied the renewal of his passport on the ground that he had forfeited his U.S. citizenship by voting in a foreign election as specified by the 1940 Nationality Act.

The Supreme Court held 5–4 that he could not be deprived of U.S. citizenship without his consent based on the unequivocal mandate of the Citizenship Clause. In *Vance v. Terrazas*, 444 U.S. 252 (1980), Terrazas, a U.S. citizen by virtue of his birth in the U.S. in 1947, applied for a certificate of Mexican nationality in 1970, renouncing his U.S. citizenship. Subsequently, he claimed that he had not truly intended to abandon his U.S. citizenship, but the U.S. Department of State determined that he had relinquished it. On appeal, the Supreme Court held 5–4 that the actual intent to relinquish U.S. citizenship had to be proven by itself, and could not be inferred from the mere performance of an act designated by Congress as expatriating (automatically causing loss of citizenship). However, the determination of such intent could be made upon a "preponderance of the evidence," rather than the more stringent standard of "clear, convincing and unequivocal evidence." Following remand, Terrazas lost his U.S. citizenship.

PRIVILEGES OR IMMUNITIES CLAUSE

The prohibition against state abridgement of "the privileges or immunities" of U.S. citizens in the Fourteenth Amendment imitates Article IV, Section 2, Clause 1, stating, "The Citizens of each State shall be entitled to all Privileges and Immunities of Citizens in the several States." Accordingly, the decisions cited there are relevant here.

In *Saenz v. Roe*, 526 U.S. 489 (1999), California, with a generous welfare program, had enacted a statute limiting the maximum welfare benefits available to new residents, for their first year of residency, to the lesser benefits they would have received in the state of their prior residency. The Supreme Court overturned the limitation, ruling 7–2 that under the clause the newly arrived residents had the right to be treated the same as long-term residents, and that the clause does not allow for degrees of citizenship based on the length of residence. The Court mentioned the majority opinion in *The Slaughter-House Cases*, 83 U.S. 36, 80 (1873), stating that one of the privileges conferred by the clause "is that a citizen of the United States can, of his own volition, become a citizen of any State of the Union by a bona fide residence therein, with the same rights as other citizens of that State."

DUE PROCESS CLAUSE

The guarantee in the Fourteenth Amendment that no state shall "deprive any person of life, liberty, or property, without due process of law" reiterates the guarantee of the Fifth Amendment that requires that the federal government afford due process of law. The Due Process Clause is used by judges to oversee the reasonableness of laws.

Procedural due process includes a person's right to be adequately notified of proceedings against him, the opportunity to be effectively heard at these proceedings, and the requirement that the proceedings be conducted and decided by an impartial tribunal. As the Supreme Court stated in *Snyder v. Massachusetts*, 291 U.S. 97, 105 (1934), a state "is free to regulate the procedure of its courts in accordance with its own conception of policy and fairness unless, in so doing, it offends some principle of justice so rooted in the traditions and conscience of our people as to be ranked as fundamental." Accordingly, a defendant's due process rights are violated by a mob-dominated trial (*Moore v. Dempsey*, 261 U.S. 86 [1923]), 6–2 vote); the prosecution's presentation of testimony known to be perjured (*Mooney v. Holohan*, 294 U.S. 103 [1938], 9–0 vote); and a criminal conviction based on a lesser standard than that of proof beyond a reasonable doubt (*In re Winship*, 397 U.S. 358 [1970], 6–3 vote).

The application of the procedural due process doctrine is further illustrated by the following cases.

1. In *Chicago, Milwaukee & St. Paul Railway Co. v. Minnesota*, 134 U.S. 418 (1890), the Supreme Court voided 6–3 state legislation that did not permit judicial review of railroad rates set by a state regulatory agency. Due process requires judicial review of agency decisions to determine their legality. In *Reagan v. Farmers' Loan & Trust Co.*, 154 U.S. 362 (1894), the Supreme Court again upheld 9–0 the right of courts to review ratemaking by state commissions.

2. In *Bi-Metallic Investment Co. v. State Board of Equalization*, 239 U.S. 441 (1915), involving an increase in the valuation of all taxable property, the Supreme Court held 9–0 that no procedural due process rights are violated in a tax levied against a large number of people without a hearing. "Where a rule of conduct applies to more than a few people, it is impracticable that everyone should have a direct voice in its adoption. The Constitution does not require all public acts to be done in town meeting or an assembly of the whole." 239 U.S. 445.

3. In *Tumey v. Ohio*, 273 U.S. 510 (1927), where the judge received a fee for each conviction, the Supreme Court ruled 9–0 that to subject a defendant to trial in a criminal case involving his liberty or property before a judge having a direct, personal, substantial interest in convicting him is a denial of due process. The same result was reached in *Ward v. Village of Monroeville*, 409 U.S. 57 (1972), where the Supreme Court held 7–2 that Ward was denied due process by being compelled to stand trial for traffic offenses before the mayor, who was responsible for village finances and whose court, through fines, forfeitures, costs and fees, provided a substantial portion of village funds.

4. In *International Shoe Co. v. Washington*, 326 U.S. 310 (1945), the company, a foreign corporation, employed salesman in the state to solicit orders from prospective customers to be accepted or rejected by the company at a point outside the state. The state sued the company to collect unpaid unemployment compensation taxes for its in-state salesman. The Supreme Court held 9–0 that the in-state activities of the company created sufficient contacts for the state to enforce against the company an obligation arising out of such activities. Such "long-arm statutes" are prevalent among the states, and permit service of process by mail against the out-of-state defendant. If the defendant fails to respond, the plaintiff can obtain a default judgment that would be enforceable against the defendant under the Full Faith and Credit Clause, Article IV, Section 1. An insufficient nexus was found in *World-Wide Volkswagen Corp. v. Woodson*, 444 U.S. 286 (1980), where the plaintiffs were injured on an interstate trip in Oklahoma due to an allegedly defective automobile purchased from the corporation in New York. The Court ruled 6–3 that there was a total absence of any affiliating circumstances necessary to support Oklahoma court jurisdiction. The corporation carried on no activity whatsoever in the state, closed no sales or performed any services there, and availed itself of none of the benefits of state law.

5. In *In re Gault*, 387 U.S. 1 (1967), the Supreme Court held 8–1 that a juvenile defendant, prior to commitment to a state industrial school for an alleged obscene telephone call, was entitled to adequate notice of hearing, right of counsel, right of confrontation and cross-examination of witnesses, and exercise of privilege against self-incrimination. A fair hearing is also required for parole revocation. *Morrissey v. Brewer*, 408 U.S. 471 (1972), 9–0 vote.

6. In *Sniadach v. Family Finance Corp.*, 395 U.S. 337 (1969), the Supreme Court held 7–1 that a state cannot constitutionally allow garnishment of wages without prior notice and hearing.

7. In *Goldberg v. Kelly*, 397 U.S. 254 (1970), the Supreme Court ruled 5–3 that a state must afford public aid recipients a pre-termination evidentiary hearing before discontinuing their aid. However, in *Board of Regents of State Colleges v. Roth*, 408 U.S. 564 (1972), a teacher, hired under a one-year contract, was told that he would not be rehired for the next year and was given no explanation for the decision or opportunity to challenge it. The Court held 5–3 that the non-tenured teacher had no property interest protected by procedural due process because there was no right to continued employment.

8. In *Fuentes v. Shevin*, 407 U.S. 67 (1972), the Supreme Court held 4–3 that state laws that allowed for the summary repossession of petitioner's property without prior notice or hearing violate procedural due process.

9. In *Goss v. Lopez*, 419 U.S. 565 (1974), the Supreme Court held 5–4 that high school students facing suspension for alleged misconduct must be given notice and afforded a hearing. Students "do not shed their constitutional rights at the schoolhouse door." 419 U.S. 574.

10. In *Bordenkircher v. Hayes*, 434 U.S. 357 (1978), the prosecutor told Hayes, who was charged with forgery, that if he would plead guilty, a five-year sentence would be recommended; otherwise the prosecutor would seek conviction of Hayes as an habitual criminal (due to past offenses) which could result in a lifetime prison sentence. Hayes refused the offer, resulting in his conviction as a habitual criminal with a lifetime sentence. On appeal, in which Hayes argued that the prosecutor's use of the plea bargaining process was coercive, the Supreme Court held 5–4 that Hayes' right to due process was not violated during plea bargaining when he elected his right to trial and was convicted as a habitual criminal.

11. In *Santosky v. Kramer*, 455 U.S. 745 (1982), the Supreme Court held 5–4 that before the state may terminate, over parental objection, the rights of parents in their natural child—a termination that interferes with a fundamental liberty interest—due process requires that the state support its allegations by at least clear and convincing evidence. Hence the lesser standard of preponderance of the evidence is insufficient.

12. In *Connecticut Department of Public Safety v. Doe*, 538 U.S. 1 (2003), the state's "Megan's Law" requires that convicted sex offenders register with the department and that the department publish on the Internet a registry showing sex offenders' names, addresses, photographs and descriptions. On appeal, the Supreme Court held 9–0 that procedural due process does not require that convicted sex offenders receive a hearing before their public disclosure on the registry. The registry merely made already public information more readily available to the public on the Internet, and did not assess the dangerousness of those listed. Thus, disclosing an offender on the registry without a hearing did not violate procedural due process.

Under the substantive due process doctrine, when government action is challenged as a violation of individual liberty, the courts balance the importance of the governmental interest being served, and the appropriateness of the government's method of implementation, against the resulting infringement of individual rights. If the government action infringes upon a fundamental right, such as racial discrimination, strict scrutiny is applied, and the action will be upheld only if it serves a compelling government interest and is narrowly tailored to further that interest. Otherwise, if the government action does not restrict a fundamental right, a rational basis test is applied. That test is satisfied if the goal is rationally related to a legitimate government purpose.

In *West Coast Hotel Co. v. Parrish*, 300 U.S. 379 (1937), the Supreme Court, in a majority opinion by Chief Justice Charles Evans Hughes, upheld 5–4 a state minimum wage law for women as a constitutional limitation on the freedom of contract because of the state's special interest in protecting the health and financial welfare of women. The decision ended a line of cases holding that the freedom of contract superseded government regulation designed to promote health and economic welfare. Among those cases, *Lochner v. New York*, 198 U.S. 45 (1905), 5–4 vote, voided law limiting working hours for bakers; *Adair v. United States*, 208 U.S. 161 (1908), 7–2 vote, and *Coppage v. Kansas*, 236 U.S. 1 (1915), 6–3 vote, upheld "yellow dog" contracts that forbade workers from joining unions; and *Adkins v. Children's Hospital*, 261 U.S. 525 (1923), 5–3 vote, voided minimum wage law for women.

Since the *Lochner* line of cases had frustrated the New Deal program, President Franklin Delano Roosevelt announced in his ninth fireside chat on March 9, 1937, his proposed legislation to increase the membership of the Supreme Court by authorizing the appointment of an additional justice to the Court for each sitting member over the age of 70½, up to a maximum of six. Shortly thereafter, on March 29, the Court issued the *West Coast Hotel* decision, in which Associate Justice Owen Roberts, switching from his previous freedom-of-contract position, joined Hughes and Associate Justices Louis Brandeis, Benjamin Cardozo and Harlan Fiske Stone to form the majority—a move that came to be known as "the switch in time that saved nine." The Court at that time was composed of four conservative members (the "Four Horsemen"), Associate Justices Pierce Butler (age 71), James Clark McReynolds (age 75), George Sutherland (age 75), and Willis Van Devanter (age 77); three liberal members (the "Three Musketeers"), Associate Justices Brandeis (age 80), Cardozo (age 66), and Stone (age 64); and Chief Justice Hughes (age 74) and Associate Justice Roberts (age 61). With the retirement of Justice Van Devanter on June 2, 1937, and his replacement by Justice Hugo Black on August 19, 1937, the Roosevelt court-packing proposal was defeated in Congress.

The application of the substantive due process doctrine is further illustrated by the following cases.

1. In *Munn v. Illinois*, 94 U.S. 113 (1877), the Supreme Court upheld 7–2 state legislation proposed by the Granger movement to regulate grain elevator rates, declaring that private businesses "affected with a public interest" may be regulated for the public good, and that any effect on interstate commerce was incidental. The Grangers were farmers opposed to the monopolistic practices of railroads and grain elevators. The *Munn* case was the most important of the six Granger cases decided by the Court on that

day, and established the precedent for government regulation of the rates and service of privately owned public utilities.

2. In *Santa Clara County v. Southern Pacific Railroad Co.*, 118 U.S. 394 (1886), the Supreme Court, in a case involving tax assessments, observed 9–0 that railroad corporations are persons within the meaning of the Fourteenth Amendment.

3. In *Allgeyer v. Louisiana*, 165 U.S. 578 (1897), the Supreme Court invalidated 9–0, under the Fourteenth Amendment, a state law prohibiting persons from entering into certain insurance contracts by mail with companies operating outside the state. "The 'liberty' mentioned in that amendment means not only the right of the citizen to be free from the mere physical restraint of his person, as by incarceration, but the term is deemed to embrace the right of the citizen to be free in the enjoyment of all his faculties, to be free to use them in all lawful ways, to live and work where he will, to earn his livelihood by any lawful calling, to pursue any livelihood or avocation, and for that purpose to enter into all contracts which may be proper, necessary, and essential to his carrying out to a successful conclusion the purposes above mentioned." 165 U.S. 589.

4. In *Holden v. Hardy*, 169 U.S. 366 (1898), the Supreme Court upheld 7–2 a Utah law limiting the working hours for miners and smelters as a legitimate exercise of the state police power due to the dangerous working conditions. The Court viewed the inherent danger of the work as distinguishing the decision from other cases of the era that invalidated workplace laws under the Due Process Clause.

5. In *Muller v. Oregon*, 208 U.S. 412 (1908), the Supreme Court upheld 9–0 state restrictions on the working hours of women as justified by the strong state interest in protecting women's health. Louis Brandeis (1856–1941), as an attorney for Oregon, filed a brief of over 115 pages that went beyond traditional legal arguments and provided statistical, historical, sociological and economic data that documented the damaging health effects on women from working long hours. Thereafter, briefs that relied on such extra-legal data became known as "Brandeis briefs." Later, Brandeis served as an associate justice of the U.S. Supreme Court (1916–1939). In *Bunting v. Oregon*, 243 U.S. 426 (1917), the Court upheld 5–3 a state law establishing a ten-hour day for factory workers and requiring time-and-a-half pay for overtime. The Court accepted the legislative determination that the law was needed to preserve worker health.

6. In *Meyer v. Nebraska*, 262 U.S. 390 (1923), the Supreme Court invalidated 7–2 a state law prohibiting the teaching of foreign languages to grade school children.

7. In *Wolff Packing Co. v. Court of Industrial Relations*, 262 U.S. 522 (1923), a Kansas law declared a compelling public interest in key industries,

such as food, clothing, energy and transportation; required compulsory arbitration of all disputes in these industries through a special court; and empowered the court to restrict strikes and employer lockouts and to fix wages and oversee working conditions. The Supreme Court invalidated the law 9–0, holding that the mere declaration that a business is affected with the public interest is not conclusive of the question as to whether its regulation is justified and comports with due process.

8. In *Pierce v. Society of the Sisters of the Holy Names of Jesus and Mary*, 268 U.S. 510 (1925), the Supreme Court invalidated 9–0 a state compulsory act that required attendance at public schools because it "unreasonably interferes with the liberty of parents and guardians to direct the upbringing and education of children under their control." 268 U.S. 534. A state may require children to attend school, but cannot mandate attendance at public schools.

9. In *Village of Euclid v. Amber Realty Co.*, 272 U.S. 365 (1926), the Supreme Court upheld 6–3 a comprehensive zoning ordinance regulating the location of businesses, industries and residences as a reasonable exercise of the police power to ensure the protection of the public health, safety, morals and welfare. However, in *Nectow v. City of Cambridge*, 277 U.S. 183 (1928), the Supreme Court held 9–0 that an otherwise constitutional zoning ordinance was unconstitutional as applied to Nectow's property because it was not indispensable to the general plan and did not promote the general welfare of the inhabitants of the city, and that, while the cost to Nectow was high, the public benefit was small.

10. In *New State Ice Co. v. Liebmann*, 285 U.S. 262 (1932), the Supreme Court invalidated 6–2 a state law declaring that the manufacture and sale of ice is a public business subject to licensing and regulation based on a showing of public need. While *New State Ice* has not been overruled, it may have been superseded by decisions that uphold broad legislative authority to regulate business activity. The case is memorable for the dissent of Justice Louis Brandeis, joined in by Justice Harlan Fiske Stone: "To stay experimentation in things social and economic is a grave responsibility. Denial of the right to experiment may be fraught with serious consequences to the nation. It is one of the happy incidents of the federal system that a single courageous state may, if its citizens choose, serve as a laboratory; and try novel and social and economic experiments without risk to the rest of the country." 285 U.S. 311.

11. In *Nebbia v. New York*, 291 U.S. 502 (1934), the Supreme Court upheld 5–4 state retail price regulation for milk because the price controls were not "arbitrary, discriminatory, or demonstrably irrelevant" to the state policy to promote the general welfare. 291 U.S. 539. A state may adopt any reasonable economic policy to promote the public welfare even though the business regulated does not fall within the category of "businesses affected with a public interest."

12. In *Watts v. Indiana*, 338 U.S. 49 (1949), the Supreme Court overturned 6–3 the murder conviction of Watts, who was held incommunicado in solitary confinement for seven days and questioned by police in relays ranging in duration from 3 to 9 hours. In *Rochin v. California*, 342 U.S. 165 (1952), the Supreme Court overturned 8–0 the conviction of Rochin for drug possession based on doctors pumping the drug capsules from his stomach against his will and on the direction of police. The Court found no distinction between a "verbal confession extracted by physical abuse and a confession wrested from defendant's body by physical abuse." 342 U.S. 167.

13. In *Williamson v. Lee Optical Company*, 348 U.S. 483 (1955), the Supreme Court upheld 8–0 an Oklahoma statute prohibiting any person not a licensed optometrist or ophthalmologist from fitting, duplicating or replacing lenses for eyeglasses without a prescription. "The day is gone when this Court uses the Due Process Clause of the Fourteenth Amendment to strike down state laws, regulatory of business or industrial conditions, because they may be unwise, improvident, or out of harmony with a particular school of thought.... We emphasize again what Chief Justice Waite said in *Munn v. Illinois*, 94 U.S. 113, 134, 'For protection against abuses by legislatures the people must resort to the polls, not the courts.'" 348 U.S. 488.

14. In *Ferguson v. Skrupa*, 372 U.S. 726 (1963), the Supreme Court upheld 9–0 the right of a state to prohibit debt adjusting, whereby a debtor agrees to pay a fee to an adjustor who then pays the debtor's creditor. The state contended that the practice would lead to grave abuses against distressed debtors, especially those in the lower income brackets. The Court disavowed assessing the wisdom of state regulation of economic activity.

15. As to exculpatory evidence, the Supreme Court in *Brady v. Maryland*, 373 U.S. 83 (1963), held 7–2 that the suppression by the prosecution of evidence favorable to the accused violates due process where the evidence is material either to guilt or to punishment, irrespective of the good faith or bad faith of the prosecution. In *Kyles v. Whitley*, 514 U.S. 419 (1995), the Court held 5–4 that the prosecutor has an obligation to discover, preserve and communicate with the defense any exculpatory evidence in the government's possession.

16. In *Roe v. Wade*, 410 U.S. 113 (1973), the Supreme Court upheld 7–2 the right of a woman to terminate her pregnancy by abortion as guaranteed by her right to privacy under the Due Process Clause. The Court divided the pregnancy term into three thirteen-week periods, or trimesters, in an effort to balance the state's legitimate interest in controlling abortions against a woman's right to terminate her pregnancy. During the first trimester, the woman has an unqualified right to have an abortion following consultation with her physician. During the second trimester, the state can regulate the abortion procedure to ensure the woman's health. In the third trimester,

when the fetus becomes viable, the state can restrict or proscribe abortions, except in cases where the woman's life or health is in danger. In *Webster v. Reproductive Health Services*, 492 U.S. 490 (1989), the Court upheld 5–4 state restrictions on the use of state funds, facilities and employees in performing or assisting abortions unnecessary to save the mother's life. In *Planned Parenthood of Southeastern Pennsylvania v. Casey*, 505 U.S. 833 (1992), the Court upheld 5–4 state requirements for parental consent, informed consent and 24-hour waiting period, but invalidated spousal notification prior to obtaining an abortion because it created an "undue burden" on married women seeking an abortion. In *Stenberg v. Carhart*, 530 U.S. 914 (2000), the Court invalidated 5–4 a state law criminalizing partial-birth abortions because it was vague, placed an undue burden on a woman's right to have an abortion, and did not provide an exception to preserve a woman's health. In *Gonzales v. Carhart*, 550 U.S. 124 (2007), the Court upheld 5–4 the federal Partial-Birth Abortion Ban Act of 2003 because it outlawed a specific type of abortion procedure, usually used in the second trimester, known as intact dilation and extraction (D&E) and, hence, did not impose an undue burden on the due process right (Fifth Amendment) of women to obtain an abortion. The Court ruled that the omission of a health exception for the mother was justified because Congress found that intact D&E was never medically necessary nor needed to protect maternal health.

17. In *O'Connor v. Donaldson*, 422 U.S. 563 (1975), the Supreme Court held 9–0 that states cannot confine persons to an institution without treatment if they are non-dangerous and capable of safely living by themselves or with the aid of responsible family or friends.

18. In *Moore v. East Cleveland*, 431 U.S. 494 (1977), the Supreme Court overturned 5–4 a housing ordinance limiting occupancy of a dwelling to members of a single family so defined as to exclude Moore, who lived with her son and two grandsons. Four justices ruled that the ordinance constituted an "intrusive regulation of the family" without promoting any compelling government interest. They were joined by a fifth justice who found that the ordinance constituted a taking of Moore's property without just compensation.

19. In *Carey v. Population Services International*, 431 U.S. 678 (1977), the Supreme Court invalidated 7–2 a state law criminalizing the sale of contraceptives to persons under 16, the distribution of contraceptives to persons 16 or older by anyone other than a licensed pharmacist, and the advertisement or display of contraceptives by anyone. The Court ruled that regulations burdening a decision as fundamental as to whether to bear or beget a child may be justified only by compelling state interests, and must be narrowly drawn to express only those interests, which the state had failed to achieve in this case.

20. In *Youngberg v. Romeo*, 457 U.S. 307 (1982), the Supreme Court held 9–0 that an involuntarily committed retarded person in a state institution has constitutionally protected liberty interests under the Due Process Clause to reasonably safe conditions of confinement, freedom from unreasonable bodily restraints, and such minimally adequate training as reasonably may be required for these interests.

21. In *DeShaney v. Winnebago County Department of Social Services*, 489 U.S. 189 (1989), a child was subjected to serious beatings by his father, with whom he lived. Although the county received complaints of such abuse, it did not act to remove the child from his father's custody. Finally, the father beat the child so severely that he suffered permanent brain damage rendering him profoundly retarded. The Supreme Court ruled 6–3 that the county's failure to prevent child abuse by a custodial parent does not violate the child's right to liberty under the Due Process Clause. "The Clause is phrased as a limitation on the State's power to act, not as a guarantee of certain minimal levels of safety and security. It forbids the State itself to deprive individuals of life, liberty, or property without 'due process of law,' but its language cannot fairly be extended to impose an affirmative obligation on the State to ensure that those interests do not come to harm through other means." 489 U.S. 195.

22. In *Washington v. Harper*, 494 U.S. 210 (1990), the Supreme Court held 6–3 that the Due Process Clause permits a state to treat a prison inmate, who has a serious mental illness, with antipsychotic drugs against his will, if he is dangerous to himself or others and the treatment is in his medical interest. The Court found that an internal institutional review was sufficient, and that a judicial hearing was not required.

23. In *Cruzan v. Director, Missouri Department of Health*, 497 U.S. 261 (1990), the Supreme Court upheld 5–4 the state's refusal of the parents' request to disconnect the life-support system of their daughter, who was in a "persistent vegetative state." The state had found no "clear and convincing" evidence that she would have supported such a request. The Court recognized that, while persons have a due process right to refuse medical treatment and while incompetent persons are incapable of exercising such right, the state's action designed to preserve human life was constitutional. Also, there was no guarantee that family members would always act in the best interests of incompetent patients.

24. In *Washington v. Glucksberg*, 521 U.S. 702 (1997), the Supreme Court upheld 9–0 a state ban on physician-assisted suicide because it protected the integrity and ethics of the medical profession, protected the vulnerable from mistakes, and reaffirmed the value of life. The Court reached the same result in *Vacco v. Quill*, 521 U.S. 793 (1997), under the Equal Protection Clause. On the other hand, the Supreme Court in *Gonzales v. Oregon*,

546 U.S. 243 (2006), refused 6–3 to overturn Oregon's Death with Dignity Act which legalized physician-assisted death for terminally ill patients.

25. In *BMW of North America v. Gore*, 517 U.S. 559 (1996), the Supreme Court invalidated 5–4 excessively high punitive damages of $2 million in relation to $4,000 of compensatory damages. In *State Farm Mutual Automobile Insurance Co. v. Campbell*, 538 U.S. 408 (2003), the Supreme Court invalidated 6–3 excessively high punitive damages of $145 million in relation to $1 million of compensatory damages. "Compensatory damages are intended to redress a plaintiff's concrete loss, while punitive damages are aimed at the different purposes of deterrence and retribution." 538 U.S. 408. In *Philip Morris USA v. Williams*, 549 U.S. 346 (2007), the Supreme Court held 5–4 that the "Due Process Clause forbids a State to use a punitive damages award to punish a defendant for injury that it inflicts upon nonparties," such as punitive damages for a cigarette cancer death being magnified by the harm done to "strangers to the litigation." In *Exxon Shipping Co. v. Baker*, 554 U.S. ___ (2008), the supertanker *Exxon Valdez* ran aground off the Alaskan coast in 1989, spilling millions of gallons of oil into Prince William Sound. The Supreme Court ruled 5–3 that a ratio of no more than one-to-one between compensatory and punitive damages is generally appropriate in maritime cases. Thus, the punitive damages should not exceed $507 million because Exxon had paid $507 million to landowners and fishermen as compensatory damages caused by the spill.

26. In *Lawrence v. Texas*, 539 U.S. 558 (2003), the Supreme Court invalidated 6–3 a state law criminalizing sexual intimacy by same-sex couples. "Liberty presumes an autonomy of self that includes freedom of thought, belief, expression, and certain intimate conduct." 539 U.S. 562. This decision overruled *Bowers v. Hardwick*, 478 U.S. 186 (1986), upholding 5–4 a Georgia law criminalizing homosexual sex in private between consenting adults.

27. In *Caperton v. A. T. Massey Coal Company, Inc.*, 556 U.S. ___ (2009), the Supreme Court held 5–4 that state court justice Brent Benjamin should have recused himself from participating in the decision of a case involving a party who was a major contributor in supporting the election campaign of the justice. Benjamin voted with the 3–2 majority in favor of the contributor's company. Such an extraordinary situation presents a serious risk of bias in violation of the due process guarantee for fair and impartial adjudication.

28. In *District Attorney's Office for the Third Judicial District v. Osborne*, 557 U.S. ___ (2009), the Supreme Court held 5–4 that there is no due process right for a criminal defendant to obtain post-conviction access to the state's DNA evidence, used in his conviction, for more advanced testing. The Court reasoned that the defendant's rights were adequately protected by state law, which provides that the defendant can overturn his conviction if there is newly-discovered evidence that clearly establishes his innocence.

The Supreme Court has used the Due Process Clause to require that the states abide by most of the guarantees in the Bill of Rights through the doctrine of selective incorporation, thereby imposing much the same fundamental obligations on the state governments as are required of the federal government. Otherwise, there would have been a substantial lack of uniformity in the guarantees afforded by the federal and state constitutions. The extent of incorporation is shown by the following cases.

1. Establishment of Religion Clause, First Amendment, incorporated as applicable to the states in *Everson v. Board of Education of Ewing Township*, 330 U.S. 1 (1947).

2. Free Exercise of Religion Clause, First Amendment, incorporated as applicable to the states in *Cantwell v. Connecticut*, 310 U.S. 296 (1940).

3. Freedom of Speech Clause, First Amendment, incorporated as applicable to the states in *Gitlow v. New York*, 268 U.S. 652 (1925).

4. Freedom of the Press Clause, First Amendment, incorporated as applicable to the states in *Near v. Minnesota*, 283 U.S. 697 (1931).

5. Freedom of Assembly Clause, First Amendment, incorporated as applicable to the states in *De Jonge v. Oregon*, 299 U.S. 353 (1937).

6. Freedom of Petition Clause, First Amendment, incorporated as applicable to the states in *Edwards v. South Carolina*, 372 U.S. 229 (1963).

7. Right to Bear Arms, Second Amendment, incorporation, as applicable to the states, anticipated following *District of Columbia v Heller*, 554 U.S. __ (2008).

8. Quartering of Soldiers, Third Amendment, incorporated as applicable to the states in *Engblom v. Carey*, 677 F2d 957 (2d Cir 1982).

9. Search and Seizure Clause, Fourth Amendment, incorporated as applicable to the states in *Wolf v. Colorado*, 338 U.S. 25 (1949). Exclusionary rule applied to the states in *Mapp v. Ohio*, 367 U.S. 643 (1961).

10. Warrant Clause, Fourth Amendment, incorporated as applicable to the states in *Aguilar v. Texas*, 378 U.S. 108 (1964).

11. Grand Jury Clause, Fifth Amendment, not incorporated as applicable to the states. It is unlikely that the clause will be incorporated because the Supreme Court in *Hurtado v. California*, 110 U.S. 516 (1884), has ruled 8–1 that a criminal proceeding based on accusations by a prosecutor and a preliminary hearing before a judge, rather than a grand jury indictment, is an adequate protection of due process under the Fourteenth Amendment.

12. Double Jeopardy Clause, Fifth Amendment, incorporated as applicable to the states in *Benton v. Maryland*, 395 U.S. 784 (1969).

13. Self-Incrimination Clause, Fifth Amendment, incorporated as applicable to the states in *Malloy v. Hogan*, 378 U.S. 1 (1964).

14. Just Compensation Clause, Fifth Amendment, incorporated as

applicable to the states in *Chicago, Burlington & Quincy Railroad Co. v. City of Chicago*, 166 U.S. 226 (1897). This was the first incorporation of the Bill of Rights as applicable to the states.

15. Speedy Trial Clause, Sixth Amendment, incorporated as applicable to the states in *Klopfer v. North Carolina*, 386 U.S. 213 (1967).

16. Public Trial Clause, Sixth Amendment, incorporated as applicable to the states in *In re Oliver*, 333 U.S. 257 (1948).

17. Jury Trial Clause, Sixth Amendment, incorporated as applicable to the states in *Parker v. Gladden*, 385 U.S. 363 (1966).

18. Notice of Accusation Clause, Sixth Amendment, incorporated as applicable to the states in *In re Oliver*, 333 U.S. 257 (1948).

19. Confrontation Clause, Sixth Amendment, incorporated as applicable to the states in *Pointer v. Texas*, 380 U.S. 400 (1965).

20. Compulsory Process Clause, Sixth Amendment, incorporated as applicable to the states in *Washington v. Texas*, 388 U.S. 14 (1967).

21. Right to Counsel Clause, Sixth Amendment, incorporated as applicable to the states in *Powell v. Alabama*, 287 U.S. 45 (1932), in capital cases; *Gideon v. Wainwright*, 372 U.S. 335 (1963), in felony cases; and *Argersinger v. Hamlin*, 407 U.S. 25 (1972), in cases permitting imprisonment.

22. Trial by Jury in Common Law Cases, Seventh Amendment, not incorporated as applicable to the states. *Minneapolis & St. Louis R. Co. v. Bombolis*, 241 U.S. 211 (1916).

23. Excessive Bail and Fines Clauses, Eighth Amendment, not incorporated as applicable to the states. However, the majority opinion in *Schilb v. Kuebel*, 404 U.S. 357 (1971), stated that "the Eighth Amendment's proscription of excessive bail has been assumed to have application to the States through the Fourteenth Amendment." 404 U.S. 365.

24. Cruel and Unusual Punishment Clause, Eighth Amendment, incorporated as applicable to the states in *Robinson v. California*, 370 U.S. 660 (1962).

EQUAL PROTECTION CLAUSE

The guarantee in the Fourteenth Amendment that no state shall "deny to any person within its jurisdiction the equal protection of the laws" requires that the states must apply the law equally and cannot give undue preference to one person or class of persons over another. The clause restrains government actions and not those of private citizens. However, to reach private conduct, the Congress has enacted the Civil Rights Acts of 1964 and 1968 under the powers conferred by the Commerce Clause (Article I, Section 8, Clause 3) and the Enforcement Clause of the Fourteenth Amendment.

The Supreme Court has defined three levels of scrutiny in applying the Equal Protection Clause, the genesis of which is found in footnote four of the majority opinion of Associate Justice Harlan Fiske Stone in *United States v. Carolene Products*, 304 U.S. 144 (1938). In the footnote, he applied minimal scrutiny to economic regulation (rational basis test), but suggested strict scrutiny for legislation that violates specifically enumerated constitutional rights, makes it more difficult to achieve change through normal political processes, or is aimed at "discrete and insular minorities," who lack the usual protections of the political process. The levels of scrutiny are as follws:

1. The highest level, strict scrutiny, applies to suspect classifications, such as race, religion, or interfering with fundamental rights such as voting or travel. Under strict scrutiny law is deemed unconstitutional unless it is narrowly tailored to serve a compelling government interest. For example, in *Loving v. Virginia*, 388 U.S. 1 (1967), the Supreme Court invalidated 9–0 a state ban on interracial marriage, finding that such racial discrimination is "odious to a free people" and is subject to "the most rigid scrutiny" under the Equal Protection Clause. Also, in *Adarand Constructors v. Pena*, 515 U.S. 200 (1995), the Supreme Court held 5–4 that all racial classifications, whether imposed by federal, state or local authorities, must pass strict scrutiny, meaning that they "must serve a compelling government interest, and must be narrowly tailored to further that interest." 515 U.S. 235.

2. The second level, intermediate scrutiny, applies to gender, and a law addressing such a classification is unconstitutional unless it is substantially related to the achievement of an important government objective. An example is *Craig v. Boren*, 429 U.S. 190 (1976), in which the Supreme Court ruled 7–2 that a state law, establishing different minimum drinking ages for men at 21 years and women at 18 years, was an unconstitutional gender classification which was not supported by any substantial relationship between the law and maintaining traffic safety.

3. The third level relies on the rational basis test for subjects where the government needs only to show that the challenged classification is rationally related to serving a legitimate government interest. In *Railway Express Agency v. New York*, 336 U.S. 106 (1949), the Supreme Court upheld 9–0 a city ordinance forbidding the sale of advertisements on the exterior sides of commercial trucks, unless the advertising concerns the truck operator's own business. The Court found that the prohibition of such advertising was rationally related to promoting traffic safety by reducing driver distractions, and that the exemption of advertising concerning the truck operator's own business did not violate the Equal Protection Clause. However, in *City of Cleburne v. Cleburne Living Center*, 473 U.S. 432 (1985), the Supreme Court held 9–0 that the denial of a permit to Cleburne Living Center to operate a home for the mentally retarded was premised on an irrational prejudice against the mentally retarded and, hence, a violation of the Equal Protection Clause under the rational basis test.

• AGE ISSUES. In *Massachusetts Board of Retirement v. Murgia*, 427 U.S. 307 (1976), involving a police officer in excellent health who was forced to retire at age 50, the Supreme Court held 7–1 that there was no violation of the Equal Protection Clause because the state mandatory retirement law rationally furthered the purpose of protecting the public by assuring the physical preparedness of state police officers. In *Gregory v. Ashcroft*, 501 U.S. 452 (1991), the Court held 7–2 that a state law requiring state judges to retire at age 70 does not violate the Equal Protection Clause or the federal Age Discrimination in Employment Act (ADEA). The authority of a state's people to determine the qualifications of their most important government officials lies "at the heart of representative government," and is reserved under the Tenth Amendment and guaranteed by the Guarantee Clause of Article IV. For Congress to intrude in this area, it must make its intention to do so "unmistakably clear" in the ADEA.

• MARRIAGE ISSUES. In addition to the *Loving* case above, the Supreme Court in *Zablocki v. Redhail*, 434 U.S. 374 (1978), overturned 8–1 a state statute that prohibited the marriage of a parent who was delinquent in child support payments. Ruling that the prohibition violated the Equal Protection Clause, the Court reaffirmed the fundamental right of marriage. In *Orr v. Orr*, 440 U.S. 268 (1979), the Court invalidated 6–3 a state law that required husbands to pay alimony, but not wives. In *Wengler v. Druggists Mutual Insurance Co.*, 446 U.S. 142 (1980), the Court invalidated 8–1 a state workers' compensation law denying a widower benefits on his wife's work-related death unless he is incapacitated or dependent on her earnings, but granting a widow death benefits without proof of dependence on her husband's earnings. In *Turner v. Safley*, 482 U.S. 78 (1987), the Court invalidated 9–0 a prison regulation prohibiting inmates from marrying without the permission of the warden as a violation of their constitutional right to marry and as not related to any legitimate penal concern.

• RACIAL ISSUES. The Supreme Court in *Strauder v. West Virginia*, 100 U.S. 303 (1880), ruled 7–2 that the exclusion of individuals from juries solely because of their race is a violation of the Equal Protection clause. The same result was reached in *Hernandez v. Texas*, 347 U.S. 475 (1954), 9–0 vote, with respect to the exclusion of Mexican-Americans and all other racial groups. The discriminatory use of peremptory challenges in jury selection is addressed under the Jury Trial Clause of the Sixth Amendment. The Supreme Court has held that the clause is violated when a state or municipality prejudicially applies a law that is race-neutral on its face so as to sharply reduce the number of Chinese laundries (*Yick Wo v. Hopkins*, 118 U.S. 356 [1886], 9–0 vote); offers in-state legal education to whites, but not blacks (*Missouri ex rel. Gaines v. Canada*, 305 U.S. 337 [1938], 6–2 vote); provides grossly unequal law school to blacks (*Sweatt v. Painter*, 339 U.S. 629 [1950],

9–0 vote); segregates participation of black at white college (*McLaurin v. Oklahoma State Regents*, 339 U.S. 637 [1950], 9–0 vote); prohibits unmarried interracial cohabitation, but not unmarried same-race cohabitation (*McLaughlin v. Florida*, 379 U.S. 184 [1964], 9–0 vote); racially segregates prisoners in prisons and jails (*Lee v. Washington*, 390 U.S. 333 [1968], 9–0 vote); and removes child custody from the natural mother upon her remarriage to a person of another race (*Palmore v. Sidoti*, 466 U.S. 429 [1984], 9–0 vote). Also, the Supreme Court has ruled that the state may not enforce racially restrictive covenants regarding residential occupancy. *Shelley v. Kraemer*, 334 U.S. 1 (1948), 6–0 vote.

In *Brown v. Board of Education of Topeka*, 347 U.S. 483 (1954), the Supreme Court ruled 9–0 that the racial segregation of students in public schools violates the Equal Protection Clause because separate facilities are inherently unequal. This decision overturned *Plessy v. Ferguson*, 163 U.S. 537 (1896), 7–1 vote, which upheld the constitutionality of racial segregation in public accommodations under the doctrine of "separate but equal." In *Bolling v. Sharp*, 347 U.S. 497 (1954), the Supreme Court ruled 9–0 that racial segregation in the public schools of the District of Columbia denied blacks due process of law as guaranteed by the Fifth Amendment. The Court recognized that, while the Fifth Amendment did not contain an Equal Protection Clause like the Fourteenth Amendment, "the concepts of equal protection and due process, both stemming from our American ideal of fairness, are not mutually exclusive." In effect, the Court made a "reverse incorporation" of the Equal Protection Clause of the Fourteenth Amendment into the Fifth Amendment. The Supreme Court in *Brown v. Board of Education II*, 349 U.S. 294 (1955), delegated 9–0 to the district courts the task of carrying out school desegregation "with all deliberate speed." However, in *Alexander v. Holmes County Board of Education*, 396 U.S. 19 (1969), the Supreme Court declared 9–0 that the "with all deliberate speed" formula was no longer constitutionally permissible, and that the racial segregation of southern schools must end immediately.

In *Cooper v. Aaron*, 358 U.S. 1 (1958), the Supreme Court held 9–0 that no scheme of racial discrimination is legal "where there is state participation through any arrangement, management, funds or property." 358 U.S. 4. The Supreme Court has invalidated programs that failed to racially desegregate school systems: *Griffin v. County School Board of Prince Edward County*, 377 U.S. 218 (1964), 9–0 vote, tuition grants and tax credits; *Green v. County School Board of New Kent County*, 391 U.S. 430 (1968), 9–0 vote, freedom of choice plans; *Monroe v. Board of Commissioners of City of Jackson*, 391 U.S. 450 (1968), 9–0 vote, free-transfer plans; and *Wright v. Council of City of Emporia*, 407 U.S. 451 (1972), 5–4 vote, realignment of school districts. The Court in *Swann v. Charlotte-Mecklenburg County Board of Education*, 402

U.S. 1 (1971), upheld 9–0 the redrawing of school zones and the busing of students among schools to create racial balance within the schools as an appropriate means to achieve desegregation. However, in *Milliken v. Bradley*, 418 U.S. 717 (1974), the Court overturned 5–4 a multi-school district desegregation plan for the busing of inner-city minority children to school districts outside Detroit in the absence of a showing that such outlying school districts had promoted racial segregation.

In *Burton v. Wilmington Parking Authority*, 365 U.S. 715 (1961), the Supreme Court held 6–3 that the refusal of a restaurant to serve a black person constituted state action in violation of the Equal Protection Clause because the restaurant was an integral part of a public building devoted to a public parking service that was owned and operated by a state agency. In contrast, the Court in *Moose Lodge v. Irvis*, 407 U.S. 163 (1972), held 6–3 that the refusal of service to a black person in the dining room of a private club in a private building did not violate the clause. The holding of a state liquor license by the club did not sufficiently implicate the state in the club's racially discriminatory guest practices so as to make such practices "state action" within the purview of the clause.

On the issue of *affirmative action*, the Supreme Court in *Regents of the University of California v. Bakke*, 438 U.S. 265 (1978), upheld 5–4 the constitutionality of affirmative action programs in using race as a factor in admissions, but held that the rigidity of a racial quota system violated the Equal Protection Clause and Title VI of the 1964 Civil Rights Act. The University had a policy of reserving 16 of 100 seats for minority applicants, resulting in the rejection of Bakke, a white male, although he had grade and test scores significantly higher than some of the minority applicants. The Court found that this policy amounted to a quota, whereas race should be only one element in the selection process. In *Fullilove v. Klutznick*, 448 U.S. 448 (1980), Congress, in the Public Works Employment Act of 1977, provided for a 10 percent "set aside" for minority businesses. The Supreme Court upheld 6–3 the set aside as a valid exercise of congressional authority—under the Spending and Commerce Clauses, Article I, Section 8, Clauses 1 & 3, and the Fourteenth Amendment's Enforcement Clause (Section 5)—where the Congress had found a history of racial discrimination. In *Metro Broadcasting Inc. v. Federal Communications Commission*, 497 U.S. 547 (1990), the Supreme Court upheld 5–4 the FCC's minority preference policies to promote broadcast diversity and increase minority ownership of broadcasting companies. However, in the absence of such congressional authority, the Supreme Court in *Wygant v. Jackson Board of Education*, 476 U.S. 267 (1986), held 5–4 that the Equal Protection Clause barred the board from laying off white teachers with more seniority than minority ones. The board had failed to justify the racial classification with a compelling government interest, and failed to demonstrate that the means chosen were narrowly tailored to achieve that purpose. In *Richmond v. J. A. Croson Co.*, 488 U.S. 469 (1989), the Court held 6–3 that state and local government programs to help minority-owned businesses cannot use rigid racial quotas and must be limited to correcting documented examples of past discrimination. The Court reasoned: "The dream of a Nation of equal citizens in a society where race is irrelevant to personal opportunity and achievement would be lost in a mosaic of shifting preferences based on inherently unmeasurable claims of past wrongs." 488 U.S. 505.

In *Gratz v. Bollinger*, 539 U.S. 244 (2003), the Supreme Court held 6–3 that the University of Michigan's use of racial preferences in undergraduate admissions violated the Equal Protection Clause and Title VI of the 1964 Civil Rights Act because the automatic preference for admission of under-represented minorities was not narrowly tailored and did not provide individualized consideration. In *Grutter v. Bollinger*, 539 U.S. 306 (2003), the Court held 5–4 that the university's use of racial preferences in law school admissions did not violate the Equal Protection Clause and Title VI because the school conducted a highly individualized review of each applicant that ensures that all factors that may contribute to diversity are meaningfully considered without race being the controlling factor. In *Parents Involved in Community Schools v. Seattle School District No. 1*, 551 U.S. 701 (2007), the school district allowed students to apply to any high school of their choice. However, in order to maintain racial diversity a school's population could not exceed approximately 40 percent white and 60 percent non-white. To obtain this racial balance, either white or non-white students would be assigned to a high school as needed to achieve this goal. The Supreme Court 5–4 invalidated this student assignment plan, ruling that it does not meet the narrowly tailored and compelling government interest requirements for diversity because it is used only to achieve racial balance.

In *Ricci v. DeStefano*, 557 U.S. ___ (2009), the Supreme Court held 5–4 that city officials discriminated against 18 firefighters (17 white, one Hispanic) when they rejected a promotions test in which whites had outscored minorities. The court ruled that employers must have a "strong basis in evidence" under Title VII of the 1964 Civil Rights Act that a test is unfair to minorities rather than simply relying on outcomes that show a disparate impact. The Equal Protection Clause was not relied on in *Ricci*.

• ELECTORAL ISSUES. In *Baker v. Carr*, 369 U.S. 186 (1962), the Supreme Court held 6–2 that federal courts must consider on the merits suits challenging the apportionment of state legislatures as "justiciable" issues under the Equal Protection Clause, thereby abandoning the prior practice of treating such issues as "political questions" not subject to judicial review.

In *Gray v. Sanders*, 372 U.S. 368 (1963), the Court held 8–1 that party primary elections must afford equal voting status according to the standard of "one person, one vote"—a standard that was extended to the apportionment of both houses of bicameral state legislatures (*Reynolds v. Sims*, 377 U.S. 566 [1964], 8–1 vote), and to the apportionment of congressional districts (*Wesberry v. Sanders*, 376 U.S. 1 [1964], 6–3 vote). However, the Supreme Court in *Mahan v. Howell*, 410 U.S. 315, 322 (1973), recognized 5–3 greater population flexibility for state legislative reapportionment than for congressional redistricting.

The Supreme Court in *Fortson v. Dorsey*, 379 U.S. 433 (1965), upheld 8–1 the combination of single- and multi-member senatorial districts of substantially equal population. In *Rogers v. Lodge*, 458 U.S. 613 (1982), the Court invalidated 6–3 the at-large election of county commissioners as a device to further racial discrimination, and upheld establishment of single-member districts. In *Hunt v. Cromartie*, 532 U.S. 234 (2001), the Court ruled 5–4 that an irregularly drawn congressional district, which included several areas with many black voters, did not violate the Equal Protection Clause if drawn to reflect political, rather than racial, identification. In *Bush v. Gore*, 531 U.S. 98 (2000), the Court voided the statewide manual recount of ballots ordered by the Florida court on the ground that there was no uniform standard for election officials to apply in the recount, thereby violating the Equal Protection and Due Process Clauses. In *Crawford v. Marion County Election Board*, 553 U.S. 181 (2008), the Court held 6–3 that a state law that requires voters to present either state or federal photo identification does not unduly burden their right to vote, and is justified by the state interest in preventing voter fraud.

In *Kramer v. Union Free School District No. 15*, 395 U.S. 621 (1969), the Supreme Court held 6–3 that a state may not limit school district voting to resident owners of real property or parents of public school children and, hence, an adult resident in his parents' home is entitled to vote. Also, the Court in *Cipriano v. City of Houma*, 395 U.S. 701 (1969), invalidated 9–0 a state law allowing only property taxpayers to vote on the issuance of revenue bonds by a municipal utility system. However, in *Associated Enterprises, Inc. v. Toltec District*, 410 U.S. 743 (1973), the Court upheld 6–3 the limitation of the voting franchise to property owners in the creation and maintenance of a state watershed improvement district, for which they bear the primary burden and share the benefits. In *Richardson v. Ramirez*, 418 U.S. 24 (1974), the Court ruled 6–3 that state disenfranchisement of convicted felons who have completed their sentences and paroles does not violate the Equal Protection Clause. However, in *Hunter v. Underwood*, 471 U.S. 222 (1985), the Court held 8–0 that a state's felony disenfranchisement provision will violate the Equal Protection Clause if it can be shown that the provision was enacted for a racially discriminatory purpose.

- GENDER ISSUES. In *Reed v. Reed*, 404 U.S. 71 (1971), the Supreme Court held 7–0 that administrators of estates cannot be named in a way that discriminates between sexes, such as preferring males over females. In *Cleveland Board of Education v. LaFleur*, 414 U.S. 632 (1974), the Court invalidated 7–2 overly restrictive maternity leave policies in public schools, such as requiring pregnant teachers to take unpaid leave beginning five months before the expected birth and ending at the school semester after the child was three months old. In *Frontiero v. Richardson*, 411 U.S. 677 (1973), the Court held 8–1 that the military cannot differentiate benefits based on gender. In *Stanton v. Stanton*, 421 U.S. 7 (1975), Utah, for the purpose of determining length of child support in divorce cases, provided that males achieved maturity at 21, and females at 18. The Court invalidated 8–1 this distinction, finding no rational justification for the age difference. In *Personnel Administrator of Massachusetts v. Feeney*, 442 U.S. 256 (1979), the Court upheld 7–2 a state law giving hiring preference to veterans over non-veterans, denying Feeney's claim of gender discrimination because so few women held veteran status. The Court found that the law served "legitimate and worthy purposes" and that the distinction was between veterans and non-veterans, not between men and women. In *Michael M. v. Superior Court of Sonoma County*, 450 U.S. 464 (1981), the Court upheld 5–4 a state statutory rape law, providing that when two persons between the ages of 14 and 17 engage in heterosexual intercourse, the male is guilty, but not the female. In *Mississippi University for Women v. Hogan*, 458 U.S. 718 (1982), the Court held 5–4 that the exclusion of men from enrolling in the university's nursing school violated the Equal Protection Clause. In *Johnson v. Transportation Agency of Santa Clara County*, 480 U.S. 616 (1987), the Court held 6–3 that, under the Civil Rights Act of 1964, a sex-based affirmative action plan can be used to overcome the effects of past job discrimination based on gender. Sex was only one factor among many in making promotion decisions, and no quota system was established. In *United States v. Virginia*, 518 U.S. 515 (1996), the Court held 7–1 that the Virginia Military Institute's male-only admission policy violated the Equal Protection Clause. The Court also found that VMI's proposal to establish a parallel women's-only academy at a private women's college was constitutionally inadequate because it would lack the stature and prestige of VMI.
- ILLEGITIMATE CHILDREN ISSUES. In *Levy v. Louisiana*, 391 U.S. 68 (1968), state law denied a suit by illegitimate children for the wrongful death of their mother, while permitting such a suit by legitimate children. The Supreme Court held 6–3 that the denial of the right of recovery by illegitimate children creates an invidious discrimination contravening the Equal Protection Clause because legitimacy or illegitimacy of birth has no relation to the wrong allegedly inflicted on the mother. In *Stanley v. Illinois*, 405 U.S.

645 (1972), state law provided that children of unmarried fathers, upon the death of the mother, are declared wards of the state and placed in guardianship without a hearing on parental fitness, whereas such a hearing is required before the state assumes custody of children of married or divorced parents and unmarried mothers. The Supreme Court held 5–2 that such disparate treatment constitutes a denial of equal protection of the law. In *Gomez v. Perez*, 409 U.S. 535 (1973), the Court held 7–2 that a state law denying the right of paternal support to illegitimate children while granting it to legitimate children violates the Equal Protection Clause. In *New Jersey Welfare Rights Organization v. Cahill*, 411 U.S. 619 (1973), the Court held 8–1 that a state program limiting welfare benefits to married parents with children denies equal protection to illegitimate children. In *Clark v. Jeter*, 486 U.S. 456 (1988), the Court invalidated 9–0 a state law requiring illegitimate children seeking support from their fathers to prove their paternity within six years of birth, whereas legitimate children could seek support at any time. Also, the six-year statute of limitations did not "necessarily provide a reasonable opportunity to assert a claim on behalf of an illegitimate child." 486 U.S. 464.

• INDIGENT/AFFORDABILITY ISSUES. The Supreme Court in *Griffin v. Illinois*, 351 U.S. 12 (1956), held 5–4 that indigent defendants convicted of armed robbery were entitled to receive a free transcript of their trial proceedings in order to effectuate their appeal; and in *Mayer v. Chicago*, 404 U.S. 189 (1971), the court extended this ruling 7–0 to require free transcripts for indigent defendants convicted of misdemeanors. In *Bullock v. Carter*, 405 U.S. 134 (1972), candidates for local office in the Texas Democratic primary election were required to pay fees as high as $8,900 to have their names printed on the ballots. The Supreme Court held 7–0 that the fee system contravenes the Equal Protection Clause because it eliminates legitimate potential candidates who cannot afford the filing fees.

In *Maher v. Roe*, 432 U.S. 464 (1977), the Supreme Court held 6–3 that the Equal Protection Clause does not require a state participating in the Medicaid program to pay the expenses incident to non-therapeutic abortions for indigent women simply because it has made a policy choice to subsidize the medical expenses incident to pregnancy and childbirth. Financial need alone does not identify a suspect class for purposes of equal protection analysis.

• SEXUAL ISSUES. In *Skinner v. Oklahoma*, 316 U.S. 535 (1942), the state statute allowed for the sterilization of persons convicted three or more times of felonies involving moral turpitude. The Supreme Court ruled 9–0 that the statute violated the Equal Protection Clause because white-collar crimes, such as embezzlement, were excluded from such punishment. While the

Skinner decision did not specifically overrule *Buck v. Bell*, 274 U.S. 200 (1927), which upheld 8–1 the compulsory sterilization of the mentally retarded, *Skinner* did discourage such sterilizations. Justice Oliver Wendell Holmes, in writing for the majority in *Buck*, stated: "It is better for all the world, if instead of waiting to execute degenerate offspring for crime, or to let them starve for their imbecility, society can prevent those who are manifestly unfit from continuing their kind. The principle that sustains compulsory vaccination is broad enough to cover cutting the Fallopian tubes. Three generations of imbeciles are enough." 274 U.S. 207. The case was the subject of the 1994 movie: *Against Her Will: The Carrie Buck Story.*

In *Eisenstadt v. Baird*, 405 U.S. 438 (1972), the Supreme Court invalidated 6–1 a state law prohibiting the distribution of contraceptives to unmarried persons. The Court held that the law's distinction between single and married persons failed to satisfy the "rational basis test" of the Equal Protection Clause. In *Romer v. Evans*, 517 U.S. 620 (1996), the Court invalidated 6–3 a state constitutional amendment precluding any governmental action to protect homosexuals and bisexuals from discrimination based on their sexual orientation. The Court held that the Equal Protection Clause was violated because the amendment was not rationally related to any legitimate government interest.

- INDEBTEDNESS ISSUE. In *Bearden v. Georgia*, 461 U.S. 660 (1983), the Supreme Court held 9–0 that if a state determines a fine or restitution to be the appropriate penalty for a crime, it may not thereafter imprison a person solely because he lacks the resources to pay the fine or restitution. However, if the person has willfully refused to pay the fine or restitution when he has the resources to pay or has failed to make a sufficient effort to obtain the money through employment or borrowing, the state is justified in using imprisonment as a sanction to enforce collection.
- PICKETING ISSUES. In *Police Department of Chicago v. Mosley*, 408 U.S. 92 (1972), the Supreme Court invalidated 9–0 a city ordinance prohibiting all picketing within 150 feet of a school, except peaceful picketing in a labor dispute, as violative of the Equal Protection Clause because it makes an impermissible distinction between peaceful labor picketing and other peaceful picketing. *Mosley* was followed in *Carey v. Brown*, 447 U.S. 455 (1980), where the Court voided 6–3 a state law that prohibited picketing of residences, but exempted peaceful picketing of places of employment involved in labor disputes. The law discriminated between lawful and unlawful conduct based upon the content of the picketer's communication.
- RESIDENT ISSUES. In *Shapiro v. Thompson*, 394 U.S. 618 (1969), the Supreme Court invalidated 6–3 a state law denying welfare benefits to those failing to satisfy a one-year residency requirement, as a violation of

the fundamental right to travel as guaranteed by the Equal Protection Clause. In *Graham v. Richardson*, 403 U.S. 365 (1971), the Court held 9–0 that state laws that placed conditions on welfare benefits due to citizenship and imposed durational residency requirements on aliens violated the Equal Protection Clause. In *Sugarman v. Dougall*, 413 U.S. 634 (1973), the Court invalidated 8–1 a New York law providing that only U.S. citizens may hold permanent positions in the competitive class of state civil service. The Court ruled that the law barred aliens without justification, and was not limited to the accomplishment of substantial state interests. In *Zobel v. Williams*, 457 U.S. 55 (1982), the Court invalidated 8–1 the Alaska mineral income dividend distribution plan under which each adult resident receives one dividend unit for each year of residency subsequent to 1959, the first year of Alaska statehood. The Court found that the plan violated the Equal Protection Clause because it created fixed distinctions between earlier and later residents, based on their length of residency in the state, and that such inequality did not rationally further a legitimate state purpose. In *Plyler v. Doe*, 457 U.S. 202 (1982), the Court invalidated 5–4 a Texas law denying funding for the education of illegal immigrant children because the law did not serve a compelling state interest. While they were not citizens, they were persons within the ambit of the Equal Protection Clause.

• PUBLIC SCHOOL FUNDING ISSUE. In *San Antonio Independent School District v. Rodriguez*, 411 U.S. 1 (1973), the Supreme Court held 5–4 that reliance on property taxes to fund public schools does not violate the Equal Protection Clause even though it results in funding disparities for the poorer school districts. The Court applied the rational basis test, found no invidious discrimination since the funding mechanism was similar to that used by other states, and ruled that the "Equal Protection Clause does not require absolute equality or precisely equal advantages." 411 U.S. 24.

• PHYSICIAN-ASSISTED SUICIDE. The Supreme Court in *Vacco v. Quill*, 521 U.S. 793 (1997), upheld 9–0 New York's ban on physician-assisted suicide under the Equal Protection Clause. Recognizing a "distinction between refusing treatment and assisting a suicide" the court maintained that valid public interests—including "prohibiting intentional killing and preserving life; preventing suicide; maintaining physicians' role as their patients' healers; protecting vulnerable people from indifference, prejudice, and psychological and financial pressure to end their lives; and avoiding a possible slide toward euthanasia"—were sufficient to satisfy a rational legislative classification. 521 U.S. 794. The Court reached the same result in *Washington v. Glucksberg*, 521 U.S. 702 (1997), under the Due Process Clause.

Under the leadership of Earl Warren (1881–1974) as the 14th Chief Justice (1953–1969), the Supreme Court aggressively expanded its role with particular emphasis on extending to the states guarantees of the Bill of Rights, as incorporated by the Due Process and Equal Protection Clauses of the Fourteenth Amendment, as reflected by the following chronology.

1. *Brown v. Board of Education of Topeka*, 347 U.S. 483 (1954), banned racial segregation in public schools.

2. *Bolling v. Sharpe*, 347 U.S. 497 (1954), banned racial segregation in public schools in the District of Columbia by attributing an equal protection component to the Fifth Amendment.

3. *Yates v. United States*, 354 U.S. 298 (1957), overturned criminal convictions for conspiring to overthrow the federal government, holding that "advocacy and teaching of forcible overthrow as an abstract principle" is protected free speech.

4. *Trop v. Dulles*, 356 U.S. 86 (1958), banned punishments that conflicted with "the evolving standards of decency that mark the progress of a maturing society."

5. *Gomillion v. Lightfoot*, 364 U.S. 339 (1960), invalidated irregular electoral district boundaries drawn to deprive blacks of political power.

6. *Mapp v. Ohio*, 367 U.S. 643 (1961), incorporated the exclusionary rule of the Search and Seizure Clause, Fourth Amendment, as applicable to the states.

7. *Baker v. Carr*, 369 U.S. 186 (1962), required federal courts to consider on the merits suits challenging the apportionment of state legislatures as "justiciable" issues subject to judicial review.

8. *Engel v. Vitale*, 370 U.S. 421 (1962), banned nondenominational prayer in public schools.

9. *Robinson v. California*, 370 U.S. 660 (1962), incorporated the Cruel and Unusual Clause, Eighth Amendment, as applicable to the states.

10. *Edwards v. South Carolina*, 372 U.S. 229 (1963), incorporated the Freedom of Petition Clause, First Amendment, as applicable to the states.

11. *Gideon v. Wainwright*, 372 U.S. 335 (1963), required that indigent non-capital criminal defendants receive publicly-funded counsel.

12. *Gray v. Sanders*, 372 U.S. 368 (1963), required that party primary elections afford equal voting status according to the standard of "one person, one vote."

13. *Abington School District v. Schempp*, 374 U.S. 203 (1963), banned reading of Bible verses in public schools.

14. *Sherbert v. Verner*, 374 U.S. 398 (1963), overturned state denial of unemployment compensation to a Seventh-Day Adventist who was fired for refusing to work on Saturday, the Sabbath Day of her faith.

15. *Wesberry v. Sanders*, 376 U.S. 1 (1964), required that the apportionment of congressional districts reflect the standard of "one person, one vote."

16. *Reynolds v. Sims*, 377 U.S. 566 (1964), required that the apportionment of both houses of bicameral state legislatures reflect the standard of "one person, one vote."

17. *Malloy v. Hogan*, 378 U.S. 1 (1964), incorporated the Self-Incrimination Clause, Fifth Amendment, as applicable to the states.

18. *Aguilar v. Texas*, 378 U.S. 108 (1964), incorporated the Warrant Clause, Fourth Amendment, as applicable to the states.

19. *Escobedo v. Illinois*, 378 U.S. 478 (1964), required that criminal suspects be provided counsel during police interrogations.

20. *Pointer v. Texas*, 380 U.S. 400 (1965), incorporated the Confrontation Clause, Sixth Amendment, as applicable to the states.

21. *Griswold v. Connecticut*, 381 U.S. 479 (1965), established a right to privacy in marital relations.

22. *South Carolina v. Katzenbach*, 383 U.S. 301 (1966), upheld the Voting Rights Act of 1965 that established extensive federal oversight of elections in states with a history of discriminatory voting practices, including the prohibition of any voting practice changes without advance federal approval (preclearance).

23. *Miranda v. Arizona*, 384 U.S. 436 (1966), required that police advise a suspect in custody of his rights prior to interrogation.

24. *Parker v. Gladden*, 385 U.S. 363 (1966), incorporated the Jury Trial Clause, Sixth Amendment, as applicable to the states.

25. *Klopfer v. North Carolina*, 386 U.S. 213 (1967), incorporated the Speedy Trial Clause, Sixth Amendment, as applicable to the states.

26. *Loving v. Virginia*, 388 U.S. 1 (1967), invalidated a state ban on interracial marriage.

27. *Washington v. Texas*, 388 U.S. 14 (1967), incorporated the Compulsory Process Clause, Sixth Amendment, as applicable to the states.

28. *Katz v. United States*, 389 U.S. 347 (1967), required that police obtain a search warrant for wiretapping conversation in public telephone booth.

29. *Green v. County School Board*, 391 U.S. 430 (1968), invalidated "freedom of choice" plan that failed to racially desegregate a school system.

30. *Tinker v. Des Moines School District*, 393 U.S. 503 (1969), permitted wearing of armbands in public school as a form of symbolic protest.

31. *Benton v. Maryland*, 395 U.S. 784 (1969), incorporated the Double Jeopardy Clause, Fifth Amendment, as applicable to the states.

Earl Warren is buried in the Arlington National Cemetery, Arlington, Virginia, in the western part of Section 21, adjacent to Lawton Drive. His tombstone bears this inscription: "Where there is injustice, we should correct it; where there is poverty, we should eliminate it; where there is corruption, we should stamp it out; where there is violence, we should punish it; where there is neglect, we should provide care; where there is war, we should restore peace; and wherever corrections are achieved, we should add them permanently to our storehouse of treasures."

Earl Warren is second in significance only to John Marshall in the development if constitutional law.

APPORTIONMENT OF REPRESENTATIVES CLAUSE

Section 2 of the Fourteenth Amendment overrode the "three-fifths" count of Article I, Section 2, Clause 3, by fully counting former slaves in the apportionment of members of the House of Representatives, and thereby increasing the political power of the former slave states. The provision for proportional reduction in representation in the House for states that denied males, 21 years and older, the right to vote, except for rebellion or other crime, was not enforced irrespective of widespread black disenfranchisement. In *Richardson v. Ramirez*, 418 U.S. 24 (1974), the Supreme Court relied on the above "other crime" voter disqualification in upholding 6–3 state disenfranchisement of convicted felons who have completed their sentences and paroles.

DISQUALIFICATION FOR REBELLION CLAUSE

Section 3 of the Fourteenth Amendment prohibits the holding of federal or state office by a federal or state official who had previously sworn allegiance to the United States and then engaged in insurrection or rebellion against the United States or given aid or comfort to its enemies. The Congress was authorized to remove this disability by a two-thirds vote of each House.

The General Amnesty Act of 1872, 17 Statutes 142, removed the political disabilities from all but about 500 of the Confederate leaders. Many of these were subsequently restored by special acts, and in 1898 a general amnesty law removed the disabilities from the remainder. 30 Statutes 432.

DEBTS INCURRED DURING REBELLION CLAUSE

Section 4 of the Fourteenth Amendment confirmed the validity of the public debt incurred by the United States in waging the Civil War, and prohibited the payment of the debt incurred by the Confederacy or any claim for the loss of slaves.

ENFORCEMENT CLAUSE

Section 5 authorizes the enforcement of the Fourteenth Amendment by congressional legislation.

In *Katzenbach v. Morgan*, 384 U.S. 641 (1966), the Supreme Court upheld 7–2 a provision of the Voting Rights Act of 1965 stating that no person who had completed the sixth grade in an accredited Puerto Rican school could be denied the right to vote because of the inability to read or write English. The Court found that the banning of literacy tests, in order to prevent abuses in voter registration, was appropriate legislation under Section 5 of the Fourteenth Amendment. Earlier, the Supreme Court in *Lassiter v. Northampton Election Board*, 360 U.S. 45 (1959), had held 9–0 that a state may, consistent with the Equal Protection Clause, apply a literacy test to all voters irrespective of race.

In *City of Boerne v. Flores*, 521 U.S. 507 (1997), a Catholic archbishop sued local zoning authorities under the Religious Freedom Restoration Act (RFRA) of 1993 for denial of a permit to expand his church in a historic preservation district governed by an ordinance regulating new construction. The Supreme Court invalidated 6–3 the state application of the RFRA as exceeding congressional enforcement power under Section 5 of the Fourteenth Amendment by seeking to expand the free exercise of religion beyond the degree to which it had been recognized by the Court. The Court found a lack of "congruence and proportionality" between the alleged constitutional wrong and the congressional remedy to correct it. The Court held that it has the sole power to define the substantive rights under the Free Exercise of Religion Clause of the First Amendment. Congress cannot enforce a constitutional right by altering its meaning. There is no evidence that the ordinance favored one religion over another or that it was based on hostility to free religious exercise. However, in *Gonzales v. O Centro Espirita Beneficiente Uniao do Vegetal*, 546 U.S. 418 (2006), the Supreme Court upheld 8–0 the federal application of the RFRA by permitting a religious organization's use of an otherwise illegal drug for religious purposes due to the failure of the federal government to prove a compelling interest in regulating the use of the drug for religious purposes. RFRA was interpreted as requiring the examination of individual religious claims and the granting of exceptions to general laws where no compelling government interest is shown.

In *Kimel v. Florida Board of Regents*, 528 U.S. 62 (2000), the Supreme Court held 5–4 that, although the Age Discrimination in Employment Act of 1967 (ADEA) states congressional intent to abrogate the state's sovereign immunity under the Eleventh Amendment in suits for money damages, the abrogation exceeded congressional authority under Section 5 of the Fourteenth Amendment because the discrimination complained of was rationally based on age. The same result was reached in *Board of Trustees of the University of Alabama v. Garrett*, 531 U.S. 365 (2001), where the Supreme Court held 5–4 that suits in federal court by state employees to recover money damages by reason of state failure to comply with the Americans with Disabilities Act of 1990 (ADA) are barred by the Eleventh Amendment. The Court ruled that "in order to authorize private individuals to recover damages against the States, there must be a pattern of discrimination by the

States which violates the Fourteenth Amendment, and the remedy imposed by Congress must be congruent and proportional to the targeted violation." 531 U.S. 374. The Court found that these requirements were not met.

However, in *Tennessee v. Lane*, 541 U.S. 509 (2004), the plaintiffs, Tennesseans who could not access the upper floors in state courthouses, were seeking money damages under the ADA. The Supreme Court held 5–4 that the ADA did not violate the state sovereign immunity doctrine of the Eleventh Amendment because Congress had sufficient evidence that the disabled were being denied those fundamental rights that are protected by the Due Process Clause of the Fourteenth Amendment and subject to enforcement by Section 5 thereof. The Court found that the remedies required of the state were reasonable in making such accommodations, and that here the ADA was a "reasonable prophylactic measure, reasonably targeted to a legitimate end."

The Family and Medical Leave Act of 1993 (FMLA), enacted by Congress under the Commerce Clause (Article I, Section 8, Clause 3) and Section 5 of the Fourteenth Amendment, allows an employee to take unpaid leave due to a serious health condition that renders him unable to perform his job, or due to the need to care for a sick family member or to care for a new child by birth, adoption or foster care. An employee whose rights have been violated may sue his employer for money damages and equitable relief. In *Nevada Department of Human Resources v. Hibbs*, 538 U.S. 721 (2003), the Supreme Court upheld 6–3 the abrogation of state sovereign immunity by FMLA because it was narrowly targeted to combat gender-based discrimination in the workplace where Congress found that working women usually bear the primary responsibility for family caretaking.

Amendment XV
Racial Suffrage

Ratified February 3, 1870

Section 1. The right of citizens of the United States to vote shall not be denied or abridged by the United States or by any State on account of race, color, or previous condition of servitude.

Section 2. The Congress shall have power to enforce this article by appropriate legislation.

The Fifteenth Amendment was the last of the three Reconstruction Amendments, and was adopted to give male voters the right to vote regardless of race, color or previous condition of servitude. Previously, the states had held the total responsibility for determining voter qualifications.

In *Guinn v. United States*, 238 U.S. 347 (1915), Oklahoma law required persons to pass a literacy test in registering to vote, but exempted from the test those voters whose grandfathers had been eligible to vote on or before January 1, 1866. Since the Civil War had ended in May 1865, the grandfather clause primarily favored white voters while discriminating against black ones whose grandfathers had been slaves without the right to vote. Accordingly, the Supreme Court ruled 8–0 that the grandfather clause exemption for literacy tests was repugnant to the Fifteenth Amendment because illiterate whites were able to vote, but not illiterate blacks. In response to the *Guinn* decision in 1915, Oklahoma passed the 1916 voter registration law providing that all citizens qualified to vote in 1916 who failed to register during the 12-day period between April 30 and May 11, 1916, would be perpetually disenfranchised, except those who voted in 1914. Thus citizens, primarily white people, who were registered to vote in 1914, due to the invalidated grandfather clause or otherwise, remained entitled to vote. The Supreme Court in *Lane v. Wilson*, 307 U.S. 268 (1939), struck down 6–2 the 1916 law as being in violation of the Fifteenth Amendment due to the automatic grant of voting rights to many white citizens while discriminating against many black citizens by providing them only 12 days in which to register.

In *Rice v. Cayetano*, 528 U.S. 495 (2000), the Supreme Court ruled 7–2 that the state cannot restrict eligibility to vote in elections for trustees of the state Office of Hawaiian Affairs to persons of Hawaiian ancestry because it creates a race-based voting qualification in violation of the Fifteenth Amendment.

In *Smith v. Allwright*, 321 U.S. 649 (1944), the Texas Democratic Party, a voluntary organization, allowed only whites to participate in its primary elections. Since Texas was a one-party state, winning the primary election was tantamount to winning the general election. The Supreme Court held 8–1 that denying blacks the right to vote in primary elections violated the Fifteenth Amendment because primaries were an integral part of the state election procedures. Public activities, such as elections, are subject to constitutional scrutiny even if they are managed by private organizations. *Allwright* followed *Nixon v. Herndon*, 273 U.S. 536 (1927), in which the Court invalidated 9–0, on equal protection grounds, a Texas law that forbade blacks from voting in the Democratic primary election for the nomination of candidates for election in the ensuing general election. In an effort to preserve the all-white primary, Texas empowered the Democratic party to determine voter qualifications for the primary which the Supreme Court overturned 5–4 as state action in *Nixon v. Condon*, 286 U.S. 73 (1932).

The *Allwright* doctrine was extended in *Terry v. Adams*, 345 U.S. 461 (1953), in which the Supreme Court invalidated 8–1 an unofficial county primary (the Jaybird Primary) for the selection of candidates for public office, held by a private, all-white club that performed a public function despite the lack of state regulation.

In *Gomillion v. Lightfoot*, 364 U.S. 339 (1960), the state of Alabama redrew city electoral district boundaries from a square to a 28-sided shape to exclude blacks from the city limits and place them in a primarily black district. The Supreme Court ruled 9–0 that the redistricting violated the Fifteenth Amendment because it sought to deprive blacks of political power. In *Mobile v. Bolden*, 446 U.S. 55 (1980), Bolden argued that the election of city commissioners at-large, rather than by single-member districts, unfairly diluted the voting strength of black citizens. The Supreme Court upheld 6–3 the at-large election in the absence of proof that the disputed plan was conceived or operated as a purposeful device to further racial discrimination. "The Fifteenth Amendment does not entail the right to have Negro candidates elected." 446 U.S. 65.

As to congressional enforcement power under Section 2 of the Fifteenth Amendment, the Supreme Court in *South Carolina v. Katzenbach*, 383 U.S. 301 (1966), upheld 8–1 the Voting Rights Act of 1965 that established extensive federal oversight of elections in states with a history of discriminatory voting practices, including the prohibition of any voting practice changes without advance federal approval (preclearance). The decision established congressional power to proscribe a class of suspect practices without the courts having to find them to be unconstitutional in every instance. In *Northwest Austin Municipal Utility District No. 1 v. Holder*, 557 U.S. ___ (2009), the Supreme Court declined 8–1 to rule on the constitutionality of the preclearance requirement for voting practice changes under the Voting Rights Act of 1965 by relying on the doctrine of constitutional avoidance. The doctrine provides that a court should avoid ruling on a constitutional issue if the case may be resolved on non-constitutional grounds (*Escambia County v. McMillan*, 466 U.S. 48 [1984], 8–0 vote). Accordingly, the Court interpreted the Act to permit all political subdivisions, including the district, to seek exemption from the preclearance requirement (9–0 vote). However, the Court, while recognizing the historic accomplishments of the Act, stated that it raises serious constitutional concerns because the preclearance requirement causes an unprecedented intrusion into areas of state and local responsibility; and that the current burdens imposed by preclearance must be justified by current needs.

Amendment XVI
Income Tax

Ratified February 3, 1913

The Congress shall have power to lay and collect taxes on incomes, from whatever source derived, without apportionment among the several States, and without regard to any census or enumeration.

Prior to the Sixteenth Amendment, congressional power to tax income was defined by three provisions.

1. Article I, Section 2, Clause 3, provided that "[r]epresentatives and direct taxes shall be apportioned among the several States ... according to their respective Numbers...."

2. Article I, Section 8, Clause 1, provided that "[t]he Congress shall have Power To lay and collect Taxes, Duties, Imposts and Excises ... but all Duties, Imposts and Excises shall be uniform throughout the United States."

3. Article I, Section 9, Clause 4, provided that "[n]o Capitation, or other direct, Tax shall be laid, unless in Proportion to the Census or Enumeration herein before directed to be taken."

Congress, during the Civil War, levied an income tax on individuals, without apportionment of the tax among the states according to population. In *Springer v. United States*, 102 U.S. 586 (1881), the Supreme Court upheld 7–0 the income tax, rejecting the claim that it was a direct tax prohibited by the Constitution unless apportioned among the states. The Court ruled that only taxes on real estate and capitation taxes (fixed amount per person) were direct taxes. Income taxes were considered to be excises (indirect taxes), whose imposition required geographical uniformity, but not apportionment. However, in *Pollock v. Farmers' Loan & Trust Co.*, 157 U.S. 429 (1895), the Supreme Court greatly limited congressional authority to levy an unapportioned income tax by holding 5–4 that a tax on income from real and personal property, such as rent, interest or dividends, should be treated as a tax on the property itself and, therefore, it was a direct tax that required apportionment. *Pollock* made the source of income (such as property or wages) relevant in determining whether the tax was direct or indirect, and thus frustrated the ability of Congress to impose a comprehensive income tax. Accordingly, *Pollock* was overturned by the Sixteenth Amendment, which clarified that there was no requirement for the apportionment of income taxes, irrespective of source. The apportionment requirement for other direct taxes was not disturbed by the Amendment.

In *Commissioner v. Glenshaw Glass Co.*, 348 U.S. 426 (1955), taxpayers sought to exclude punitive damages as taxable gross income under the Internal Revenue Code. In denying the taxpayers relief, the Supreme Court gave a broad interpretation of taxable gross income (except that which is specifically exempted) by holding 7–1 that it included all "undeniable accessions to wealth, clearly realized, and over which the taxpayers have complete dominion." 348 U.S. 431.

The Sixteenth Amendment (1913) was the first of the four amendments adopted during the Progressive Era. The others are the Seventeenth Amendment for the popular election of senators (1913), the Eighteenth Amendment for the prohibition of intoxicating liquors (1919), and the Nineteenth Amendment for woman suffrage (1920).

Amendment XVII
Popular Election of Senators

Ratified April 8, 1913

The Senate of the United States shall be composed of two Senators from each State, elected by the people thereof, for six years; and each Senator shall have one vote. The electors in each State shall have the qualifications requisite for electors of the most numerous branch of the State legislatures.

When vacancies happen in the representation of any State in the Senate, the executive authority of such State shall issue writs of election to fill such vacancies: *Provided*, That the legislature of any State may empower the executive thereof to make temporary appointments until the people fill the vacancies by election as the legislature may direct.

This amendment shall not be so construed as to affect the election or term of any Senator chosen before it becomes valid as part of the Constitution.

The Seventeenth Amendment supersedes Article I, Section 3, Clause 1, by providing that senators shall be chosen by direct popular vote, instead of by state legislatures; and amends Clause 2 of Section 3 by providing that a state legislature may empower the governor to make a temporary appointment to fill a vacancy until an election can be held. The Amendment altered the balance of power between the federal and state governments, as intended by the framers, by insulating senators from the direct influence of state legislatures and their concern for states' rights. In senatorial election campaigns, the state legislatures became just one more interest group in a broad array of those seeking to affect the outcome of the election.

Amendment XVIII
Prohibition of Intoxicating Liquors

Ratified January 16, 1919

Section 1. After one year from the ratification of this article the manufacture, sale, or transportation of intoxicating liquors within, the importation thereof into, or the exportation thereof from the United States and all territory subject to the jurisdiction thereof for beverage purposes is hereby prohibited.

Section 2. The Congress and the several States shall have concurrent power to enforce this article by appropriate legislation.

Section 3. This article shall be inoperative unless it shall have been ratified as an amendment to the Constitution by the legislatures of the several States, as provided in the Constitution, within seven years from the date of the submission hereof to the States by the Congress.

The National Prohibition Act of 1919, also known as the Volstead Act, provided for the enforcement of the Eighteenth Amendment under stringent penalties and defined intoxicating liquors as those containing more than one half of one percent of alcohol by volume. The Act exempted wine used for religious sacraments and liquor prescribed by physicians as medicine. Alcohol for industrial use was required to be denatured to prevent human consumption. The Act permitted continued private possession of alcoholic beverages acquired prior to Prohibition as well as home fermentation of fruit juices to produce cider or wine for personal use. The constitutionality of the Act was upheld by the Supreme Court in the *National Prohibition Cases*, 253 U.S. 350 (1920).

In *Dillon v. Gloss*, 256 U.S. 368 (1921), the Supreme Court ruled 9–0 that Congress may impose a deadline for ratification, as provided in Section 3 of the Eighteenth Amendment, and that the date of ratification, not its proclamation, determines the effectiveness of the Amendment.

The Eighteenth Amendment to the Constitution is the only one that has been repealed (Twenty-first Amendment, [1933]).

Amendment XIX
Woman Suffrage

Ratified August 18, 1920

The right of citizens of the United States to vote shall not be denied or abridged by the United States or by any State on account of sex.

Congress shall have power to enforce this article by appropriate legislation.

The Nineteenth Amendment repeated the language of the Fifteenth Amendment, except that "race, color, or previous condition of servitude" was replaced by "sex."

The original Constitution did not grant or deny women suffrage, but left the determination of voter qualifications to the states. Article I, Section 2, Clause 1, in the case of House elections, provides that "the Electors in each State shall have the Qualifications requisite for Electors of the most numerous Branch of the State Legislature." Article II, Section 1, Clause 2, provides that "[e]ach State shall appoint, in such Manner as the Legislature thereof may direct," the number of presidential electors to which the state is entitled. The Constitution was gender-neutral, with masculine pronouns interpreted to include the feminine, except that for the first time the Fourteenth Amendment, Section 2, used the extent of disenfranchisement of males, 21 years of age or older (other than for rebellion or other crime), as the measure for proportional reduction in House representation.

In *Minor v. Happersett*, 88 U.S. 162 (1874), the Supreme Court upheld 9–0 the Missouri law, limiting suffrage to male citizens, as not an infringement of Minor's civil rights under the Fourteenth Amendment, irrespective of her citizenship. The Court ruled that, at the time of the adoption of the Amendment, suffrage was not coextensive with citizenship, nor was it at the time of the adoption of the Constitution.

In *Leser v. Garnett*, 258 U.S. 130 (1922), the Supreme Court held 9–0 that the Nineteenth Amendment was constitutionally adopted. In response to the contention that several states voting for ratification were disqualified from doing so due to their constitutions prohibiting woman suffrage, the Court ruled that the ratifying state legislatures were acting in federal capacity under the Constitution which transcended any state limitations. In response to the contention that two state ratifications were invalid for failure to follow state legislative procedures, the Court ruled, first, that the contention was moot because of subsequent state ratifications and, second, that the acceptance of the two state ratifications by the Secretary of State as valid was conclusive, rendering the issue non-justiciable.

Amendment XX
Term Endings; Presidential Succession

Ratified January 23, 1933

Section 1. The terms of the President and Vice President shall end at noon on the 20th day of January, and the terms of Senators and Representatives at noon on the 3d day of January, of the years in which such terms would have ended if this article had not been ratified; and the terms of their successors shall then begin.

Section 2. The Congress shall assemble at least once in every year, and such meeting shall begin at noon on the 3d day of January, unless they shall by law appoint a different day.

Section 3. If, at the time fixed for the beginning of the term of the President, the President elect shall have died, the Vice President elect shall become President. If a President shall not have been chosen before the time fixed for the beginning of his term, or if the President elect shall have failed to qualify, then the Vice President elect shall act as President until a President shall have qualified; and the Congress may by law provide for the case wherein neither a President elect nor a Vice President elect shall have qualified, declaring who shall then act as President, or the manner in which one who is to act shall be selected, and such person shall act accordingly until a President or Vice President shall have qualified.

Section 4. The Congress may by law provide for the case of the death of any of the persons from whom the House of Representatives may choose a President whenever the right of choice shall have devolved upon them, and for the case of the death of any of the persons from whom the Senate may choose a Vice President whenever the right of choice shall have devolved upon them.

Section 5. Sections 1 and 2 shall take effect on the 15th day of October following the ratification of this article.

Section 6. This article shall be inoperative unless it shall have been ratified as an amendment to the Constitution by the legislatures of three-fourths of the several States within seven years from the date of its submission.

TERM ENDINGS CLAUSE

The Twentieth Amendment reduced the amount of time between the general election in November and the beginning of the presidential, vice presidential and congressional terms. The original Constitution specified the length of terms, but not their beginning. Nor did it fix the date of the general election. The terms of Representatives are fixed at two years (Article I, Section 2, Clause 1), Senators at six years (Article I, Section 3, Clause 1), and the President and Vice President at four years (Article II, Section 1, Clause 1). Following the ratification of the Constitution on June 21, 1788, the Confederation Congress on September 13, 1788, set the date for the choosing of presidential electors as January 7, 1789, the date for the electors to vote for the President and the Vice President as February 4, 1789, and the date for the Constitution to become operative as March 4, 1789. Thus began the terms of the President, the Vice President, the Senators, and the Representatives.

Initially, the states determined the times for the choosing and the voting of presidential electors, as well as for the election of Representatives, and the choosing of Senators by the state legislatures; nevertheless, all terms were determined from the base date of March 4, 1789. In 1845, the Congress fixed the date of general elections for presidential electors to be held quadrennially on "the Tuesday after the first Monday in November" in even-numbered years. 3 *U.S. Code*, § 1. The November date was selected to benefit a rural, agrarian society because it occurred after the harvests but before severe winter weather. Later, the Congress also fixed this November date, biennially, for the election of Representatives (2 *U.S. Code*, § 7), and for the choosing of Senators by direct popular vote following the ratification of the Seventeenth Amendment in 1913 (2 *U.S. Code*, § 1).

As transportation and communication improved substantially over the years, the four months' delay between the general election and the beginning of the new terms became excessive, especially when the public demanded a rapid change in course following an election.

Another problem was the short "lame duck" congressional sessions that occurred between the general elections in even-numbered years and the term beginnings on the following March 4. The original Constitution provided that the Congress would assemble each year on the first Monday in December, unless otherwise provided by law. Article I, Section 4, Clause 2. This resulted in congressional sessions following the general elections, in which defeated members and those not seeking reelection ("lame ducks") could continue to serve until March 4, producing an undesirable legislative situation in which they were no longer accountable to voters. The Congress could have solved this problem legislatively by simply postponing assembly until March 4, but it failed to do so. Also, "lame duck" sessions, although shortened, are not completely eliminated by the Twentieth Amendment since Congress may still assemble between the general election and the following January 3 (the new term ending date for congressional members under the Amendment).

However, the ratification of Section 1 of the Twentieth Amendment is required for the one-time reduction of the presidential and vice presidential terms from March 4 to January 20, and the congressional terms from March 4 to January 3.

Presidential Succession Clause

Section 3 of the Twentieth Amendment amends Article II, Section 1, Clause 6, to clarify presidential succession. The Vice President shall become the President in the event of the death of the President-elect. If a President-elect has not been chosen by the beginning of the term or if the President-elect fails to qualify, then the Vice President-elect shall act as President until a President has qualified. In the event that neither a President-Elect nor a Vice President-Elect has qualified by the beginning of the term, then the Congress is authorized to select a person to act as President until a President or Vice President shall have qualified.

Pursuant to the authorization of Section 3, the Congress repealed the Presidential Succession Act of 1886 with the enactment of the Presidential Succession Act of 1947, which prescribed the line of succession beginning with the Speaker of the House of Representatives, the President Pro Tempore of the Senate, the Secretaries of State, the Treasury, and Defense, the Attorney General, the Postmaster General, and the Secretaries of the Interior, Agriculture, Commerce and Labor. The Act has been amended, and currently prescribes the following line of succession: Speaker of the House, President Pro Tempore of the Senate, Secretaries of State, the Treasury, and Defense, Attorney General, Secretaries of the Interior, Agriculture, Commerce, Labor, Health and Human Services, Housing and Urban Development, Transportation, Energy, Education, Veterans' Affairs, and Homeland Security. 3 USC, Sec 19.

Section 4 of the Twentieth Amendment amends Article II, Section 1, Clause 3, as amended by the Twelfth Amendment, with respect to the Electoral College, to authorize the Congress to determine presidential and vice presidential succession in the event of the death of any of the persons from whom the House of Representatives may choose as the President, and in the event of the death of any of the persons from whom the Senate may choose as the Vice President.

Pursuant to Section 5 of the Twentieth Amendment, Sections 1 and 2, concerning term endings and congressional assembly, became effective on October 15, 1933, due to the Amendment's ratification on January 23, 1933. Since the general election was held on November 8, 1932, the first meeting of the 73rd Congress and the inauguration of President Franklin D. Roosevelt and Vice President John Nance Garner were still held on March 4, 1933. Under Section 1, the first congressional terms began with the 74th Congress on January 3, 1935, and the first presidential and vice presidential terms began on January 20, 1937.

Section 6 of the Twentieth Amendment specifies that the method of ratification shall be by three-fourths of the state legislatures (Article V), and that seven years shall be the time limit for ratification.

Amendment XXI
Repeal of Amendment XVIII re Prohibition

Ratified December 5, 1933

Section 1. The eighteenth article of amendment to the Constitution of the United States is hereby repealed.

Section 2. The transportation or importation into any State, Territory, or possession of the United States for delivery or use therein of intoxicating liquors, in violation of the laws thereof, is hereby prohibited.

Section 3. This article shall be inoperative unless it shall have been ratified as an amendment to the Constitution by conventions in the several States, as provided in the Constitution, within seven years from the date of the submission hereof to the States by the Congress.

The Twenty-first Amendment is the only one that was ever ratified to explicitly repeal an earlier amendment to the Constitution—the Eighteenth Amendment, prohibition of intoxicating liquors (1919).

Under Section 1, the Supreme Court in *United States v. Chambers*, 291 U.S. 217 (1934), ruled 9–0 that the National Prohibition Act, to the extent based on congressional authority granted by the Eighteenth Amendment, became inoperative and, therefore, prosecutions for violation of the Act, including proceedings on appeal, continued or begun after ratification of the

Twenty-first Amendment must be dismissed for lack of jurisdiction. However, the ruling did not apply to final judgments rendered prior to ratification. The purpose of Section 2 is to preserve state, territory and possession jurisdiction over intoxicating beverages.

In *Craig v. Boren*, 429 U.S. 190 (1976), the Supreme Court ruled 7–2 that a state law establishing different minimum drinking ages for men (21 years) and women (18 years) was an unconstitutional gender classification which was not supported by any substantial relationship between the law and maintaining traffic safety. The Court found that in such a case the Twenty-first Amendment does not override the Equal Protection Clause of the Fourteenth Amendment. In *South Dakota v. Dole*, 483 U.S. 203 (1987), the Court held 7–2 that the Twenty-first Amendment does not prohibit Congress from denying federal highway funds to states that did not enact a national minimum drinking age. The Court reasoned that the offer of benefits is not coercion that inappropriately invades state sovereignty. In *44 Liquormart, Inc. v. Rhode Island*, 517 U.S. 484 (1996), the Court invalidated 9–0 a state law banning the advertisement of retail liquor prices as an infringement of the sellers' freedom of speech under the First Amendment. The Twenty-first Amendment may not be applied to impinge on the freedom of speech guarantee.

In *Granholm v. Heald*, 544 U.S. 460 (2005), the Supreme Court invalidated 5–4 state laws that permitted in-state wineries to sell wine directly to consumers but restricted out-of-state wineries from doing the same. The Court held that the Twenty-first Amendment in such a case does not override the Commerce Clause. "The aim of the Twenty-first Amendment was to allow States to maintain an effective and uniform system for controlling liquor by regulating its transportation, importation, and use. The Amendment did not give States the authority to pass nonuniform laws in order to discriminate against out-of-state goods, a privilege they had not enjoyed at any earlier time." 544 U.S. 484.

In *Capital Cities Cable, Inc. v. Crisp*, 467 U.S. 691 (1984), the Supreme Court held 9–0 that a state ban against in-state cable television systems retransmitting out-of-state cable signals containing alcoholic beverage commercials violated the Commerce and Supremacy Clauses (Article I, Section 8, Clause 3; Article VI, Clause 2). The state ban was in conflict with regulations adopted by the Federal Communications Commission (FCC) under the Communications Act of 1934 to promote the flow of interstate broadcast signals. The Court reasoned that conflicts between the state role under the Twenty-first Amendment and federal law requires a balancing test which in this case favors the FCC's policy in insuring widespread availability of diverse cable services throughout the U.S. in comparison with the state interest in limiting alcoholic beverage advertising. In *Bacchus Imports, Ltd. v.*

Dias, 468 U.S. 263 (1984), the Court invalidated 5–3 a state tax on alcohol products, but exempted certain locally produced ones, ruling that a "cardinal rule of Commerce Clause jurisprudence" is that no state may impose a tax which discriminates against interstate commerce. The Court stated that the central purpose of the Twenty-first Amendment was not to empower states to favor local liquor industry by erecting barriers to competition.

As provided in Section 3, the Twenty-first Amendment is the only amendment thus far ratified by conventions held in the several states, rather than being ratified by the state legislatures (Article V). The state convention route was selected by the Congress out of the concern that state legislatures would be more susceptible to the temperance lobby.

Amendment XXII
Presidential Term Limit

Ratified February 27, 1951

Section 1. No person shall be elected to the office of the President more than twice, and no person who has held the office of President, or acted as President, for more than two years of a term to which some other person was elected President shall be elected to the office of President more than once. But this Article shall not apply to any person holding the office of President when this Article was proposed by Congress, and shall not prevent any person who may be holding the office of President, or acting as President, during the term within which this Article becomes operative from holding the office of President or acting as President during the remainder of such term.

Section 2. This Article shall be inoperative unless it shall have been ratified as an amendment to the Constitution by the legislatures of three-fourths of the several States within seven years from the date of its submission to the States by the Congress.

The Twenty-second Amendment resulted from Franklin D. Roosevelt being elected to four terms for service from 1933 to 1945, during the Great Depression and World War II, thereby breaking the two-term tradition established by President George Washington in serving from 1789 to 1797.

The Amendment prohibits a President from being elected to more than two terms, a total of eight years. However, a person may serve up to ten years if he assumes a former president's term of two years or less. For example, a President serving during the last two years of his predecessor's term (vacated by death or resignation) could then be twice elected to the office. The two-term limitation usually erodes a President's power and influence during the second term because he has no chance for reelection.

Amendment XXIII
Presidential Electors for the District of Columbia

Ratified March 29, 1961

Section 1. The District constituting the seat of Government of the United States shall appoint in such manner as Congress may direct:

A number of electors of President and Vice President equal to the whole number of Senators and Representatives in Congress to which the District would be entitled if it were a State, but in no event more than the least populous State; they shall be in addition to those appointed by the States, but they shall be considered, for the purposes of the election of President and Vice President, to be electors appointed by a State; and they shall meet in the District and perform such duties as provided by the twelfth article of amendment.

Section 2. The Congress shall have the power to enforce this article by appropriate legislation.

Under the Enclave Clause (Article I, Section 8, Clause 17), the Congress exercises exclusive authority over the District of Columbia. Although residents of the District have all the obligations of citizenship, such as the payment of taxes and serving in the military, they did not have the right to vote in national elections until the ratification of the Twenty-third Amendment. Under the Amendment, citizens of the District have the right to vote for presidential and vice presidential electors in addition to those selected by the states. The number of the District's electors cannot exceed that of the state with the smallest population, which means three electors, irrespective of the population of the District.

The Amendment does not make the District of Columbia a state, or give the District any other attributes of statehood, or change the exclusive legislative control of the Congress.

Amendment XXIV
Poll Tax Prohibition

Ratified January 23, 1964

Section 1. The right of citizens of the United States to vote in any primary or other election for President or Vice President, for electors for President or Vice President, or for Senator or Representative in Congress, shall not be denied or abridged by the United States or any State by reason of failure to pay any poll tax or other tax.

Section 2. The Congress shall have power to enforce this article by appropriate legislation.

The Twenty-fourth Amendment prohibits the Congress and the states from requiring the payment of a tax to vote in federal elections. The Amendment overrode, as to federal elections, *Breedlove v. Suttles*, 302 U.S. 277 (1937), in which the Supreme Court ruled 9–0 that poll taxes did not violate the Fourteenth and Fifteenth Amendments. In *Harper v. Virginia State Board of Elections*, 383 U.S. 663 (1966), the Court finished off the *Breedlove* precedent by striking down poll taxes in state and local elections, holding 6–3 that making voter affluence an electoral standard violated the Equal Protection Clause of the Fourteenth Amendment. In *Harman v. Forssenius*, 380 U.S. 528 (1965), the Court invalidated 9–0 a state statute that gave federal voters the choice of either paying a poll tax or filing a certificate of residence six months prior to an election. The Court found that this was an onerous procedural requirement to avoid paying the poll tax and, hence, conflicted with the Twenty-fourth Amendment.

Amendment XXV
Presidential Succession

Ratified February 10, 1967

Section 1. In case of the removal of the President from office or of his death or resignation, the Vice President shall become President.

Section 2. Whenever there is a vacancy in the office of the Vice President, the President shall nominate a Vice President who shall take office upon confirmation by a majority vote of both Houses of Congress.

Section 3. Whenever the President transmits to the President pro tempore of the Senate and the Speaker of the House of Representatives his written declaration that he is unable to discharge the powers and duties of his office, and until he transmits to them a written declaration to the contrary, such powers and duties shall be discharged by the Vice President as Acting President.

Section 4. Whenever the Vice President and a majority of either the principal officers of the executive departments or of such other body as Congress may by law provide, transmit to the President pro tempore of the Senate and the Speaker of the House of Representatives their written declaration that the President is unable to discharge the powers and duties of his office, the Vice President shall immediately assume the powers and duties of the office as Acting President.

Thereafter, when the President transmits to the President pro tempore of the Senate and the Speaker of the House of Representatives his written declaration that no inability exists, he shall resume the powers and duties of his office unless the Vice President and a majority of either the principal officers of the executive department or of such other body as Congress may by law provide, transmit within four days to the President pro tempore of the Senate and the Speaker of the House of Representatives their written declaration that the President is unable to discharge the powers and duties of his office. Thereupon Congress shall decide the issue, assembling within forty-eight hours for that purpose if not in session. If the Congress, within twenty-one days after receipt of the latter written declaration, or, if Congress is not in session, within twenty- one days after Congress is required to assemble, determines by two-thirds vote of both Houses that the President is unable to discharge the powers and duties of his office, the Vice President shall continue to discharge the same as Acting President; otherwise, the President shall resume the powers and duties of his office.

The Twenty-fifth Amendment was ratified after the assassination of President John F. Kennedy on November 22, 1963, in Dallas, Texas.

Section 1 clarified the ambiguity of the original Article II, Section 1, Clause 6, and confirmed the prior eight precedents for presidential succession, by providing that the Vice President becomes the President, and not the Acting President, upon the death, removal or resignation of the President.

Section 2 established for the first time a procedure for filling vacancies in the office of the Vice President by requiring the President to nominate a Vice President who would take office upon the confirmation by majority vote of both Houses of Congress. Otherwise, the vacancy would exist until filled by the next quadrennial presidential and vice presidential election. This procedure was used in 1973 when President Richard Nixon nominated Gerald R. Ford to succeed Vice President Spiro T. Agnew, who had resigned because of criminal bribery charges, and Congress confirmed the nomination. It was used again in 1974 when President Nixon resigned because of the Watergate scandal. Vice President Ford became President and nominated Nelson A. Rockefeller as Vice President, and Congress confirmed the nomination. For the first time in history, neither the President nor Vice President had been chosen by the electors.

Sections 3 and 4 address the problem of presidential disability. Under Section 3, when the President advises Congress that he is "unable to discharge the powers and duties" of his office, the Vice President assumes the role of Acting President until such time as the President may seek to reclaim his office by asserting that he is again able to discharge the powers and duties thereof. This provision has been used when the President undergoes surgery where anesthesia is administered.

Section 4 addresses the problem when the President is unable or unwilling to acknowledge his inability to discharge the powers and duties of his office, such as when President James Garfield was comatose after being shot in 1881, and when President Woodrow Wilson was incapacitated by a stroke in 1919. Incapacity could also result from insanity or emotional instability. If the Vice President and a majority of the presidential cabinet members determine that the President is incapacitated, the Vice President immediately becomes the Acting President. The President may challenge this determination by declaring to Congress that no incapacity exists and resuming the office of President, unless the Vice President and a majority of the presidential cabinet members dispute the President's assertion of capacity. Thereupon, the Congress must promptly resolve the issue. If a two-thirds majority of each House, within the time prescribed, votes that the President is incapacitated, he remains as President, but is stripped of his powers and duties, and the Vice President continues to serve as the Acting President. Otherwise, the President continues in office with his powers and duties restored. If the President loses, he may try again later in which case the whole process starts over again.

Section 4 also authorizes the Congress to replace a majority of the presidential cabinet members with a majority of "such other body as Congress may by law provide" to act with the Vice President.

Amendment XXVI
Voting Age Fixed at Eighteen

Ratified July 1, 1971

Section 1. The right of citizens of the United States, who are eighteen years of age or older, to vote shall not be denied or abridged by the United States or by any State on account of age.

Section 2. The Congress shall have power to enforce this article by appropriate legislation.

In the 1970 renewal of the Voting Rights Act of 1965, Congress reduced the age qualification to 18 for voting in all federal, state and local elections. The Supreme Court in *Oregon v. Mitchell*, 400 U.S. 112 (1970), held 5–4 that Congress may set the voting age requirement in federal elections, but not for state and local elections. The decision presented a major problem in the election process because 21 was the minimum age prescribed by the vast majority of the states. Accordingly, two voter registration lists would have to be maintained, one for those under age 21 for federal elections, and one for those age 21 and older for federal, state and local elections. Also, special federal election ballots would have to be provided for those under 21. In order to avoid this dilemma for the 1972 general election, Congress proposed the Twenty-sixth Amendment on March 23, 1971, and three-fourths of the state legislatures ratified it 107 days later on July 1, 1971, the shortest ratification period in U.S. history.

Amendment XXVII
Congressional Compensation

Ratified May 7, 1992

No law, varying the compensation for the services of the Senators and Representatives, shall take effect, until an election of Representatives shall have intervened.

The Twenty-seventh Amendment provides that no change in congressional compensation may become effective until after the next biennial congressional election, so that members of Congress have to face the electorate before the compensation can be increased.

The Congress on September 24, 1789, submitted to the states twelve proposed amendments to the Constitution. The first one was the Congressional Apportionment Amendment that proposed the revision of Article I, Section 2, Clause 3, by establishing the following formula for increasing the number of Representatives in accord with population growth: one Representative for every 30,000 persons, until the House had 100 members; then one Representative for every 40,000 persons, until the House had 200 members; and when the population increased to 50,000 persons for each Representative, Congress would establish new ratios for the apportionment of Representatives. The Congressional Apportionment Amendment was not ratified and now exists in limbo because no deadline for ratification was specified. However, the Amendment is unnecessary because the phrase "The Number of Representatives shall not exceed one for every thirty Thousand" (Article I, Section 2, Clause 3) is interpreted to mean that that there shall be at least thirty thousand persons for each Representative. To avoid the House membership's becoming unwieldy, the Congress passed a law in 1911 that fixed the House membership at 435.

The second one submitted to the states was the Congressional Compensation Amendment, which did not receive enough votes for ratification by the time the remaining ten amendments were ratified on December 15, 1791. Accordingly, these amendments were renumbered as I through X and became known as the Bill of Rights. While the Congressional Compensation Amendment had continuing merit, it languished until 1982 when Gregory Watson, a student at the University of Texas at Austin, discovered the amendment and launched a national campaign that resulted in its ratification as the Twenty-seventh Amendment on May 7, 1992, more than 202 years after its submission to the states in 1789.

In *Coleman v. Miller*, 307 U.S. 433 (1939), the Supreme Court held 7–2 that constitutional amendments are considered pending before the states indefinitely unless Congress establishes a deadline within which the states must act. Congress, and not the courts, is responsible for deciding if an amendment has been validly ratified.

In *Boehner v. Anderson*, 30 F 3d 156 (DC Cir 1994), the court held that periodic cost of living adjustment (COLA) pay increases for members of Congress pursuant to the Ethics Reform Act of 1989 did not violate the Twenty-seventh Amendment because the initial pay raises took effect after an election had intervened, and each subsequent COLA is not an additional law, but becomes effective pursuant to the 1989 Act. In *Schaffer v. Clinton*, 240 F 3d 878 (10th Cir 2001), cert denied, *Schaffer v. O'Neill*, 534 U.S. 992 (2001), the court held that members of Congress receiving a COLA lacked standing to challenge it under the Amendment because they suffered no actual injury. They can remit to the Treasury the portion of the pay they believe to be unconstitutional, or work within the political system to seek the repeal of the COLA.

Appendix A
Supreme Court Justices, 1789–2010

Each listing shows tenure and appointing president; 112 total.

Chief Justices, Seat 1

John Jay, 1789–1795, by President George Washington

John Rutledge, 1795, by President George Washington

Oliver Ellsworth, 1796–1800, by President George Washington

John Marshall, 1801–1835, by President John Adams

Roger Taney, 1836–1864, by President Andrew Jackson

Salmon Chase, 1864–1873, by President Abraham Lincoln

Morrison Waite, 1874–1888, by President Ulysses S. Grant

Melville Fuller, 1888–1910, by President Grover Cleveland

Edward D. White, 1910–1921, by President William Howard Taft

William Howard Taft, 1921–1930, by President Warren G. Harding

Charles Evans Hughes, 1930–1941, by President Herbert Hoover

Harlan Fiske Stone, 1941–1946, by President Franklin D. Roosevelt

Frederick M. Vinson, 1946–1953, by President Harry S. Truman

Earl Warren, 1953–1969, by President Dwight D. Eisenhower

Warren E. Burger, 1969–1986, by President Richard Nixon

William H. Rehnquist, 1986–2005, by President Ronald Reagan

John G. Roberts, 2005–Present, by President George W. Bush

Associate Justices, Seat 2

James Wilson, 1789–1798, by President George Washington

Bushrod Washington, 1799–1829, by President John Adams

Henry Baldwin, 1830–1844, by President Andrew Jackson

Robert C. Grier, 1846–1870, by President James K. Polk

William Strong, 1870–1880, by President Ulysses S. Grant

William B. Woods, 1881–1887, by President Rutherford B. Hayes

Lucius Lamar, 1888–1893, by President Grover Cleveland

Howell E. Jackson, 1893–1895, by President Benjamin Harrison

Rufus W. Peckham, 1896–1909, by President Grover Cleveland

Horace H. Lurton, 1910–1914, by President William Howard Taft

James C. McReynolds, 1914–1941, by President Woodrow Wilson

James F. Byrnes, 1941–1942, by President Franklin D. Roosevelt

Wiley B. Rutledge, 1943–1949, by President Franklin D. Roosevelt

Sherman Minton, 1949–1956, by President Harry S. Truman

William J. Brennan, 1956–1990, by President Dwight D. Eisenhower

David H. Souter, 1990–2009, by President George H. W. Bush

Sonia Sotomayor, 2009–Present, by President Barack Obama

Associate Justices, Seat 3

William Cushing, 1790–1810, by President George Washington

Joseph Story, 1812–1845, by President James Madison

Levi Woodberry, 1845–1851, by President James K. Polk

Benjamin R. Curtis, 1851–1857, by President Millard Fillmore

Nathan Clifford, 1858–1881, by President James Buchanan

Horace Gray, 1882–1902, by President Chester A. Arthur

Oliver Wendell Holmes, 1902–1932, by President Theodore Roosevelt

Benjamin N. Cardozo, 1932–1938, by President Herbert Hoover

Felix Frankfurter, 1939–1962, by President Franklin D. Roosevelt

Arthur J. Goldberg, 1962–1965, by President John F. Kennedy

Abe Fortas, 1965–1969, by President Lyndon B. Johnson

Harry A. Blackmun, 1970–1994, by President Richard Nixon

Stephen G. Breyer, 1994–Present, by President William Clinton

Associate Justices, Seat 4

John Blair, 1790–1795, by President George Washington

Samuel Chase, 1796–1811, by President George Washington

Gabriel Duvall, 1811–1835, by President James Madison

Philip P. Barbour, 1836–1841, by President Andrew Jackson

Peter V. Daniel, 1842–1860, by President Martin Van Buren

Samuel F. Miller, 1862–1890, by President Abraham Lincoln

Henry B. Brown, 1891–1906, by President Benjamin Harrison

William H. Moody, 1906–1910, by President Theodore Roosevelt

Joseph R. Lamar, 1911–1916, by President William Howard Taft

Louis D. Brandeis, 1916–1939, by President Woodrow Wilson

William O. Douglas, 1939–1975, by President Franklin D. Roosevelt

John Paul Stevens, 1975–2010, by President Gerald Ford

Elena Kagan, 2010–Present by President Barack Obama

Associate Justices, Seat 5

John Rutledge, 1790–1791, by President George Washington

Thomas Johnson, 1792–1793, by President George Washington

William Paterson, 1793–1806, by President George Washington

Henry B. Livingston, 1807–1823, by President Thomas Jefferson

Smith Thompson, 1823–1843, by President James Monroe

Samuel Nelson, 1845–1872, by President John Tyler

Ward Hunt, 1873–1882, by President Ulysses S. Grant

Samuel Blatchford, 1882–1893, by President Chester A. Arthur

Edward D. White, 1894–1910, by President Glover Cleveland

Willis Van Devanter, 1911–1937, by President William Howard Taft

Hugo Black, 1937–1971, by President Franklin D. Roosevelt

Lewis F. Powell, Jr., 1972–1987, by President Richard Nixon

Anthony M. Kennedy, 1988–Present, by President Ronald Reagan

Associate Justices, Seat 6*

James Iredell, 1790–1799, by President George Washington

Alfred Moore, 1800–1804, by President John Adams

William Johnson, Jr., 1804–1834, by President Thomas Jefferson

James M. Wayne, 1835–1867, by President Andrew Jackson

Joseph P. Bradley, 1870–1892, by President Ulysses S. Grant

George Shiras, Jr., 1892–1903, by President Benjamin Harrison

William R. Day, 1903–1922, by President Theodore Roosevelt

Pierce Butler, 1923–1939, by President Warren G. Harding

Frank Murphy, 1940–1949, by President Franklin D. Roosevelt

Tom C. Clark, 1949–1967, by President Harry S. Truman

Thurgood Marshall, 1967–1991, by President Lyndon B. Johnson

Clarence Thomas, 1991–Present, by President George H. W. Bush

Associate Justices, Seat 7

Thomas Todd, 1807–1826, by President Thomas Jefferson

Robert Trimble, 1826–1828, by President John Quincy Adams

John McLean, 1830–1861, by President Andrew Jackson

Noah H. Swayne, 1862–1881, by President Abraham Lincoln

Stanley Matthews, 1881–1889, by President James Garfield

David J. Brewer, 1890–1910, by President Benjamin Harrison

Charles Evans Hughes, 1910–1916, by President William Howard Taft

John H. Clarke, 1916–1922, by President Woodrow Wilson

George Sutherland, 1922–1938, by President Warren G. Harding

Stanley F. Reed, 1938–1957, by President Franklin D. Roosevelt

Charles E. Whittaker, 1957–1962, by President Dwight D. Eisenhower

Byron R. White, 1962–1993, by President John F. Kennedy

Ruth B. Ginsburg, 1993–Present, by President William Clinton

Associate Justices, Seat 8

John McKinley, 1838–1852, by President Martin Van Buren

John A. Campbell, 1853–1861, by President Franklin Pierce

David Davis, 1862–1877, by President Abraham Lincoln

John Marshall Harlan, 1877–1911, by President Rutherford B. Hayes

Mahlon Pitney, 1912–1922, by President William Howard Taft

Edward T. Sanford, 1923–1930, by President Warren G. Harding

Owen J. Roberts, 1930–1945, by President Herbert Hoover

Harold H. Burton, 1945–1958, by President Harry S. Truman

Potter Stewart, 1958–1981, by President Dwight D. Eisenhower

Sandra Day O'Connor, 1981–2006, by President Ronald Reagan

Samuel A. Alito, 2006–Present, by President George W. Bush

Associate Justices, Seat 9

Stephen J. Field, 1863–1897, by President Abraham Lincoln

Joseph McKenna, 1898–1925, by President William McKinley

Harlan Fiske Stone, 1925–1941, by President Calvin Coolidge

Robert H. Jackson, 1941–1954, by President Franklin D. Roosevelt

John Marshall Harlan II, 1955–1971, by President Dwight D. Eisenhower

William H. Rehnquist, 1972–1986, by President Richard Nixon

Antonin Scalia, 1986–Present, by President Ronald Reagan

*Seat 6 reflects the service of Iredell, Moore, Johnson and Wayne pursuant to the Judiciary Act of 1789, its abolishment by the Judicial Circuits Act of 1866, and the service of the other Justices pursuant to the Circuit Judges Act of 1869.

Associate Justice, Seat Abolished

John Catron, 1837–1865, by President Andrew Jackson
(This seat was abolished in 1866 when the number of Justices was reduced from 10 to 9.)

Chief Justices Rutledge, White, Hughes, Stone and Rehnquist also served as Associate Justices. The two top nominators of justices were George Washington (11) and Franklin D. Roosevelt (9).

Appendix B

Text of the Constitution

Ratified June 21, 1788
(Titles and editorial notes have been added to the original text.)

Preamble

We the People of the United States, in Order to form a more perfect Union, establish Justice, insure domestic Tranquility, provide for the common defense, promote the general Welfare, and secure the Blessings of Liberty to ourselves and our Posterity, do ordain and establish this Constitution for the United States of America.

Article I
The Legislative Branch

Section 1. Legislative Vesting. All legislative Powers herein granted shall be vested in a Congress of the United States, which shall consist of a Senate and House of Representatives.

Section 2, Clause 1, House of Representatives. The House of Representatives shall be composed of Members chosen every second Year by the People of the several States, and the Electors in each State shall have the Qualifications requisite for Electors of the most numerous Branch of the State Legislature.

Section 2, Clause 2, Qualifications for Representatives. No Person shall be a Representative who shall not have attained to the Age of twenty five Years, and been seven Years a Citizen of the United States, and who shall not, when elected, be an Inhabitant of that State in which he shall be chosen.

Section 2, Clause 3, Apportionment, Enumeration, Allocation of Representatives. [Representatives and direct Taxes shall be apportioned among the several States which may be included within this Union, according to their respective Numbers, which shall be determined by adding to the whole Number of free Persons, including those bound to Service for a Term of Years, and excluding Indians not taxed, three fifths of all other Persons.*] The actual Enumeration shall be made within three Years after the first Meeting of the Congress of the United States, and within every subsequent Term of ten Years, in such Manner as they shall by Law direct. The Number of Representatives shall not exceed one for every thirty Thousand, but each State shall have at Least one Representative; and until such enumeration shall be made, the State of New Hampshire shall be entitled to chuse three, Massachusetts eight, Rhode-Island and Providence Plantations one, Connecticut five, New-York six, New Jersey four, Pennsylvania eight, Delaware one, Maryland six, Virginia ten, North Carolina five, South Carolina five, and Georgia three.

Section 2, Clause 4, Vacancies. When vacancies happen in the Representation from any State, the Executive Authority thereof shall issue Writs of Election to fill such Vacancies.

Section 2, Clause 5, Speaker of the House, Impeachment. The House of Representatives shall chuse their Speaker and other Officers; and shall have the sole Power of Impeachment.

Section 3, Clause 1, Senate. The Senate of the United States shall be composed of two Senators from each State, [chosen by the Legislature thereof†] for six Years; and each Senator shall have one Vote.

Section 3, Clause 2, Senatorial Classes and Vacancies. Immediately after they shall be assembled in Consequence of the first Election, they shall be divided as equally as may be into three Classes. The Seats of the Senators of the first Class shall be vacated at the Expiration of the second Year, of the second Class at the Expiration of the fourth Year, and of the third Class at the Expiration of the sixth Year, so that one third may be chosen every second Year; [and if Vacancies happen by Resignation, or otherwise, during the Recess of the Legislature of any State, the Executive thereof may make temporary Appointments until the next Meeting of the Legislature, which shall then fill such Vacancies.§]

Section 3, Clause 3, Qualifications for Senators. No Person shall be a Senator who shall not have attained to the Age of thirty Years, and been

*The bracketed language was changed by the Fourteenth Amendment, Section 2, relating to apportionment of Representatives, and the Sixteenth Amendment relating to income taxes without apportionment.
†The bracketed language was changed by the Seventeenth Amendment providing for the popular election of Senators.)
§The bracketed language was changed by the Seventeenth Amendment, Clause 2.

nine Years a Citizen of the United States, and who shall not, when elected, be an Inhabitant of that State for which he shall be chosen.

Section 3, Clause 4, Vice President as Presiding Officer. The Vice President of the United States shall be President of the Senate, but shall have no Vote, unless they be equally divided.

Section 3, Clause 5, President Pro Tempore. The Senate shall chuse their other Officers, and also a President pro tempore, in the Absence of the Vice President, or when he shall exercise the Office of President of the United States.

Section 3, Clause 6, Trial of Impeachment. The Senate shall have the sole Power to try all Impeachments. When sitting for that Purpose, they shall be on Oath or Affirmation. When the President of the United States is tried, the Chief Justice shall preside: And no Person shall be convicted without the Concurrence of two thirds of the Members present.

Section 3, Clause 7, Punishment for Impeachment. Judgment in Cases of Impeachment shall not extend further than to removal from Office, and disqualification to hold and enjoy any Office of honor, Trust or Profit under the United States: but the Party convicted shall nevertheless be liable and subject to Indictment, Trial, Judgment and Punishment, according to Law.

Section 4, Clause 1, Election Regulations. The Times, Places and Manner of holding Elections for Senators and Representatives, shall be prescribed in each State by the Legislature thereof; but the Congress may at any time by Law make or alter such Regulations, except as to the Places of chusing Senators.

Section 4, Clause 2, Meetings of Congress. The Congress shall assemble at least once in every Year, and such Meeting shall be on the [*first Monday in December], unless they shall by Law appoint a different Day.

Section 5, Clause 1, Qualifications and Quorum. Each House shall be the Judge of the Elections, Returns and Qualifications of its own Members, and a Majority of each shall constitute a Quorum to do Business; but a smaller Number may adjourn from day to day, and may be authorized to compel the Attendance of absent Members, in such Manner, and under such Penalties as each House may provide.

Section 5, Clause 2, Rules and Expulsion. Each House may determine the Rules of its Proceedings, punish its Members for disorderly Behaviour, and, with the Concurrence of two thirds, expel a Member.

Section 5, Clause 3, House Journal. Each House shall keep a Journal of its Proceedings, and from time to time publish the same, excepting such Parts as may in their Judgment require Secrecy; and the Yeas and Nays of the Members of either House on any question shall, at the Desire of one fifth of those Present, be entered on the Journal.

Bracketed date was changed by the Twentieth Amendment, Section 2.

Section 5, Clause 4, Adjournment. Neither House, during the Session of Congress, shall, without the Consent of the other, adjourn for more than three days, nor to any other Place than that in which the two Houses shall be sitting.

Section 6, Clause 1, Compensation, Privilege from Arrest, Speech and Debate. The Senators and Representatives shall receive a Compensation for their Services, to be ascertained by Law, and paid out of the Treasury of the United States. They shall in all Cases, except Treason, Felony and Breach of the Peace, be privileged from Arrest during their Attendance at the Session of their respective Houses, and in going to and returning from the same; and for any Speech or Debate in either House, they shall not be questioned in any other Place.

Section 6, Clause 2, Sinecure, Incompatibility. No Senator or Representative shall, during the Time for which he was elected, be appointed to any civil Office under the Authority of the United States, which shall have been created, or the Emoluments whereof shall have been encreased during such time; and no Person holding any Office under the United States, shall be a Member of either House during his Continuance in Office.

Section 7, Clause 1, Origination. All Bills for raising Revenue shall originate in the House of Representatives; but the Senate may propose or concur with Amendments as on other Bills.

Section 7, Clause 2, Presentment of Bills, Pocket Veto. Every Bill which shall have passed the House of Representatives and the Senate, shall, before it become a Law, be presented to the President of the United States; If he approve he shall sign it, but if not he shall return it, with his Objections to that House in which it shall have originated, who shall enter the Objections at large on their Journal, and proceed to reconsider it. If after such Reconsideration two thirds of that House shall agree to pass the Bill, it shall be sent, together with the Objections, to the other House, by which it shall likewise be reconsidered, and if approved by two thirds of that House, it shall become a Law. But in all such Cases the Votes of both Houses shall be determined by Yeas and Nays, and the Names of the Persons voting for and against the Bill shall be entered on the Journal of each House respectively. If any Bill shall not be returned by the President within ten Days (Sundays excepted) after it shall have been presented to him, the Same shall be a Law, in like Manner as if he had signed it, unless the Congress by their Adjournment prevent its Return, in which Case it shall not be a Law.

Section 7, Clause 3, Presentment of Resolutions. Every Order, Resolution, or Vote to which the Concurrence of the Senate and House of Representatives may be necessary (except on a question of Adjournment) shall be presented to the President of the United States; and before the Same shall take Effect, shall be approved by him, or being disapproved by him, shall be repassed by two thirds of the Senate and House of Representatives, according to the Rules and Limitations prescribed in the Case of a Bill.

Section 8, Clause 1, Taxes, Spending. The Congress shall have Power To lay and collect Taxes, Duties, Imposts and Excises, to pay the Debts and provide for the common Defence and general Welfare of the United States; but all Duties, Imposts and Excises shall be uniform throughout the United States;

Clause 2, Borrowing. To borrow Money on the credit of the United States;

Clause 3, Commerce. To regulate Commerce with foreign Nations, and among the several States, and with the Indian Tribes;

Clause 4, Naturalization, Bankruptcy. To establish an uniform Rule of Naturalization, and uniform Laws on the subject of Bankruptcies throughout the United States;

Clause 5, Coinage, Weights and Measures. To coin Money, regulate the Value thereof, and of foreign Coin, and fix the Standard of Weights and Measures;

Clause 6, Counterfeiting. To provide for the Punishment of counterfeiting the Securities and current Coin of the United States;

Clause 7, Post Office. To establish Post Offices and post Roads;

Clause 8, Patent and Copyright. To promote the Progress of Science and useful Arts, by securing for limited Times to Authors and Inventors the exclusive Right to their respective Writings and Discoveries;

Clause 9, Inferior Courts. To constitute Tribunals inferior to the supreme Court;

Clause 10, Define and Punish. To define and punish Piracies and Felonies committed on the high Seas, and Offences against the Law of Nations;

Clause 11, Declare War, Marque and Reprisal, Captures. To declare War, grant Letters of Marque and Reprisal, and make Rules concerning Captures on Land and Water;

Clause 12, Army. To raise and support Armies, but no Appropriation of Money to that Use shall be for a longer Term than two Years;

Clause 13, Navy. To provide and maintain a Navy;

Clause 14, Military Regulations. To make Rules for the Government and Regulation of the land and naval Forces;

Clause 15, Militia. To provide for calling forth the Militia to execute the Laws of the Union, suppress Insurrections and repel Invasions;

Clause 16, Organizing Militia. To provide for organizing, arming, and disciplining, the Militia, and for governing such Part of them as may be employed in the Service of the United States, reserving to the States respectively, the Appointment of the Officers, and the Authority of training the Militia according to the discipline prescribed by Congress;

Clause 17, Enclave. To exercise exclusive Legislation in all Cases whatsoever, over such District (not exceeding ten Miles square) as may, by Cession of particular States, and the Acceptance of Congress, become the Seat of the Government of the United States, and to exercise like Authority over all Places purchased by the Consent of the Legislature of the State in which the Same shall be, for the Erection of Forts, Magazines, Arsenals, dock–Yards, and other needful Buildings;—And

Clause 18, Necessary and Proper. To make all Laws which shall be necessary and proper for carrying into Execution the foregoing Powers, and all other Powers vested by this Constitution in the Government of the United States, or in any Department or Officer thereof.

Section 9, Clause 1, Slave Trade. The Migration or Importation of such Persons as any of the States now existing shall think proper to admit, shall not be prohibited by the Congress prior to the Year one thousand eight hundred and eight, but a Tax or duty may be imposed on such Importation, not exceeding ten dollars for each Person.

Section 9, Clause 2, Habeas Corpus. The Privilege of the Writ of Habeas Corpus shall not be suspended, unless when in Cases of Rebellion or Invasion the public Safety may require it.

Section 9, Clause 3, Bill of Attainder, Ex Post Facto Law. No Bill of Attainder or ex post facto Law shall be passed.

Section 9, Clause 4, Direct Taxes. [No Capitation, or other direct, Tax shall be laid, unless in Proportion to the Census or Enumeration herein before directed to be taken.*]

Section 9, Clause 5, Export Taxation. No Tax or Duty shall be laid on Articles exported from any State.

Section 9, Clause 6, Port Preference. No Preference shall be given by any Regulation of Commerce or Revenue to the Ports of one State over those of another; nor shall Vessels bound to, or from, one State, be obliged to enter, clear, or pay Duties in another.

Section 9, Clause 7, Appropriations. No Money shall be drawn from the Treasury, but in Consequence of Appropriations made by Law; and a regular Statement and Account of the Receipts and Expenditures of all public Money shall be published from time to time.

Section 9, Clause 8, Titles of Nobility, Emoluments. No Title of Nobility shall be granted by the United States: And no Person holding any Office of Profit or Trust under them, shall, without the Consent of the Congress, accept of any present, Emolument, Office, or Title, of any kind whatever, from any King, Prince, or foreign State.

Section 10, Clause 1, State Absolute Prohibitions. No State shall enter

*The bracketed language was repealed by the Sixteenth Amendment authorizing the income tax.

into any Treaty, Alliance, or Confederation; grant Letters of Marque and Reprisal; coin Money; emit Bills of Credit; make any Thing but gold and silver Coin a Tender in Payment of Debts; pass any Bill of Attainder, ex post facto Law, or Law impairing the Obligation of Contracts, or grant any Title of Nobility.

Section 10, Clause 2, Import-Export. No State shall, without the Consent of the Congress, lay any Imposts or Duties on Imports or Exports, except what may be absolutely necessary for executing it's inspection Laws: and the net Produce of all Duties and Imposts, laid by any State on Imports or Exports, shall be for the Use of the Treasury of the United States; and all such Laws shall be subject to the Revision and Controul of the Congress.

Section 10, Clause 3, Compact. No State shall, without the Consent of Congress, lay any Duty of Tonnage, keep Troops, or Ships of War in time of Peace, enter into any Agreement or Compact with another State, or with a foreign Power, or engage in War, unless actually invaded, or in such imminent Danger as will not admit of delay.

Article II
The Executive Branch

Section 1, Clause 1, Executive Power. The executive Power shall be vested in a President of the United States of America. He shall hold his Office during the Term of four Years, and, together with the Vice President, chosen for the same Term, be elected, as follows:

Section 1, Clause 2, Presidential Electors. Each State shall appoint, in such Manner as the Legislature thereof may direct, a Number of Electors, equal to the whole Number of Senators and Representatives to which the State may be entitled in the Congress: but no Senator or Representative, or Person holding an Office of Trust or Profit under the United States, shall be appointed an Elector.

Section 1, Clause 3, Electoral College. [The Electors shall meet in their respective States, and vote by Ballot for two Persons, of whom one at least shall not be an Inhabitant of the same State with themselves. And they shall make a List of all the Persons voted for, and of the Number of Votes for each; which List they shall sign and certify, and transmit sealed to the Seat of the Government of the United States, directed to the President of the Senate. The President of the Senate shall, in the Presence of the Senate and House of Representatives, open all the Certificates, and the Votes shall then be counted. The Person having the greatest Number of Votes shall be the President, if such Number be a Majority of the whole Number of Electors appointed; and if there be more than one who have such Majority, and have an equal Number of Votes, then the House of Representatives shall immediately chuse by Ballot one of them for President; and if no Person have a Majority, then from the five highest on the List the said House shall in like Manner chuse the President. But in chusing the President, the Votes shall be taken by States, the Representation from each State having one Vote; A quorum for this Purpose shall consist of a Member or Members from two thirds of the States, and a Majority of all the States shall be necessary to a Choice. In every Case, after the Choice of the President, the Person having the greatest Number of Votes of the Electors shall be the Vice President. But if there should remain two or more who have equal Votes, the Senate shall chuse from them by Ballot the Vice President.*]

Section 1, Clause 4, Presidential Elector Vote. The Congress may determine the Time of chusing the Electors, and the Day on which they shall give their Votes; which Day shall be the same throughout the United States.

Section 1, Clause 5, Presidential Eligibility. No Person except a natural born Citizen, or a Citizen of the United States, at the time of the Adoption of this Constitution, shall be eligible to the Office of President; neither shall any Person be eligible to that Office who shall not have attained to the Age of thirty five Years, and been fourteen Years a Resident within the United States.

Section 1, Clause 6, Presidential Succession. [In Case of the Removal of the President from Office, or of his Death, Resignation, or Inability to discharge the Powers and Duties of the said Office, the Same shall devolve on the Vice President, and the Congress may by Law provide for the Case of Removal, Death, Resignation or Inability, both of the President and Vice President, declaring what Officer shall then act as President, and such Officer shall act accordingly, until the Disability be removed, or a President shall be elected.†]

Section 1, Clause 7, Presidential Compensation. The President shall, at stated Times, receive for his Services, a Compensation, which shall neither be increased nor diminished during the Period for which he shall have been elected, and he shall not receive within that Period any other Emolument from the United States, or any of them.

Section 1, Clause 8, Oath of Office. Before he enter on the Execution of his Office, he shall take the following Oath or Affirmation:—"I do solemnly swear (or affirm) that I will faithfully execute the Office of President of the United States, and will to the best of my Ability, preserve, protect and defend the Constitution of the United States."

Section 2, Clause 1, Commander in Chief, Opinions, Pardons. The President shall be Commander in Chief of the Army and Navy of the United

*The bracketed language was changed by the Twelfth Amendment.
†The bracketed language was changed by the Twentieth and Twenty-fifth Amendments.

States, and of the Militia of the several States, when called into the actual Service of the United States; he may require the Opinion, in writing, of the principal Officer in each of the executive Departments, upon any Subject relating to the Duties of their respective Offices, and he shall have Power to grant Reprieves and Pardons for Offences against the United States, except in Cases of Impeachment.

Section 2, Clause 2, Treaties, Appointments. He shall have Power, by and with the Advice and Consent of the Senate, to make Treaties, provided two thirds of the Senators present concur; and he shall nominate, and by and with the Advice and Consent of the Senate, shall appoint Ambassadors, other public Ministers and Consuls, Judges of the supreme Court, and all other Officers of the United States, whose Appointments are not herein otherwise provided for, and which shall be established by Law: but the Congress may by Law vest the Appointment of such inferior Officers, as they think proper, in the President alone, in the Courts of Law, or in the Heads of Departments.

Section 2, Clause 3, Recess Appointments. The President shall have Power to fill up all Vacancies that may happen during the Recess of the Senate, by granting Commissions which shall expire at the End of their next Session.

Section 3, State of the Union, Convening and Adjourning Congress, Receiving Ambassadors, Faithful Execution, Commissioning Officers. He shall from time to time give to the Congress Information of the State of the Union, and recommend to their Consideration such Measures as he shall judge necessary and expedient; he may, on extraordinary Occasions, convene both Houses, or either of them, and in Case of Disagreement between them, with Respect to the Time of Adjournment, he may adjourn them to such Time as he shall think proper; he shall receive Ambassadors and other public Ministers; he shall take Care that the Laws be faithfully executed, and shall Commission all the Officers of the United States.

Section 4, Impeachment. The President, Vice President and all civil Officers of the United States, shall be removed from Office on Impeachment for, and Conviction of, Treason, Bribery, or other high Crimes and Misdemeanors.

Article III
The Judicial Branch

Section 1, Judicial Vesting, Good Behavior, Compensation. The judicial Power of the United States shall be vested in one supreme Court, and in such inferior Courts as the Congress may from time to time ordain and establish. The Judges, both of the supreme and inferior Courts, shall hold their Offices during good Behaviour, and shall, at stated Times, receive for their Services a Compensation, which shall not be diminished during their Continuance in Office.

Section 2, Clause 1, Judicial Power. The judicial Power shall extend to all Cases, in Law and Equity, arising under this Constitution, the Laws of the United States, and Treaties made, or which shall be made, under their Authority;—to all Cases affecting Ambassadors, other public Ministers and Consuls;—to all Cases of admiralty and maritime Jurisdiction;—to Controversies to which the United States shall be a Party;—to Controversies between two or more States;—[between a State and Citizens of another State;*—]between Citizens of different States,—between Citizens of the same State claiming Lands under Grants of different States [and between a State, or the Citizens thereof, and foreign States, Citizens or Subjects.*]

Section 2, Clause 2, Original and Appellate Jurisdiction. In all Cases affecting Ambassadors, other public Ministers and Consuls, and those in which a State shall be Party, the supreme Court shall have original Jurisdiction. In all the other Cases before mentioned, the supreme Court shall have appellate Jurisdiction, both as to Law and Fact, with such Exceptions, and under such Regulations as the Congress shall make.

Section 2, Clause 3, Criminal Trials. The Trial of all Crimes, except in Cases of Impeachment, shall be by Jury; and such Trial shall be held in the State where the said Crimes shall have been committed; but when not committed within any State, the Trial shall be at such Place or Places as the Congress may by Law have directed.

Section 3, Clause 1, Treason. Treason against the United States, shall consist only in levying War against them, or in adhering to their Enemies, giving them Aid and Comfort. No Person shall be convicted of Treason unless on the Testimony of two Witnesses to the same overt Act, or on Confession in open Court.

Section 3, Clause 2, Punishment of Treason. The Congress shall have Power to declare the Punishment of Treason, but no Attainder of Treason shall work Corruption of Blood, or Forfeiture except during the Life of the Person attainted.

Article IV
State Relations

Section 1, Full Faith and Credit. Full Faith and Credit shall be given in each State to the public Acts, Records, and judicial Proceedings of every other State. And the Congress may by general Laws prescribe the Manner in which such Acts, Records and Proceedings shall be proved, and the Effect thereof.

The bracketed language was changed by the Eleventh Amendment.

Section 2, Clause 1, Privileges and Immunities. The Citizens of each State shall be entitled to all Privileges and Immunities of Citizens in the several States.

Section 2, Clause 2, Interstate Extradition. A Person charged in any State with Treason, Felony, or other Crime, who shall flee from Justice, and be found in another State, shall on Demand of the executive Authority of the State from which he fled, be delivered up, to be removed to the State having Jurisdiction of the Crime.

Section 2, Clause 3, Fugitive Slaves. [No Person held to Service or Labour in one State, under the Laws thereof, escaping into another, shall, in Consequence of any Law or Regulation therein, be discharged from such Service or Labour, but shall be delivered up on Claim of the Party to whom such Service or Labour may be due.*]

Section 3, Clause 1, New States. New States may be admitted by the Congress into this Union; but no new State shall be formed or erected within the Jurisdiction of any other State; nor any State be formed by the Junction of two or more States, or Parts of States, without the Consent of the Legislatures of the States concerned as well as of the Congress.

Section 3, Clause 2, Territory, Property. The Congress shall have Power to dispose of and make all needful Rules and Regulations respecting the Territory or other Property belonging to the United States; and nothing in this Constitution shall be so construed as to Prejudice any Claims of the United States, or of any particular State.

Section 4, Guarantee of Republican Government. The United States shall guarantee to every State in this Union a Republican Form of Government, and shall protect each of them against Invasion; and on Application of the Legislature, or of the Executive (when the Legislature cannot be convened), against domestic Violence.

Article V
The Amendment Process

Article V, Amendments. The Congress, whenever two thirds of both Houses shall deem it necessary, shall propose Amendments to this Constitution, or, on the Application of the Legislatures of two thirds of the several States, shall call a Convention for proposing Amendments, which, in either Case, shall be valid to all Intents and Purposes, as Part of this Constitution, when ratified by the Legislatures of three fourths of the several States, or by Conventions in three fourths thereof, as the one or the other Mode of Ratification may be proposed by the Congress; Provided that no Amendment which may be made prior to the Year One thousand eight

---

The bracketed language was overturned by the Thirteenth Amendment prohibiting slavery.

hundred and eight shall in any Manner affect the first and fourth Clauses in the Ninth Section of the first Article; and that no State, without its Consent, shall be deprived of its equal Suffrage in the Senate.

Article VI
The Supremacy of the Constitution

Clause 1, Debt Assumption. All Debts contracted and Engagements entered into, before the Adoption of this Constitution, shall be as valid against the United States under this Constitution, as under the Confederation.

Clause 2, Supreme Law of the Land. This Constitution, and the Laws of the United States which shall be made in Pursuance thereof; and all Treaties made, or which shall be made, under the Authority of the United States, shall be the supreme Law of the Land; and the Judges in every State shall be bound thereby, any Thing in the Constitution or Laws of any State to the Contrary notwithstanding.

Clause 3, Loyalty. The Senators and Representatives before mentioned, and the Members of the several State Legislatures, and all executive and judicial Officers, both of the United States and of the several States, shall be bound by Oath or Affirmation, to support this Constitution; but no religious Test shall ever be required as a Qualification to any Office or public Trust under the United States.

Article VII
The Ratification Process

Clause 1, Ratification. The Ratification of the Conventions of nine States, shall be sufficient for the Establishment of this Constitution between the States so ratifying the Same.

Clause 2, Subscription. Done in Convention by the Unanimous Consent of the States present the Seventeenth Day of September in the Year of our Lord one thousand seven hundred and Eighty seven and of the Independence of the United States of America the Twelfth In witness whereof We have hereunto subscribed our Names, (The names of the signers are shown here without the abbreviations used in the actual signatures.)

Attest: William Jackson, Secretary

George Washington, President of the Convention, Deputy
   from Virginia

New Hampshire: John Langdon, Nicholas Gilman

Massachusetts: Nathaniel Gorham, Rufus King

Connecticut: William Samuel Johnson, Roger Sherman

New York: Alexander Hamilton

New Jersey: William Livingston, David Brearley, William Paterson, Jonathan Dayton

Pennsylvania: Benjamin Franklin, Thomas Mifflin, Robert Morris, George Clymer, Thomas Fitzsimons, Jared Ingersoll, James Wilson, Gouverneur Morris

Delaware: George Read, Gunning Bedford, Jr., John Dickinson, Richard Bassett, Jacob Broom

Maryland: James McHenry, Daniel of St. Thomas Jenifer, Daniel Carroll

Virginia: John Blair, James Madison, Jr.

North Carolina: William Blount, Richard Dobbs Spaight, Hugh Williamson

South Carolina: John Rutledge, Charles Cotesworth Pinckney, Charles Pinckney, Pierce Butler

Georgia: William Few, Abraham Baldwin

Amendments to the Constitution

Amendment I
The Five Freedoms of Religion, Speech, Press, Assembly and Petition

Ratified December 15, 1791

Congress shall make no law respecting an establishment of religion, or prohibiting the free exercise thereof; or abridging the freedom of speech, or of the press; or the right of the people peaceably to assemble, and to petition the Government for a redress of grievances.

Amendment II
Right to Bear Arms

Ratified December 15, 1791

A well regulated Militia, being necessary to the security of a free State, the right of the people to keep and bear Arms, shall not be infringed.

Amendment III
Quartering of Soldiers

Ratified December 15, 1791

No Soldier shall, in time of peace be quartered in any house, without the consent of the Owner, nor in time of war, but in a manner to be prescribed by law.

Amendment IV
Search and Seizure, Warrants

Ratified December 15, 1791

The right of the people to be secure in their persons, houses, papers, and effects, against unreasonable searches and seizures, shall not be violated, and no Warrants shall issue, but upon probable cause, supported by Oath or affirmation, and particularly describing the place to be searched, and the persons or things to be seized.

Amendment V
The Five Rights of Grand Jury, Protection from Double Jeopardy, Protection from Self-Incrimination, Due Process, and Just Compensation

Ratified December 15, 1791

No person shall be held to answer for a capital, or otherwise infamous crime, unless on a presentment or indictment of a Grand Jury, except in cases arising in the land or naval forces, or in the Militia, when in actual service in time of War or public danger; nor shall any person be subject for the same offence to be twice put in jeopardy of life or limb; nor shall be compelled in any criminal case to be a witness against himself, nor be deprived of life, liberty, or property, without due process of law; nor shall private property be taken for public use, without just compensation.

Amendment VI
Seven Rights of the Accused, Criminal Court Procedures

Ratified December 15, 1791

In all criminal prosecutions, the accused shall enjoy the right to a speedy and public trial, by an impartial jury of the State and district wherein the crime shall have been committed, which district shall have been previously ascertained by law, and to be informed of the nature and cause of the accusation; to be confronted with the witnesses against him; to have compulsory process for obtaining witnesses in his favor, and to have the Assistance of Counsel for his defence.

Amendment VII
Trial by Jury in Common Law Cases

Ratified December 15, 1791

In Suits at common law, where the value in controversy shall exceed twenty dollars, the right of trial by jury shall be preserved, and no fact tried by a jury, shall be otherwise re-examined in any Court of the United States, than according to the rules of the common law.

Amendment VIII
Cruel and Unusual Punishment

Ratified December 15, 1791

Excessive bail shall not be required, nor excessive fines imposed, nor cruel and unusual punishments inflicted.

Amendment IX
Retention of Unenumerated Rights by the People

Ratified December 15, 1791

The enumeration in the Constitution, of certain rights, shall not be construed to deny or disparage others retained by the people.

Amendment X
Power Reserved to States or People

Ratified December 15, 1791

The powers not delegated to the United States by the Constitution, nor prohibited by it to the States, are reserved to the States respectively, or to the people.

Amendment XI
Suits Against a State

Ratified February 7, 1795

The Judicial power of the United States shall not be construed to extend to any suit in law or equity, commenced or prosecuted against one of the United States by Citizens of another State, or by Citizens or Subjects of any Foreign State.

Amendment XII
Electoral College

Ratified June 15, 1804

The Electors shall meet in their respective states, and vote by ballot for President and Vice-President, one of whom, at least, shall not be an inhabitant of the same state with themselves; they shall name in their ballots the person voted for as President, and in distinct ballots the person voted for as Vice-President, and they shall make distinct lists of all persons voted for as President, and of all persons voted for as Vice-President, and of the number of votes for each, which lists they shall sign and certify, and transmit sealed to the seat of the government of the United States, directed to the President of the Senate;—The President of the Senate shall, in the presence of the Senate and House of Representatives, open all the certificates and the votes shall then be counted;—The person having the greatest number of votes for President, shall be the President, if such number be a majority of the whole number of Electors appointed; and if no person have such majority, then from the persons having the highest numbers not exceeding three on the list of those voted for as President, the House of Representatives shall choose immediately, by ballot, the President. But in choosing the President, the votes shall be taken by states, the representation from each state having one vote; a quorum for this purpose shall consist of a member or members from two-thirds of the states, and a majority of all the states shall be necessary to a choice. [And if the House of Representatives shall not choose a President whenever the right of choice shall devolve upon them, before the fourth day of March next following, then the Vice-President shall act as President, as in the case of the death or other constitutional disability of the President.—*] The person having the greatest number of votes as Vice-President, shall be the Vice-President, if such number be a majority of the whole number of Electors appointed, and if no person have a majority, then from the two highest numbers on the list, the Senate shall choose the Vice-President; a quorum for the purpose shall consist of two-thirds of the whole number of Senators, and a majority of the whole number shall be necessary to a choice. But no person constitutionally ineligible to the office of President shall be eligible to that of Vice-President of the United States.

---

*The bracketed language was changed by the Twentieth Amendment, Sections 1 and 3, including the change of the presidential inauguration from March 4 to January 20.

Amendment XIII
Slavery Abolition

Ratified December 6, 1865

Section 1, Slavery Abolition Clause. Neither slavery nor involuntary servitude, except as a punishment for crime whereof the party shall have been duly convicted, shall exist within the United States, or any place subject to their jurisdiction.

Section 2, Enforcement Clause. Congress shall have power to enforce this article by appropriate legislation.

Amendment XIV
Citizenship, Privileges or Immunities, Due Process, Equal Protection

Ratified July 9, 1868

Section 1, Citizenship, Privileges or Immunities, Due Process, Equal Protection Clauses. All persons born or naturalized in the United States, and subject to the jurisdiction thereof, are citizens of the United States and of the State wherein they reside. No State shall make or enforce any law which shall abridge the privileges or immunities of citizens of the United States; nor shall any State deprive any person of life, liberty, or property, without due process of law; nor deny to any person within its jurisdiction the equal protection of the laws.

Section 2, Apportionment of Representatives Clause. Representatives shall be apportioned among the several States according to their respective numbers, counting the whole number of persons in each State, excluding Indians not taxed. But when the right to vote at any election for the choice of electors for President and Vice-President of the United States, Representatives in Congress, the Executive and Judicial officers of a State, or the members of the Legislature thereof, is denied to any of the male inhabitants of such State, [being twenty-one years of age,*] and citizens of the United States, or in any way abridged, except for participation in rebellion, or other crime, the basis of representation therein shall be reduced in the proportion which the number of such male citizens shall bear to the whole number of male citizens twenty-one years of age in such State.

Section 3, Disqualification for Rebellion Clause. No person shall be a Senator or Representative in Congress, or elector of President and Vice-President, or hold any office, civil or military, under the United States, or

The bracketed language was changed by the Twenty-sixth Amendment reducing the voting age to eighteen years. Women were granted the right to vote by the Nineteenth Amendment.

under any State, who, having previously taken an oath, as a member of Congress, or as an officer of the United States, or as a member of any State legislature, or as an executive or judicial officer of any State, to support the Constitution of the United States, shall have engaged in insurrection or rebellion against the same, or given aid or comfort to the enemies thereof. But Congress may by a vote of two-thirds of each House, remove such disability.

Section 4, Debts Incurred During Rebellion. The validity of the public debt of the United States, authorized by law, including debts incurred for payment of pensions and bounties for services in suppressing insurrection or rebellion, shall not be questioned. But neither the United States nor any State shall assume or pay any debt or obligation incurred in aid of insurrection or rebellion against the United States, or any claim for the loss or emancipation of any slave; but all such debts, obligations and claims shall be held illegal and void.

Section 5, Enforcement Clause. The Congress shall have power to enforce, by appropriate legislation, the provisions of this article.

Amendment XV
Racial Suffrage

Ratified February 3, 1870

Section 1, Racial Suffrage Clause. The right of citizens of the United States to vote shall not be denied or abridged by the United States or by any State on account of race, color, or previous condition of servitude.

Section 2, Enforcement Clause. The Congress shall have power to enforce this article by appropriate legislation.

Amendment XVI
Income Tax

Ratified February 3, 1913

The Congress shall have power to lay and collect taxes on incomes, from whatever source derived, without apportionment among the several States, and without regard to any census or enumeration.

Amendment XVII
Popular Election of Senators

Ratified April 8, 1913

Section 1, Popular Election Clause. The Senate of the United States shall be composed of two Senators from each State, elected by the people thereof, for six years; and each Senator shall have one vote. The electors in each State shall have the qualifications requisite for electors of the most numerous branch of the State legislatures.

Section 2, Vacancies Clause. When vacancies happen in the representation of any State in the Senate, the executive authority of such State shall issue writs of election to fill such vacancies: *Provided,* That the legislature of any State may empower the executive thereof to make temporary appointments until the people fill the vacancies by election as the legislature may direct.

Section 3, Preservation of Prior Election Clause. This amendment shall not be so construed as to affect the election or term of any Senator chosen before it becomes valid as part of the Constitution.

Amendment XVIII
Prohibition of Intoxicating Liquors

Ratified January 16, 1919
Repealed December 5, 1933

Section 1, Prohibition Clause. After one year from the ratification of this article the manufacture, sale, or transportation of intoxicating liquors within, the importation thereof into, or the exportation thereof from the United States and all territory subject to the jurisdiction thereof for beverage purposes is hereby prohibited.

Section 2, Concurrent Jurisdiction Clause. The Congress and the several States shall have concurrent power to enforce this article by appropriate legislation.

Section 3, Ratification Clause. This article shall be inoperative unless it shall have been ratified as an amendment to the Constitution by the legislatures of the several States, as provided in the Constitution, within seven years from the date of the submission hereof to the States by the Congress. (The Eighteenth Amendment was repealed by the Twenty-first Amendment in 1933.)

Amendment XIX
Woman Suffrage

Ratified August 18, 1920

Woman Suffrage Clause. The right of citizens of the United States to vote shall not be denied or abridged by the United States or by any State on account of sex.

Enforcement Clause. Congress shall have power to enforce this article by appropriate legislation.

Amendment XX
Term Endings, Presidential Succession

Ratified January 23, 1933

Section 1, Term Endings Clause. The terms of the President and Vice President shall end at noon on the 20th day of January, and the terms of Senators and Representatives at noon on the 3d day of January, of the years in which such terms would have ended if this article had not been ratified; and the terms of their successors shall then begin.

Section 2, Congressional Assembly Clause. The Congress shall assemble at least once in every year, and such meeting shall begin at noon on the 3d day of January, unless they shall by law appoint a different day.

Section 3, Presidential Succession Clause. If, at the time fixed for the beginning of the term of the President, the President elect shall have died, the Vice President elect shall become President. If a President shall not have been chosen before the time fixed for the beginning of his term, or if the President elect shall have failed to qualify, then the Vice President elect shall act as President until a President shall have qualified; and the Congress may by law provide for the case wherein neither a President elect nor a Vice President elect shall have qualified, declaring who shall then act as President, or the manner in which one who is to act shall be selected, and such person shall act accordingly until a President or Vice President shall have qualified.

Section 4, Congressional Role in Presidential Succession. The Congress may by law provide for the case of the death of any of the persons from whom the House of Representatives may choose a President whenever the right of choice shall have devolved upon them, and for the case of the death of any of the persons from whom the Senate may choose a Vice President whenever the right of choice shall have devolved upon them.

Section 5, Effective Date Clause. Sections 1 and 2 shall take effect on the 15th day of October following the ratification of this article.

Section 6, Ratification Clause. This article shall be inoperative unless it shall have been ratified as an amendment to the Constitution by the legislatures of three-fourths of the several States within seven years from the date of its submission.

Amendment XXI
Repeal of Amendment XVIII Re Prohibition

Ratified December 5, 1933

Section 1, Repeal Clause. The eighteenth article of amendment to the Constitution of the United States is hereby repealed.

Section 2, State Jurisdiction Clause. The transportation or importation into any State, Territory, or possession of the United States for delivery or use therein of intoxicating liquors, in violation of the laws thereof, is hereby prohibited.

Section 3, Ratification Clause. This article shall be inoperative unless it shall have been ratified as an amendment to the Constitution by conventions in the several States, as provided in the Constitution, within seven years from the date of the submission hereof to the States by the Congress.

Amendment XXII
Presidential Term Limit

Ratified February 27, 1951

Section 1, Presidential Term Limit Clause. No person shall be elected to the office of the President more than twice, and no person who has held the office of President, or acted as President, for more than two years of a term to which some other person was elected President shall be elected to the office of the President more than once. But this Article shall not apply to any person holding the office of President when this Article was proposed by the Congress, and shall not prevent any person who may be holding the office of President, or acting as President, during the term within which this Article becomes operative from holding the office of President or acting as President during the remainder of such term.

Section 2, Ratification Clause. This Article shall be inoperative unless it shall have been ratified as an amendment to the Constitution by the legislatures of three-fourths of the several States within seven years from the date of its submission to the States by the Congress.

Amendment XXIII
Presidential Electors for District of Columbia

Ratified March 29, 1961

Section 1, Presidential Elector Clause. The District constituting the seat of Government of the United States shall appoint in such manner as Congress may direct:

A number of electors of President and Vice President equal to the whole number of Senators and Representatives in Congress to which the District would be entitled if it were a State, but in no event more than the least populous State; they shall be in addition to those appointed by the States, but they shall be considered, for the purposes of the election of President and Vice President, to be electors appointed by a State; and they shall meet in the District and perform such duties as provided by the twelfth article of amendment.

Section 2, Enforcement Clause. The Congress shall have power to enforce this article by appropriate legislation.

Amendment XXIV
Poll Tax Prohibition

Ratified January 23, 1964

Section 1, Poll Tax Prohibition Clause. The right of citizens of the United States to vote in any primary or other election for President or Vice President, for electors for President or Vice President, or for Senator or Representative in Congress, shall not be denied or abridged by the United States or any State by reason of failure to pay any poll tax or other tax.

Section 2, Enforcement Clause. The Congress shall have power to enforce this article by appropriate legislation.

Amendment XXV
Presidential Succession

Ratified February 10, 1967

Section 1, Presidential Succession Clause. In case of the removal of the President from office or of his death or resignation, the Vice President shall become President.

Section 2, Vice Presidential Vacancy Clause. Whenever there is a vacancy in the office of the Vice President, the President shall nominate a Vice President who shall take office upon confirmation by a majority vote of both Houses of Congress.

Section 3, Voluntary Declaration of Presidential Incapacity Clause. Whenever the President transmits to the President pro tempore of the Senate and the Speaker of the House of Representatives his written declaration that he is unable to discharge the powers and duties of his office, and until he transmits to them a written declaration to the contrary, such powers and duties shall be discharged by the Vice President as Acting President.

Section 4, Involuntary Declaration of Presidential Incapacity Clause. Whenever the Vice President and a majority of either the principal officers of the executive departments or of such other body as Congress may by law provide, transmit to the President pro tempore of the Senate and the Speaker of the House of Representatives their written declaration that the President is unable to discharge the powers and duties of his office, the Vice President shall immediately assume the powers and duties of the office as Acting President.

Thereafter, when the President transmits to the President pro tempore of the Senate and the Speaker of the House of Representatives his written declaration that no inability exists, he shall resume the powers and duties of his office unless the Vice President and a majority of either the principal officers of the executive department or of such other body as Congress may by law provide, transmit within four days to the President pro tempore of the Senate and the Speaker of the House of Representatives their written declaration that the President is unable to discharge the powers and duties of his office. Thereupon Congress shall decide the issue, assembling within forty-eight hours for that purpose if not in session. If the Congress, within twenty-one days after receipt of the latter written declaration, or, if Congress is not in session, within twenty-one days after Congress is required to assemble, determines by two-thirds vote of both Houses that the President is unable to discharge the powers and duties of his office, the Vice President shall continue to discharge the same as Acting President; otherwise, the President shall resume the powers and duties of his office.

Amendment XXVI
Voting Age Fixed at Eighteen

Ratified July 1, 1971

Section 1, Voting Age Eighteen Clause. The right of citizens of the United States, who are eighteen years of age or older, to vote shall not be denied or abridged by the United States or by any State on account of age.

Section 2, Enforcement Clause. The Congress shall have power to enforce this article by appropriate legislation.

Amendment XXVII
Congressional Compensation

Ratified May 7, 1992

No law, varying the compensation for the services of the Senators and Representatives, shall take effect, until an election of Representatives shall have intervened.

Bibliography

Adickes, Roland. *The United States Constitution and Citizens' Rights: The Interpretation and Mis-Interpretation of the American Contract for Governance.* Jefferson NC: McFarland, 2001.

Beeman, Richard. *Plain, Honest Men: The Making of the American Constitution.* New York: Random House, 2009.

Bowen, Catherine Drinker. *Miracle at Philadelphia: The Story of the Constitutional Convention, May to September 1787.* Boston: Little, Brown, 1966.

Burns, James MacGregor. *Packing the Court: The Rise of Judicial Power and the Coming Crisis of the Supreme Court.* New York: Penguin, 2009.

Charles, Patrick J. *The Second Amendment: The Intent and Its Interpretation by the States and the Supreme Court.* Jefferson, NC: McFarland, 2009.

Chemerinsky, Erwin. *Constitutional Law: Principles and Policies.* 3rd ed. New York: Wolters Kluwer, 2006.

Cooke, Edward F. *A Detailed Analysis of the Constitution.* 6th ed. Lanham, MD: Rowman & Littlefield, 1995.

Currie, David P. *The Constitution of the United States: A Primer for the People.* 2d ed. Chicago: University of Chicago Press, 2000.

DeLeo, John. *The Student's Guide to Understanding Constitutional Law.* Belmont, CA: Cengage Learning, 2005.

Federal Judicial Center. *www.fjc.gov.*

Gutzman, Kevin R.C. *The Politically Incorrect Guide to the Constitution.* Washington, DC: Regnery, 2007.

Hall, Kermit L. *The Oxford Guide to United States Supreme Court Decisions,* 2nd ed. New York: Oxford University Press, 2009.

_____, and John J. Patrick. *The Pursuit of Justice: Supreme Court Decisions That Shaped America.* New York: Oxford University Press, 2006.

Hartman, Gary. *Landmark Supreme Court Cases: The Most Influential Decisions of the Supreme Court of the United States.* New York: Checkmark, 2006.

Holder, Angela Roddey. *The Meaning of the Constitution.* 2d ed. New York: Hauppauge, 1987.

Hudson, David L., Jr. *The Handy Supreme Court Answer Book.* Canton, MI: Visible Ink, 2008.

Irons, Peter. *A People's History of the Supreme Court.* New York: Viking, 1999.

_____, and Stephanie Guitton. *May It Please the Court: The Most Significant Oral Arguments Made Before the Supreme Court Since 1955.* New York: New Press, 1993.

Jost, Kenneth. *The Supreme Court, A to Z.* 4th ed. Washington, DC: CQ Press, 2006.

Journal of Supreme Court History. Washington, DC: Published three times a year (March, July and November) on behalf of the Supreme Court Historical Society.

Levy, Leonard Williams. *Original Intent and the Framers' Constitution.* Chicago. Ivan R. Dee, 2000.

Levy, Robert A., and William Mellor. *The Dirty Dozen: How Twelve Supreme Court Cases Radically Expanded Government and Eroded Freedom.* New York: Sentinel, 2008.

Lieberman, Jethro K. *A Practical Companion to the Constitution: How the Supreme Court Has Ruled on Issues from Abortion to Zoning.* Berkeley: University of California Press, 1999.

Lipsky, Seth. *The Citizen's Constitution: An Annotated Guide.* New York: Basic, 2009.

McCloskey, Robert G. *The American Supreme Court.* Revised by Sanford Levinson. Chicago: University of Chicago Press, 2005.

Meese, Edwin III. *The Heritage Guide to the Constitution.* Washington: Regnery, 2005.

Monk, Linda R. *The Words We Live By: Your Annotated Guide to the Constitution.* New York: Hyperion, 2003.

Oyez Project. *www.oyez.org.*

Padover, Saul. *The Living U.S. Constitution.* New York: Mentor, 1953.

Rosen, Jeffrey. *The Supreme Court: The Personalities and Rivalries That Defined America.* New York: Times Books/ Henry Holt, 2007.

Schwartz, Bernard. *A History of the Supreme Court.* New York: Oxford University Press, 1995.

Supreme Court of the United States. *www.supremecourtus.gov.*

Toobin, Jeffrey. *The Nine: Inside the Secret World of the Supreme Court.* New York: Anchor, 2008.

Trachtman, Michael G. *The Supremes' Greatest Hits: The 37 Supreme Court Cases That Most Directly Affect Your Life.* Rev. and updated ed. New York: Sterling, 2009.

Vile, John R. *A Companion to the United States Constitution and Its Amendments.* 3d ed. Westport, CT: Praeger, 2001.

Index of Cases

General Index

280

LaVergne, TN USA
02 February 2011
214852LV00003B/2/P